Numerical and Computational Methods in Structural Engineering and Mechanics

Numerical and Computational Methods in Structural Engineering and Mechanics

Guest Editors

Joaquim Infante Barbosa
José Alberto Rodrigues

MDPI

Basel • Beijing • Wuhan • Barcelona • Belgrade • Novi Sad • Cluj • Manchester

Guest Editors

Joaquim Infante Barbosa
IDMEC, Instituto Superior
Técnico
Universidade de Lisboa
Lisboa
Portugal

José Alberto Rodrigues
CIMA and Department of
Mathematics
Instituto Superior de
Engenharia de Lisboa – ISEL
Polytechnic University of
Lisbon
Lisboa
Portugal

Editorial Office

MDPI AG
Grosspeteranlage 5
4052 Basel, Switzerland

This is a reprint of the Special Issue, published open access by the journal *Mathematics* (ISSN 2227-7390), freely accessible at: https://www.mdpi.com/journal/mathematics/special_issues/Struct_Eng_Mech.

For citation purposes, cite each article independently as indicated on the article page online and as indicated below:

Lastname, A.A.; Lastname, B.B. Article Title. *Journal Name* **Year**, *Volume Number*, Page Range.

ISBN 978-3-7258-3891-2 (Hbk)
ISBN 978-3-7258-3892-9 (PDF)
https://doi.org/10.3390/books978-3-7258-3892-9

Contents

About the Editors

Joaquim Infante Barbosa

Joaquim Infante Barbosa is currently a retired Full Professor at ISEL – Instituto Superior de Engenharia de Lisboa, Polytechnic University of Lisbon. He is a Senior Researcher at IDMEC – Instituto Superior Técnico, University of Lisbon and CIMOSM - Centro de Investigação em Modelação e Optimização de Sistemas Multifuncionais, Instituto Superior de Engenharia de Lisboa, Polytechnic University of Lisbon. He obtained a Master's degree in Mechanical Engineering from Instituto Superior Técnico in 1984, and completed his PhD in Mechanical Engineering in 1993 at the University of Lisbon Instituto Superior Técnico. He was a post-doctorate at the Department of Mechanical Engineering of Texas A&M University in 1999. His scientific interests include the finite element method, structural optimization, computational mechanics, symbolic computation, composite materials, and functionally graded materials. He has been the chairman and member of a number of scientific conferences related to Numerical and Symbolic Computation for mechanics and engineering. He has published more than 40 articles in international peer-reviewed journals and participates or has participated as a researcher in 20 projects.

José Alberto Rodrigues

José Alberto Rodrigues completed his PhD in Sciences, specializing in Mathematics, at the University of Minho Department of Mathematics and Applications. He also has a Master's degree in Applied Mathematics from the University of Lisbon Instituto Superior Técnico, and a Bachelor's degree in Mathematics from the University of Lisbon Faculty of Sciences. He is an Associate Professor at the Instituto Superior de Engenharia de Lisboa, Polytechnic University of Lisbon. His main areas of interest are mathematical analysis, applied mathematics, and scientific computing. He has publications devoted to mathematical modelling and numerical methods, more specifically in Isogeometric Analysis techniques, and didactic books devoted to Calculus and Numerical Analysis for undergraduate students. He is a staff member of the Research Centre on Modelling and Optimization of Multifunctional Systems (CIMOSM, ISEL). He is currently an integrated member of the Center for Research in Mathematics and Applications (CIMA).

mathematics

MDPI

Editorial

Editorial: Advances in Mathematical Modeling for Structural Engineering and Mechanics

Joaquim Infante Barbosa [1,2,*] and José Alberto Rodrigues [3,*]

1 CIMOSM, ISEL—Centro de Investigação em Modelação e Optimização de Sistemas Multifuncionais, Instituto Superior de Engenharia de Lisboa, 1959-007 Lisboa, Portugal
2 IDMEC, IST—Instituto de Engenharia Mecânica, Instituto Superior Técnico, Universidade de Lisboa, 1049-001 Lisboa, Portugal
3 CIMA e Departamento de Matemática—Instituto Superior de Engenharia de Lisboa, Rua Conselheiro Emídio Navarro, 1, 1959-007 Lisbon, Portugal
* Correspondence: joaquim.barbosa@tecnico.ulisboa.pt (J.I.B.); jose.rodrigues@isel.pt (J.A.R.)

Mathematical modeling is a cornerstone in addressing complex problems across science and engineering, showcasing its inherently multidisciplinary nature. In structural engineering and mechanics, the development of robust and precise numerical schemes has been instrumental in deepening our understanding of physical phenomena and driving innovation in computational methodologies. This Special Issue is dedicated to exploring advanced mathematical modeling approaches that tackle the diverse challenges faced in these fields.

1. Central Themes

A key focus of this issue is the automation and systematization of complex mechanical problems, which are essential for reducing computational effort and achieving significant time savings. The integration of numerical and computational techniques has further enhanced problem-solving efficiency, enabling engineers and researchers to address intricate structural issues with greater precision. Additionally, the development of hybrid analytical–numerical methods has provided powerful tools that combine theoretical rigor with computational adaptability, advancing the field significantly.

2. Scope of Contributions

The contributions in this Special Issue span a wide array of topics, including:

- The design of robust computational methods and simulations;
- Parameter fitting techniques;
- Inverse problem strategies in differential equations;
- Numerical simulations in structural engineering;
- Optimization of complex structural systems, and;
- Integrated computational methods that bridge mathematical theory with engineering applications.

3. Innovative Research Highlights

The articles featured in this issue exemplify the innovative approaches researchers are taking to address critical challenges in structural engineering and mechanics. Notable studies include:

Received: 5 March 2025
Accepted: 6 March 2025
Published: 12 March 2025

Citation: Barbosa, J.I.; Rodrigues, J.A. Editorial: Advances in Mathematical Modeling for Structural Engineering and Mechanics. *Mathematics* **2025**, *13*, 936. https://doi.org/10.3390/math13060936

1. **Biomimetic optimization**: a study extending the meshless natural-neighbor radial-point interpolation method, which applies a bi-evolutionary, bone-remodeling-inspired algorithm to optimize automotive parts, highlighting the synergy between computational mechanics and biomimetic principles.
2. **Deep learning in diagnostics**: a novel fault diagnosis method for rolling bearings that utilizes Swin Transformer and Generalized S Transform, showcasing the potential of deep learning in engineering diagnostics.
3. **Fluid–structure interactions**: numerical simulations of shock waves in gas-water interactions, offering valuable insights into fluid–structure interactions crucial for various engineering applications.
4. **Innovative material design**: investigations into auxetic lattice structures for impact absorption, emphasizing the importance of innovative material design in mechanical engineering.
5. **Computational efficiency:** a p-refinement method leveraging transition elements to enhance finite element applications, demonstrating advancements in computational efficiency.
6. **Open-source tools**: the introduction of Seismo-VLAB, an open-source software with new capabilities for soil–structure interaction analysis, underscoring the importance of accessible computational tools in engineering research.

4. Additional Contributions

Other significant studies include:

- **Advanced composite materials**: free vibration analysis of stiffened functionally graded graphene-reinforced composite multilayer cylindrical panels, providing insights into advanced composite materials.
- **Structural connections**: experimental and numerical analyses of in-line connections in structural elements, offering valuable data for improving connection performance.
- **AI in mechanical engineering**: a self-evolving neural network-based control technique for vibration suppression in carbon nanotubes, showcasing the intersection of artificial intelligence and mechanical engineering.
- **Fracture mechanics**: a comprehensive review of multi-crack fracture mechanics, consolidating experimental, theoretical, and numerical advancements in the field.

5. Conclusions

The diverse range of topics covered in this Special Issue reflects the evolving landscape of mathematical modeling in structural engineering and mechanics. By integrating computational advancements with engineering principles, these studies pave the way for future innovations in the field. We extend our gratitude to all contributors, reviewers, and researchers whose dedication and expertise have enriched this collection, providing valuable resources for further exploration and development in mathematical modeling and engineering mechanics. We also acknowledge the excellent collaboration with the publisher, the constant assistance provided by the MDPI associate editors in bringing this project to completion, and the great support of the Managing Editor of this Special Issue, Ms. Helene Hu.

Conflicts of Interest: The authors declare no conflicts of interest.

List of Contributions

1. Alsaade, F.; Al-zahrani, M.; Yao, Q.; Jahanshahi, H. A Self-Evolving Neural Network-Based Finite-Time Control Technique for Tracking and Vibration Suppression of a Carbon Nanotube. *Mathematics* **2023**, *11*, 1581. https://doi.org/10.3390/math11071581.
2. Birdean, C.; Both, I.; Mărginean, I.; Cernescu, A. Understanding In-Line Connections Behavior from Experimental and Numerical Analyses on Rectangular and Circular Hollow Section Elements. *Mathematics* **2023**, *11*, 3416. https://doi.org/10.3390/math11153416.
3. Zhou, Y.; Zhang, Y.; Nyasha Chirukam, B.; Li, J.; Lu, C.; Babaei, M.; Asemi, K. Free Vibration Analyses of Stiffened Functionally Graded Graphene-Reinforced Composite Multilayer Cylindrical Panel. *Mathematics* **2023**, *11*, 3662. https://doi.org/10.3390/math11173662.
4. Kusanovic, D.; Seylabi, E.; Ayoubi, P.; Nguyen, K.; Garcia-Suarez, J.; Kottke, A.; Asimaki, D. Seismo-VLAB: An Open-Source Software for Soil–Structure Interaction Analyses. *Mathematics* **2023**, *11*, 4530. https://doi.org/10.3390/math11214530.
5. Shahriar, A.; Mostafa, A. A p-Refinement Method Based on a Library of Transition Elements for 3D Finite Element Applications. *Mathematics* **2023**, *11*, 4954. https://doi.org/10.3390/math11244954.
6. Széles, L.; Horváth, R.; Cveticanin, L. Research on Auxetic Lattice Structure for Impact Absorption in Machines and Mechanisms. *Mathematics* **2024**, *12*, 1983. https://doi.org/10.3390/math12131983.
7. Wu, Z.; Zhang, D.; Yan, J.; Pang, J.; Sun, Y. Numerical Simulation of Shock Wave in Gas–Water Interaction Based on Nonlinear Shock Wave Velocity Curve. *Mathematics* **2024**, *12*, 3268. https://doi.org/10.3390/math12203268.
8. Wang, Z.; Li, D.; Zhong, Y.; Liu, Y.; Shao, Y. Review of Experimental, Theoretical and Numerical Advances in Multi-Crack Fracture Mechanics. *Mathematics* **2024**, *12*, 3881. https://doi.org/10.3390/math12243881.
9. Yan, J.; Zhu, X.; Wang, X.; Zhang, D. A New Fault Diagnosis Method for Rolling Bearings with the Basis of Swin Transformer and Generalized S Transform. *Mathematics* **2025**, *13*, 45. https://doi.org/10.3390/math13010045.
10. Oliveira, C.; Pais, A.; Belinha, J. Extending the Meshless Natural-Neighbour Radial-Point Interpolation Method to the Structural Optimization of an Automotive Part Using a Bi-Evolutionary Bone-Remodelling-Inspired Algorithm. *Mathematics* **2025**, *13*, 178. https://doi.org/10.3390/math13020178.

mathematics

Article

A Self-Evolving Neural Network-Based Finite-Time Control Technique for Tracking and Vibration Suppression of a Carbon Nanotube

Fawaz W. Alsaade [1,*], Mohammed S. Al-zahrani [2], Qijia Yao [3] and Hadi Jahanshahi [4,*]

1 Department of Computer Science, College of Computer Sciences and Information Technology, King Faisal University, Al-Ahsa 31982, Saudi Arabia
2 Department of Computer Networks and Communications, College of Computer Sciences and Information Technology, King Faisal University, Al-Ahsa 31982, Saudi Arabia; malzahrani@kfu.edu.sa
3 School of Automation and Electrical Engineering, University of Science and Technology Beijing, Beijing 100083, China; qijia_yao@ustb.edu.cn
4 Department of Mechanical Engineering, University of Manitoba, Winnipeg, MB R3T 5V6, Canada
* Correspondence: falsaade@kfu.edu.sa (F.W.A.); jahanshahi.hadi90@gmail.com (H.J.)

Abstract: The control of micro- and nanoscale systems is a vital yet challenging endeavor because of their small size and high sensitivity, which make them susceptible to environmental factors such as temperature and humidity. Despite promising methods proposed for these systems in literature, the chattering in the controller, convergence time, and robustness against a wide range of disturbances still require further attention. To tackle this issue, we present an intelligent observer, which accounts for uncertainties and disturbances, along with a chatter-free controller. First, the dynamics of a carbon nanotube (CNT) are examined, and its governing equations are outlined. Then, the design of the proposed controller is described. The proposed approach incorporates a self-evolving neural network-based methodology and the super-twisting sliding mode technique to eliminate the uncertainties' destructive effects. Also, the proposed technique ensures finite-time convergence of the system. The controller is then implemented on the CNT and its effectiveness in different conditions is investigated. The numerical simulations demonstrate the proposed method's outstanding performance in both stabilization and tracking control, even in the presence of uncertain parameters of the system and complicated disturbances.

Keywords: carbon nanotubes; Chebyshev Neural Network; self-evolving algorithm; vibration control; super-twisting sliding mode

MSC: 34H05; 37N35; 93C40; 92B20

Citation: Alsaade, F.W.; Al-zahrani, M.S.; Yao, Q.; Jahanshahi, H. A Self-Evolving Neural Network-Based Finite-Time Control Technique for Tracking and Vibration Suppression of a Carbon Nanotube. *Mathematics* **2023**, *11*, 1581. https://doi.org/10.3390/math11071581

Academic Editors: Joaquim Infante Barbosa and José Alberto Rodrigues

Received: 20 February 2023
Revised: 13 March 2023
Accepted: 21 March 2023
Published: 24 March 2023

1. Introduction

CNTs have a high aspect ratio, high tensile strength, and high thermal and electrical conductivity, which makes them ideal for use in advanced materials and devices [1,2]. They have been used to create strong and lightweight materials, as well as in high-performance electronics. They can also be used as a catalyst in chemical reactions and have been studied as a potential solution for environmental problems such as air and water purification [3,4].

The control of CNTs has been an active area of research in recent years, and many studies have been conducted on developing control strategies for CNTs in different fields such as mechanical systems, chemical systems, and electrical systems [5,6]. One of the main challenges is the lack of understanding of the dynamics and properties of CNTs at the nanoscale, which can make it difficult to predict and control their behavior [7,8]. Additionally, the high aspect ratio of CNTs makes them very flexible and sensitive to external forces, which can make them difficult to control. Furthermore, the control of CNTs requires the ability to account for the effects of uncertainties and disturbances, which can be challenging [9]. Due to these issues, research in this field is ongoing and new control schemes are being developed to address these challenges [10].

Nowadays, machine learning approaches have revolutionized technologies in many fields of study. With the advancement of computing power and the availability of large datasets, machine learning algorithms can learn patterns, make predictions, and automate decision-making processes with remarkable accuracy [11]. This has led to significant breakthroughs in various fields [12–14]. Also, as a stepping stone in most machine learning-based techniques, neural networks have been widely used in various control applications to tackle complex and nonlinear systems [15,16]. For instance, Chen et al. [17] have used neural networks in their study to identify the generalized kernel representations and to design the intelligent fault diagnosis schemes. Neural networks are also used to approximate the mathematical model of the system and improve the control performance [18,19]. The ability of neural networks to learn and generalize from data makes them particularly useful in the control of systems that are difficult to model or have a large number of uncertain parameters [20,21]. In the control of nano/microsystems, neural networks have been used to compensate for the effects of uncertainties and disturbances on the system's behavior. They can also be used to estimate the system's dynamic, which can be used to improve the performance of the system [22,23]. Neural networks can be used in combination with traditional control methods such as feedback control, adaptive control, and model predictive control to improve control performance [24]. Furthermore, neural networks can also be used in the identification of system parameters, which can be used to improve the accuracy of the control strategy [25].

Some of the achievements in the literature include the development of control schemes that can effectively deal with the small size and unique properties of CNTs. For instance, recently in [26], an adaptive sliding mode control scheme has been developed which is able to work well under highly uncertain cases in which all parameters are uncertain and the uncertainties cannot be separated from the control force. In that study, a double electrostatic actuators scheme has been used and a decoupling scheme that can suppress the vibration of CNTs in multiple directions has been designed. Also, in [27], piezoelectric patches have been used as sensors to measure the displacement of the beam and actuators to implement control forces for vibration control. A model-free adaptive fuzzy sliding mode controller has been utilized to suppress the vibration of the rotating CNT-reinforced composite beam. In addition, since the state vector cannot be measured for control purposes and only the piezoelectric sensor's output is available, a model-free adaptive fuzzy sliding mode observer has been proposed here to estimate the system's state vector. These control schemes have been successful in achieving precise control of CNTs and have been shown to have excellent performance in numerical simulations. Despite these advances, there are still areas where improvements can be made. Chattering and handling various types of uncertainties remain persistent challenges for control engineers. This is particularly true for discontinuous disturbances, which many of the existing methods are unable to effectively deal with. The high sensitivity of nanosystems means that even small disturbances can have a significant impact on their performance, and the presence of chattering can significantly detract from their performance [28]. As a result, further research is needed to develop control methods that can effectively handle chattering and deal with a wide range of uncertainties, including discontinuous disturbances, to ensure the optimal performance of nano- and microscale systems.

Motivated by the aforementioned factors, in the current study we take advantage of the universal approximation of neural networks and propose an intelligent and smooth controller for stabilization and tracking control of CNT. We use Chebyshev Neural Network (ChNN) which is a specific type of artificial neural network that utilizes the Chebyshev polynomial as the activation function [29]. It has been demonstrated to have faster convergence and superior approximation ability compared to traditional neural networks. The Chebyshev polynomial activation function can approximate the complex function to an arbitrary degree of accuracy and its simple form reduces the risk of overfitting and enhances the robustness of the network. The ChNN has been successfully used in various areas such as system identification, function approximation, and control systems, and has shown impressive results in terms of accuracy, generalization ability, and stability [30,31].

The proposed control method for CNTs tackles the challenges posed by the small size of these systems and their sensitivity to environmental factors like temperature and humidity. This approach improves the performance of the controller and makes it more robust to changes in the system's properties. The numerical results of the implementation of the controller on CNTs are a testament to the proposed method's superior performance. The finite-time control strategy guarantees the closed-loop system to converge to the desired state in a finite time, regardless of the initial conditions, making them more robust in unknown conditions. This feature is especially important in the case of CNTs as the properties of CNTs can change with time due to environmental factors.

The rest of the article is structured as follows: Section 2 covers the modeling and mathematical representation of a CNT. In Section 3, the design process of the controller and its guaranteed stability are discussed. Then, in Section 4, the proposed controller is applied to the system in various uncertain scenarios for stabilization and tracking control. Finally, Section 5 concludes with summarizing remarks and prospects.

2. Modeling and Mathematical Formulation of the System

This section presents an overview of the system model of the CNT and the mathematical formulation used to describe its dynamics. The governing equations of motion for the CNT and the continuum mechanics principles applied to the CNT system are also presented. The scheme of a clamped–clamped single-walled CNT that uses electrostatic actuation to transport viscous fluid is illustrated in Figure 1.

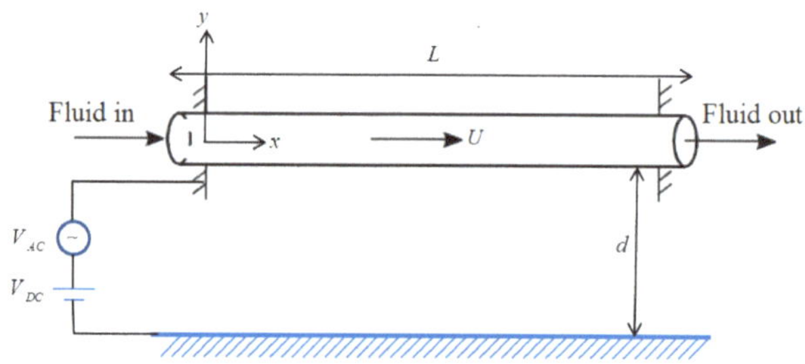

Figure 1. An illustration of a single-walled CNT.

The tubular structure being analyzed has a slender shape and undergoes planar motions, represented by $w(x,\ t)$ where x is the location and t is the time variable. The fluid flow velocity inside the CNT is represented by U. The governing nonlinear partial differential equation (PDE) and its appropriate boundary conditions have been derived by utilizing Hamilton's principle to study the CNT dynamics, taking into account the nonlocal effects. The following equation represents this governing equation and its corresponding boundary conditions [32]:

$$\begin{aligned}&\left(1+c\frac{\partial}{\partial t}\right)EI\frac{\partial^4 w}{\partial x^4}+\left[MU^2-N+PA(1-2v)+M\frac{\partial U}{\partial t}(L-x)\right]\frac{\partial^2 w}{\partial x^2}+(M+m)\frac{\partial^2 w}{\partial t^2}+2MU\frac{\partial^2 w}{\partial x\partial t}\\&-rA\left(U\frac{\partial^3 w}{\partial x^3}+\frac{\partial^3 w}{\partial x^2\partial t}\right)-(e_0a)^2\left[(M+m)\frac{\partial^4 w}{\partial x^2\partial t^2}+MU^2\frac{\partial^4 w}{\partial x^4}+2MU\frac{\partial^4 w}{\partial x^3\partial t}\right]=q_{elec}-(e_0a)^2\frac{\partial^2 q_{elec}}{\partial x^2}\end{aligned} \tag{1}$$

$$\begin{cases} w=w'=0atx=0\\ w=w'=0atx=L\end{cases} \tag{2}$$

where L signifies the length of the CNT, while EI represents its flexural rigidity. The viscoelastic nature of the CNT is denoted by c, and its Poisson ratio is shown as υ. The

CNT's mass per unit length is indicated by m, and the impact of the nonlocal elastic stress field on its behavior is symbolized by e_0. The static tension in the pipe is designated as N. For the fluid being conveyed at the end of the CNT, A stands for the cross-sectional area, M for its mass per unit length, r for its viscosity, and P for its internal pressure. The external electrostatic force affecting the CNT is represented by q_{elec} [33].

$$q_{elec} = \frac{\pi\varepsilon_0 v^2}{\sqrt{(d-w)(d-w+2R)}arccosh^2\left(1+\frac{d-w}{R}\right)}, \tag{3}$$

In the equation, ε_0 is the permittivity of the vacuum coefficient, with a value of 8.854×10^{-12} (C^2/Nm^2). The applied electrostatic voltage is represented by v, and the distance between the two electrodes is represented by d. The nonlinear PDE governing the CNT (1) was converted into a dimensionless form using the following dimensionless quantities.

$$\begin{gathered}\eta = \frac{w}{d}, \xi = \frac{x}{L}, \tau = \left(\frac{EI}{M+m}\right)^{1/2}\frac{t}{L^2}, \overline{R} = \frac{R}{d}, u_f = \left(\frac{M}{EI}\right)^{1/2} LU, \alpha = \left(\frac{EI}{M+m}\right)^{1/2}\frac{c}{L^2}, \\ T = \frac{NL^2}{EI} - \frac{PAL^2}{EI}(1-2v), \beta = \frac{rA}{(EIM)^{1/2}}, M_r = \left(\frac{M}{M+m}\right)^{1/2}, e_n = \frac{e_0 a}{L}, \overline{V} = \frac{v}{\sqrt{\frac{d^2EI}{\pi\varepsilon_0 L^4}}},\end{gathered} \tag{4}$$

These non-dimensional parameters are used to simplify the equation of motion and make it easier to analyze. By expressing the variables in a dimensionless form, it is possible to compare the results from different scenarios and to understand the underlying physics of the CNT's behavior more clearly. This is particularly useful when studying nonlinear systems such as the CNT, as it enables one to identify and analyze the key factors that affect the system's behavior. The dimensionless equation of motion is given by

$$\begin{aligned}&\alpha\frac{\partial^5\eta}{\partial\xi^4\partial\tau} + \frac{\partial^4\eta}{\partial\xi^4} + \left[u_f^2 - T + M_r\dot{u}_f(1-\xi)\right]\frac{\partial^2\eta}{\partial\xi^2} + \frac{\partial^2\eta}{\partial\tau^2} + 2M_r u_f\frac{\partial^2\eta}{\partial\xi\partial\tau} \\ &-\beta\left(u_f\frac{\partial^3\eta}{\partial\xi^3} + M_r\frac{\partial^3\eta}{\partial\xi^2\partial\tau}\right) - e_n^2\left(\frac{\partial^4\eta}{\partial\xi^2\partial\tau^2} + u_f^2\frac{\partial^4\eta}{\partial\xi^4} + 2M_r u_f\frac{\partial^4\eta}{\partial\xi^3\partial\tau}\right) = \\ &+\frac{\overline{V}^2}{\sqrt{(1-\eta)(1-\eta+2\overline{R})}arccosh^2\left(1+\frac{1-\eta}{\overline{R}}\right)} \\ &-e_n^2\frac{\partial^2\eta}{\partial\xi^2}\left(\frac{\overline{V}^2}{\sqrt{(1-\eta)(1-\eta+2\overline{R})}arccosh^2\left(1+\frac{1-\eta}{\overline{R}}\right)}\right),\end{aligned} \tag{5}$$

It has been assumed that the fluid's velocity, u_f, fluctuates in a periodic manner. To simplify the analysis, this velocity has been transformed into a dimensionless form, which is presented as:

$$\alpha u_f = u_0[1 + \mu cos(\omega\tau)] \tag{6}$$

In the equation, the fluid's average speed is represented by u_0, and the amplitude and frequency of its harmonic fluctuation are represented by μ and ω, respectively.

By applying the Galerkin method to the nonlinear PDE of the CNT, the complex and highly nonlinear equation is reduced to a set of simple and manageable nonlinear ordinary differential equations (ODEs). The Galerkin method is a mathematical technique that is used to simplify the solution of partial differential equations. This makes it possible to analyze the system and gain insights into its behavior. The equation of motion was discretized using the first and most significant mode shape of the CNT. This means that only the first and most significant pattern of vibration of the CNT has been considered in the analysis. This is a common practice in the analysis of linear and nonlinear systems, as it enables one to focus on the most important aspect of the system and simplify the analysis. It means that the governing PDE is broken down into smaller parts that can be more easily solved.

$$\eta(\xi,\tau) = \varphi(\xi)Q(\tau) \tag{7}$$

where the spatial and temporal parts of the deflection of the CNT are represented by $\varphi(\xi)$ and $Q(\tau)$, respectively, where $\varphi(\xi)$ satisfies the boundary conditions of the CNT.

The Taylor series has been used to express the external electrostatic force of the CNT as follows:

$$\frac{1}{\sqrt{(1-\eta)(1-\eta+2\overline{R})arccosh^2\left(1+\frac{1-\eta}{\overline{R}}\right)}} = 0.1537 + 0.2374\eta + 0.6081\eta^2 + 2.1650\eta^3 + \ldots. \tag{8}$$

The Taylor series is a mathematical tool that allows one to represent a function as an infinite sum of terms, where each term is a function of one or more variables raised to a certain power. In this case, the external electrostatic force of the CNT is represented as a sum of infinite terms, each term depending on the electrostatic voltage, v, and the electrode's distance, d. By expressing the external electrostatic force in this way, it becomes possible to study its properties and behavior in detail. Additionally, it allows one to analyze how the force changes as the applied voltage and distance between electrodes change. This leads to the final form of the nonlinear ODE as follows:

$$\ddot{Q} + (C_c + C_d)\dot{Q} + (K_c + K_d)Q = \overline{V}^2\left[a_1 + a_2Q + a_3Q^2 + a_4Q^3\right] \tag{9}$$

For more details on the parameters in Equation (9) refer to [34]. The electrostatic actuation which includes both a direct current voltage (v_{DC}) and an alternating current harmonic voltage (v_{AC}) component is given by:

$$v = v_{DC} + v_{AC}cos(\Omega t) = v_{DC} + v_{AC}(t) \tag{10}$$

Supposing $v_{AC} << v_{DC} \rightarrow v_{AC}^2 \approx 0$, results in

$$v^2 = v_{DC}^2 + 2v_{DC}v_{AC}(t) \tag{11}$$

Thus, Equation (9) can be reformulated as

$$\begin{aligned} &\ddot{Q} + (C_c + C_d)\dot{Q} + (K_c + K_d)Q = \overline{\overline{V}}^2\left[a_1 + a_2Q + a_3Q^2 + a_4Q^3\right] \\ &+2\frac{\overline{\overline{V}}^2}{v_{DC}}v_{AC}(t)\left[a_1 + a_2Q + a_3Q^2 + a_4Q^3\right] \end{aligned} \tag{12}$$

in which

$$\overline{\overline{V}} = \frac{v_{DC}}{\sqrt{\frac{d^2EI}{\pi\varepsilon_0L^4}}} \tag{13}$$

3. Proposed Control Methodology

In this section, a novel control method, referred to as a neural network-based finite-time super-twisting sliding mode technique, has been proposed for the vibration control of a CNT. This approach utilizes the electrostatic actuation as the implemented control signal and utilizes a neural network to accurately estimate the system's states. The stability of the proposed controller design is also proven in this section.

The proposed technique has several advantages over traditional control methods, including its ability to effectively handle the nonlinearity and uncertainty present in the CNT system, as well as its robustness to external disturbances. Additionally, it utilizes a finite-time convergence algorithm, which ensures that the system reaches the desired equilibrium state within a finite time (not exponential convergence), regardless of initial conditions or system parameters. Furthermore, by using a self-evolving neural network, it can improve control performance by reducing the effect of measurement noise and system uncertainties.

The state space equation of the system by defining $Q = x_1, \dot{Q} = \dot{x}_1 = x_2$ and $v_{AC} = u$ has been rewritten as follows:

$$\begin{cases} \dot{x}_1 = x_2 \\ \dot{x}_2 = -C_c x_2 - K_c x_1 + \overline{\overline{V}}^2 \left[a_1 + a_2 x_1 + a_3 x_1^2 + a_4 x_1^3\right] + \\ \quad 2\frac{\overline{\overline{V}}^2}{v_{DC}} \left[a_1 + a_2 x_1 + a_3 x_1^2 + a_4 x_1^3\right] u + d(\tau) \end{cases} \tag{14}$$

where $d(\tau) = d_0(\tau) - K_d x_1 - C_d x_2$ represents the compound disturbance, which includes external disturbance and uncertainties. Without losing generality, we rewrite the general state space of the system as follows:

$$\begin{cases} \dot{x}_i = x_{i+1} i = 1, 2, \cdots, n-1 \\ \dot{x}_n = f(x) + g(x)u + d(t) \\ y = x_1 \end{cases} \tag{15}$$

3.1. ChNN

A ChNN is a type of neural network that is designed to work with signals represented on a Chebyshev basis. In a ChNN, the input signal is first transformed into the Chebyshev basis using Chebyshev polynomials. Chebyshev polynomials are a set of orthogonal polynomials that are defined on a specific interval, usually [−1, 1]. They have several useful properties, such as rapid convergence and a high degree of smoothness. Using Chebyshev polynomials to represent the input signal allows the ChNN to take advantage of these properties and achieve a high degree of accuracy.

The transformed signal is then processed by the neural network, which is typically a feedforward network with one or more hidden layers. The weights and biases of the network are trained using a suitable optimization algorithm, such as backpropagation. ChNNs are particularly effective in nonlinear system modeling, where they can achieve a high degree of accuracy with a relatively small number of parameters. This is because Chebyshev polynomials are able to approximate nonlinear functions very well. Furthermore, ChNNs are able to handle signals with different scales, such as signals that contain both low-frequency and high-frequency components. Overall, a ChNN is an effective method for approximating nonlinear functions.

By taking the inputs of the ChNN as x_1 and x_2, which are the error and its time-derivative, respectively, the calculation of Chebyshev polynomials can be done using the commonly known recursive formula:

$$\Phi_{i+1}(x_i) = 2x_i \Phi_i(x_i) - \Phi_{i-1}(x_i) \tag{16}$$

in which the first Chebyshev polynomial is $\Phi_0(x_i)$ considered to be constant and equal to 1, and the second one is considered as $2x_i, 2x_i + 1$, or $2x_i - 1$, in the literature. Here we set $\Phi_1(x_i) = 2x_i$. The basis function in the Chebyshev polynomial is considered as:

$$H = [\Phi_0(x_1).\Phi_1(x_1).\Phi_2(x_1). \ldots .\Phi_n(x_1). \ldots \Phi_1(x_m).\Phi_2(x_m). \ldots . \Phi_n(x_m)] \tag{17}$$

The Chebyshev polynomials are ordered by n, and the neural network has m inputs as they are illustrated in Figure 2. A non-linear function $G(x) \in \mathbb{R}^m$ is estimated by a ChNN as

$$\hat{F}(x) = W^* H(x) + \varepsilon \tag{18}$$

where W^* represents the optimal weight matrix of the ChNN and ε represents the ChNN's bounded approximation error.

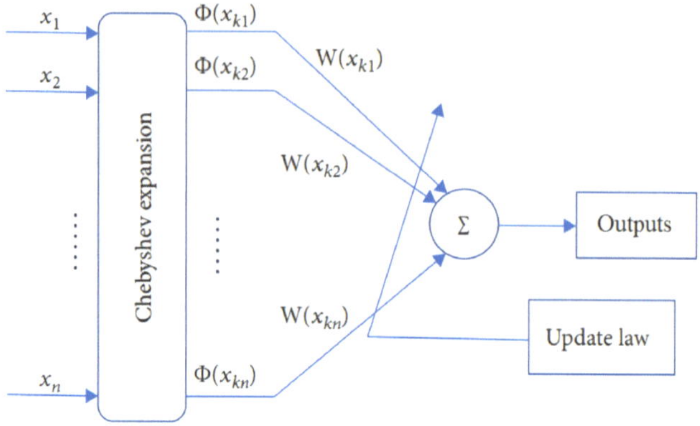

Figure 2. The configuration of the ChNN.

3.2. *Super-Twisting Finite-Time SMC*

The super-twisting algorithm, introduced in [35] is a widely sliding mode control and observation technique. Here are some of the advantages of the super-twisting sliding mode controllers:

- High accuracy in controlling dynamic systems,
- Robustness against uncertainties,
- Simplicity in implementation,
- Finite-time stability properties.

In this work, we present a reliable controller for CNTs by leveraging the universal approximation capability of neural networks and the robustness of super-twisting sliding mode controllers. By combining these two powerful techniques, we aim to achieve improved control performance. The difference between the actual response and the desired response of the system is represented by the tracking error as follows:

$$e(t) = x_1(t) - x_d(t) \tag{19}$$

Here, $x_d\ (t)$ represents the desired value of the state $x(t)$. The sliding surface is defined as:

$$s_t(t) = \tau e(t) + \dot{e}(t), \tag{20}$$

In this equation, the constant τ is a user-defined positive value. If the user-defined parameter (τ) of the sliding surface satisfies the Routh–Hurwitz stability condition, then the sliding surface will be considered stable. Our proposed solution for system (1) is a self-evolving finite-time super-twisting controller which is given by:

$$\begin{aligned} u_c &= -g^{-1}(x)\Big(f(x) - \dot{x}_{1d} + u_{st1} + \hat{d} + \tau e(t)\Big), \\ u_{st1} &= -k_1|s_t|^{\frac{1}{2}} sign(s_t) + u_{st2} \\ \dot{u}_{st2} &= -k_2 sign(s_t) \end{aligned} \tag{21}$$

The parameters k_1 and k_2 are both positive used-defined parameters in this equation. Additionally, the difference between the estimated weights and the actual weights is referred to as the error of weight estimation which is given by:

$$\widetilde{W} = W^* - \hat{W} \tag{22}$$

As it is shown in Figure 2, the neural network needs an updating law to evolve based on the new condition. The following adaptive law describes the proposed process to evolve the weights of the neural network:

$$\dot{\hat{W}} = -\gamma\, s_t \phi \tag{23}$$

where γ is a positive design parameter. It is noteworthy that the proposed control technique eliminates the need for a training phase, which is typically required in many other control techniques. This means that the system can start operating immediately without any prior knowledge of the system's dynamics or control parameters. This is achieved by using a sophisticated updating law to adjust the network's weights based on the current state of the system and its desired output.

Theorem 1. *The control law (21) ensures that the closed-loop system states (15) attain the desired value within a specified time.*

Proof. Equation (24) represents the time derivative of the sliding surface.

$$\begin{aligned} \dot{s}_t &= \left(\tau\dot{e}(t) + f(x) + g(x)u_c - \dot{x_{1d}}\right) \\ &= \left(\tau\dot{e}(t) + f(x) - \left(f(x) - \dot{x}_{1d} + u_{st1} + \hat{d} + \tau\dot{e}(t)\right) - \dot{x_{1d}}\right) \\ &= \left(-u_{st1} + d - \hat{d}\right) \end{aligned} \tag{24}$$

In accordance with Equation (18), we know $d - \hat{d} = d - \hat{W}\phi = \varepsilon$ which results in

$$\dot{s}_t = -u_{st1} + \varepsilon \tag{25}$$

Hence, substituting the proposed u_{st1} one can reach the following equations:

$$\begin{aligned} \dot{s}_t &= -k_1|s_t|^{\frac{1}{2}} sign(s_t) + u_{st2} + \varepsilon \\ \dot{u}_{st2} &= -k_2 sign(s_t) \end{aligned} \tag{26}$$

in which ε is a bounded estimation error. By introducing $w_1 = s_t$ and $w_2 = u_{st2}$ as new variables and reformulating the equation, we obtain

$$\begin{aligned} \dot{w}_1 &= -k_1|w_1|^{\frac{1}{2}} sign(w_1) + w_2 + \varepsilon \\ \dot{w}_2 &= -k_2 sign(w_1) \end{aligned} \tag{27}$$

Equation (27) represents a second-order super-twisting algorithm. According to Theorem 2 in [36] we select the following Lyapunov function

$$V_0 = \varsigma^{\mathrm{T}} P \varsigma \tag{28}$$

in which P is a symmetric and positive definite matrix, V_0 is quadratic Lyapunov function, and $\varsigma = [\varsigma_1, \varsigma_2]^T = \left[|w_1|^{\frac{1}{2}} sign(w_1), w_2\right]^T$ in which the following equality is held for symmetric and positive definite matrix Q

$$\dot{V}_0 = -|w_1|^{\frac{1}{2}} \varsigma^{\mathrm{T}} Q \varsigma \tag{29}$$

In addition, the error trajectory will be globally ultimately bounded, and the convergence time is given by t_f as follows:

$$t_f = t_{s\Delta} + \frac{2\lambda_{max}\{P\}}{\lambda_{min}^{\frac{1}{2}}\{P\}\lambda_{min}\{Q\}} V_0^{\frac{1}{2}}(t_0) \tag{30}$$

following the procedure outlined in [36], matrices P and Q in the Lyapunov function can be chosen, ensuring that the variables w_1 and w_2 reach zero in finite time (t_f). □

Figure 3 depicts the process of implementing the proposed control scheme that incorporates the ChNN estimator. By leveraging the ChNN estimator and super-twisting algorithm, the proposed scheme can achieve enhanced performance even when faced with uncertainties in the model and external disturbance. In the following section, we will employ this control scheme to regulate the nonlinear dynamic of the CNT.

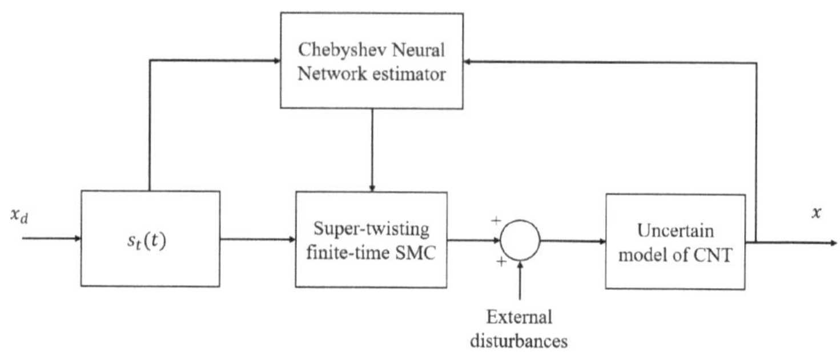

Figure 3. The block diagram of the proposed control scheme.

4. Simulation Results

The results of numerical simulations that demonstrate the proposed control method's outstanding performance on a CNT system are presented in this section. The system's parameters that have been made dimensionless are $\alpha = 0.001$, $\beta = 0.300$, $M_r = 0.800$, $T = 20$, and $e_n^2 = 0.200$. The proposed control technique's parameters are selected using a trial-and-error approach that is notably straightforward due to the technique's versatility across a broad range of parameters. This involves adjusting the control gains and evaluating the system's performance until the desired level of performance is attained. However, to achieve the best possible performance with this controller, it is advisable to utilize an evolutionary algorithm like a genetic algorithm to determine the controller's parameters. This approach considers the convergence time and control input value as objective functions to optimize the controller's performance.

4.1. Stabilization with Uncertain Parameters

In order to take to account the effects of uncertainties, the parameters C_c and K_c of the system are treated as time-varying parameters and subject to unknown perturbations as follows:

$$\Delta C_c = 0.5\sin\left(0.2t^2\right),\ \Delta K_c = 50\cos(2sqrt(t)) \tag{31}$$

The objective of this section is to maintain the stability of the CNT despite its continuously changing dynamic parameters. As shown in Figure 4, the states of the system are stabilized in a very short amount of time. This figure is meant to demonstrate that even though the parameters of the CNT system are continuously changing, the states of the system quickly stabilize and reach a stable state within a short amount of time. Figure 5, on the other hand, shows the control inputs that are applied to the CNT system in order to maintain its stability. The control signal is illustrated over time, showing the "chattering-free" behavior of the controller.

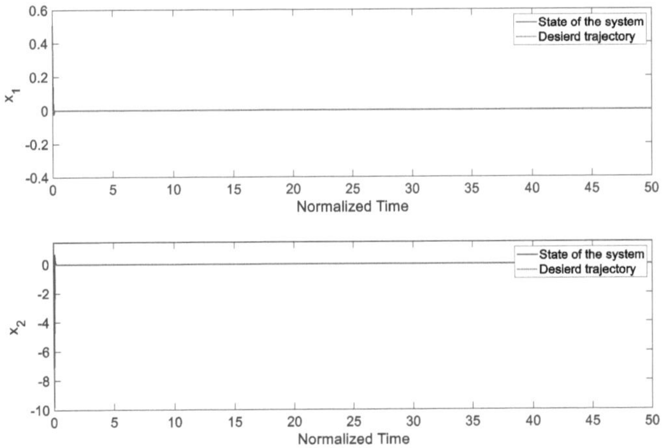

Figure 4. The states of the CNT with uncertain parameters using the suggested control technique method.

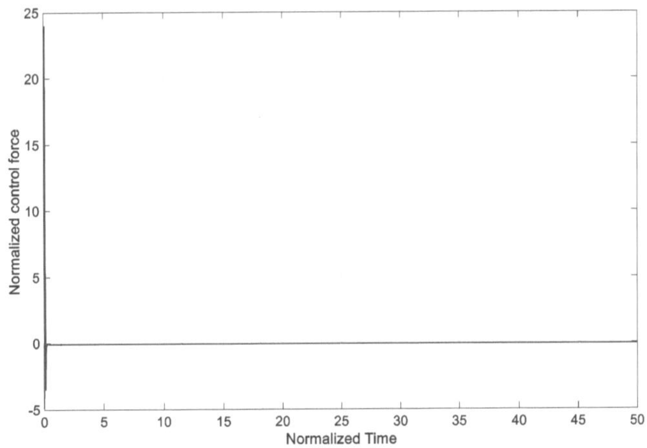

Figure 5. The control input for the CNT with uncertain parameters.

4.2. Stabilization in the Presence of Discontinuous Disturbances

In this study, we take into account the CNT in the presence of external disturbances that are complex and change over time, such as:

$$d(\tau) = 2\mathrm{sign}(\sin(0.5t)) + 0.5\cos(0.2\sqrt{t}) \tag{32}$$

The numerical results presented here effectively demonstrate the effectiveness of the proposed control strategy in maintaining the stability of the CNT system. Figure 6 clearly showcases the stabilized states of the system, even under complex disturbance conditions, highlighting the robustness of the proposed approach. Figure 7, on the other hand, presents the control signals obtained through the proposed control technique, which results in chattering-free control signals. Chattering can cause unwanted oscillations and vibrations in the system, negatively impacting its performance and reliability. The proposed control strategy, by avoiding chattering, ensures stability without sacrificing performance.

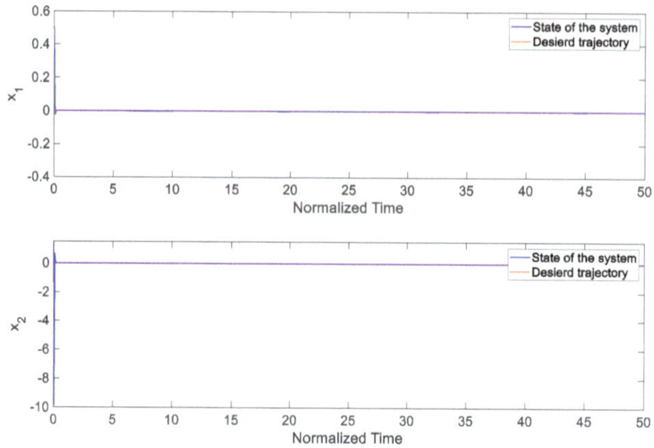

Figure 6. The states of the CNT with uncertain parameters and unknown disturbances using the suggested control technique method.

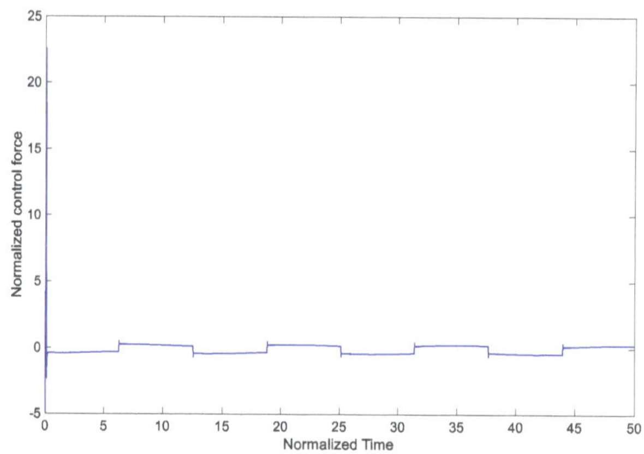

Figure 7. The control input for the CNT with uncertain parameters and unknown disturbance.

There is rigorous reason behind the smooth control signal of the proposed technique. In the proposed control scheme, the sign function is not applied directly to the system. Instead, only terms containing $k_1|s_t|^{\frac{1}{2}}sign(s_t)$ and the integral of $k_2sign(s_t)$ are present, both of which are smooth (refer to Equation (21) in the manuscript). Furthermore, since the controller stabilizes the system in finite time, the sliding surface converges to zero within a finite time. This means that the sign(s_t) function becomes zero after a short period, resulting in reduced or eliminated chattering and vibration during the stabilization process. Hence, the proposed finite-time controller offers two benefits: (a) it stabilizes the system within a finite time, and (b) it reduces or eliminates chattering in the control input signal, thereby reducing vibration in the system.

These results demonstrate the robustness and effectiveness of the proposed super-twisting sliding mode algorithm in maintaining the stability of the CNT system and have significant implications for the design of control systems in practical applications. Discontinuous disturbances can cause instability in the system and lead to poor performance, making it crucial to design a controller that can effectively handle these disturbances. It is noteworthy that many conventional controllers struggle to handle such disturbances, either due to stability criteria that they cannot meet or an increased convergence time. This highlights the importance of the proposed super-twisting sliding mode algorithm, which is able to handle discontinuous disturbances and maintain the stability of the CNT system even in challenging conditions. The results presented in the figures demonstrate the robustness and effectiveness of the proposed algorithm in these scenarios, making it a valuable contribution to the field of control systems design.

4.3. Tracking Control

To examine the efficiency of the proposed control scheme, we set a specific desired state trajectory for the system. This desired state trajectory acts as a benchmark for evaluating the performance of the proposed scheme and allows us to determine how well the system is able to track the desired path. By comparing the actual state of the system with the desired state, we can evaluate the accuracy and reliability of the proposed control strategy in achieving the desired state. This step is crucial in validating the proposed control scheme and provides insight into its ability to track a desired trajectory, a key requirement for many control systems applications.

$$x_d = 0.3sin(3t) + 0.1cos(0.5t) \tag{33}$$

Figures 8 and 9 show the system's states and chatter-free control input. The tracking control results demonstrate the proposed control scheme's ability to reach the desired performance. This is evidenced by the stable and smooth behavior of the system, as well as the control input, which does not exhibit any "chatter" or erratic behavior. This suggests that the proposed control method is effective in controlling the system and producing stable and consistent results, even in the presence of disturbances or other challenging conditions.

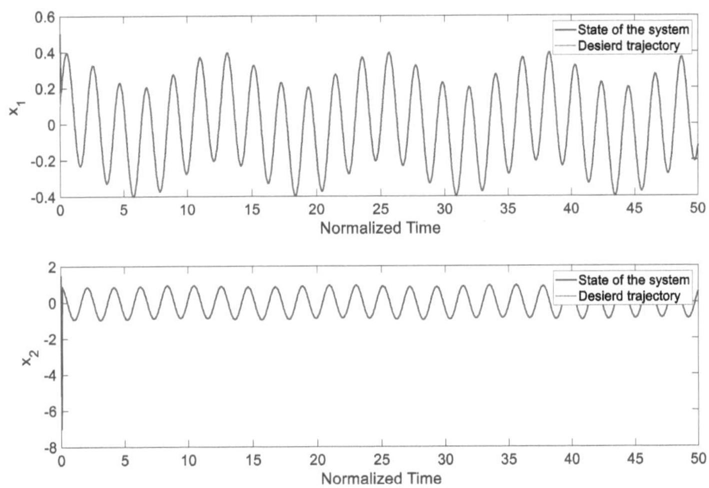

Figure 8. The states of CNT in tracking control in the presence of uncertain parameters and unknown disturbance.

In summary, this new control method provides a promising solution for the control of CNTs, which are widely used in various fields such as electronics, energy, and medicine, and the ability to control them accurately and efficiently is of great importance.

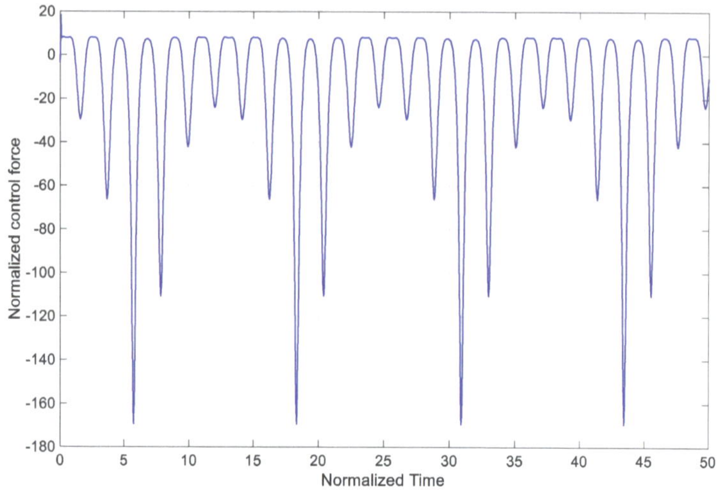

Figure 9. The control input for tracking of CNT with uncertain parameters and unknown disturbance.

5. Conclusions

We studied the stabilization and control of CNTs with dynamic parameters and unknown discontinuous uncertainties. The proposed control scheme extends the super-twisting sliding mode control and offers chattering-free and finite-time responses by leveraging the universal approximation capabilities of neural networks. The self-evolving neural network was utilized in the control algorithm to take into account the effects of disturbances and uncertainties, which helped to provide a chattering-free and finite-time response. The Lyapunov stability theorem was used to prove the finite-time convergence and stability of the system. The disturbances and uncertainties were taken into consideration in the stability analysis of the proposed control scheme. The effectiveness of the proposed scheme was assessed through various numerical simulations in different scenarios, including stabilization with time-varying parameters, stabilization in the presence of disturbances, and tracking control. Numerical simulation results confirmed the proposed control technique's theoretical claims and showed its excellent performance. Given the promising results of the proposed solution in our study, we recommend considering its application in practical scenarios in the future. Also, future enhancements to the proposed controller can include the integration of self-tuning algorithms, making it versatile and adaptable for use in various systems. Also, by incorporating fractional-order elements, the proposed controller can achieve improved performance and accuracy in capturing complex dynamic behaviors, making it more suitable for use in a wider range of systems.

Author Contributions: Conceptualization, F.W.A., M.S.A.-z., Q.Y. and H.J.; methodology, F.W.A., M.S.A.-z., Q.Y. and H.J.; software, F.W.A., M.S.A.-z., Q.Y. and H.J.; validation, F.W.A., M.S.A.-z., Q.Y. and H.J.; formal analysis, F.W.A., M.S.A.-z., Q.Y. and H.J.; writing—original draft preparation, F.W.A., M.S.A.-z., Q.Y. and H.J.; writing—review and editing, F.W.A., M.S.A.-z., Q.Y. and H.J.; supervision, F.W.A., M.S.A.-z., Q.Y. and H.J. All authors have read and agreed to the published version of the manuscript.

Funding: The authors extend their appreciation to the Deputyship for Research and Innovation, Ministry of Education in Saudi Arabia, for funding this research work (Project number INSTR005).

Data Availability Statement: No new data were created.

Conflicts of Interest: The authors declare no conflict of interest.

References

1. Anzar, N.; Hasan, R.; Tyagi, M.; Yadav, N.; Narang, J. Carbon Nanotube-A Review on Synthesis, Properties and Plethora of Applications in the Field of Biomedical Science. *Sens. Int.* **2020**, *1*, 100003. [CrossRef]
2. Andrews, R.; Weisenberger, M.C. Carbon Nanotube Polymer Composites. *Curr. Opin. Solid State Mater. Sci.* **2004**, *8*, 31–37. [CrossRef]
3. Endo, M.; Hayashi, T.; Kim, Y.A.; Muramatsu, H. Development and Application of Carbon Nanotubes. *Jpn. J. Appl. Phys.* **2006**, *45*, 4883. [CrossRef]
4. Norizan, M.N.; Moklis, M.H.; Demon, S.Z.N.; Halim, N.A.; Samsuri, A.; Mohamad, I.S.; Knight, V.F.; Abdullah, N. Carbon Nanotubes: Functionalisation and Their Application in Chemical Sensors. *RSC Adv.* **2020**, *10*, 43704–43732. [CrossRef] [PubMed]
5. Wang, X.; Dong, A.; Hu, Y.; Qian, J.; Huang, S. A Review of Recent Work on Using Metal–Organic Frameworks to Grow Carbon Nanotubes. *Chem. Commun.* **2020**, *56*, 10809–10823. [CrossRef] [PubMed]
6. Brozena, A.H.; Kim, M.; Powell, L.R.; Wang, Y. Controlling the Optical Properties of Carbon Nanotubes with Organic Colour-Centre Quantum Defects. *Nat. Rev. Chem.* **2019**, *3*, 375–392. [CrossRef]
7. Mirghaffari, A.; Rahmani, B. Active Vibration Control of Carbon Nanotube Reinforced Composite Beams. *Trans. Inst. Meas. Control* **2017**, *39*, 1851–1863. [CrossRef]
8. Fadaee, M.; Talebitooti, M. Active Vibration Control of Carbon Nanotube-Reinforced Composite Beam Submerged in Fluid Using Magnetostrictive Layers. *Mech. Based Des. Struct. Mach.* **2022**, *50*, 799–816. [CrossRef]
9. Qiu, C.; Zhang, Z.; Zhong, D.; Si, J.; Yang, Y.; Peng, L.-M. Carbon Nanotube Feedback-Gate Field-Effect Transistor: Suppressing Current Leakage and Increasing on/off Ratio. *ACS Nano* **2015**, *9*, 969–977. [CrossRef]
10. Quoc, T.H.; van Tham, V.; Tu, T.M. Active Vibration Control of a Piezoelectric Functionally Graded Carbon Nanotube-Reinforced Spherical Shell Panel. *Acta Mech.* **2021**, *232*, 1005–1023. [CrossRef]
11. Zamfirache, I.A.; Precup, R.-E.; Roman, R.-C.; Petriu, E.M. Policy Iteration Reinforcement Learning-Based Control Using a Grey Wolf Optimizer Algorithm. *Inf. Sci.* **2022**, *585*, 162–175. [CrossRef]
12. Precup, R.-E.; Preitl, S.; Petriu, E.; Bojan-Dragos, C.-A.; Szedlak-Stinean, A.-I.; Roman, R.-C.; Hedrea, E.-L. Model-Based Fuzzy Control Results for Networked Control Systems. *Rep. Mech. Eng.* **2020**, *1*, 10–25. [CrossRef]
13. Chun-Yueh, L.I.N. Fuzzy AHP-Based Prioritization of the Optimal Alternative of External Equity Financing for Start-Ups of Lending Company in Uncertain Environment. *Sci. Technol.* **2022**, *25*, 133–149.
14. Chen, Y.; Chu, B.; Freeman, C.T. Iterative Learning Control for Robotic Path Following with Trial-Varying Motion Profiles. *IEEE/ASME Trans. Mechatron.* **2022**, *27*, 4697–4706. [CrossRef]
15. Suzuki, K. *Artificial Neural Networks: Industrial and Control Engineering Applications*; BoD–Books on Demand: Norderstedt, Germany, 2011; ISBN 9533072202.
16. Awodele, O.; Jegede, O. Neural Networks and Its Application in Engineering. In Proceedings of the Informing Science & IT Education Conference (InSITE) 2009, Macon, GA, USA, 12–15 June 2009; pp. 83–95.
17. Chen, H.; Liu, Z.; Alippi, C.; Huang, B.; Liu, D. Explainable Intelligent Fault Diagnosis for Nonlinear Dynamic Systems: From Unsupervised to Supervised Learning. *IEEE Trans. Neural Netw Learn. Syst.* **2022**. *early access*. [CrossRef]
18. Yousefpour, A.; Jahanshahi, H.; Munoz-Pacheco, J.M.; Bekiros, S.; Wei, Z. A Fractional-Order Hyper-Chaotic Economic System with Transient Chaos. *Chaos Solitons Fractals* **2020**, *130*, 109400. [CrossRef]
19. Meghdari, A.; Naderi, D.; Alam, M.R. Neural-Network-Based Observer for Real-Time Tipover Estimation. *Mechatronics* **2005**, *15*, 989–1004. [CrossRef]
20. Chen, S.-B.; Beigi, A.; Yousefpour, A.; Rajaee, F.; Jahanshahi, H.; Bekiros, S.; Martínez, R.A.; Chu, Y. Recurrent Neural Network-Based Robust Nonsingular Sliding Mode Control with Input Saturation for a Non-Holonomic Spherical Robot. *IEEE Access* **2020**, *8*, 188441–188453. [CrossRef]
21. Yasami, A.; Beigi, A.; Yousefpour, A. Application of Long Short-Term Memory Neural Network and Optimal Control to Variable-Order Fractional Model of HIV/AIDS. *Eur. Phys. J. Spec. Top.* **2022**, *231*, 1875–1884. [CrossRef]
22. Xu, C.; Zhang, J.; Yi, M. Optimum Design and Application of Nano-Micro-Composite Ceramic Tool and Die Materials with Improved Back Propagation Neural Network. In *Artificial Neural Networks: Industrial and Control Engineering Applications*; BoD–Books on Demand: Norderstedt, Germany, 2011; pp. 131–152.
23. Almakaeel, H.; Albalawi, A.; Desai, S. Artificial Neural Network Based Framework for Cyber Nano Manufacturing. *Manuf. Lett.* **2018**, *15*, 151–154. [CrossRef]
24. Eslami, S.; Jalili, N.; Saeidpourazar, R. A Neural Network-Based Controller for a Piezoelectrically-Actuated Nano/Micromanipulator. In *Proceedings of the Smart Materials, Adaptive Structures and Intelligent Systems*; ASME: New York, NY, USA, 2008; Volume 43321, pp. 539–546.
25. Wang, B.; Liu, J.; Alassafi, M.O.; Alsaadi, F.E.; Jahanshahi, H.; Bekiros, S. Intelligent Parameter Identification and Prediction of Variable Time Fractional Derivative and Application in a Symmetric Chaotic Financial System. *Chaos Solitons Fractals* **2022**, *154*, 111590. [CrossRef]
26. Wang, Y.; Wang, Z.; Zhang, X. Robust Active Vibration Suppression of Single-Walled Carbon Nanotube Using Adaptive Sliding-Mode Control and Electrostatic Actuators. *J. Vib. Control* **2022**, *29*, 1387–1399. [CrossRef]
27. Rahmani, B. Adaptive Fuzzy Sliding Mode Control for Vibration Suppression of a Rotating Carbon Nanotube-Reinforced Composite Beam. *J. Vib. Control* **2018**, *24*, 2447–2463. [CrossRef]

28. Yang, W.; Ratinac, K.R.; Ringer, S.P.; Thordarson, P.; Gooding, J.J.; Braet, F. Carbon Nanomaterials in Biosensors: Should You Use Nanotubes or Graphene? *Angew. Chem. Int. Ed.* **2010**, *49*, 2114–2138. [CrossRef]
29. Mall, S.; Chakraverty, S. Chebyshev Neural Network Based Model for Solving Lane–Emden Type Equations. *Appl. Math. Comput.* **2014**, *247*, 100–114. [CrossRef]
30. Wang, B.; Jahanshahi, H.; Dutta, H.; Zambrano-Serrano, E.; Grebenyuk, V.; Bekiros, S.; Aly, A.A. Incorporating Fast and Intelligent Control Technique into Ecology: A Chebyshev Neural Network-Based Terminal Sliding Mode Approach for Fractional Chaotic Ecological Systems. *Ecol. Complex.* **2021**, *47*, 100943. [CrossRef]
31. Lu, K.; Li, T.; Zhang, L. Active Attitude Fault-Tolerant Tracking Control of Flexible Spacecraft via the Chebyshev Neural Network. *Trans. Inst. Meas. Control* **2019**, *41*, 925–933. [CrossRef]
32. Liang, F.; Su, Y. Stability Analysis of a Single-Walled Carbon Nanotube Conveying Pulsating and Viscous Fluid with Nonlocal Effect. *Appl. Math. Model.* **2013**, *37*, 6821–6828. [CrossRef]
33. Fakhrabadi, M.M.S.; Rastgoo, A.; Ahmadian, M.T. Size-Dependent Instability of Carbon Nanotubes under Electrostatic Actuation Using Nonlocal Elasticity. *Int. J. Mech. Sci.* **2014**, *80*, 144–152. [CrossRef]
34. Yousefpour, A.; Vahidi-Moghaddam, A.; Rajaei, A.; Ayati, M. Stabilization of Nonlinear Vibrations of Carbon Nanotubes Using Observer-Based Terminal Sliding Mode Control. *Trans. Inst. Meas. Control* **2020**, *42*, 1047–1058. [CrossRef]
35. Levant, A. Sliding Order and Sliding Accuracy in Sliding Mode Control. *Int. J. Control* **1993**, *58*, 1247–1263. [CrossRef]
36. Moreno, J.A.; Osorio, M. Strict Lyapunov Functions for the Super-Twisting Algorithm. *IEEE Trans. Autom. Control* **2012**, *57*, 1035–1040. [CrossRef]

mathematics

Article

Understanding In-Line Connections Behavior from Experimental and Numerical Analyses on Rectangular and Circular Hollow Section Elements

Calin-Ioan Birdean [1], Ioan Both [2,*], Ioan Mărginean [2] and Anghel Cernescu [1]

1 Department of Mechanics and Strength of Materials, Politehnica University of Timisoara, 300222 Timisoara, Romania; calin.birdean@student.upt.ro (C.-I.B.); anghel.cernescu@upt.ro (A.C.)
2 Department of Steel Structures and Structural Mechanics, Politehnica University of Timisoara, 300224 Timisoara, Romania; ioan.marginean@upt.ro
* Correspondence: ioan.both@upt.ro

Abstract: Depending on the connection type, especially semi-rigid connections, the analyses of building structures offer accurate results function of the rigidity and ductility. The present paper analyzes the in-line connection of rectangular and circular hollow sections, categorized as semi-rigid connections, suitable for an architectural design of invisible joints. For such connection the standards do not cover an explicit design method. Experimental bending tests were performed on rectangular and circular hollow sections having the end plate fixed inside the profile and bolted by four and one high-strength bolts, respectively. The joint separation represents a serviceability criterion which was monitored using digital image correlation technique. Based on experimental results, a numerical model was validated using the finite element method. After the validation of the numerical model based on the experimental results, a parametric investigation was conducted to study the influence of the access hole, the preload level, the end plate thickness, and the axial force. The results show the small influence of the bolt preload, but the end plate thickness was of major importance. A reduction of the assembly rigidity was also caused by the manhole. The study shows the feasibility of the connection configuration with the end plate positioned inside the hollow profile.

Keywords: in-line connection; experimental test; finite element analyses; joint separation; parametric study

MSC: 65Z05

Citation: Birdean, C.-I.; Both, I.; Mărginean, I.; Cernescu, A. Understanding In-Line Connections Behavior from Experimental and Numerical Analyses on Rectangular and Circular Hollow Section Elements. *Mathematics* **2023**, *11*, 3416. https://doi.org/10.3390/math11153416

Academic Editors: Joaquim Infante Barbosa and José Alberto Rodrigues

Received: 16 July 2023
Revised: 30 July 2023
Accepted: 3 August 2023
Published: 5 August 2023

1. Introduction

For an attractive aspect of steel structures, rectangular or circular hollow sections are welded leading to a continuous aspect of the structure. This solution involves specialized manpower and requires more time for erecting. Bolted connections provide sufficient capacity and rigidity if used for hollow sections with end plates extended outside of the profile perimeter as presented by [1]. By positioning the bolts only within the perimeter of the profile, the response of the connection is highly affected by lowering both the rigidity and the capacity. Nevertheless, the bolted connection has the advantage of a reduced erecting time compared to the welded connection.

In the case of T joints where distribution of moment is very important, the rigidity of welded joints for hollow sections reduces, if the axial force leads to stresses close to the yielding of material [2]. Similar studies were conducted to determine the bending capacity, rotational stiffness and ductility for high strength steel connection which proved the need for reduction coefficients only for few welding types [3].

When different profiles of tubular sections are connected by welding, the push–pull local mechanism is the common failure mode for which the rotational stiffness may be of high importance. Design methods for T joints were suggested by Szlendak [4], but the in-line connection failure mode, which is the current interest, is very different as the web of the element is not an influencing factor.

For the continuity connection of tubular sections, end plates connected by bolts can be used. The thickness effect on the prying force for bolted flange connection with the bolts positioned outside the profile perimeter was shown by Liu et al. [5]. The study also presented flange thicknesses, bolt edge distances, flange edge widths, and bolt hole diameters influence, both experimentally as well as numerically.

For high levels of forces, inner and outer bolts can be used for the flange connection of hollow sections as presented by Li et al. [6]. This connection exhibits a more direct stress distribution.

Another improved connection was presented by Deng et al. [7], the external double-layered flange connection, which overcomes the brittle fracture and the lamellar tearing of traditional flange connections.

Such connections are highly used for steel antenna towers [8] either for unipole or truss configurations, and for modular steel constructions and the joints types presented in [9]. Among these connections, the hidden joints are of interest due to their aesthetic aspect. Due to the small distance between the compressed area and the tensioned bolt, the rigidity of such connections is limited, and the joint is considered a semi-rigid joint. For structures with semi-rigid joints, the real deformation of the structure is obtained only if the rigidity of the joints is considered. The influence of the axial and bending level on the rigidity of the semi-rigid joints was presented in [10].

Structures with hollow sections require supplementary strength for seismic design. An innovative dismountable joint based on container corner fitting is proposed by Lian et al. [11] and its seismic performance is investigated based on FE analysis. The study showed a simplified connection that substitutes the bolt modeling with multiple connectors.

The stability of square hollow sections in comparison to concrete-filled steel tubes used in the case of modular construction was presented by Chen et al. [12] for which the connections are also similar to the section dimensions. These connections usually use high-strength bolts, but a 20% lighter cast–steel connector can be used without compromising the strength needed to satisfy the design loads [13].

In a numerical study, Urbonas and Daniunas [14] showed that the inclination of the beam, and quantity and location of bolts have a significant influence on joint rigidity.

The aesthetic aspect of the element can be maintained using an end plate with the same perimeter as the hollow profile as presented by Both et al. [15], where the failure modes, both welding and bolt failure, were also highlighted after an experimental testing program on in-line connections of rectangular hollow sections. This configuration is susceptible to lamellar tearing [16]; thus, the current studied configuration eliminated this risk.

In addition, the prying forces developing in these connections represent a risk factor, and the force in the bolt can be calculated using the relations developed by [17]. The current configuration eliminates the development of the prying forces as the end plates are not in contact.

Based on the classical strain iteration algorithm for cross sections, in practice, the assessment of the capacity can be determined using the method developed by Stephan and Stutzki [18]. The method is suitable for computer programs but the magnitude of the joint separation in the tensioned area is not available, although it can be a serviceability criterion for design.

These in-line connections are mostly used for axial force transfer between the elements, but bending can also occur. Thus, the response of these joints to flexural loading is necessary to be studied either for the resistance or for the deformation.

The paper presents the response of an in-line bolted connection with the end plate positioned inside a rectangular or circular hollow section at 2 mm from the profile end plane, with access through a hand hole. Based on experimental results, a numerical model is defined using the finite element method. After the validation of the numerical model based on the experimental results, a parametric investigation is conducted to study the influence of the access hole, the preload level, the end plate thickness, and the axial force.

2. Materials and Methods (Experimental Tests)

As the results of the numerical simulation are based on experimental results, the following relates to the testing data.

Two tests were performed on each rectangular hollow section (RHS) and circular hollow section (CHS) specimen subjected to bending. The length of the specimen was different resulting in the loading position and the boundary conditions presented in Figure 1. Both supports allowed free rotation while only one allowed horizontal displacements.

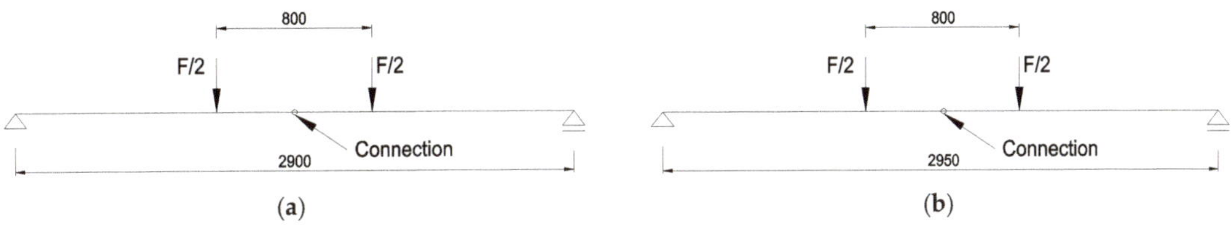

Figure 1. Static scheme for: (**a**) RHS; (**b**) CHS.

Each tested specimen implied two assemblies connected in the middle of the span. The rectangular specimens considered the RHS250 × 150 × 8 profile, with the details of the specimen presented in Figure 2.

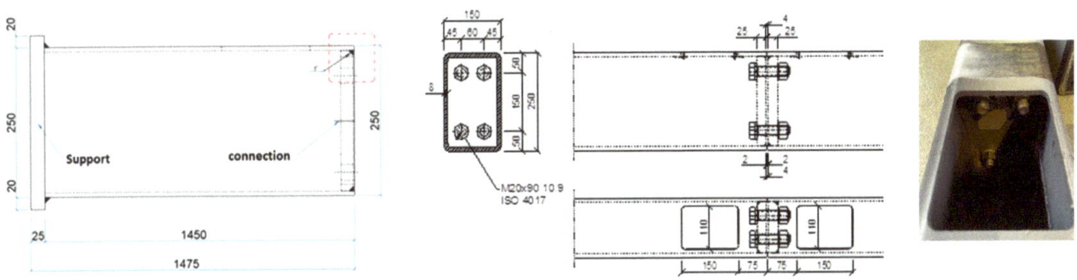

Figure 2. Details of RHS specimen.

The circular specimen considered the CHS114.3 × 10 profile, with the details of the specimen presented in Figure 3.

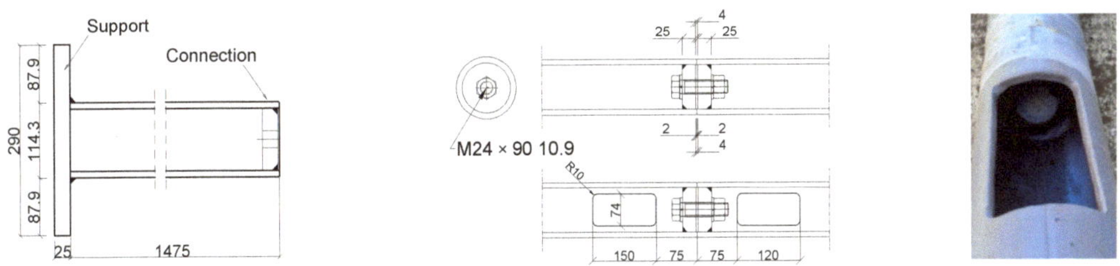

Figure 3. Details of CHS specimen.

Each element assembly had a cut of 150 mm long and a width of 110 mm and 74 mm for the RHS and CHS specimens, respectively. The RHS was connected using four M20 gr.

10.9 bolts, while the CHS was connected by one M24 gr. 10.9 bolt. The torque wrench was set to introduce a 130 kN preload force.

It must be mentioned that the end plates had a thickness of 25 mm and were inserted in the profiles at a distance of 2 mm from the profile end, to allow perfect contact between the hollow sections and avoid contact between the welding of the end plates.

The entire setup of the experimental tests is presented in Figure 4. A supplementary structure (yellow structure) was assembled to avoid out-of-plane displacements of the actuator and the specimens.

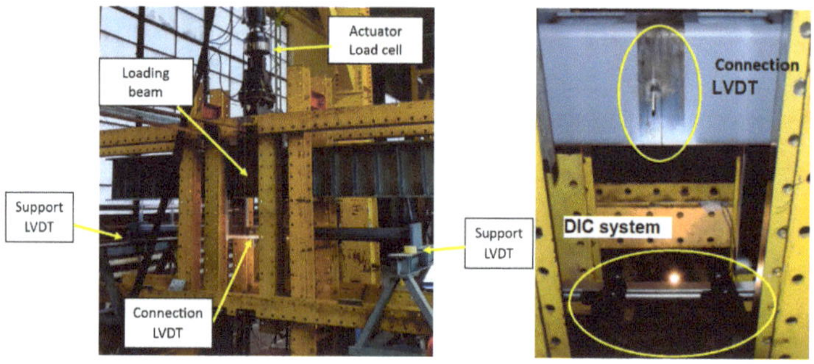

Figure 4. Test setup.

The recordings of the experimental tests consist of the vertical displacements at the supports and midspan, and the force obtained from the actuator. The vertical displacements were measured by linear variable displacement transducer (LVDT) while the force was measured by the actuator load cell.

The transmission of loading forces was achieved by means of devices that allowed the loading points to rotate freely. In the case of RHS profiles, the device contains a roller and parts to distribute the load over the entire width of the upper flange, Figure 5a, while for CHS profiles, a steel part was cut out to transmit the loads to the upper contour of the profile, Figure 5b.

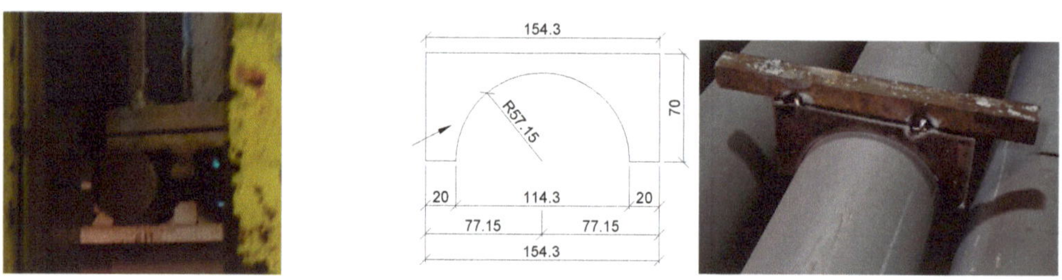

(a) (b)

Figure 5. Loading devices for: (a) RHS; (b) CHS.

The mechanical properties of the base material were determined according to ISO 6892-1 [19] on two specimens extracted from the specimen profiles as presented in Figure 6. Due to the available equipment, the specimens from the bolts were manufactured as presented in Figure 6c and they do not respect the proportionality factor.

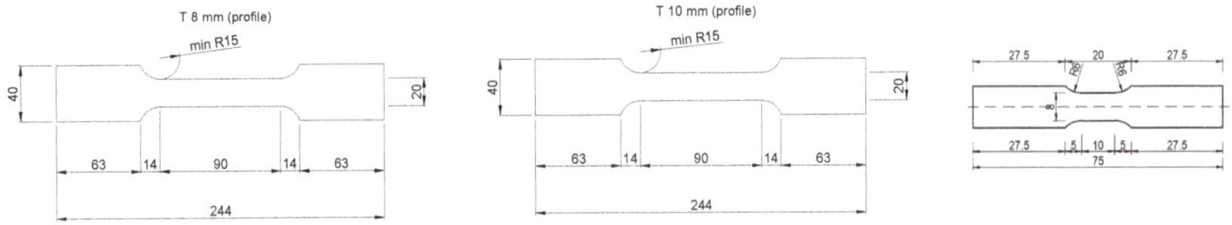

(a) (b) (c)

Figure 6. Tensile tests specimen for: (**a**) RHS; (**b**) CHS; (**c**) bolts.

The material characteristic curves are presented in Figure 7 where a small ductility is observed for the material of the CHS profile. Because the bolt tensile specimen is smaller than the standard specimen, the elongation of the material cannot be considered similar to the base material of the profiles.

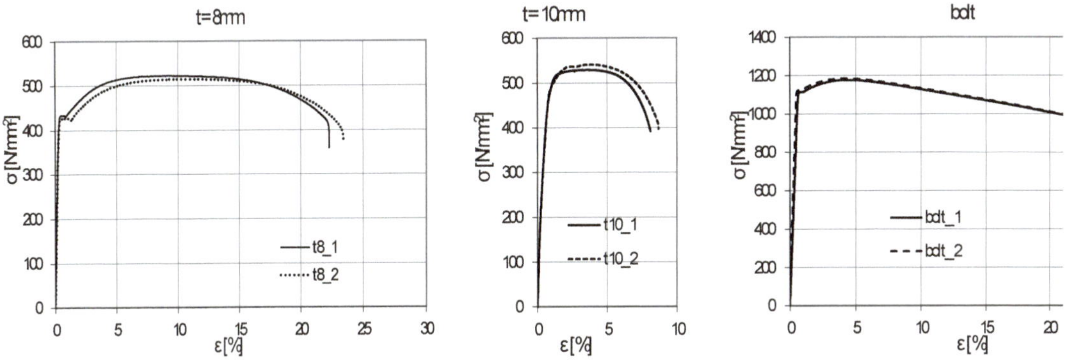

(a) (b) (c)

Figure 7. Base material characteristic curves for: (**a**) RHS; (**b**) CHS; (**c**) bolt.

A major necking was observed for the material of the RHS profile compared to the necking of the material of the CHS profile in Figure 8, which explains the small ductility of the CHS material in the characteristic curve.

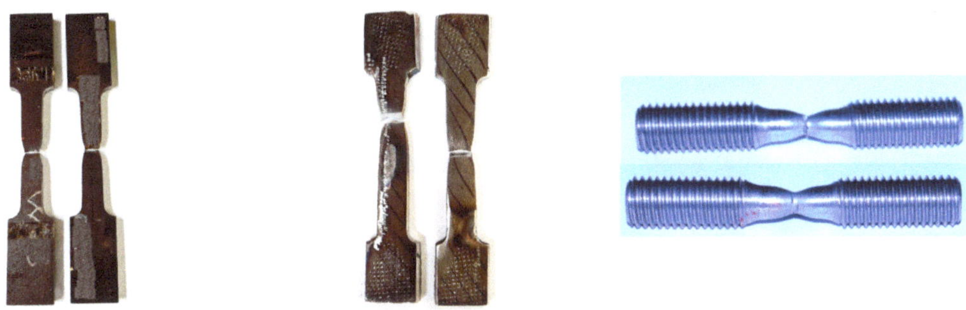

(a) (b) (c)

Figure 8. Fracture of the tensile specimens for: (**a**) RHS; (**b**) CHS; (**c**) bolt.

Based on the testing recordings, the following yield point and tensile strength were determined:

- 441–553 N/mm^2—RHS;

- 496–535 N/mm^2—CHS;
- 396–516 N/mm^2—end plate;
- 1119–1184 N/mm^2—bolt.

By transforming the characteristic curves into true stress-true strain, using the relations provided by Eurocode 1993-1-5 [20], the final value of the tensile strength used in the numerical model is 605, 564, 557, and 1231 N/mm^2, for the RHS, CHS, end plate and bolt, respectively.

The secondary interest of the experiments is the joint separation of the two hollow sections. Due to bolt pretensioning, the hollow sections should not separate immediately after loading. This parameter represents a serviceability limit state criterion. To monitor the joint separation, the digital image correlation (DIC) technique was employed with the system provided by isiSys GmbH. Black dots on a white background were applied on the tensioned side of each specimen to obtain the speckle pattern, Figure 9. Two virtual extensometers were defined by connecting two virtual gauges defined on each side of the connection.

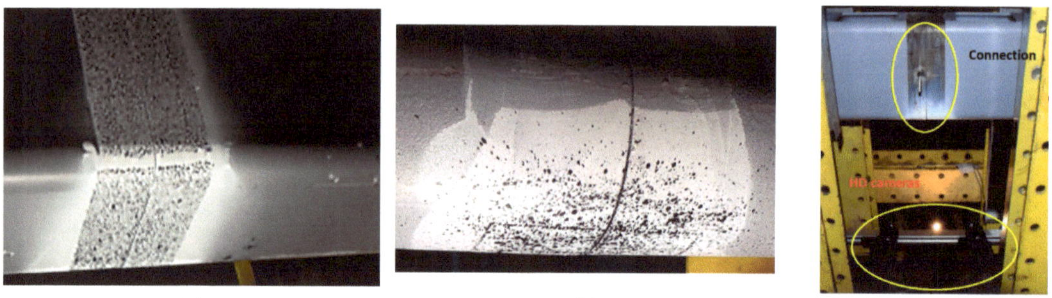

(**a**) (**b**) (**c**)

Figure 9. (**a**) Speckle pattern for RHS; (**b**) speckle pattern for CHS; (**c**) setup for the DIC system.

The DIC allows the displacement monitoring of the virtual gauges and the distance between them by using VIC Gauge 3D v7 software as well as the strain in the monitored area by using VIC 3D on the images captured by the high-resolution cameras.

3. Materials and Methods (Numerical Simulations)

The finite element analysis was conducted using Abaqus 2017 [21] software. The principle for using numerical analysis is to avoid expensive physical tests to evaluate the effect of different parameters. Numerical analyses can be performed in various formulations but the most effective is desired. An optimization has to be found between the precision and the complexity of the model. The current study simulates the connection between hollow sections which, from the experimental tests, was proven to reach the maximum capacity at bolt failure. Because stability phenomena are not influencing the response of the assembly, the standard static analysis is employed and, as it will be shown, will provide accurate results. Based on the validated model which provides similar results as the data recording during the experiment, the effect of the access hole, bolt preload, and end plate thickness is assessed.

Three-dimensional solid elements were defined as parts of the assembly similar to the entire experimental specimen (Figures 10 and 11 for RHS and CHS, respectively). The static, general solver was employed for the analysis during loading.

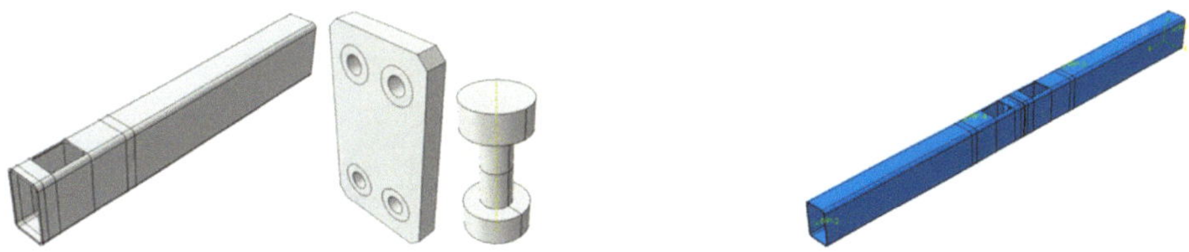

(**a**) (**b**)

Figure 10. Finite element model for RHS: (**a**) individual parts; (**b**) assembly.

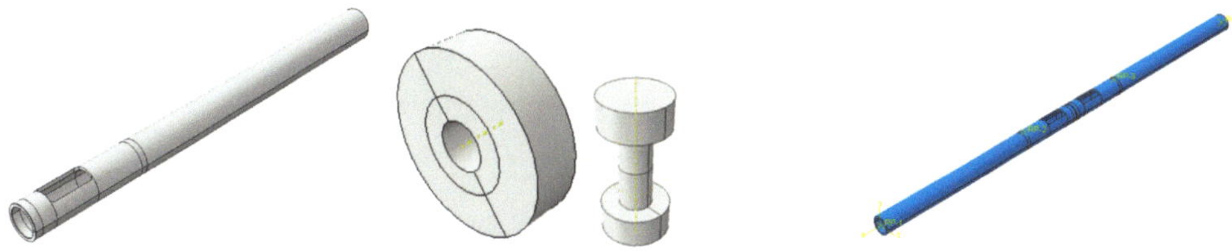

(**a**) (**b**)

Figure 11. Finite element model for CHS: (**a**) individual parts; (**b**) assembly.

The material properties considered an elasticity modulus of 210,000 N/mm^2 while the strength and deformation were defined with the true stress obtained from the tensile tests as presented in Table 1.

Table 1. Mechanical properties for the finite element model.

Material	Yield Stress $R_{p0.2}$ [N/mm^2]	True Tensile Strength R_m [N/mm^2]	Percentage Plastic Extension at Maximum Force A_g [%]
t = 8 (RHS)	441	605	8
t = 10 (CHS)	496	564	4
End plate	396	557	10
Bolt	1119	1231	5

The contact interaction was defined for normal and tangential behavior. The tangential contact defined with a *Penalty* friction formulation, with isotropic directionality, and a 0.1 friction coefficient. The theoretical relation for such contact is given in Abaqus Documentation [21] with an equivalent tangential stress being less than the critical tangential stress which is proportional to the contact pressure by the friction coefficient, see Equation (1). The stiff elastic behavior was modeled by the *stiff elastic behavior* for which the condition is not applied pointwise but weighted over a small area. This allowable maximum elastic slip is considered the default value of 0.5% of the average length of all contact elements [21].

$$\tau_{eq} = \sqrt{\tau_1^2 + \tau_2^2} < \mu \cdot p = \tau_{crit} \quad (1)$$

For the normal behavior, the *Hard* contact formulation was selected with the default direct method as a constraint enforcement method which attempts to strictly enforce a given pressure–overclosure behavior per constraint, without approximation or use of augmentation iterations. In addition, separation after contact was allowed.

The contact was defined as *surface-to-surface* interactions for the following pairs: bolt head and first end plate, bolt nut, and second end plate, hollow section ends in contact (Figure 12).

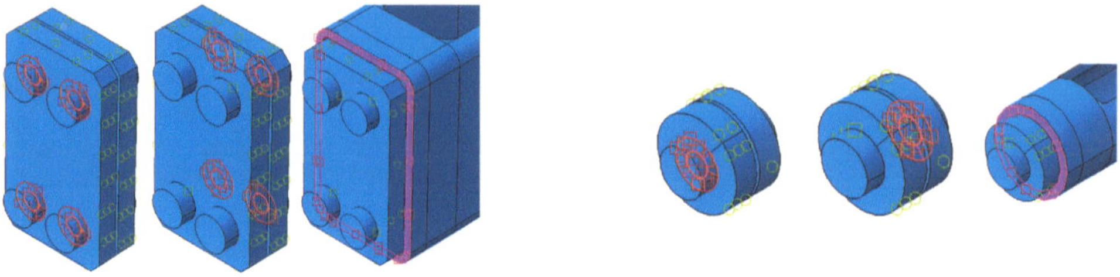

(**a**) (**b**)

Figure 12. Contact interactions: (**a**) RHS; (**b**) CHS.

A pinned and a roller support were defined at the assembly ends using a coupling constraint controlled by a reference point (Figure 13).

(**a**) (**b**)

Figure 13. Support conditions: (**a**) RHS; (**b**) CHS.

The loading areas are defined also in a kinematic coupling constraint controlled by reference points which have an imposed vertical displacement of 50 mm (Figure 14).

(**a**) (**b**)

Figure 14. Loading areas for: (**a**) RHS; (**b**) CHS.

The end plate was connected to the RHS or CHS profile using the Tie constraint. Supplementary, contact interactions are necessary to be defined between the bolts and the end plate, and between the two hollow profiles which are in contact.

The contact interaction was defined as normal and tangential behavior, allowing separation after contact. The tangential contact was defined with a 0.1 friction coefficient.

Each part was meshed with C3D8R (an 8-node linear brick, reduced integration, hourglass control) finite element type. The size of the element was approximately 5 mm, with smaller elements being defined for the bolts, allowing 2 elements on the thickness of the hollow element wall (Figure 15). In order to reduce the computation time, the length of the finite element in the longitudinal direction was increased.

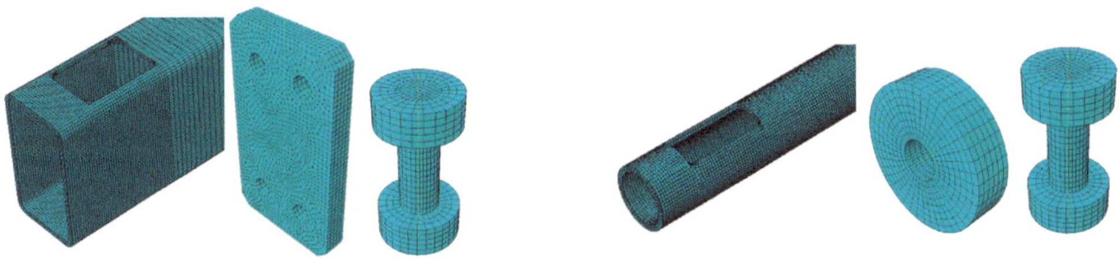

(**a**) (**b**)

Figure 15. FEM mesh for parts: (**a**) RHS; (**b**) CHS.

For the bolts, a preload of 130 kN was defined in a separate step before the applied load, analyzed in a static step. The preload propagation was modified to "Fix at current length" for the following analyzing steps, to allow the development of internal stress in the bolts due to bending of the specimen.

4. Results

4.1. Experimental Results

From the recordings of the experimental tests, Force-Displacement curves were obtained as presented in Figure 16. Of course, the capacity of the RHS is bigger than the capacity of the CHS as well as the rigidity. It must be mentioned that the observed failure mode for both sections was bolt failure but the RHS specimen showed a redundant behavior due to the number of bolts, while the CHS specimen had a brittle failure mode, after the shank fracture the entire assembly could not resist any force. The failure mode of the bolts used in the RHS connection is the thread stripping while for the CHS connection is the shank fracture, as presented in Figure 16.

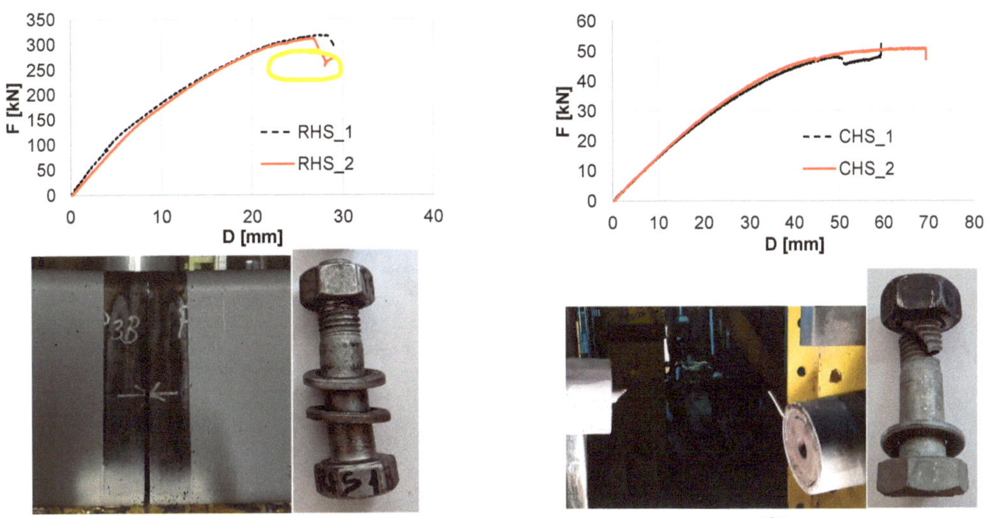

(**a**) (**b**)

Figure 16. Force displacement curves and failure modes: (**a**) RHS; (**b**) CHS.

The DIC results are presented in Figure 17. Comparing the two graphs, it is observed that the increased rigidity of the RHS maintains the profiles in contact for a significant amount of force, approximately 50% of the maximum force. On the other hand, the CHS connection starts to separate in the tensioned area from the initial stage of loading.

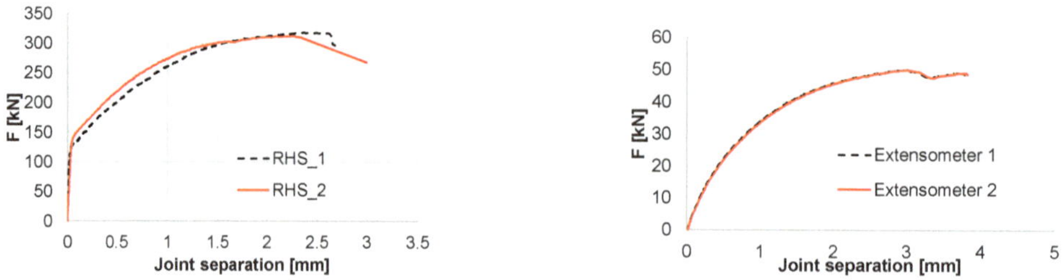

(a) (b)

Figure 17. Joint separation recorded during experiments: (**a**) RHS; (**b**) CHS.

It must be mentioned that the separation is recorded after the pretensioning of the bolts which means that the initial compressive stress in the hollow profiles is not captured by the DIC system. Nevertheless, the compressive deformation of the profiles due to bolt pretension has a small value which can be determined by the numerical analysis.

4.2. Numerical Results

With the aforementioned parameters of the numerical model, the results of the finite element analysis are presented in Figure 18. The results of the numerical analysis follow in good accordance with the experimental results; thus, the model is considered to be validated for further studies.

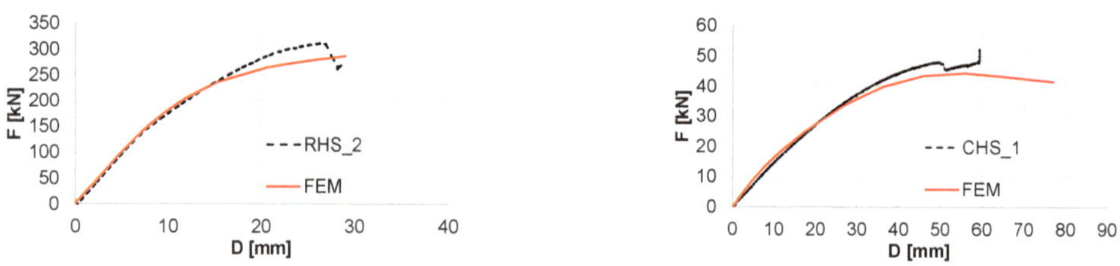

(a) (b)

Figure 18. Experimental vs. FEM analysis: (**a**) RHS; (**b**) CHS.

The FEM model allows the assessment of stress distribution within the connection and furthermore, the bolts (Figure 19). Due to the flexibility of the end plate, a nonuniform distribution of the stress is observed on the profile contact for RHS, opposite to the CHS where the preload leads to a uniform pressure between the two profiles. Even in this stage, the bolts of the RHS connection are subjected to bending.

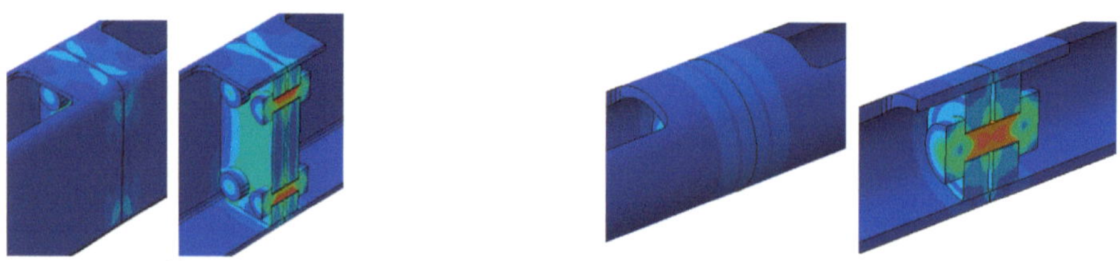

(a) (b)

Figure 19. Stress caused by preload in the profile and in the bolts for: (**a**) RHS; (**b**) CHS.

By extracting the longitudinal displacements of the nodes close to the connection and adding the absolute value of the displacements of the two nodes, the joint separation was obtained (Figure 20). It must be mentioned that the preload introduced an initial deformation of 0.045 mm and 0.004 for the RHS and CHS, respectively. These values were subtracted from the final joint separation as the deformations in the experiment were not included in the recordings of the DIC system.

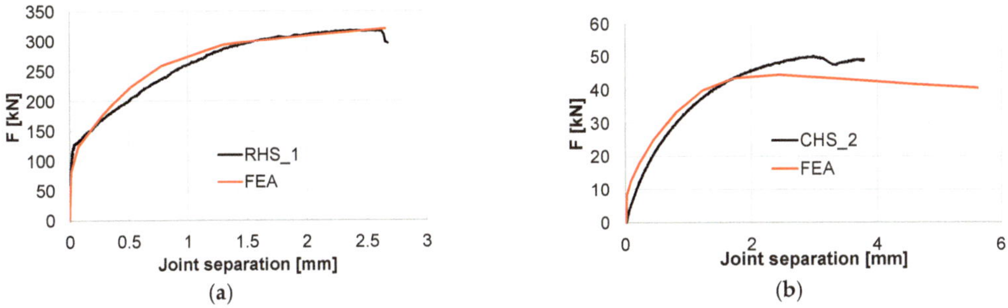

Figure 20. Joint separation: (**a**) RHS; (**b**) CHS.

For the RHS, the joint separation obtained by the FEA closely follows the recordings during the experiment, especially the first stage of the experiment where the two profiles are kept in contact. The CHS connection response obtained from the FEA is similar to the RHS analysis, showing an initial stage where the profiles are in contact, a phenomenon that was not observed in the experiment of CHS.

4.3. Parametric Study

4.3.1. Hand Hole Effect

A continuous hollow section was defined to study the influence of the hand-hole necessary for bolt assembling. This handhole is commonly covered by a plate connected by 2 small screws to plates welded to the interior of the hollow walls.

The results show an increased rigidity of the assembly but a similar maximum force for both RHS and CHS (Figure 21).

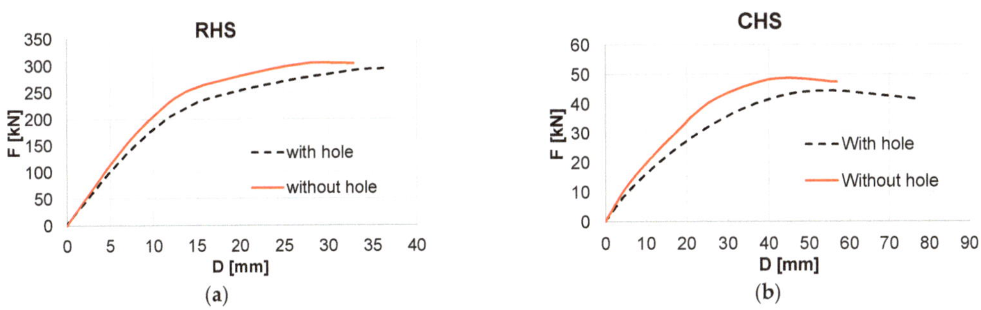

Figure 21. Hand hole effect: (**a**) RHS; (**b**) CHS.

4.3.2. Bolt Preload Effect

Bolt preload is required to have contact between profiles and perfect alignment at the time of assembling the structure. The RHS connection allows several bolts to be used while the CHS connections, which are usually of smaller sections, allow the use of one bolt. By considering different levels of preload, 0.3 ×, 0.5 ×, and 0.7 × Fy, where Fy is the nominal grade 10.9 yield force, the effect of the bolt preload was studied. A slightly significant increase of rigidity was observed for the RHS connection with the bolt preloaded at 200 kN, while for the other cases, the change of rigidity is neglectable, Figure 22.

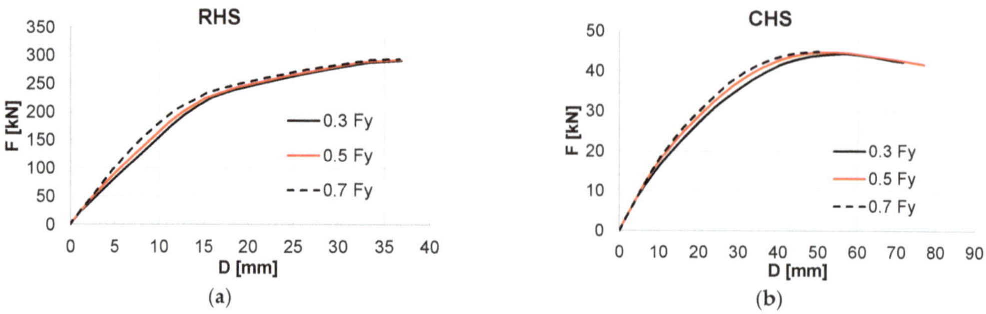

Figure 22. Bolt preload effect on capacity: (**a**) RHS; (**b**) CHS.

Although the bolt preload effect on the capacity and the rigidity of the specimen is not significant, the joint separation, which is a serviceability criterion, is improved for the CHS connection, as depicted in Figure 23.

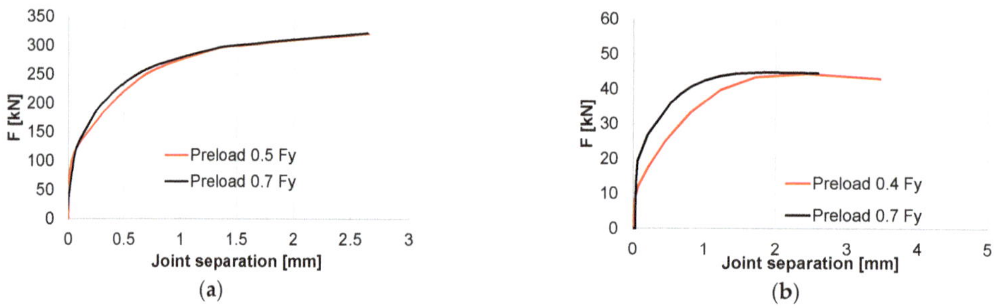

Figure 23. Bolt preload effect on joint separation: (**a**) RHS; (**b**) CHS.

4.3.3. End Plate Thickness Effect

Although the two connections have different capacities, the end plate thicknesses considered for the parametric study were in the same range due to constructional reasons.

A significant loss of capacity is observed for the RHS connection although the initial rigidity is maintained at the same value. The CHS connection shows a 10% loss of capacity for similar plate thicknesses but for lower thicknesses the capacity reduces drastically, Figure 24.

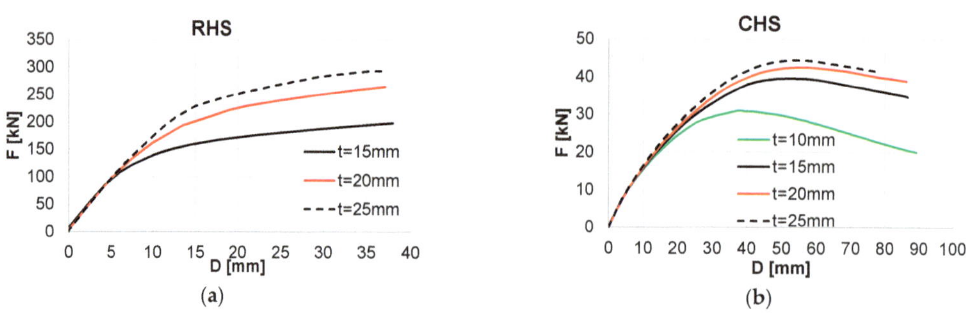

Figure 24. End plate thickness effect: (**a**) RHS; (**b**) CHS.

Similarly, the rigidity of the connection starts to decrease after 50% of the maximum force. Due to the singular bolt of the CHS connection, the curve shows an increased softening with the smaller thickness.

5. Discussion

The current study intended to highlight the response, in terms of capacity and joint separation, and the failure mode of an in-line connection for rectangular and circular hollow sections with an end plate welded inside the tubular section. In such a configuration the bolted connection is not visible leading to an aesthetic visual effect. Similar studies were performed in the literature [15], with the end plate having external dimensions similar to the hollow section, resulting in a connection prone to welding failure.

Nevertheless, with a reduced lever arm of the bolts to resist the bending deformation of the joint, the capacity of the connection is limited. Experimental tests were conducted on two similar specimens for an RHS of 250 × 150 × 8 with an end plate of 25 mm and four bolts M20 gr. 10.9 and two specimens for a CHS of 114.3 × 10 with an end plate of 25 mm and one bolt M24 gr. 10.9. The two tests lead to similar results showing trustful results. By applying two symmetrical forces with respect to the connection, pure bending was the only internal force in the connection. The tested specimen was monitored by linear displacement transducers to obtain the midspan deflection while the force was monitored by the actuator loadcell. To record the joint separation, the digital image correlation technique was employed. Tensile tests were also performed to obtain the real mechanical properties of the base material of the RHS, CHS, and bolt.

From the experimental tests, the failure mode of the connection was observed in Figure 16. Both typologies failed by bolt fracture but the RHS, due to the multitude of bolts, experienced a safer collapse of the connection while the CHS profiles, connected by one bolt, completely detached from the connection. Force displacement curves were obtained from the acquisition system and joint separation was measured by the virtual extensometers of the DIC system.

The results of the experimental tests represent the basis of the numerical simulations performed by Abaqus [21]. As the failure mode of the specimens is bolt failure, static general analyses lead to satisfactory results if the preload force in the bolt was introduced. With the real material properties, the numerical analyses of the specimens showed good agreement with the experimental results both in terms of rigidity and capacity (Figure 18). By comparing the joint separation recorded by the DIC system to the FEM model, the RHS specimens also showed a good agreement, with minor separation until 35% of the maximum force, while, experimentally, the CHS connection started separating immediately after load application although numerically, the preload limited the separation until 20% of the maximum force applied.

The validated numerical models were then used for a parametric study considering: (i) the existence of an access hole for the bolt tightening, (ii) bolt preload, and (iii) end plate thickness.

A small increase of the capacity was observed for the specimens without the access hole, as the weak component was the bolt resistance, but a significant decrease in the deformation was observed especially for the CHS (Figure 21). Of course, the decreased rigidity due to an access hole was the proportion of the missing material in the position of maximum bending moment. For the maximum force applied, an increase of 9% resulted for the CHS while the RHS had a similar capacity.

For the three levels of preload, 0.3, 0.5, and 0.7 of the nominal yield force of the bolts used in the connection, M20 gr 10.9 and M24 gr 10.9, for the RHS and CHS, respectively, the flexibility of the end plate for RHS led to a neglectable influence on both rigidity and capacity of the connection, but the joint separation was reduced for the CHS, which has a more rigid end plate compared to the area of the cross-section of the hollow section (Figure 22).

The major influence on the connection response was represented by the end plate thickness. For flexible end plate 10 mm for CHS and 15 mm for RHS, the capacity was reduced by 34% and 32%, respectively. In the numerical simulation, although the contact was maintained for the first 20% of the maximum force, the joint separation was almost three times larger than for a rigid end plate (Figure 24).

The maximum forces obtained for different levels of preload and for the end plate thickness are summarized in Figure 25. The previously mentioned observations are observed in these graphs.

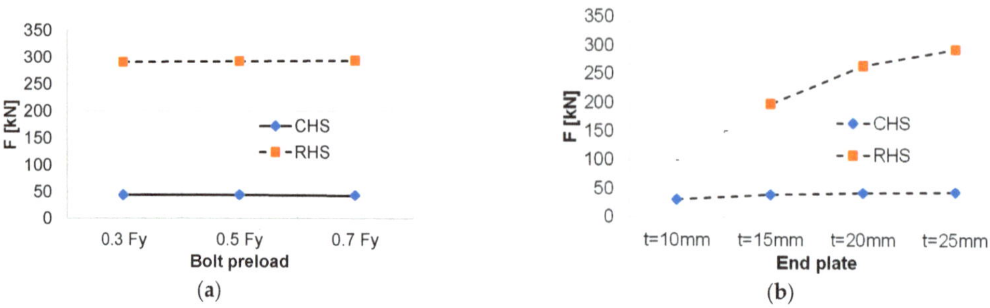

Figure 25. Maximum forces: (**a**) bolt preload; (**b**) end plate thickness.

The standards do not offer explicit design methods for these in-line connections although their use is becoming greater for aesthetic reasons. Based on the method presented by Stephan and Stutzki [18], the computer program GAS [22] allows the design of the connection but it does not offer any information about the joint separation. An estimation of the deformation in the joint can be related to the position of the neutral axis provided by the program. In Figure 26, the neutral axis for the RHS and CHS connections are presented considering the material properties obtained in the tensile tests and the preload of the bolts in the experiment. The defined bending moments to reach this position of the neutral axis were 41.5 and 5.25 kNm for the RHS and CHS, respectively. By determining the values of the bending moment according to Figure 1, the values corresponding to the inflection point in Figure 20 are 42.9 and 4.6 kNm. It can be seen that the values were very close; thus, the numerical model can predict the joint separation.

Figure 26. Position of neutral axis according to [18]: (**a**) RHS; (**b**) CHS.

Although the discussions were focused on RHS and CHS, it must be mentioned that the two typologies are related to the size of the elements. The small size of rectangular hollow sections can also be used with only one bolt for the connection, and large circular hollow sections can have several bolts connecting the end plate inserted in the hollow section.

6. Conclusions

Depending on the purpose of the structure, the response of the in-line connection of hollow sections can relate to capacity, rigidity, and/or joint separation. The current study presents a feasible configuration of the in-line connection for which a continuous aspect of the connected elements can be obtained. Without a standardized design method, it is shown that a simple numerical model can predict the response of the connection as validated based on the experimental results and analytical formulation.

Depending on the size of the element one or several bolts can be used for the connection. The connections using one bolt are prone to catastrophic failure as the connection has no redundant links.

The parameters affecting the capacity and the rigidity of the connection are the end plate thickness while the access hole and the preload affect in a small amount only the rigidity.

The parameters affecting the joint separation are the preload, if the end plate is not flexible, and the end plate thickness. Without a great material expense, a rigid end plate can reduce the joint separation as well as a controlled preload of the bolt.

Either rectangular or circular hollow section, the size of the element dictates the connection configuration which in any case has a smaller capacity than a continuous element due to the bolted connection, or a smaller rigidity due to the access holes.

Author Contributions: Conceptualization, C.-I.B. and A.C.; data curation, C.-I.B. and I.B.; funding acquisition, C.-I.B.; investigation, C.-I.B., I.B. and I.M.; methodology, I.B. and I.M.; resources, A.C.; software, C.-I.B.; supervision, A.C.; validation, C.-I.B., I.B. and A.C.; writing—original draft, C.-I.B.; writing—review and editing, I.B., I.M. and A.C. All authors have read and agreed to the published version of the manuscript.

Funding: This paper was financially supported by the project "Network of excellence in applied research and innovation for doctoral and postdoctoral programs/InoHubDoc", a project co-funded by the European Social Fund financing agreement no. POCU/993/6/13/153437.

Data Availability Statement: Data unavailable.

Conflicts of Interest: The authors declare no conflict of interest.

References

1. Liu, X.C.; He, X.N.; Wang, H.X.; Yang, Z.W.; Pu, S.H.; Ailin, Z. Bending-shear performance of column-to-column bolted-flange connections in prefabricated multi-high-rise steel structures. *J. Constr. Steel Res.* **2018**, *145*, 28–48. [CrossRef]
2. Garifullin, M.; Pajunen, S.; Mela, K.; Heinisuo, M.; Havula, J. Initial in-plane rotational stiffness of welded RHS T joints with axial force in main member. *J. Constr. Steel Res.* **2017**, *139*, 353–362. [CrossRef]
3. Havula, J.; Garifullin, M.; Heinisuo, M.; Mela, K.; Pajunen, S. Moment-rotation behavior of welded tubular high strength steel T joint. *Eng. Struct.* **2018**, *172*, 523–537. [CrossRef]
4. Szlendak, J. Beam-column welded RHS connections. *Thin-Walled Struct.* **1991**, *12*, 63–80. [CrossRef]
5. Liu, X.C.; He, X.N.; Wang, H.X.; Zhang, A.L. Compression-bend-shearing performance of column-to-column bolted-flange connections in prefabricated multi-high-rise steel structures. *Eng. Struct.* **2018**, *160*, 439–460. [CrossRef]
6. Li, Q.; Xu, C.; Luo, Z.; Huang, F.; An, Y.; Zhang, D.; Liu, P. Experiment and design methodology of an IODR flange connection under bending load. *J. Constr. Steel Res.* **2023**, *201*, 107744. [CrossRef]
7. Deng, H.-Z.; Li, C.; Song, X.-Q.; Li, F.; Fu, P.-C. Tensile resistance and design model of an external double-layered flange connection. *J. Constr. Steel Res.* **2019**, *161*, 309–327. [CrossRef]
8. Radu, D.; Feier, A. Steel antenna towers—From designing to manufacturing optimization. *Mater. Sci. Eng.* **2018**, *399*, 012047. [CrossRef]
9. Nadeem, G.; Safiee, N.A.; Bakar, N.A.; Karim, I.A.; Nasir, N.A.M. Connection design in modular steel construction: A review. *Structures* **2021**, *33*, 3239–3256. [CrossRef]
10. Urbonas, K.; Daniūnas, A. Behaviour of semi-rigid steel beam-to-beam joints under bending and axial forces. *J. Constr. Steel Res.* **2006**, *62*, 1244–1249. [CrossRef]
11. Lian, J.-Y.; Deng, E.-F.; He, J.-M.; Cai, L.-M.; Gao, S.-C.; Zhou, J.-J. Numerical analysis on seismic performance of corner fitting connection in modular steel building. *Structures* **2021**, *33*, 1659–1676. [CrossRef]
12. Chen, Y.; Hou, C.; Peng, J. Stability study on tenon-connected SHS and CFST columns in modular construction. *Steel Compos. Struct.* **2019**, *30*, 185–199.
13. Dhanapal, J.; Ghaednia, H.; Das, S.; Velocci, J. Structural performance of state-of-the-art VectorBloc modular connector under axial loads. *Eng. Struct.* **2019**, *183*, 496–509. [CrossRef]
14. Urbonas, K.; Daniūnas, A. Numerical tests of steel beam-to-column semi-rigid connections. *J. Civ. Eng. Manag.* **2003**, *9*, 292–296. [CrossRef]

15. Both, I.; Nunes, D.L.; Ivan, A.; Vucicevic, D. The Response of In-Line Connection of RHS Sections Subjected to Bending and Shear. In *Modern Technologies for the 3rd Millennium*; Nistor, S., Popoviciu, G.A., Eds.; Editografica S R L: Bologna, Italy, 2019; pp. 117–122. Available online: https://www.webofscience.com/wos/woscc/full-record/WOS:000617030100020 (accessed on 5 November 2022).
16. Feier, A.; Chivu, O.R. Lamellar tearing observations regarding the applications of European standards in the field of welded steel constructions. *Rev. De Chim.* **2018**, *69*, 352–1354. [CrossRef]
17. Huang, F.; Zhang, D.; Hong, W.; Li, B. Mechanism and calculation theory of prying force for flexible flange connection. *J. Constr. Steel Res.* **2017**, *132*, 97–107. [CrossRef]
18. Stephan, S.; Stutzki, C. A General Method for the Design of Bolted Connections for Space Frames. In Proceedings of the Fifth International Conference on Space Structures, Guildford, UK, 29 August 2002.
19. *EN ISO 6892-1*; Metallic Materials—Tensile Testing. Part 1: Method of Test at Room Temperature. CEN: Brussels, Belgium, 2009.
20. *EN 1993-1-5*; Eurocode 3: Design of Steel Structures—Part 1–5: Plated Structural Elements. CEN: Brussels, Belgium, 2006.
21. *Dassault Systemes, Abaqus 6.14 Documentation*; Simulia Systems: Providence, RI, USA, 2014.
22. *Gartner Steel and Glass*; Josef Gartner GmbH: Bayern, Germany, 2023.

mathematics

Article

Free Vibration Analyses of Stiffened Functionally Graded Graphene-Reinforced Composite Multilayer Cylindrical Panel

Yuhua Zhou [1], Yanhu Zhang [1], Brighton Nyasha Chirukam [2], Jianwei Li [1,*], Congshan Lu [3], Masoud Babaei [4,*] and Kamran Asemi [5]

1 Institute of Advanced Manufacturing and Modern Equipment Technology, Jiangsu University, Zhenjiang 212000, China; zhou839@yahoo.com (Y.Z.); yanhuzhang08121@gmail.com (Y.Z.)
2 School of Mechanical Engineering, Xi'an Technological University, Xi'an 710021, China; brightonnchirukam05686@gmail.com
3 School of Mechanical Engineering, Jiangsu University, Zhenjiang 212000, China; congshanlu01@gmail.com
4 Department of Mechanical Engineering, University of Eyvanekey, Eyvanekey 99888-35918, Iran
5 Department of Mechanical Engineering, Islamic Azad University, North Tehran Branch, Tehran 1477893855, Iran; k.asemi@iau-tnb.ac.ir
* Correspondence: ujs_zhyh@126.com (J.L.); masoudbabaei@eyc.ac.ir (M.B.)

Abstract: In this paper, the free vibration response of a stiffened functionally graded graphene nanoplatelet (GPL)-reinforced composite multilayer cylindrical shell panel is studied for the first time. The shell is stiffened by both stringers and rings. Additionally, the effect of reinforcing the shell panel, ring and stinger with GPLs is independently studied. Halpin–Tsai relations are employed to evaluate the mechanical properties of the shell panel, rings and stringers. The first-order shear deformation shell theory, accompanied by the Lekhnitsky smeared stiffener model, using the numerical finite element method and Hamilton principle, is employed to develop the governing motion equations of the shell panel. Four different types of GPL patterns, including FG-A, FG-X, FG-O and UD, are assumed across the thickness of the shell panel, rings and stringers. The effects of different factors, including various weight fractions and patterns of GPLs nanofillers, the geometry of the shell panel and stiffeners and two displacement boundary conditions, on the natural frequencies of the shell panel, have been studied.

Keywords: free vibration; stiffened; functionally graded; graphene-reinforced composite multilayer cylindrical panel; FSDT; FEM

MSC: 37M05

Citation: Zhou, Y.; Zhang, Y.; Nyasha Chirukam, B.; Li, J.; Lu, C.; Babaei, M.; Asemi, K. Free Vibration Analyses of Stiffened Functionally Graded Graphene-Reinforced Composite Multilayer Cylindrical Panel. *Mathematics* **2023**, *11*, 3662. https://doi.org/10.3390/math11173662

Academic Editors: Joaquim Infante Barbosa and José Alberto Rodrigues

Received: 1 August 2023
Revised: 18 August 2023
Accepted: 22 August 2023
Published: 24 August 2023

1. Introduction

Nowadays, reinforcement plays an important role in different industries, such as aerospace, marine and automotive industries. These reinforcements can be divided into two major groups. In the first group, the structure is stiffened by another external shape, such as a ring or stringer. The external stiffener can be fabricated with the same or different material as the original structure. These stiffeners can be connected to the original structure with glue, welding, screws or rivets. Due to the fact that these connections may cause a stress concentration, the original structure and stiffeners can be manufactured integrally. In the second group, the structure is reinforced with nanoparticles. These nanoparticles are added to the metallic or polymeric matrix during the process of fabrication, and metallic or polymeric nanocomposite structures are manufactured. These reinforcements can be added to various shapes, including plate, beam and shell-type structures and increase the dynamic and static efficiency of the structure. Among these structures, shell-type structures are widely applied as a part of sophisticated shapes, such as aircraft, rockets, submarines, etc. Due to these structures being continuously subjected to dynamic loads, it is essential to study the vibration response and natural frequencies of shell-type-reinforced structures. There are a lot of investigations related to the natural frequency responses of stiffened structures. First, the articles are reviewed that are related to the vibration behavior of the first group. For instance, natural frequencies of ring-and-stringer-stiffened conical shells with simply supported boundary conditions are presented numerically and experimentally by Crenwelge and Muster [1]. Nayak, Satpathy and Tripathy [2] presented free vibrations of stiffened plates using the numerical finite element method (FEM). The effect of several parameters, such as the number and orientation of stiffeners, aspect ratio, boundary conditions and stiffener depth to plate thickness ratio on the free vibration of stiffened plates are investigated. Based on laminated composite shell theories and utilizing FEM, Nayak and Bandyopadhyay [3] performed a comprehensive investigation of the free vibration responses of laminated composite stiffened shallow shells. Sinha et al. [4] employed experimental and numerical approaches to present the natural frequencies of laminated composite stiffened plates by changing the numbers, types and orientation of stiffeners. Nayak and Bandyopadhyay [5] developed an FE formulation for the natural frequency characteristics of stiffened conoidal shells. The effects of various stiffened geometries on the free vibration response of conoidal shells were examined. The free vibration response of shells of revolution stiffened by stringers employing a finite strip method was reported by Naghsh, Saadatpour and Azhari [6]. They understood that reinforcing the shells with stringers could increase or decrease the natural frequency. Quoc, Van Tham and Tu [7] studied the free vibration behavior of a stiffened functionally graded (FG) porous cylindrical shell under different boundary conditions on the basis of first-order shear deformation theory (FSDT), Lekhnitsky's smeared stiffener assumptions and the Galerkin method. Samanta and Mukhopadhyay [8] surveyed the natural frequencies of stiffened shells by applying FSDT and the FE technique. Mustafa and Ali [9] applied an energy method for the natural frequencies of stiffened circular cylindrical shells based on FSDT. Al-Najafi and Warburton [10] presented the natural frequency characteristics of ring-stiffened cylindrical shells by applying Flügge's shell theory and using the Rayleigh–Ritz approach. Zarei, Rahimi and Hemmatnezhad [11] performed a comprehensive investigation, including numerical, experimental and analytical approaches, to evaluate natural frequencies of grid-stiffened truncated composite conical shells using FSDT. Their analytical procedure was conducted in accordance with the Ritz method. Additionally, Zarei, Rahimi and Hemmatnezhad [12] used the same methodology and solution to investigate the free vibration response of stiffened composite joined conical–cylindrical shells. Aris and Ahmadi [13] performed an investigation on the natural frequency results of stiffened rotating FGM conical shells under thermal conditions in accordance with higher-order shear deformation theory (HSDT) and applying the Galerkin method. Based on Donnell's thin shell theory and employing the Galerkin procedure, the free vibration behavior of grid-stiffened composite truncated spherical shells was reported by Ansari, Hemmatnezhad and Taherkhani [14]. Tu Tran et al. [15] employed FSDT, together with the Galerkin method and Lekhnitsky's smeared stiffener technique, to analyze natural frequencies of stiffened FG circular cylindrical shells supported by a Pasternak elastic foundation for various boundary conditions subjected to a thermal environment. The free vibration analysis of laminated stiffened cylindrical panels based on FSDT and utilizing FEM was surveyed by Tuan, Quoc and Tu, [16]. Nguyen and Hoang [17] analytically presented the free vibration response of a stiffened FG cylindrical shell supported on an elastic foundation based on FSDT, the Galerkin method and the Lekhnitsky smeared stiffener technique. Qin Li et al. [18] employed FSDT and an analytical solution based on Rayleigh–Ritz to study the free vibration of a stiffened cylindrical shell under general boundary conditions. Bich, Van Dung and Nam [19] investigated the vibration response of eccentrically stiffened FG cylindrical panels based on classical shell theory by employing the analytical method. The natural frequency response of stiffened cylindrical shells in accordance with higher-order theory determined by applying the Carrera unified formulation (CUF) was examined by Carrera, Zappino and Filippi [20]. Lugovoi and Prokopenko [21] studied the impact of an elastic foundation and reinforcement on the vibration response of shallow shells with a rectangular planform. Shahani and Kiarasi [22] studied the influence of a ring and stringer on the stability of thin cylindrical shells based on FSDT numerically and experimentally.

This literature review denotes that in the most of research, the connection between the original structure and reinforcements is considered ideal without screws, rivets and welding. Therefore, in most of them, Lekhnitsky's smeared stiffener technique is applied for analysis. Now, the articles are reviewed which are related to the second group of reinforcements or to reinforcing with nanoparticles. As lots of investigations have been developed for the dynamic and static analyses of the structures which are reinforced with various nanoparticles, those studies are mentioned here that are related to the vibration behavior of plate and shell-type structures which are reinforced by Graphene platelets (GPLs). In detail, the vibration responses of polymeric composite shells reinforced by GPLs integrated with piezoelectric patches including electroelastic nonlinearities were presented by Rao, Schmidt and Schröder [23]. Van Do and Lee [24] employed the Bézier extraction-based isogeometric method to predict the natural frequencies of FG-GPLs multilayered composite cylindrical shell panels by applying FSDT. Amirabadi, Farhatnia, Eftekhari and Hosseini-Ara [25] used third-order shear deformation theory (TSDT) and the generalized differential quadrature method (GDQM) to obtain the free vibration responses of FG-GPL-reinforced conical shells under a rotational velocity and various displacement boundary conditions. Jamalabadi et al. [26] calculated the fundamental natural frequencies of FG-GPL-reinforced composite conical panels supported by a elastic foundation using FSDT and 2D-GDQ methods. Salehi, Gholami and Ansari [27] presented the nonlinear free vibration response of FG porous cylindrical shells reinforced by GPLs considering initial imperfections utilizing HSDT. Yang et al. [28] employed FSDT, the Galerkin approach and harmonic balance method to predict the nonlinear free vibration results of FG-GPL-reinforced composite conical shells. Van Do and Lee [29] developed HSDT to investigate static response and the natural frequencies of multilayer spherical and cylindrical panels reinforced by GPLs in accordance with the isogeometric procedure. Employing FSDT and Ritz's method, the free vibration of GPL-reinforced composite doubly curved shells was presented by Esmaieli and Kiani [30]. Baghbadorani and Kiani [31] used the Donnell kinematic relations, FSDT and Navier solutions for the free vibration response of FG cylindrical shells reinforced with GPLs. Dong et al. [32] studied the influences of axial load and rotational velocity on the nonlinear free vibration response of graded-graphene-reinforced cylindrical shells based on the nonlinear Donnell shell theory and by employing the Galerkin approach. Based on a similar methodology and solution, the natural frequency responses of FG-GPL-reinforced porous nanocomposite cylindrical shells with rotational velocity were presented by Dong et al. [33]. Song et al. [34] employed the second-order shear deformation theory in curvilinear coordinate and analytical solution based on harmonic response to investigate wave dispersion responses of FG-GPL curved viscoelastic panels. Sobhani et al. [35] employed FSDT and GDQ methods to evaluate the vibration behavior of graphene oxide powder composites joined paraboloidal–cylindrical shells with different boundary conditions. The effect of initial imperfection on the active control of FG-GPL cylindrical shells with piezoelectric layers due to the application of a proportional derivative smart controller was reported by Zare et al. [36].

Rezaei Pajand, Sobhani and Masoodi [37] investigated the vibrational response of joined conical–conical shells made of FGM based on FSDT and employing the GDQM. In another work, based on the same theory and methodology, Sobhani and Avcar [38] performed an investigation on the influence of various nanofiller materials (CNTs, GNPs, and GOPs) on the natural frequencies of nanocomposite cylindrical shells. Sobhani, Masoodi and Ahmad Pari [39] analyzed the free-damped vibration of GPL nanocomposite joined conical–conical–cylindrical-shell marine-like structures in accordance with FSDT and Donnell's simplifications. The governing equations of the structure were obtained by employing the Hamilton principle. Finally, GDQM was applied for solving the governing equations of the structure. Based on the first-order shear deformation hypothesis and

GDQM, wave frequency responses of the nanocomposite-linked hemispherical–conical-shell underwater-like bodies with the impacts of two types of graphene-based nanofillers were reported by Sobhani, Masoodi and Ahmad Pari [40]. Sobhani, Masoodi and Ahmad Pari [41] employed FDST as the theory and GDQM as a solution to evaluate the circumferential vibration analysis of nano-porous-sandwich assembled spherical–cylindrical–conical shells under elastic boundary conditions. Sobhani, Masoodi and Civalek [42] simulated the vibrational response of a jet engine cowl shell-like structure based on FSDT by employing GDQM as a numerical approach. Sobhani [43] used (FSDT) and the general shell hypothesis (GSH) to investigate the free vibration of combined paraboloidal–conical air vehicle segment shell-type structures. The governing equations of the structure were obtained by employing the Hamilton principle. Finally, GDQM was applied for solving the governing equations of combined paraboloidal–conical air vehicle segment shell-type structures. Song et al. [44] presented an analytical solution based on the perturbation technique to investigate buckling and postbuckling of biaxially compressed functionally graded multilayer graphene nanoplatelet-reinforced polymer composite plates. Within the framework of the first-order shear deformation plate theory, Song et al. [45] presented an analytical solution based on the Navier method for the free and forced vibrations of functionally graded polymer composite plates reinforced with graphene nanoplatelets. Wang, Ye and Zu [46] studied the nonlinear vibration of metal foam cylindrical shells reinforced with graphene platelets based on the improved Donnell nonlinear shell theory by applying the Galerkin approach. Chai and Wang [47] presented an analytical solution for the traveling wave vibration of graphene platelet-reinforced porous joined conical–cylindrical shells in a spinning motion based on Donnell's shell theory. Ye and Wang [48] employed the Galerkin procedure and Donnell's nonlinear shell theory to analyze the nonlinear forced vibration of functionally graded graphene platelet-reinforced metal foam cylindrical shells: internal resonances. By using the Galerkin method, the nonlinear forced vibration of the simply supported functionally graded porous nanocomposite thin plates reinforced with graphene platelets based on the Kirchhoff assumptions was presented by Teng and Wang [49]. Wang et al. [50] presented an efficient method for the vibration and stability analysis of rectangular plates axially moving in fluid based on the Kirchhoff plate theory and utilizing the finite element method. Based on Donnell's shell theory and using the Rayleigh–Ritz method, a general approach for the free vibration analysis of spinning joined conical–cylindrical shells with arbitrary boundary conditions was examined by Chai and Wang [51]. Safarpour, Rahimi and Alibeigloo [52] studied the free vibration and static responses of FG-GPL-truncated conical and cylindrical shells by applying 3D elasticity theory and using GDQM as a solution method. Babaei et al. [53] presented the natural frequency responses of a FG-GPL cylindrical shell panel based on the 3D theory of elasticity by applying FEM according to the Rayleigh–Ritz approach. Based on the same procedure and solution, Kiarasi et al. [54] investigated the free vibration of FG-GPL joined conical–cylindrical shells. Zhang, Wang and Li [55] used FEM, the 3D theory of elasticity and the Rayleigh–Ritz method to calculate the natural frequencies amounts of FG-GPL joined hemispherical–cylindrical–hemispherical shell vessels. Zu et al. [56] analyzed the vibration suppression performance of fiber-reinforced polymer spherical–cylindrical shells with GPL coatings under thermal conditions by applying the FSDT and Rayleigh–Ritz technique.

The above literature review shows that reinforcing the structures with nanoparticles and stiffening them using a ring and stringer have a great effect on the natural frequency response of the structures, but no investigation has been presented pertaining to the effect of both of them on the behavior of the structures yet. In this study, the free vibration of stiffened functionally graded graphene-reinforced composite multilayer cylindrical shell panels has been investigated for the first time. In this study, the shell panel, rings and stingers are reinforced with GPLs independently. Reinforcing the rings and stringers in addition to the shell panel is one of the novel points of the present study. Four various distributions of GPLs across the thickness of cylindrical panel, rings and stringers are considered. Lekhnitsky's smeared stiffener technique is assumed for obtaining the governing equations of the stiffened FG-GPL cylindrical shell panel. By employing the Hamilton principle in conjunction with FSDT, the governing motion equations of the shell are developed and solved via FEM. The effects of several factors such as the weight fractions of GPLs, various GPL patterns for the cylindrical panel, rings and stringers, different boundary conditions, and the effect of the geometry of the panel and stiffeners on the natural frequencies of stiffened FG-GPL cylindrical shell panel have been investigated. In detail, the maximum influences of the GPL pattern and the weight fraction of GPLs on the natural frequencies of the structure were approximately 60% and 118%, respectively. Additionally, the influence of strengthening the shell with GPLs was much greater than that of stiffening it with ring and stringers.

2. Deriving the Governing Equations

2.1. Definition of the Geometry and Material Properties of the Stiffened Cylindrical Shell Panel

Consider an FG-GPL multilayer cylindrical shell panel with stiffeners under compressive axial force (Figure 1). The radius, length, span angle and thickness of the structure are denoted by L, β and h, respectively. Additionally, (x, θ, z) is considered across the axial, hoop and radial axes, respectively. The shell panel is stiffened by both stringers (longitudinal stiffeners) and rings (circumferential stiffeners). Additionally, various GPL patterns are shown in Figure 1.

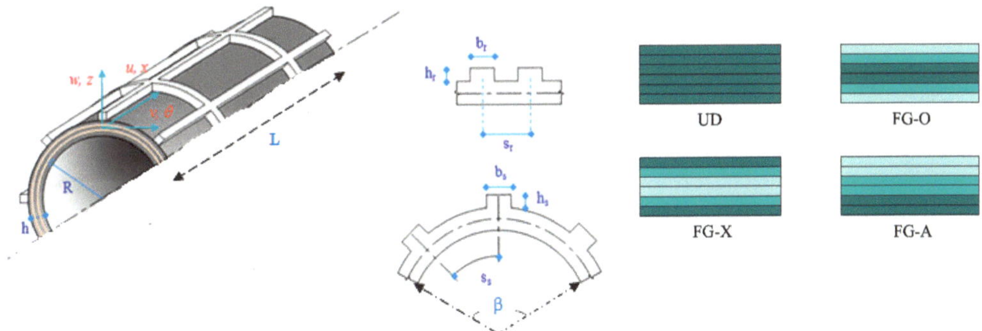

Figure 1. The geometry of the stiffened FG-GPL multilayer shell panel and the different distributions of the GPLs.

The multilayer GPL nanocomposite shell panel is assumed to have excellently bonded GPL-RC layers. In this research, it is considered that the shell panel is reinforced by GPLs. Each layer of the shell panel consists of a combination of GPLs as a nanofiller and a matrix made of an isotropic polymer. Due to the elimination of the stress concentration, rings and stringers are made of the same isotropic polymeric matrix used in the shell panel. GPLs are uniformly or non-uniformly distributed in the polymer matrix. Hence, the weight fraction of the nano-fillers (GPLs) varies in terms of being functionally graded across the radial direction of the shell panel. It is supposed that the shell panel is constructed of NL layers. Four different functions of the volume fraction of FG GPL-RCs are considered: FG-A, O, X, and a uniform pattern (UD). For UD, the GPL weight fraction is the same for each layer. Therefore, UD represents a homogeneous isotropic GPL-RC structure. In the FG patterns, the weight fraction of GPL has a linear variation across the thickness of the shell panel. For FG-X, the weight fraction of GPLs at the inner and outer layers is the maximum while this is different for the FG-O where the weight fraction for mid-layers is the maximum. Furthermore, for A-GPLRC, the weight fraction at the inner layers is the maximum and by distancing from it, the number of GPLs continuously decreases, and the outer surface of shell has the lowest number of GPLs. The equal weight fraction for different GPL distributions may be estimated as follows [57,58].

$$\begin{aligned} &U-GPLRC \quad V_{GPL}^{(k)}=V_{GPL}^{*} \\ &X-GPLRC \quad V_{GPL}^{(k)}=4\,V_{GPL}^{*}(0.5+|K-(N_L+1)/2\,)|/(2+N_L) \\ &O-GPLRC \quad V_{GPL}^{(k)}=4\,V_{GPL}^{*}((N_L+1)/2-|K-(N_L+1)/2 \\ &A-GPLRC \quad V_{GPL}^{(k)}=2\,V_{GPL}^{*}K/(N_L+1) \end{aligned} \tag{1}$$

Here, V_{GPL}^{K} represents the volume content of GPLs in each layer of the shell panel. In Equation (1), K will change from 1 to N_L. V_{GPL}^{K} shows the volume fraction of nanofillers in the shell, and may be evaluated as follows [59]:

$$V_{GPL}^{*}=\frac{\Delta_{GPL}\rho_m}{\Delta_{GPL}\rho_m+\rho_{GPL}-\Delta_{GPL}\rho_{GPL}} \tag{2}$$

where in the above equation, ρ_{GPL} and ρ_m are the mass density of the nanofillers and polymeric matrix, respectively, and Δ_{GPL} is the weight fraction of the nanofillers. It is mentioned that due to the prevention of agglomeration phenomena, the maximum amount of Δ_{GPL} should be lower than 1%.

Based on the Halpin–Tsai micromechanics estimation [60–63], Young's modulus of the shell panel is described as the following relations:

$$E=\frac{3}{8}\left(\frac{1+\varepsilon_L^{GPL}\eta_L^{GPL}V_{GPL}}{1-\eta_L^{GPL}V_{GPL}}\right)E_m+\frac{5}{8}\left(\frac{1+\varepsilon_W^{GPL}\eta_W^{GPL}V_{GPL}}{1-\eta_W^{GPL}V_{GPL}}\right) \tag{3}$$

$$\varepsilon_L^{GPL}=\frac{2l_{GPL}}{t_{GPL}} \tag{4}$$

$$\varepsilon_w^{GPL}=\frac{2w_{GPL}}{t_{GPL}} \tag{5}$$

$$\eta_L^{GPL}=\frac{E_{GPL}-E_m}{E_{GPL}+\varepsilon_L^{GPL}E_m} \tag{6}$$

$$\eta_W^{GPL}=\frac{E_{GPL}-E_m}{E_{GPL}+\varepsilon_W^{GPL}E_m} \tag{7}$$

where E_{GPL} and E_m are the Young's modulus of elasticity of the nanofillers and matrix, respectively. Additionally, l_{GPL}, W_{GPL}, t_{GPL} and V_{GPL} are the length, width, thickness and the volume fraction of the nanofillers, respectively. The rule of mixture estimation is employed to evaluate the Poisson's ratio and the mass density of the GPL-RC [64,65]:

$$\rho=\rho_{GPL}V_{GPL}+\rho_m(1-V_{GPL}) \tag{8}$$

$$v=v_{GPL}V_{GPL}+v_m(1-V_{GPL}) \tag{9}$$

where v_{GPL} and v_m are the Poisson's ratio of the nanofillers and matrix, respectively. The shear modulus, G, of the shell part is expressed as below [66–70]:

$$G=\frac{E}{2(1+v)} \tag{10}$$

2.2. Governing Equations (FSDT—Virtual Work Principle)

In this section, FSDT is considered to describe the displacement components. Additionally, Lekhnitsky's smeared stiffener assumptions are employed to present the relation between the shell panel with its rings and stringers. In this theory, the transverse normal values at the mid-plane of the plate remain straight and rotate such that they do not remain perpendicular to the mid-surface after deformation. Applying the FSDT of the shells, the displacement constituents of the shell are considered to be as follows [71]:

$$\begin{aligned} u(x,\theta,z,t) &= u_0(x,\theta,t) + z\ \varphi_x(x,\theta,t) \\ v(x,\theta,z,t) &= v_0(x,\theta,t) + z\ \varphi_\theta(x,\theta,t) \\ w(x,\theta,z,t) &= w_0(x,\theta,t) \end{aligned} \quad (11)$$

where u_0, v_0, and w_0 are the displacement components of the mid-plane of the shell panel along the axial, circumferential and radial directions, respectively. Additionally, $\varphi_x(x,\theta,t)$ and $\varphi_\theta(x,\theta,t)$ are the rotations of the mid-plane of the shell around the θ and x axes, respectively. Additionally, according to the FSDT, the kinematic relations are as follows:

$$\begin{aligned} \varepsilon_x &= \varepsilon_x^0 + z\,k_x \\ \varepsilon_\theta &= \varepsilon_\theta^0 + z\,k_\theta \\ \gamma_{x\theta} &= \gamma_{x\theta}^0 + z\,k_{x\theta} \\ \gamma_{\theta z} &= \gamma_{\theta z}^0 \\ \gamma_{xz} &= \gamma_{xz}^0 \end{aligned} \quad (12)$$

where

$$\begin{aligned} &\varepsilon_x^0 = \tfrac{\partial u_0}{\partial x}; && k_x = \tfrac{\partial \varphi_x}{\partial x}; && \varepsilon_\theta^0 = \tfrac{\partial v_0}{R\partial\theta} + \tfrac{w_\circ}{R}; \\ &k_\theta = \tfrac{\partial \varphi_\theta}{R\partial\theta}; && \gamma_{x\theta}^0 = \tfrac{\partial u_\circ}{R\partial\theta} + \tfrac{\partial v_\circ}{\partial x}; && k_{x\theta} = \tfrac{\partial \varphi_x}{R\partial\theta} + \tfrac{\partial \varphi_\theta}{\partial x}; \\ &\gamma_{\theta z} = \varphi_\theta + \tfrac{\partial w_\circ}{R\partial\theta} - \tfrac{v_\circ}{R}; && \gamma_{xz}^0 = \varphi_x + \tfrac{\partial w_\circ}{\partial x}; \end{aligned} \quad (13)$$

According to the Lekhnitsky approach, the resultant force and moments for the FG-GPL cylindrical shell panel with stiffeners are considered as follows [72]:

$$\begin{aligned} N_x &= (A_{11} + \tfrac{E_s A_s}{S_s})\varepsilon_x^0 + A_{12}\varepsilon_\theta^0 + (B_{11} + \tfrac{E_s A_s z_s}{S_s})k_x + B_{12}k_\theta \\ N_\theta &= A_{12}\varepsilon_x^0 + (A_{22} + \tfrac{E_r A_r}{S_r})\varepsilon_\theta^0 + B_{12}k_x + (B_{22} + \tfrac{E_r A_r z_r}{S_r})k_\theta \\ N_{x\theta} &= A_{66}\gamma_{x\theta}^0 + B_{66}k_{x\theta} \\ M_x &= (B_{11} + \tfrac{E_s A_s z_s}{S_s})\varepsilon_x^0 + B_{12}\varepsilon_\theta^0 + (D_{11} + \tfrac{E_s I_s}{S_s})k_x + D_{12}k_\theta \\ M_\theta &= B_{12}\varepsilon_x^0 + (B_{22} + \tfrac{E_r A_r z_r}{S_r})\varepsilon_\theta^0 + D_{12}k_x + (D_{22} + \tfrac{E_r I_r}{S_r})k_\theta \\ M_{x\theta} &= B_{66}\gamma_{x\theta}^0 + D_{66}k_{x\theta} \\ &\begin{cases} Q_\theta = k_s(A_{44} + \tfrac{G_r A_r}{S_r})\gamma_{\theta z} \\ Q_x = k_s(A_{55} + \tfrac{G_s A_s}{S_s})\gamma_{xz} \end{cases} \end{aligned} \quad (14)$$

where

$$\begin{aligned} &A_{11} = A_{22} = \int_{-\frac{h}{2}}^{\frac{h}{2}} \tfrac{E}{1-v^2}dz; && B_{11} = B_{22} = \int_{-\frac{h}{2}}^{\frac{h}{2}} \tfrac{E}{1-v^2}zdz; && D_{11} = D_{22} = \int_{-\frac{h}{2}}^{\frac{h}{2}} \tfrac{E}{1-v^2}z^2dz; \\ &A_{12} = \int_{-\frac{h}{2}}^{\frac{h}{2}} \tfrac{vE}{1-v^2}dz; && B_{12} = \int_{-\frac{h}{2}}^{\frac{h}{2}} \tfrac{vE}{1-v^2}zdz; && D_{12} = \int_{-\frac{h}{2}}^{\frac{h}{2}} \tfrac{vE}{1-v^2}z^2dz; \\ &A_{66} = \int_{-\frac{h}{2}}^{\frac{h}{2}} \tfrac{E}{2[1+v]}dz; && B_{66} = \int_{-\frac{h}{2}}^{\frac{h}{2}} \tfrac{E}{2[1+v]}zdz; && D_{66} = \int_{-\frac{h}{2}}^{\frac{h}{2}} \tfrac{E}{2[1+v]}z^2dz; \\ &A_{44} = A_{55} = \int_{-\frac{h}{2}}^{\frac{h}{2}} \tfrac{E}{2[1+v]}dz; \\ &I_s = \tfrac{b_s h_s^3}{12} + A_s z_s^2; && I_r = \tfrac{b_r h_r^3}{12} + A_r z_r^2; && z_s = \pm\tfrac{h_s+h}{2}; \quad z_r = \pm\tfrac{h_r+h}{2} \end{aligned} \quad (15)$$

The elasticity and the rigidity modulus of the stringers and the rings are defined as Es and Gs, and Er and Gr, respectively. The joints between the stiffeners (ribs and stringers) and the cylindrical shell panel are considered continuously and the cylindrical panel and stiffeners including the rings and stringers are made of the same material. It is mentioned that for the Lekhnitsky approach, the original structure and stiffeners can be manufactured integrally. Additionally, for the rings and stringers, the uniaxial state of stress is considered. $k_s = 5/6$ is the shear correction factor. Additionally, the height and width of the rings and stringers are considered as follows: hr and br, and hs and bs, respectively. The areas of cross-section of the stringers and rings are denoted by As and Ar, respectively. In addition, the distances between two adjacent stringers and each ring are denoted by Ss and Sr, respectively; the distances between the centroid of an individual stringer and ring from the mid-surface of the shell panel are indicated by zs and zr, respectively. The forces and moments resultants in matrix form are as follows:

$$\begin{gathered}
\left\{\begin{array}{l} N_x \\ N_\theta \\ N_{x\theta} \\ M_x \\ M_\theta \\ M_{x\theta} \end{array}\right\} = \begin{bmatrix} \overline{A}_{11} & \overline{A}_{12} & 0 & \overline{B}_{11} & \overline{B}_{12} & 0 \\ \overline{A}_{12} & \overline{A}_{22} & 0 & \overline{B}_{12} & \overline{B}_{22} & 0 \\ 0 & 0 & \overline{A}_{66} & 0 & 0 & \overline{B}_{66} \\ \overline{B}_{11} & \overline{B}_{12} & 0 & \overline{D}_{11} & \overline{D}_{12} & 0 \\ \overline{B}_{12} & \overline{B}_{22} & 0 & \overline{D}_{12} & \overline{D}_{22} & 0 \\ 0 & 0 & \overline{B}_{66} & 0 & 0 & \overline{D}_{66} \end{bmatrix} \left\{\begin{array}{l} \varepsilon_x^0 \\ \varepsilon_\theta^0 \\ \gamma_{x\theta}^0 \\ k_x \\ k_\theta \\ k_{x\theta} \end{array}\right\}, \\
\left\{\begin{array}{l} Q_\theta \\ Q_x \end{array}\right\} = k_s \begin{bmatrix} \overline{A}_{44} & 0 \\ 0 & \overline{A}_{55} \end{bmatrix} \left\{\begin{array}{l} \gamma_{\theta z} \\ \gamma_{xz} \end{array}\right\} \\
\overline{A} = \begin{bmatrix} \overline{A}_{11} & \overline{A}_{12} & 0 \\ \overline{A}_{12} & \overline{A}_{22} & 0 \\ 0 & 0 & \overline{A}_{66} \end{bmatrix}, \\
\overline{B} = \begin{bmatrix} \overline{B}_{11} & \overline{B}_{12} & 0 \\ \overline{B}_{12} & \overline{B}_{22} & 0 \\ 0 & 0 & \overline{B}_{66} \end{bmatrix}, \\
\overline{D} = \begin{bmatrix} \overline{D}_{11} & \overline{D}_{12} & 0 \\ \overline{D}_{12} & \overline{D}_{22} & 0 \\ 0 & 0 & \overline{D}_{66} \end{bmatrix}, \bar{e} = k_s \begin{bmatrix} \overline{A}_{44} & 0 \\ 0 & \overline{A}_{55} \end{bmatrix}
\end{gathered} \tag{16}$$

$$\begin{aligned}
&\overline{A}_{11} = A_{11} + \tfrac{E_s A_s}{S_s}; \quad \overline{A}_{12} = A_{12}; \quad \overline{A}_{22} = A_{22} + \tfrac{E_r A_r}{S_r}; \quad \overline{A}_{66} = A_{66}; \\
&\overline{A}_{44} = A_{44} + \tfrac{G_r A_r}{S_r}; \quad \overline{A}_{55} = A_{55} + \tfrac{G_s A_s}{S_s}; \\
&\overline{B}_{11} = B_{11} + \tfrac{E_s A_s z_s}{S_s}; \quad \overline{B}_{12} = B_{12}; \\
&\overline{B}_{22} = B_{22} + \tfrac{E_r A_r z_r}{S_r}; \quad \overline{B}_{66} = B_{66} \\
&\overline{D}_{11} = D_{11} + \tfrac{E_s I_s}{S_s}; \quad \overline{D}_{12} = D_{12}; \\
&\overline{D}_{22} = D_{22} + \tfrac{E_r I_r}{S_r}; \quad \overline{D}_{66} = D_{66}
\end{aligned}$$

For extending the governing equations of the shell panel, the virtual work principle is employed:

$$\int_0^t (\delta K - \delta U) dt = 0 \tag{17}$$

$$K = \frac{1}{2} \int_S \left[\int_{-\frac{h}{2}}^{\frac{h}{2}} \rho_{eq} (\dot{u} + \dot{v} + \dot{w}) dz \right] R d\theta dx,$$

$$U = \frac{1}{2} \int_S \left[N_x \varepsilon_x^0 + N_\theta \varepsilon_\theta^0 + N_{x\theta} \gamma_{x\theta}^0 + M_x k_x + M_\theta k_\theta + M_{x\theta} k_{x\theta} + Q_\theta \gamma_{\theta z} + Q_x \gamma_{xz} \right] R d\theta dx,$$

$$\rho_{eq} = \rho_{Sh} + \left(\frac{A_s}{s_s h}\right)\rho_s + \left(\frac{A_r}{s_r h}\right)\rho_r$$

where K is the kinetic energy of the structure and U is the strain energy. Additionally, ρ_{Sh}, ρ_s and ρ_r are the mass density of the shell, rings and stringers, respectively, and can be evaluated using Equation (8). The variation of kinetic energy is as follows:

$$\delta K = \int_s \left[\int_{-\frac{h}{2}}^{\frac{h}{2}} \rho_{eq}(\ddot{u}\,\delta u + \ddot{v}\,\delta v + \ddot{w}\,\delta w)dz \right] Rd\theta dx, \quad (18)$$

where

$$\begin{cases} \delta u &= \delta u_0 + z\delta\varphi_x \\ \delta v &= \delta v_0 + z\delta\varphi_\theta \\ & \delta w = \delta w_0 \end{cases} \quad \begin{cases} \ddot{u} &= \frac{\partial^2 u_0}{\partial t^2} + z\frac{\partial^2 \varphi_x}{\partial t^2} \\ \ddot{v} &= \frac{\partial^2 v_0}{\partial t^2} + z\frac{\partial^2 \varphi_\theta}{\partial t^2} \\ & \ddot{w} = \frac{\partial^2 w_0}{\partial t^2} \end{cases}$$

$$\delta K = \int\int_{-\frac{h}{2}}^{\frac{h}{2}} \rho_{eq}\Big(\left(\tfrac{\partial^2 u_0}{\partial t^2} + z\tfrac{\partial^2 \varphi_x}{\partial t^2}\right)(\delta u_0 + z\delta\varphi_x) + \left(\tfrac{\partial^2 v_0}{\partial t^2} + z\tfrac{\partial^2 \varphi_\theta}{\partial t^2}\right)(\delta v_0 + z\delta\varphi_\theta) + \tfrac{\partial^2 w_0}{\partial t^2}\delta w_0\Big) R\,dz\,d\theta\,dx \quad (19)$$

The strain energy for the stiffened FG-GPL multilayer cylindrical shell panel is presented as

$$U = \iint \left\{ \begin{matrix} N_x\varepsilon_x^0 + N_\theta\,\varepsilon_\theta^0 + N_{x\theta}\gamma_{x\theta}^0 + M_x K_x + M_\theta K_\theta + \\ M_{x\theta}K_{x\theta} + Q_x\gamma_{xz} + Q_\theta\gamma_{\theta z} \end{matrix} \right\} R\,dx\,d\theta \quad (20)$$

Equation (20) may be presented in the following matrix form:

$$U = \left([N_x, N_\theta, N_{X\theta}] \begin{bmatrix} \varepsilon_x^0 \\ \varepsilon_\theta^0 \\ \gamma_{x\theta}^0 \end{bmatrix} + [M_x, M_\theta, M_{X\theta}] \begin{bmatrix} K_x \\ K_\theta \\ K_{x\theta} \end{bmatrix} + [Q_x\ Q_\theta] \begin{bmatrix} \gamma_{XZ} \\ \gamma_{\theta Z} \end{bmatrix} \right) Rdxd\theta \quad (21)$$

Additionally, the kinematic relations (Equations (12) and (13)) may be presented in the following matrix form:

$$\begin{bmatrix} \varepsilon_x \\ \varepsilon_\theta \\ \gamma_{x\theta} \end{bmatrix} = \begin{bmatrix} \varepsilon_x^0 \\ \varepsilon_\theta^0 \\ \gamma_{x\theta}^0 \end{bmatrix} + Z \quad \begin{bmatrix} K_x \\ K_\theta \\ K_{x\theta} \end{bmatrix} = \begin{bmatrix} \frac{\partial}{\partial x} & 0 & 0 & Z\frac{\partial}{\partial x} & 0 \\ 0 & \frac{1}{R}\frac{\partial}{\partial\theta} & \frac{1}{R} & 0 & Z\frac{1}{R}\frac{\partial}{\partial\theta} \\ \frac{1}{R}\frac{\partial}{\partial\theta} & \frac{\partial}{\partial x} & 0 & Z\frac{1}{R}\frac{\partial}{\partial\theta} & Z\frac{\partial}{\partial x} \end{bmatrix} \begin{bmatrix} U_0 \\ V_0 \\ W_0 \\ \varphi_x \\ \varphi_\theta \end{bmatrix} = d_1 Q$$

$$\begin{bmatrix} \gamma_{xz}^0 \\ \gamma_{\theta z}^0 \end{bmatrix} = \begin{bmatrix} 0 & 0 & \frac{\partial}{\partial x} & 1 & 0 \\ 0 & \frac{-1}{R} & \frac{1}{R}\frac{\partial}{\partial\theta} & 0 & 1 \end{bmatrix} \begin{bmatrix} U_0 \\ V_0 \\ W_0 \\ \varphi_x \\ \varphi_\theta \end{bmatrix} = d_2 Q, \quad \begin{bmatrix} \varepsilon_x^0 \\ \varepsilon_\theta^0 \\ \gamma_{x\theta}^0 \end{bmatrix} = \begin{bmatrix} \frac{\partial}{\partial x} & 0 & 0 & 0 & 0 \\ 0 & \frac{1}{R}\frac{\partial}{\partial\theta} & \frac{1}{R} & 0 & 0 \\ \frac{1}{R}\frac{\partial}{\partial\theta} & \frac{\partial}{\partial x} & 0 & 0 & 0 \end{bmatrix} \begin{bmatrix} U_0 \\ V_0 \\ W_0 \\ \varphi_x \\ \varphi_\theta \end{bmatrix} = d_3 Q \quad (22)$$

$$\begin{bmatrix} K_x \\ K_\theta \\ K_{x\theta} \end{bmatrix} = \begin{bmatrix} 0 & 0 & 0 & \frac{\partial}{\partial x} & 0 \\ 0 & 0 & 0 & 0 & \frac{1}{R}\frac{\partial}{\partial\theta} \\ 0 & 0 & 0 & \frac{1}{R}\frac{\partial}{\partial\theta} & \frac{\partial}{\partial x} \end{bmatrix} \begin{bmatrix} U_0 \\ V_0 \\ W_0 \\ \varphi_x \\ \varphi_\theta \end{bmatrix} = d_4 Q \qquad Q = \begin{bmatrix} U_0 \\ V_0 \\ W_0 \\ \varphi_x \\ \varphi_\theta \end{bmatrix}$$

Hence, by substituting Equation (22) into (21), the strain energy can be expressed as follows:

$$\delta U = \int \Big(\left((d_3Q)^T\overline{A}^T + (d_4Q)^T\overline{B}^T \right)(d_3\delta Q) + \left((d_3Q)^T\overline{B}^T + (d_4Q)^T\overline{D}^T \right)(d_4\delta Q) + (d_2Q)^T\overline{e}^T(d_2\delta Q) \Big) R\,dx\,d\theta \quad (23)$$

3. Finite Element Modeling

FEM as a numerical solution is employed to solve the governing equations of the stiffened FG-GPL multilayer cylindrical shell panel. A two-dimensional four-noded element with 20 DOfs is used to discretize the shell panel. Additionally, a local-coordinate system (ξ, η) across the x and θ axes is employed for the shape functions.

The global and natural coordinates are related via the following relations [73]:

$$\xi = \frac{2(x - x_c)}{L^{(e)}} \quad \eta = \frac{2(\theta - \theta_c)}{\beta^{(e)}} \tag{24}$$

where $-1 \le \xi,\ \eta \le 1$ are along the x and θ axes, respectively. $L^{(e)}$ and $\beta^{(e)}$ are the length and span angle of each element, respectively. Additionally, θ_c and x_c are the circumferential and axial coordinates of the center of each element. The approximation functions in terms of the natural coordinates and the displacement components of each element are presented as follows:

$$\begin{Bmatrix} \Psi_1 \\ \Psi_2 \\ \Psi_3 \\ \Psi_4 \end{Bmatrix} = \frac{1}{4} \begin{Bmatrix} (1+\xi)(1-\eta) \\ (1+\xi)(1+\eta) \\ (1-\xi)(1+\eta) \\ (1-\xi)(1-\eta) \end{Bmatrix} \tag{25}$$

$$\left(\begin{pmatrix} \Psi_1 & \cdots & 0 \\ \vdots & \ddots & \vdots \\ 0 & \cdots & \Psi_1 \end{pmatrix} \cdots \begin{pmatrix} \Psi_4 & \cdots & 0 \\ \vdots & \ddots & \vdots \\ 0 & \cdots & \Psi_4 \end{pmatrix} \right) \begin{Bmatrix} u_{01} \\ v_{01} \\ w_{01} \\ \varphi_{x1} \\ \varphi_{\theta 1} \\ \vdots \\ u_{04} \\ v_{04} \\ w_{04} \\ \varphi_{x4} \\ \varphi_{\theta 4} \end{Bmatrix} = \Psi\ q(e)$$

where $\Psi_n, n = 1,2,3,4$ are the components of the shape functions, and Ψ is the matrix of the shape functions. u_{0i}, v_{0i}, w_{0i}, φ_{xi} and $\varphi_{\theta i}$ are the nodal DOFs and are estimated as

$$\begin{gathered} u_0 = \sum_{i=1}^{4} \Psi_i U_{0i} \ \ v_0 = \sum_{i=1}^{4} \Psi_i V_{0i} \ \ w_0 = \sum_{i=1}^{4} \Psi_i W_{0i} \\ \varphi_x = \sum_{i=1}^{4} \Psi_i \theta_{xi} \ \ \varphi_\theta = \sum_{i=1}^{4} \Psi_i \theta_{\theta i} \end{gathered} \tag{26}$$

Substituting Equation (26) into Equations (19) and (23), the Hamilton's principle in Equation (17) can be rewritten as below.

$$\begin{gathered} \int_{\Omega_0^e} \left[\left((d_3\Psi)^T \overline{A}^T (d_3\Psi) + (d_4\Psi)^T \overline{B}^T (d_3\Psi) + (d_3\Psi)^T \overline{B}^T (d_4\Psi) \right.\right. \\ \left.\left. + (d_4\Psi)^T \overline{D}^T \left(d_4\Psi\right) + (d_2\Psi)^T \overline{e}^T d_2\Psi \right) q^{(e)} + \Psi^T I \Psi \ddot{q}^{(e)} \right] R dx d\theta = 0 \\ \mathrm{I} = \begin{bmatrix} \mathrm{I}_0 & 0 & 0 & \mathrm{I}_1 & 0 \\ 0 & \mathrm{I}_0 & 0 & 0 & \mathrm{I}_1 \\ 0 & 0 & \mathrm{I}_0 & 0 & 0 \\ \mathrm{I}_1 & 0 & 0 & \mathrm{I}_2 & 0 \\ 0 & \mathrm{I}_1 & 0 & 0 & \mathrm{I}_2 \end{bmatrix}, \begin{Bmatrix} \mathrm{I}_0 \\ \mathrm{I}_1 \\ \mathrm{I}_2 \end{Bmatrix} = \int_{-\frac{h}{2}}^{\frac{h}{2}} \begin{Bmatrix} 1 \\ z \\ z^2 \end{Bmatrix} \rho_{eq} dz \end{gathered} \tag{27}$$

Additionally, by replacing $d_2\Psi = B_2, d_3\Psi = B_3, d_4\Psi = B_4$ in Equation (27), and by sorting it, Equation (28) is derived for a cylindrical panel element:

$$(\boldsymbol{k}_1 + \boldsymbol{k}_2 + \boldsymbol{k}_3)^{(e)} q^{(e)} + \boldsymbol{M}^{(e)} \ddot{q}^{(e)} = 0 \tag{28}$$

where

$$
\begin{aligned}
M^e &= \int_{\Omega_0^e} \Psi^T I \Psi \, R \, dx \, d\theta \\
k_1^e &= \int \left[B_3^T \overline{A}^T + B_4^T \overline{B}^T B_3 \right] R \, dx \, d\theta \\
k_2^e &= \int \left[B_3^T \overline{B}^T B_4 + B_4^T \overline{D}^T B_4 \right] R \, dx \, d\theta. \\
k_3^e &= \int \left[B_2^T \overline{e}^T B_2 \right] R \, dx \, d\theta
\end{aligned} \tag{29}
$$

After evaluating the element matrices of each element, and via the summation of these matrices, the finite element model of the stiffened FG-GPL multilayer cylindrical panel is as follows

$$(\boldsymbol{k}_1 + \boldsymbol{k}_2 + \boldsymbol{k}_3) q + \boldsymbol{M} \ddot{q} = 0 \tag{30}$$

Finally, for the free vibration problem, the following eigenvalue problem is considered.

$$\left((\boldsymbol{k}_1 + \boldsymbol{k}_2 + \boldsymbol{k}_3) - \boldsymbol{M} \omega^2 \right) q = 0 \tag{31}$$

where in Equation (31), ω represents the circular natural frequencies of the stiffened shell panel and q is its mode shapes.

The details of the solution procedure for the free vibration problem (Equation (31)) are as follows:

1. Calculating the stiffness and mass matrices of each element according to Equation (29);
2. Assembling the stiffness and mass matrices of each element to obtain the final stiffness and mass matrices of the shell;
3. Applying the Sparse command on the matrices to reduce the size of matrices and also the computation time;
4. Applying displacement boundary conditions on the Sparse matrices according to Equation (32);
5. Solving the eigenvalue problem (Equation (31)) to obtain the natural frequencies and mode shapes. To solve Equation (31) in Matlab software, the command eigs ($k_1 + k_2 + k_3$, M; number of desired mode shapes, 0) is used. Briefly, 0 means that the lowest natural frequency close to 0 is desired. In this study, number of desired mode shapes = 6.

In this study, the following displacement boundary conditions for a cylindrical panel are considered:

$$
\begin{array}{l}
\text{When all edges of the cylindrical shell panel are clamped (CCCC), the following can be observed:} \\
u_0,\ v_0,\ w_0,\ \varphi_x,\ \varphi_\theta = 0 \quad at (x = 0, \theta), (x = L, \theta), (x, \theta = 0), (x, \theta = \beta) \\
\text{Additionally, when all edges of the structure are simply supported (SSSS):} \\
u_0,\ w_0 = 0 \qquad at \ (x = 0, \theta), (x = L, \theta) \\
v_0,\ w_0 = 0 \qquad at \ (x, \theta = 0), (x, \theta = \beta)
\end{array} \tag{32}
$$

4. Numerical Results and Discussion

4.1. Verification of Results

The vibration analysis of a stiffened cylindrical panel reinforced by a graphene platelet has not been investigated so far. Hence, for verification purposes, numerical results are derived for a homogenous stiffened cylindrical panel with a ring and stringer for free-boundary conditions. For this target, the weight fraction of GPLs in the present study should be considered zero. Additionally, the geometries and mechanical properties of the cylindrical panel of Ref [8] are considered (E = 209 GPa, υ = 0.3, ρ = 7800 kg/m^3). Then, the natural frequencies of the cylindrical panel with rings and stringers are obtained and compared with those obtained by Samanta and Mukhopadhyay [8]. This compression is given in Table 1 and shows excellent agreement. In [8], a flat shell element with a combination of a DKT (discrete Kirchhoff's triangle) plate-bending element and Allman's plane stress triangle is employed to model the problem. The bending element was a six-noded triangle with 12 degrees of freedom, while in the present study, FSDT with four-noded shell element is used. Hence, the difference between the present results and those of the reference is related to the different theories that are employed in this investigation and that of Samanta and Mukhopadhyay [8].

Table 1. A comparison of the natural frequencies of a stiffened shell between the present results and those of the reference Samanta and Mukhopadhyay [8].

Natural Frequencies (Hz)	ω_1	ω_2	ω_3	ω_4	ω_5	ω_6
Samanta and Mukhopadhyay [8]	144	247	374	559	593	678
(Present)	138	241	369	554	587	669

4.2. Numerical Results

In this section, the first six natural frequencies of the stiffened multilayer cylindrical panel reinforced by GPLs are presented. The influences of various parameters including four different patterns of the GPLs for the shell panel, rings and stringers, various weight fractions of GPLs, two different boundary conditions and various numbers of the ring and stringer on the free vibration response of the structure are examined. The geometries and mechanical properties of the stiffened FG-GPL multilayer cylindrical panel are assumed to be as follows:

Mechanical property:

$E_m = 3$ GPa, $\rho_m = 1200\ \mathrm{kg/m^3}$, $\upsilon_m = 0.34$ for epoxy, and $E_{GPL} = 1.01$ TPa, $\rho_{GPL} = 1062.5\ \mathrm{kg/m^3}$, $\upsilon_{GPL} = 0.186$, $w_{GPL} = 1.5$ μm, $l_{GPL} = 2.5$ μm, $t_{GPL} = 1.5$ nm for GPLs.

(a) Geometry of the cylindrical panel: L = 2, R = 0.5, $\theta = 120^{\circ}$
(b) Geometry of the rings and stringers: $h_s = 0.02$, $b_s = 0.04$, hr = 0.02, $b_r = 0.04$

The convergence of the finite element results of the present research is investigated through comparing the results of the successive refinement of the element size. In this regard, results are compared for meshes with an adequate fixed number of elements along the θ axis but with various numbers of elements in the axial direction. Table 2 demonstrates that applying 50 × 30 elements through the (n_x, n_θ) direction is enough to obtain convergent results.

Table 2. Convergence study of the fundamental natural frequency for the stiffened cylindrical panel structure (SSSS boundary condition; $S_s = 0.378$, $S_r = 0.5$, $\Delta = 1$ wt. %, GPL X for the structure, and GPL O for rings and stringers).

Number of Elements for Structure (n_x, n_θ)	30 × 30	40 × 30	50 × 30
ω_1	326.82	312.24	310.32

The influences of the various GPL patterns for the cylindrical panel shell and the rings and stringers on the natural frequencies of the structure are given in Table 3 (SSSS boundary condition; $S_s = 0.378$, $S_r = 0.5$, Nr = Ns = 5, and $\Delta = 1$ wt. %). As can be seen from this table, the pattern of GPLX for the cylindrical panel shell in conjunction with GPLX for the ring and stringer has the highest number of natural frequencies of the structure among various GPL patterns for the cylindrical panel, ring and stringer while the pattern of GPLUD for the cylindrical panel shell in conjunction with GPLUD for the rings and stringer has the lowest number of natural frequencies. These differences are approximately 60% and can be useful for engineers in their design. On the other hand, when the concentration of the nano-fillers on the top and bottom of the structure is more than in the middle, the structure will be accorded more rigidity and stiffness. Additionally, for each pattern of reinforcement of the cylindrical shell panel, the maximum and minimum natural frequencies belong to the shells when their rings and stringers are reinforced with the GPLX distribution and

GPLUD, respectively. Additionally, the effect of reinforcing the shell panel with GPLs on the overall stiffness of the structure is more dominant than that in the case where the rings and stringers are reinforced by GPLs. Furthermore, in each pattern of reinforcement for the cylindrical shell panel except for GPL-UD, the numbers of natural frequencies of the structure are close to each other when the reinforcement of the rings and stringers is GPL-O and GPL-A. The effect of various weight fractions of GPLs on the natural frequencies of the structure is depicted in Table 4. In this case, the patterns of reinforcement for the shell panel, rings and stringers are the same. By increasing the weight fraction of nano-fillers (from 0 to 0.01) for different GPL patterns, the number of natural frequencies of the structure significantly increases (by approximately 118% for the GPL-X pattern). The influence of increasing the weight fraction of the nano-fillers on the number of natural frequencies of the structure for GPL-X is greater than that of the other patterns while the impact of increasing the weight fraction of the nano-fillers on the number of natural frequencies of the structure for GPL-UD is smaller than that of the other patterns. Table 5 shows the impact of various boundary conditions on the natural frequencies of the structure (S_s = 0.378, S_r = 0.5, Nr = Ns = 5, and Δ = 1 wt. %). It is obvious from this table that the CCCC boundary condition has higher natural frequencies than does the SSSS boundary condition due to the fact that the CCCC boundary condition provides more rigidity than does the SSSS boundary condition. Table 6 indicates the influences of the number of rings and stringers on the natural frequencies of the stiffened cylindrical shell panel for two different boundary conditions (the GPLX pattern for the cylindrical panel; ring and stringer; Δ = 1 wt. %). By increasing the number of rings and stringers, the natural frequencies are changed a little. It is interesting that the number of fundamental frequencies of the structure for the CCCC boundary condition is increased a little by increasing the number of rings and stringers while the number of the fundamental frequencies of the structure for the SSSS boundary condition is decreased a little by increasing the numbers of rings and stringers. On the other hand, stiffening the shell with a ring and stringer may decrease or increase the natural frequencies of the structure a little depending on the boundary condition.

Table 3. The influences of various GPL patterns for the cylindrical panel shell and ring and stringer on the natural frequencies (Hz) of the structure (SSSS boundary condition; S_s = 0.378, S_r = 0.5; Δ = 1 wt. %).

GPL Pattern for Cylindrical Panel Shell	GPL Pattern for Ring and Stringer	ω_1	ω_2	ω_3	ω_4	ω_5	ω_6
GPL-UD	UD	225.13	374.82	435.39	452.77	465.65	592.43
	X	258.75	433.25	504.36	578.56	593.13	769.27
	O	242.31	420.88	499.98	524.44	560.05	673.14
	A	228.54	390.43	467.24	488.34	497.22	626.46
GPL-X	UD	282.76	479.21	539.81	599.99	633.12	710.47
	X	362.55	614.98	697.29	731.08	766.46	968.71
	O	310.32	550.74	642.12	675.84	700.48	893.65
	A	299.47	494.32	566.36	620.11	658.22	760.33
GPL-O	UD	240.88	390.15	470.46	506.42	525.84	631.26
	X	281.65	480.67	553.57	595.72	616.71	744.64
	O	276.18	466.74	549.34	588.07	600.39	730.12
	A	265.94	441.46	526.25	567.66	580.35	700.49

Table 3. *Cont.*

GPL Pattern for Cylindrical Panel Shell	GPL Pattern for Ring and Stringer	ω_1	ω_2	ω_3	ω_4	ω_5	ω_6
GPL-A	UD	226.83	362.49	432.72	450.24	478.55	600.06
	X	273.56	471.82	520.18	590.88	601.56	716.77
	O	233.14	420.13	500.72	541.57	550.22	680.48
	A	230.13	400.78	474.30	500.94	510.74	635.33

Table 4. The impact of different weight fractions of GPLs on the natural frequencies (Hz) of the structure (SSSS boundary condition; $S_s = 0.378$; $S_r = 0.5$).

GPL Pattern for Cylindrical Panel, Ring and Stringer	Δ_{GPL} %	ω_1	ω_2	ω_3	ω_4	ω_5	ω_6
GPL-X	0	166.66	277.03	322.22	347.9	355.28	438.51
	0.5	312.06	529.61	600.86	630.17	660.34	834.48
	1	362.55	614.98	697.29	731.08	766.46	968.71
GPL-A	0	166.66	277.03	322.22	347.9	355.28	438.51
	0.5	203.53	357.14	423.21	446.42	455.35	566.94
	1	230.13	400.78	474.30	500.94	510.74	635.33
GPL-UD	0	166.66	277.03	322.22	347.9	355.28	438.51
	0.5	187.55	311.66	378.26	400.12	420.18	493.33
	1	225.13	374.82	435.39	452.77	465.65	592.43
GPL-O	0	166.66	277.03	322.22	347.9	355.28	438.51
	0.5	230.47	391.59	473.27	498.30	500.42	634.78
	1	276.18	466.74	549.34	588.07	600.39	730.12

Table 5. The impact of various boundary conditions on the natural frequencies (Hz) of the structure ($S_s = 0.378$; $S_r = 0.5$; $\Delta = 1$ wt. %).

GPL Pattern for Cylindrical Panel, Ring and Stringer	Boundary Condition	ω_1	ω_2	ω_3	ω_4	ω_5	ω_6
GPL-X	cccc	696.26	912.85	1057.23	1145.3	1175.5	1289.4
	ssss	362.55	614.98	697.29	731.08	766.46	968.71
GPL-UD	cccc	421.96	557.72	647.13	702.76	720.33	793.83
	ssss	225.13	374.82	435.39	452.77	465.65	592.43
GPL-O	cccc	524.44	884.23	1032.75	1134.88	1140.55	1350.62
	ssss	276.18	466.74	549.34	588.07	600.39	730.12
GPL-A	cccc	391.63	700.45	860.27	930.18	969.31	1235.77
	ssss	230.13	400.78	474.30	500.94	510.74	635.33

Table 6. The impact of increasing the number of rings and stringers on the natural frequencies (Hz) of the structure (GPL-X for shell panel, ring and stringer, Δ = 1 wt. %).

Boundary Condition	Number of Ring and Stringer	ω_1	ω_2	ω_3	ω_4	ω_5	ω_6
CCCC	Nr = Ns = 5	696.26	912.85	1057.23	1145.3	1175.5	1289.4
	Nr = Ns = 7	697.12	913.00	1053.84	1140.72	1176.02	1284.37
	Nr = Ns = 10	698.23	913.78	1049.6	1136.8	1177.6	1280
SSSS	Nr = Ns = 5	362.55	614.98	697.29	731.08	766.46	968.71
	Nr = Ns = 7	360.01	613.47	690.33	727.66	767.13	969.47
	Nr = Ns = 10	359.62	613.2	685.22	719.85	770.11	971.13

5. Conclusions

The natural frequencies of stiffened cylindrical shell panels reinforced with graphene platelets have been studied for the first time. Four GPL patterns including GPL-X, GPL-O, GPL UD, and GPL-A were considered along with the shell thickness of the cylindrical panel, rings and stringers. Based on first-order shear deformation theory and by employing FEM based on the Hamilton principle and the Rayleigh–Ritz method, the governing equations of the structure were obtained and solved. The influences of GPL patterns for the cylindrical panel, rings and stringers, the weight fraction of nanofillers, various boundary conditions and different numbers of stringers and rings on the natural frequencies of a stiffened cylindrical shell panel reinforced with a graphene platelet have been studied.

Remarkable findings which can be used in practical applications are as follows:

(a) Maximum and minimum natural frequencies were related to GPL-X and GPL-UD, respectively;
(b) The effect of reinforcing the shell panel with GPLs on the overall stiffness of the structure was more dominant than that in the case that the rings and stringers were reinforced by GPLs. The maximum influences of the GPL patterns and weight fraction of GPLs on the natural frequencies of the structure were approximately 60% and 118%, respectively;
(c) By increasing the weight fraction of GPLs, the number of natural frequencies of the structure for the GPL-X pattern was increased to more than that of other GPL distributions;
(d) The CCCC boundary condition had higher natural frequencies than did the SSSS boundary condition;
(e) Reinforcement including rings and stringers may decrease or increase the natural frequencies of the structure depending on the boundary condition;
(f) By increasing the number of rings and stringers, the natural frequencies were changed a little;
(g) The influences of strengthening the shell with GPLs was much greater than that of stiffening it with rings and stringers.
(h) In each pattern of reinforcement for the cylindrical shell panel except for GPL-UD, the numbers of natural frequencies of the structure were close to each other when the reinforcement of rings and stringers were considered to be GPL-O and GPL-A. This means that for these cases, they can be used interchangeably.

Author Contributions: Conceptualization, J.L.; Methodology, Y.Z. (Yuhua Zhou), Y.Z. (Yanhu Zhang), C.L. and M.B.; Software, Y.Z. (Yuhua Zhou), Y.Z. (Yanhu Zhang), B.N.C., J.L., C.L. and K.A.; Validation, Y.Z. (Yuhua Zhou), B.N.C. and K.A.; Formal analysis, Y.Z. (Yuhua Zhou) and Y.Z. (Yanhu Zhang); Investigation, Y.Z. (Yuhua Zhou), Y.Z. (Yanhu Zhang), B.N.C., C.L. and K.A.; Resources, C.L.; Writing—original draft, Y.Z. (Yuhua Zhou), Y.Z. (Yanhu Zhang) and B.N.C.; Writing—review & editing, J.L., C.L., M.B. and K.A.; Visualization, Y.Z. (Yanhu Zhang); Supervision, J.L. and M.B.; Project administration, J.L. and M.B. All authors have read and agreed to the published version of the manuscript.

Funding: This work was supported by Natural Science Research of Jiangsu Higher Education Institutions of China (no. 18KJB510007) and Senior Talent Foundation of Jiangsu University (no. 16JDG037).

Acknowledgments: This work was supported by Natural Science Research of Jiangsu Higher Education Institutions of China (no. 18KJB510007) and Senior Talent Foundation of Jiangsu University (no. 16JDG037).

Conflicts of Interest: The authors declare no conflict of interest.

References

1. Crenwelge, O.E., Jr.; Muster, D. Free vibrations of ring-and-stringer-stiffened conical shells. *J. Acoust. Soc. Am.* **1969**, *46*, 176–185. [CrossRef]
2. Nayak, A.N.; Satpathy, L.; Tripathy, P.K. Free vibration characteristics of stiffened plates. *Int. J. Adv. Struct. Eng.* **2018**, *10*, 153–167. [CrossRef]
3. Nayak, A.N.; Bandyopadhyay, J.N. Free Vibration of Laminated Composite Stiffened Shallow Shells. In *Toughened Composites*; CRC Press: Boca Raton, FL, USA, 2022; pp. 261–276.
4. Sinha, L.; Mishra, S.S.; Nayak, A.N.; Sahu, S.K. Free vibration characteristics of laminated composite stiffened plates: Experimental and numerical investigation. *Compos. Struct.* **2020**, *233*, 111557. [CrossRef]
5. Nayak, A.N.; Bandyopadhyay, J.N. Free vibration analysis and design aids of stiffened conoidal shells. *J. Eng. Mech.* **2022**, *128*, 419–427. [CrossRef]
6. Naghsh, A.; Saadatpour, M.M.; Azhari, M. Free vibration analysis of stringer stiffened general shells of revolution using a meridional finite strip method. *Thin Walled Struct.* **2015**, *94*, 651–662. [CrossRef]
7. Quoc, T.H.; Van Tham, V.; Tu, T.M. Free Vibration of Stiffened Functionally Graded Porous Cylindrical Shell Under Various Boundary Conditions. In *Modern Mechanics and Applications*; Springer: Singapore, 2022; pp. 347–361.
8. Samanta, A.; Mukhopadhyay, M. Free vibration analysis of stiffened shells by the finite element technique. *Eur. J. Mech. A Solids* **2004**, *23*, 159–179. [CrossRef]
9. Mustafa, B.A.J.; Ali, R. An energy method for free vibration analysis of stiffened circular cylindrical shells. *Comput. Struct.* **1989**, *32*, 355–363. [CrossRef]
10. Al-Najafi, A.M.J.; Warburton, G.B. Free vibration of ring-stiffened cylindrical shells. *J. Sound Vib.* **1970**, *13*, 9–25. [CrossRef]
11. Zarei, M.; Rahimi, G.H.; Hemmatnezhad, M. Free vibrational characteristics of grid-stiffened truncated composite conical shells. *Aerosp. Sci. Technol.* **2020**, *99*, 105717. [CrossRef]
12. Zarei, M.; Rahimi, G.H.; Hemmatnezhad, M. On the free vibrations of joined grid-stiffened composite conical-cylindrical shells. *Thin Walled Struct.* **2021**, *161*, 107465. [CrossRef]
13. Aris, H.; Ahmadi, H. Using the higher-order shear deformation theory to analyze the free vibration of stiffened rotating FGM conical shells in a thermal environment. *Thin Walled Struct.* **2023**, *183*, 110366. [CrossRef]
14. Ansari, E.; Hemmatnezhad, M.; Taherkhani, A. Free vibration analysis of grid-stiffened composite truncated spherical shells. *Thin Walled Struct.* **2023**, *182*, 110237. [CrossRef]
15. Tran, M.T.; Nguyen, V.L.; Pham, S.D.; Rungamornrat, J. Free vibration of stiffened functionally graded circular cylindrical shell resting on Winkler–Pasternak foundation with different boundary conditions under thermal environment. *Acta Mech.* **2020**, *231*, 2545–2564. [CrossRef]
16. Tuan, T.A.; Quoc, T.H.; Tu, T.M. Free vibration analysis of laminated stiffened cylindrical panels using finite element method. *Vietnam J. Sci. Technol.* **2016**, *54*, 771–784. [CrossRef]
17. Nguyen, V.L.; Hoang, T.P. Analytical solution for free vibration of stiffened functionally graded cylindrical shell structure resting on elastic foundation. *SN Appl. Sci.* **2019**, *1*, 1–12. [CrossRef]
18. Li, X.-Q.; Zhang, W.; Yang, X.-D.; Song, L.-K. A unified approach of free vibration analysis for stiffened cylindrical shell with general boundary conditions. *Math. Probl. Eng.* **2019**, *2019*, 4157930. [CrossRef]
19. Bich, D.H.; Van Dung, D.; Nam, V.H. Nonlinear dynamical analysis of eccentrically stiffened functionally graded cylindrical panels. *Compos. Struct.* **2012**, *94*, 2465–2473. [CrossRef]
20. Carrera, E.; Zappino, E.; Filippi, M. Free vibration analysis of thin-walled cylinders reinforced with longitudinal and transversal stiffeners. *J. Vib. Acoust.* **2013**, *135*, 011019. [CrossRef]
21. Lugovoi, P.Z.; Prokopenko, N.Y. Influence of reinforcement and elastic foundation on the vibrations of shallow shells with rectangular planform. *Int. Appl. Mech.* **2011**, *47*, 714–719. [CrossRef]
22. Shahani, A.R.; Kiarasi, F. Numerical and Experimental Investigation on Post-buckling Behavior of Stiffened Cylindrical Shells with Cutout subject to Uniform Axial Compression. *J. Appl. Comput. Mech.* **2023**, *9*, 25–44.
23. Rao, M.N.; Schmidt, R.; Schröder, K.U. Forced vibration analysis of FG-graphene platelet reinforced polymer composite shells bonded with piezoelectric layers considering electroelastic nonlinearities. In *Smart Materials, Adaptive Structures and Intelligent Systems*; Society of Mechanical Engineers: New York, NY, USA, 2018; Volume 51944, p. V001T03A006.
24. Van Do, V.N.; Lee, C.-H. Bézier extraction based isogeometric analysis for bending and free vibration behavior of multilayered functionally graded composite cylindrical panels reinforced with graphene platelets. *Int. J. Mech. Sci.* **2020**, *183*, 105744. [CrossRef]

25. Amirabadi, H.; Farhatnia, F.; Eftekhari, S.A.; Hosseini-Ara, R. Free vibration analysis of rotating functionally graded GPL-reinforced truncated thick conical shells under different boundary conditions. *Mech. Based Des. Struct. Mach.* **2020**, *50*, 3821–3852. [CrossRef]
26. Jamalabadi, M.Y.A.; Borji, P.; Habibi, M.; Pelalak, R. Nonlinear vibration analysis of functionally graded GPL-RC conical panels resting on elastic medium. *Thin Walled Struct.* **2021**, *160*, 107370. [CrossRef]
27. Salehi, M.; Gholami, R.; Ansari, R. Nonlinear Resonance of Functionally Graded Porous Circular Cylindrical Shells Reinforced by Graphene Platelet with Initial Imperfections Using Higher-Order Shear Deformation Theory. *Int. J. Struct. Stab. Dyn.* **2022**, *22*, 2250075. [CrossRef]
28. Yang, S.; Hao, Y.; Zhang, W.; Yang, L.; Liu, L. Nonlinear vibration of functionally graded graphene platelet-reinforced composite truncated conical shell using first-order shear deformation theory. *Appl. Math. Mech.* **2021**, *42*, 981–998. [CrossRef]
29. Van Do, V.N.; Lee, C.-H. Static bending and free vibration analysis of multilayered composite cylindrical and spherical panels reinforced with graphene platelets by using isogeometric analysis method. *Eng. Struct.* **2020**, *215*, 110682. [CrossRef]
30. Esmaeili, H.R.; Kiani, Y. Vibrations of graphene platelet reinforced composite doubly curved shells subjected to thermal shock. *Mech. Based Des. Struct. Mach.* **2022**, 1–30. [CrossRef]
31. Baghbadorani, A.A.; Kiani, Y. Free vibration analysis of functionally graded cylindrical shells reinforced with graphene platelets. *Compos. Struct.* **2021**, *276*, 114546. [CrossRef]
32. Dong, Y.; Zhu, B.; Wang, Y.; Li, Y.; Yang, J. Nonlinear free vibration of graded graphene reinforced cylindrical shells: Effects of spinning motion and axial load. *J. Sound Vib.* **2018**, *437*, 79–96. [CrossRef]
33. Dong, Y.; Li, X.; Gao, K.; Li, Y.; Yang, J. Harmonic resonances of graphene-reinforced nonlinear cylindrical shells: Effects of spinning motion and thermal environment. *Nonlinear Dyn.* **2020**, *99*, 981–1000. [CrossRef]
34. Song, J.; Karami, B.; Shahsavari, D.; Civalek, Ö. Wave dispersion characteristics of graphene reinforced nanocomposite curved viscoelastic panels. *Compos. Struct.* **2021**, *277*, 114648. [CrossRef]
35. Sobhani, E.; Masoodi, A.R.; Dimitri, R.; Tornabene, F. Free vibration of porous graphene oxide powder nano-composites assembled paraboloidal-cylindrical shells. *Compos. Struct.* **2023**, *304*, 116431. [CrossRef]
36. Zare, R.; Najaafi, N.; Habibi, M.; Ebrahimi, F.; Safarpour, H. Influence of imperfection on the smart control frequency characteristics of a cylindrical sensor-actuator GPLRC cylindrical shell using a proportional-derivative smart controller. *Smart Struct. Syst. Int. J.* **2020**, *26*, 469–480.
37. Rezaiee Pajand, M.; Sobhan, E.; Masoodi, A. Vibrational behavior of exponentially graded joined conical-conical shells. *Steel Compos. Struct.* **2022**, *43*, 603–623.
38. Sobhani, E.; Avcar, M. The influence of various nanofiller materials (CNTs, GNPs, and GOPs) on the natural frequencies of Nanocomposite Cylindrical Shells: A comparative study. *Mater. Today Commun.* **2022**, *33*, 104547. [CrossRef]
39. Sobhani, E.; Masoodi, A.R.; Ahmadi-Pari, A.R. Free-damped vibration analysis of graphene nano-platelet nanocomposite joined conical-conical-cylindrical shell marine-like structures. *Ocean. Eng.* **2022**, *261*, 112163. [CrossRef]
40. Sobhani, E.; Masoodi, A.R.; Ahmadi-Pari, A.R. Wave frequency responses estimate of the nanocomposite linked hemispherical-conical shell underwater-like bodies with the impacts of two types of graphene-based nanofillers. *Ocean Eng.* **2022**, *262*, 112329. [CrossRef]
41. Sobhani, E.; Masoodi, A.R.; Ahmadi-Pari, A.R. Circumferential vibration analysis of nano-porous-sandwich assembled spherical-cylindrical-conical shells under elastic boundary conditions. *Eng. Struct.* **2022**, *273*, 115094. [CrossRef]
42. Sobhani, E.; Masoodi, A.R.; Civalek, Ö. On vibrational-based numerical simulation of a jet engine cowl shell-like structure. *Mech. Adv. Mater. Struct.* **2022**, *30*, 4016–4027. [CrossRef]
43. Sobhani, E. On the vibrational analysis of combined paraboloidal-conical air vehicle segment shell-type structures. *Aerosp. Sci. Technol.* **2022**, *129*, 107823. [CrossRef]
44. Song, M.; Yang, J.; Kitipornchai, S.; Zhu, W. Buckling and postbuckling of biaxially compressed functionally graded multilayer graphene nanoplatelet-reinforced polymer composite plates. *Int. J. Mech. Sci.* **2017**, *131*, 345–355. [CrossRef]
45. Song, M.; Kitipornchai, S.; Yang, J. Free and forced vibrations of functionally graded polymer composite plates reinforced with graphene nanoplatelets. *Compos. Struct.* **2017**, *159*, 579–588. [CrossRef]
46. Wang, Y.Q.; Ye, C.; Zu, J.W. Nonlinear vibration of metal foam cylindrical shells reinforced with graphene platelets. *Aerosp. Sci. Technol.* **2019**, *85*, 359–370. [CrossRef]
47. Chai, Q.; Wang, Y.Q. Traveling wave vibration of graphene platelet reinforced porous joined conical-cylindrical shells in a spinning motion. *Eng. Struct.* **2022**, *252*, 113718. [CrossRef]
48. Ye, C.; Wang, Y.Q. Nonlinear forced vibration of functionally graded graphene platelet-reinforced metal foam cylindrical shells: Internal resonances. *Nonlinear Dyn.* **2021**, *104*, 2051–2069. [CrossRef]
49. Teng, M.W.; Wang, Y.Q. Nonlinear forced vibration of simply supported functionally graded porous nanocomposite thin plates reinforced with graphene platelets. *Thin Walled Struct.* **2021**, *164*, 107799. [CrossRef]
50. Wang, Y.; Wu, H.; Yang, F.; Wang, Q. An efficient method for vibration and stability analysis of rectangular plates axially moving in fluid. *Appl. Math. Mech.* **2021**, *42*, 291–308. [CrossRef]
51. Chai, Q.; Wang, Y.Q. A general approach for free vibration analysis of spinning joined conical–cylindrical shells with arbitrary boundary conditions. *Thin Walled Struct.* **2021**, *168*, 108243. [CrossRef]

52. Safarpour, M.; Rahimi, A.R.; Alibeigloo, A. Static and free vibration analysis of graphene platelets reinforced composite truncated conical shell, cylindrical shell, and annular plate using theory of elasticity and DQM. *Mech. Based Des. Struct. Mach.* **2020**, *48*, 496–524. [CrossRef]
53. Babaei, M.; Kiarasi, F.; Tehrani, M.S.; Hamzei, A.; Mohtarami, E.; Asemi, K. Three dimensional free vibration analysis of functionally graded graphene reinforced composite laminated cylindrical panel. *Proc. Inst. Mech. Eng. Part L J. Mater. Des. Appl.* **2022**, *236*, 1501–1514. [CrossRef]
54. Kiarasi, F.; Babaei, M.; Mollaei, S.; Mohammadi, M.; Asemi, K. Free vibration analysis of FG porous joined truncated conical-cylindrical shell reinforced by graphene platelets. *Adv. Nano Res.* **2021**, *11*, 361–380.
55. Zhang, D.; Wang, Y.; Li, L. Free Vibration Response of FG Porous Joined Hemispherical–Cylindrical–Hemispherical Shell Vessels Reinforced by Graphene Platelet. *Int. J. Struct. Stab. Dyn.* **2022**, *23*, 2350025. [CrossRef]
56. Zu, X.; Gao, Z.; Zhao, J.; Wang, Q.; Li, H. Vibration Suppression Performance of FRP Spherical-Cylindrical Shells with Porous Graphene Platelet Coating in a Thermal Environment. *Int. J. Struct. Stab. Dyn.* **2022**, *22*, 2250081. [CrossRef]
57. Asgari, G.R.; Arabali, A.; Babaei, M.; Asemi, K. Dynamic instability of sandwich beams made of isotropic core and functionally graded graphene platelets-reinforced composite face sheets. *Int. J. Struct. Stab. Dyn.* **2022**, *22*, 2250092. [CrossRef]
58. Javani, M.; Kiani, Y.; Eslami, M. Thermal buckling of FG graphene platelet reinforced composite annular sector plates. *Thin Walled Struct.* **2020**, *148*, 106589. [CrossRef]
59. Bi, S.; Zhang, E.; Babaei, M.; Tornabene, F.; Dimitri, R. The Influence of GPL Reinforcements on the Post-Buckling Behavior of FG Porous Rings Subjected to an External Pressure. *Mathematics* **2023**, *11*, 2421. [CrossRef]
60. Rostami, H.; Salami, S.J. Large amplitude free vibration of sandwich beams with flexible core and FG Graphene Platelet Reinforced Composite (FG-GPLRC) face sheets based on extended higher-order sandwich panel theory. *Thin Walled Struct.* **2022**, *180*, 109999. [CrossRef]
61. Kiani, Y.; Żur, K.K. Free vibrations of graphene platelet reinforced composite skew plates resting on point supports. *Thin Walled Struct.* **2022**, *176*, 109363. [CrossRef]
62. Kiarasi, F.; Babaei, M.; Sarvi, P.; Asemi, K.; Hosseini, M.; Omidi Bidgoli, O. A review on functionally graded porous structures reinforced by graphene platelets. *J. Comput. Appl. Mech.* **2021**, *52*, 731–750.
63. Wu, H.; Zheng, Z.; Guo, J.; Li, L.; Bao, Y.; Yang, J. Axisymmetric thermal postbuckling of functionally graded graphene nanocomposite annular plates with various geometric imperfections. *Thin Walled Struct.* **2023**, *185*, 110594. [CrossRef]
64. Babaei, M.; Asemi, K.; Kiarasi, F. Static response and free-vibration analysis of a functionally graded annular elliptical sector plate made of saturated porous material based on 3D finite element method. *Mech. Based Des. Struct. Mach.* **2023**, *51*, 1272–1296. [CrossRef]
65. Van Vinh, P. A new first-order mixed beam element for static bending analysis of functionally graded graphene oxide powder-reinforced composite beams. *Structures* **2022**, *36*, 463–472. [CrossRef]
66. Arshid, E.; Amir, S.; Loghman, A. Static and dynamic analyses of FG-GNPs reinforced porous nanocomposite annular micro-plates based on MSGT. *Int. J. Mech. Sci.* **2020**, *180*, 105656. [CrossRef]
67. Babaei, M.; Kiarasi, F.; Asemi, K.; Dimitri, R.; Tornabene, F. Transient Thermal Stresses in FG Porous Rotating Truncated Cones Reinforced by Graphene Platelets. *Appl. Sci.* **2022**, *12*, 3932. [CrossRef]
68. Lam, K.Y.; Qian, W. Free vibration of symmetric angle-ply thick laminated composite cylindrical shells. *Compos. Part B Eng.* **2000**, *31*, 345–354. [CrossRef]
69. Mollaei, S.; Babaei, M.; Asemi, K. Torsional buckling of functionally graded graphene reinforced composite laminated cylindrical panel. *Arch. Appl. Mech.* **2023**, *93*, 427–435. [CrossRef]
70. Nguyen, V.L.; Limkatanyu, S.; Bui, T.Q.; Rungamornrat, J. Free vibration analysis of rotating stiffened functionally graded graphene-platelet-reinforced composite toroidal shell segments with novel four-unknown refined theories. *Int. J. Mech. Mater. Des.* **2023**, *19*, 319–350. [CrossRef]
71. Nazari, H.; Babaei, M.; Kiarasi, F.; Asemi, K. Geometrically nonlinear dynamic analysis of functionally graded material plate excited by a moving load applying first-order shear deformation theory via generalized differential quadrature method. *SN Appl. Sci.* **2021**, *3*, 1–32. [CrossRef]
72. Dong, D.T.; Van Dung, D. A third-order shear deformation theory for nonlinear vibration analysis of stiffened functionally graded material sandwich doubly curved shallow shells with four material models. *J. Sandw. Struct. Mater.* **2019**, *21*, 1316–1356. [CrossRef]
73. Zienkiewicz, O.C.; Taylor, R.L. *The Finite Element Method: Solid Mechanics*; Butterworth-Heinemann: Oxford, UK, 2000.

mathematics

MDPI

Article

Seismo-VLAB: An Open-Source Software for Soil–Structure Interaction Analyses

Danilo S. Kusanovic [1,*], Elnaz E. Seylabi [2], Peyman Ayoubi [3], Kien T. Nguyen [4], Joaquin Garcia-Suarez [5], Albert R. Kottke [6] and Domniki Asimaki [3]

1 Departamento de Obras Civiles, Universidad Técnica Federico Santa María, Valparaíso 2340000, Chile
2 Department of Civil and Environmental Engineering, University of Nevada, Reno, NV 89557, USA
3 Department of Mechanical and Civil Engineering, California Institute of Technology, Pasadena, CA 91125, USA
4 Faculty of Civil Engineering, Ho Chi Minh City University of Technology, Ho Chi Minh City 70000, Vietnam; nguyentrungkien@hcmut.edu.vn
5 Institute of Civil Engineering, Institute of Materials École Polytechnique Fédérale de Lausanne, 1015 Lausanne, Switzerland
6 Pacific Gas & Electric, San Francisco, CA 94612, USA
* Correspondence: danilo.kusanovic@usm.cl

Abstract: In the fields of structural and geotechnical engineering, improving the understanding of soil–structure interaction (SSI) effects is critical for earthquake-resistant design. Engineers and practitioners often resort to finite element (FE) software to advance this objective. Unfortunately, the availability of software equipped with boundary representation for absorbing scattered waves and ensuring consistent input ground motion prescriptions, which is necessary for accurately representing SSI effects, is currently limited. To address such limitations, the authors developed `Seismo-VLAB` (`SVL` v1.0-stable) an open-source software designed to perform SSI simulations. The methodology considers the integration of advanced techniques, including the domain decomposition method (DDM), perfectly matched layers (PMLs), and domain reduction method (DRM), in addition to parallel computing capabilities to accelerate the solution of large-scale problems. In this work, the authors provide a detailed description of the implementation for addressing SSI modeling, validate some of the `SVL`'s features needed for such purpose, and demonstrate that the coupled DRM–PML technique is a necessary condition for accurately solving SSI problems. It is expected that `SVL` provides a significant contribution to the SSI research community, offering a self-contained and versatile alternative. The software's practical application in analyzing SSI and directionality effects on 3D structures under seismic loading demonstrates its capability to model real-world earthquake responses in structural engineering.

Keywords: finite element program; soil–structure interaction; perfectly matched layer; domain reduction method; high-performance computing

MSC: 74S05; 74H15; 74G15

Citation: Kusanovic, D.S.; Seylabi, E.E.; Ayoubi, P.; Nguyen, K.T.; Garcia-Suarez, J.; Kottke, A.R.; Asimaki, D. Seismo-VLAB: An Open-Source Software for Soil–Structure Interaction Analyses. *Mathematics* **2023**, *11*, 4530. https://doi.org/10.3390/math11214530

Academic Editors: Joaquim Infante Barbosa and José Alberto Rodrigues

Received: 30 September 2023
Revised: 24 October 2023
Accepted: 30 October 2023
Published: 3 November 2023

1. Introduction

In the fields of structural and geotechnical engineering, the finite element method (or FEM, see [1–4], to name a few) is the preferred approach for approximating both linear and nonlinear responses of structures [5]. The literature consistently demonstrates that the FEM can effectively replicate the responses of physical experiments (e.g., [6–8]) as well as real-world monitored structures (e.g., [9–11]) with a high degree of accuracy. Unsurprisingly, powerful commercial software such as MSC Nastran [12], ANSYS [13], ABAQUS [14], or LS-DYNA [15] offers several sophisticated material and element libraries for modeling complex structural systems. Nevertheless, in practical civil engineering applications, it is common to lean towards the use of commercial software such as ETABS, Perform3D, SAP2000 [16–18], and FLAC [19] to handle this particular task. Typically, these software enable the modeling of the structural components with limited (usually elastic) soil materials, if they offer any. Unfortunately, these software usually fail to adequately account for wave propagation in semi-infinite domains, a critical aspect in SSI analyses. For example, the celebrated domain reduction method (or DRM, see [20–22]) proposed by Bielak et al., a powerful approach for modeling semi-infinite domains under remote excitation, is rarely available in commercial software. Similarly, the implementation of absorbing boundary conditions, such as perfectly matched layers (or PML, see [23–25]), to mitigate spurious wave reflections from far-field boundaries is often absent or limited.

The lack of numerical tools for appropriate modeling SSI problems has increased software development during the last two decades. Some software examples are Mastodon [26], Code_Aster [27], ACS-SASSI [28], Real-ESSI [29], and OpenSEES [30], to name a few. These platforms have contributed significantly by providing some capabilities to address the aforementioned limitations. However, it is worth noting that while these open-source software offers important features, several present practical challenges for users. For instance, certain software packages can be difficult to install, modifying their source code can be a formidable task due to a lack of proper comments within the source files, or implementing new features becomes cumbersome due to the source code length. Moreover, running SSI simulations with such software can often prove to be time-consuming and resource-intensive. Motivated by this need, the authors developed `Seismo-VLAB` (or `SVL`, as referenced in [31,32]), an open-source software designed to perform SSI simulations. `SVL` is developed with a focus on simplicity and good coding practices. It incorporates the Eigen C++ Template library [33], which makes it easy for users to make modifications. Additionally, implementations prioritize straightforward methods, avoiding complexity, excessive parameters, local variables, and overuse of multiple inheritances, ensuring straightforward code modifications. While `SVL` was initially created to solve computationally efficient wave propagation for earth dam problems, topographic amplification, and basin effects, it has been extended to incorporate other systems, such as building clusters and lifelines. The most important features of the software include perfectly matched layers as absorbing boundaries [24,25,34]; domain reduction for modeling wavefield incoherency in truncated domains [21]; domain decomposition for optimal parallel computing [35]; material and geometric nonlinearity [36–38]; and interfaces with message passing interface (or MPI, see [39]) and open multi-processing (or OpenMP, see [40]) parallelization.

It is believed that `SVL`'s features are necessary for efficiently solving SSI problems regarding (1) modeling of spatial variability of soil properties for uncertainty quantification in linear and nonlinear models of engineering structures [41–46], (2) inverse problems for parameter estimation as well as reliability-based performance analysis in nonlinear finite element models of engineering structures [31,47–53], (3) site response analysis for the study of amplification or deamplification of seismic waves considering topographic and basin effects [54–62], and (4) specific topics concerning SSI models with time lag effects [63], 3D seismic wave propagation [64], seismic fragility and demand hazard analyses for earth slopes [65], coupled FEM techniques for SSI analyses [66], and earthquake-induced structural pounding between buildings [67]. Thus, `SVL`'s innovativeness lies in its open-source nature, integration of advanced techniques, parallel computing capabilities, modeling of wave propagation in half-spaces, user friendliness, versatility, and applicability to diverse SSI scenarios. This combination makes `SVL` a valuable and pioneering tool for researchers and engineers in the field of soil–structure interaction. In fact, a few researchers have already used `SVL` in some peer-reviewed journals (see [68–72] as examples) for such purpose.

This work describes the most important feature requirements implemented in `SVL` for modeling half-spaces in homogeneous and heterogeneous media. A particular emphasis is placed on (a) the domain decomposition for parallel execution in cases involving large domains and (b) the symmetric hybrid PML formulation and its implementation using the Newmark-beta implicit time integration scheme. This implementation is subjected to rigorous verification by comparing results between Seismo-VLAB truncated domains with PML against those from enlarged domains with fixed boundaries. Lastly, the DRM implementation, a critical approach for modeling semi-infinite domains, is carefully examined. A comprehensive verification process follows comparing DRM-generated free-field responses with solutions from existing literature. The study concludes by utilizing the coupled DRM–PML method and the parallel computing capabilities of Seismo-VLAB to investigate SSI effects on site and structural responses for a 3D linear elastic building subjected to seismic excitation at various angles of incidence. The later application showcases the software's capability to model real-world earthquake responses in structural engineering and how these features can help to solve SSI problems in other research areas efficiently.

2. Implementation and Verification for Modeling Half-Space

Seismo-VLAB consists of two primary and self-contained processes: the Pre-Analysis and the Run-Analysis, which are depicted in Figure 1.

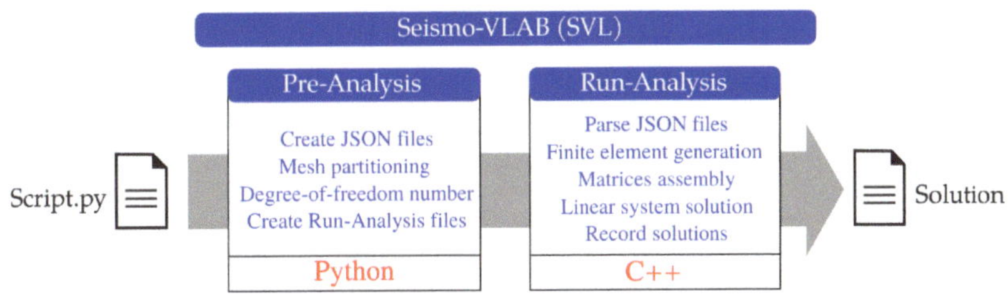

Figure 1. Seismo-VLAB global software structure. The Pre-Analysis is an interface to provide the files to be executed, and the Run-Analysis is the main core that performs the finite element analysis. The Pre-Analysis main task is to transform the Script.py into JSON input files for the Run-Analysis, which in turn converts this information into objects and executes the simulation.

The Pre-Analysis allows users to create, import, adjust, and manipulate FE models, encouraging the development of complex geometries. However, users are required to manually provide node, material, section, and element or utilize external tools to prepare this information for storage in JSON files. Conversely, the Run-Analysis performs the FE analysis, encompassing tasks such as matrix generation, assembly, linear system solution, and stores the solution. Specifically, the Run-Analysis offers the following elements:

(a) Linearized solid and structural elements such as two- and three-node truss (i.e., lin2DTruss2, lin2DTruss3, lin3DTruss2, and lin3DTruss3), three- and six-node triangular (i.e., lin2DTria3 and lin2DTria6), four- and eight-node quadrilateral (i.e., lin2DQuad4 and lin2DQuad8), four- and ten-node tetrahedron (i.e., lin3DTetra4 and lin3DTetra10), eight- and twenty-node hexahedron (i.e., lin3DHexa8 and lin3D-Hexa20), two-node frame (i.e., lin2DFrame2 and lin3DFrame2), and four-node shell (i.e., lin3DShell4) elements are currently available.

(b) Finite kinematics solid and structural elements such as two-node truss (i.e., kin-2DTruss2 and kin3DTruss2), four-node quadrilateral (i.e., kin2DQuad4), eight-node hexahedron (i.e., kin3DHexa8), and two-node frame (i.e., kin2DFrame2 and kin3D-Frame2) elements currently allow large deformation [3,73,74].

(c) The perfectly matched layer (PML) can be specified for emulating semi-infinite half-spaces in 2D and 3D simulations. Currently, four- and eight-node quadrilateral (PML2DQuad4 and PML2DQuad8), and eight- and twenty-node hexahedron (PML3DHexa8 and PML3DHexa20) elements are implemented.

The element's properties are computed using numerical integration. This process allows the selection of various quadrature rules, such as Gauss–Legendre and Gauss–Lobatto. Depending on the specific element type, the number of integration points can be chosen within a defined range: 1 to 7 for line elements (e.g., lin3DTruss2, lin3DTruss3, lin3DFrame2), 1 to 49 for area elements (e.g., lin2DTria6, lin2DQuad4, lin3DShell4, PML2DQuad4), and 1 to 343 for volume elements (e.g., lin3DTetra10, lin3DHexa8, PML-3DHexa8). This selection considers a uniform grid of points for integration.

Technical details regarding the SVL software's architecture, functionalities, and scalability are presented in [32]. This section presents the essential ingredients a numerical software (or toolbox) must have to perform parallel SSI simulations. In particular, it is demonstrated that the domain decomposition, domain reduction method, and absorbing boundary conditions are necessary to simulate truncated half-space behavior properly.

2.1. Domain Decomposition

Domain decomposition is employed to perform a parallel execution. Here, the model domain (i.e., group of objects such as Node, Element, Material, Section, and Load) is divided so that the number of elements is almost uniform across processors. The aim of performing the mesh partitioning with Metis [35] is to minimize the load imbalance [75] by distributing roughly the same number of elements across processors. However, other graph partitioning programs such as SCOTCH [76] or Zoltan [77] can be incorporated to reach the same purpose.

2.1.1. Implementation

A hypergraph, denoted as $\mathcal{H} = (\mathcal{X}, \mathcal{E})$, consists of a set of vertices, represented by $\mathcal{X}$, and hyperedges, represented by $\mathcal{E}$. In this structure [78], every hyperedge is essentially a subset of the set of vertices $\mathcal{X}$. In this regard, the k-way hypergraph partitioning problem is defined as follows: given a hypergraph $\mathcal{H} = (\mathcal{X}, \mathcal{E})$, partition set $\mathcal{X}$ into k disjoint subsets, i.e., $\mathcal{X}_1, \mathcal{X}_2, \ldots, \mathcal{X}_k$, such that $\mathcal{X} = \bigcup_{j=1}^{k} \mathcal{X}_j$. The reader may refer to [79] for more details on how this is performed. The hypergraph $\mathcal{H}$ is constructed internally using Metis subroutines, where the vertices $\mathcal{X}$ and edges $\mathcal{E}$ data in SVL are generated using the Mesh element's connectivity information. In order to minimize the processor load imbalance, a weight is specified for each vertex proportional to the number of degrees of freedom ($\mathrm{N}^{\mathrm{n}}_{\mathrm{dof}}$) of each Node. Thus, the element's load, computed as the square of the number of nodes multiplied by the number of degrees of freedom, offers an approximate measure of the computational complexity required to calculate a matrix. The latter gives a rough estimation of the relative load of an element compared to others, allowing for clustering groups of elements where the sum of individual loads is similar. This process is performed using the k-way hypergraph partitioning in Metis, from which the information is collected to construct the subdomains to be distributed to each processor. The OpenMPI [40,80–82] interface allows each partition to be sent to different processor units, so that the element mass $\mathbf{M}^{\mathrm{e}} \in \mathbb{R}^{\mathrm{N}^{\mathrm{e}}_{\mathrm{dof}} \times \mathrm{N}^{\mathrm{e}}_{\mathrm{dof}}}$, damping $\mathbf{C}^{\mathrm{e}} \in \mathbb{R}^{\mathrm{N}^{\mathrm{e}}_{\mathrm{dof}} \times \mathrm{N}^{\mathrm{e}}_{\mathrm{dof}}}$, and stiffness $\mathbf{K}^{\mathrm{e}} \in \mathbb{R}^{\mathrm{N}^{\mathrm{e}}_{\mathrm{dof}} \times \mathrm{N}^{\mathrm{e}}_{\mathrm{dof}}}$ matrices, and force $\mathbf{F}^{\mathrm{e}} \in \mathbb{R}^{\mathrm{N}^{\mathrm{e}}_{\mathrm{dof}}}$ vector ($\mathrm{N}^{\mathrm{e}}_{\mathrm{dof}}$ is the total number of degrees of freedom of the e-th element) can be generated for each subdomain. The contribution to the global stiffness matrix and force vector is assembled locally. However, the full assembly to the stiffness matrix $\mathbf{K}_{\mathrm{eff}} \in \mathbb{R}^{\mathrm{N}_{\mathrm{free}} \times \mathrm{N}_{\mathrm{free}}}$ and force vector $\mathbf{F}_{\mathrm{eff}} \in \mathbb{R}^{\mathrm{N}_{\mathrm{free}}}$ ($\mathrm{N}_{\mathrm{free}}$ is the number of free degrees of freedom) is handled by PETSc [83–85] and MUMPS [86,87] APIs.

2.1.2. Verification

The verification case considers a 3D SSI model. The soil domain size has, approximately, a horizontal length 100×100 m^2 and a vertical length 90 m. This domain is discretized using 121,944 Node, 105,825 Element, 25 Material, and 26,247 Constraint objects that allow for tying together both PML/soil and shells/soil element interfaces. Similarly, the building model size is approximately 50×50 m^2 in plan view and 60 m in elevation. The building domain is discretized using 7861 Node, 9552 Element, and 19 Section objects in total. The 3D linearized eight-node hexahedron (i.e., lin3DHexa8) elements to model the soil, and 3D linearized eight-node hexahedron perfectly matched layer (i.e., PML3DHexa8) elements to truncate the semi-infinite half-space, are employed. Moreover, 3D linearized two-node beam (i.e., lin3DFrame2) and 3D linearized four-node shell (i.e., `lin3DShell4`) elements are employed to model the building slabs, walls, columns, and beams. The finite element mesh partition is shown in Figure 2 for five (left) and eleven (right) processors, respectively. This figure also shows how elements are uniformly clustered, leading to similar colored volumes. The partitioning process does not enhance the solution's accuracy; its impact is mainly on performance in terms of execution time. Parallel simulations generally outpace their serial counterparts, making clustering, especially in linear analysis cases, beneficial for faster computation of element vectors and matrices as well as solving linear systems handled by the MUMPS and PETSc APIs.

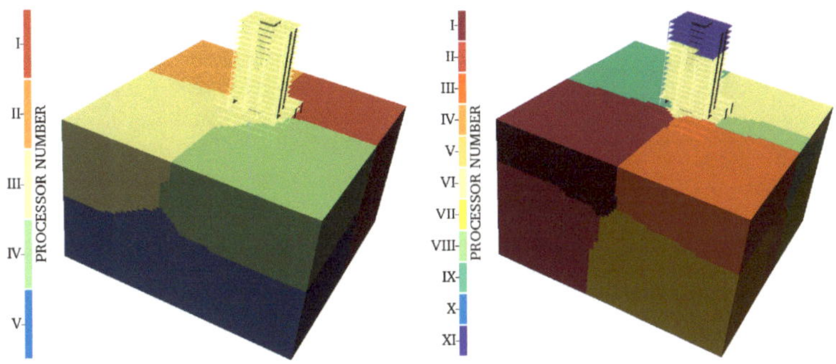

Figure 2. Domain decomposition of a 3D SSI building model using 5 (**left**) and 11 (**right**) processors.

2.2. Domain Reduction Method

The boundary element methods (BEMs) and their variants have been extensively used to investigate the problems where incident plane waves (P, SV, SH, Rayleigh) interact with canyons, basins, and buildings [88–92]. However, the majority of research efforts have focused on analyzing simple topographies and homogeneous half-spaces, which provide an oversimplified representation of the soil domain in reality. Moreover, the problem is solved in the frequency domain, making it challenging to incorporate the nonlinear behavior of both soil and structures. Currently, substructure and direct approaches employing the FEM are the most commonly used techniques for studying SSI effects. In particular, the direct approach has proven to be enormously powerful since complex foundation shapes and nonlinear responses of soil and structure are explicitly taken into account. However, one of the main problems in the direct approach is to specify consistent input ground motions inside the near field [93,94]. In general, this process involves using an FE model with enlarged domains to simulate the transition of seismic waves from far field to near field. However, addressing the near field is challenging due to the need for an accurate FE mesh that represents topographic characteristics and local soil variations. This leads to a computationally demanding task to model interactions among the structure, foundation, and soil. In this regard, the DRM developed by [21] is an effective FE methodology for modeling earthquake ground motion in highly heterogeneous localized regions.

One of the most remarkable capabilities of `SVL` is its approach for modeling the propagation of a plane wave in layered media for site amplification and 3D SSI problems in the time domain. This approach comprises two main steps: (i) the displacement fields of the incident waves in layered soils are initially obtained by, e.g., the stiffness matrix method (SMM) or thin layer method (or TML, see [95]); and (ii) these signals are subsequently fed into the domain reduction method (or DRM, as described in [21,22]), enabling the computation of effective input nodal forces for FE models. This approach, implemented in `SVL`, offers several advantages: (i) it can be applied to horizontally layered soil media and any topographical features inside the DRM layer, such as complex 3D shapes of embedded foundations, canyons, and basins; (ii) the analyses are performed in the time domain, which facilitates the use of contact interfaces and nonlinear material models; and (iii) by using DRM to map incoming waves from the far-field to the near-field domain, along with absorbing boundaries, the computational cost is significantly reduced. The proposed method is presented in more detail in [69] for the case of Rayleigh waves. This section briefly describes the framework for simulating P and SV waves in layered media using SMM and DRM.

2.2.1. Implementation

The proposed methodology to simulate SV wave propagation in layered media using FEM in the time domain is described below. Note that the process for P waves is identical, except for different polarization and wave velocities.

(a) Choose a reference incoming signal $f_0(x_0, y_0, t)$ at a reference point (x_0, y_0), propagating at an angle θ with respect to vertical axis. This time series can be a predefined or a recorded signal during a seismic event. For example, incoming signals can be obtained from the PEER Ground Motion Database, hosted at https://ngawest2.berkeley.edu/ (accessed on 2 May 2023); see [96] for details. This task is not difficult when considering linear elastic homogeneous and inhomogeneous half-space.

(b) Transform the reference signal into the frequency domain by applying the fast Fourier transform (FFT). Denote $\hat{f}_{0,j}(x_0, y_0, \omega_j)$ as the component of the transformed signal corresponding to discrete angular frequency ω_j.

(c) Calculate horizontal displacement $\hat{u}(x_0, y, \omega) = \{\hat{u}_j(x_0, y, \omega_j)\}$ and vertical displacement $\hat{v}(x_0, y, \omega) = \{\hat{v}_j(x_0, y, \omega_j)\}$ using SMM, which is described later on.

(d) Compute the horizontal displacement $\hat{u}(x, y, \omega) = \hat{u}_j(x, y, \omega_j)$ and vertical displacement $\hat{v}(x, y, \omega) = \hat{v}_j(x, y, \omega_j)$ at the DRM nodes. These free-field displacements for each ω_j are determined as follows:

$$k_j = \frac{\omega_j \sin\theta}{V_s}, \text{ and } \begin{bmatrix} \hat{u}_j(x, y, \omega_j) \\ \hat{v}_j(x, y, \omega_j) \end{bmatrix} = \begin{bmatrix} \hat{u}_j(x_0, y, \omega_j) \\ \hat{v}_j(x_0, y, \omega_j) \end{bmatrix} \exp\left(-\mathrm{i}\, k_j (x - x_0)\right), \tag{1}$$

where k_j is the horizontal wavenumber, i is the imaginary number, and $\mathrm{i}^2 = -1$. The exponential term $\exp\left(-\mathrm{i}\, k_j (x - x_0)\right)$ represents the phase lag due to finite horizontal apparent velocity when the SV wave travels through a distance $(x - x_0)$.

(e) Use inverse FFT to obtain the time histories of those displacements, $u(x, y, t)$ and $v(x, y, t)$.

(f) Calculate the effective input forces for the FEM model using DRM.

(g) Apply those input forces at the corresponding locations of the DRM layer and perform the FEM analysis.

The SMM needed in (c) is now described for a layered medium with N interfaces, i.e., N − 1 layers over a homogeneous half-space. In Figure 3a, the displacements at interfaces are obtained by solving the following system of equations:

$$\begin{bmatrix} \mathbf{K}_{11} & \mathbf{K}_{12} & \cdots & \mathbf{0} \\ \mathbf{K}_{21} & \mathbf{K}_{22} & \ddots & \vdots \\ \mathbf{0} & \ddots & \ddots & \mathbf{K}_{\mathrm{N-1,N}} \\ \mathbf{0} & \cdots & \mathbf{K}_{\mathrm{N,N-1}} & \mathbf{K}_{\mathrm{NN}} + \mathbf{K}_{\mathrm{half}} \end{bmatrix} \begin{bmatrix} \mathbf{u}_1 \\ \mathbf{u}_2 \\ \vdots \\ \mathbf{u}_{\mathrm{N}} \end{bmatrix} = \begin{bmatrix} \mathbf{0} \\ \vdots \\ \mathbf{0} \\ \mathbf{K}_{\mathrm{full}}\, \mathbf{u}^*_{\mathrm{full}} \end{bmatrix}, \tag{2}$$

where $\mathbf{K}_{\mathrm{ij}}$, $\mathbf{K}_{\mathrm{half}}$, and $\mathbf{K}_{\mathrm{full}}$ are the 2×2 component stiffness matrices of a soil layer, half-space, and imaginary full space (by joining two half-spaces), respectively; $\mathbf{u}_k$ with $1 \le k \le N$ is the displacement vector at the k-th interface; and $\mathbf{u}^*_{\mathrm{full}}$ is the displacement vector at the surface location of the half-space given free propagation of plane waves in the imaginary full space. For each frequency ω_j, $\mathbf{u}^*_{\mathrm{full}}$ is calculated as

$$\mathbf{u}^*_{\mathrm{full}} = \begin{bmatrix} \cos\theta \\ \mathrm{i}\sin\theta \end{bmatrix} \hat{f}_{0,j}(x_0, y_0, \omega_j) \exp\left(-\mathrm{i}\frac{\omega_j \cos\theta}{V_s}(y_N - y_0)\right), \tag{3}$$

where y_N is the y-coordinate of the half-space surface. Figure 3b illustrates the assembly of the element stiffness matrices of soil layers required to form the global stiffness matrix. Once the motions at the interfaces are obtained, the displacements at the interior of the soil layer are calculated by means of analytic continuation. Interested readers can refer to [95] for further details.

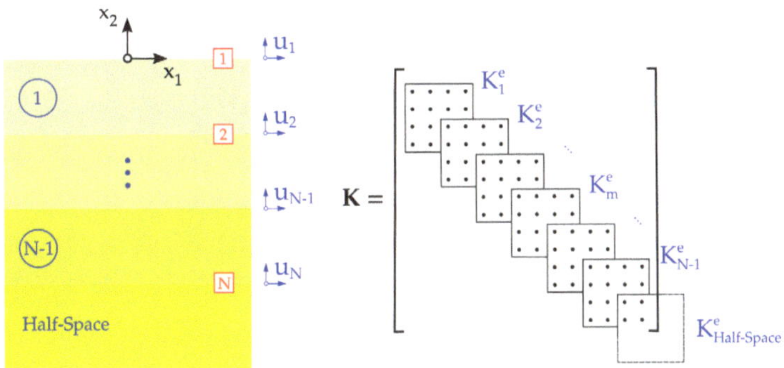

(**a**) Layered soil media (**b**) Assembly of element matrices

Figure 3. Conceptual representation of the stiffness matrix method used for free-field motion.

The derived free-field motions represented in Figure 4a (i.e., displacements, velocity, and acceleration) are subsequently used to calculate effective input forces for the FEM simulations, as is represented in Figure 4b. The generated free-field motion files can be provided in `SVL` as plain text files with columns specifying displacement, velocity, and acceleration for each component.

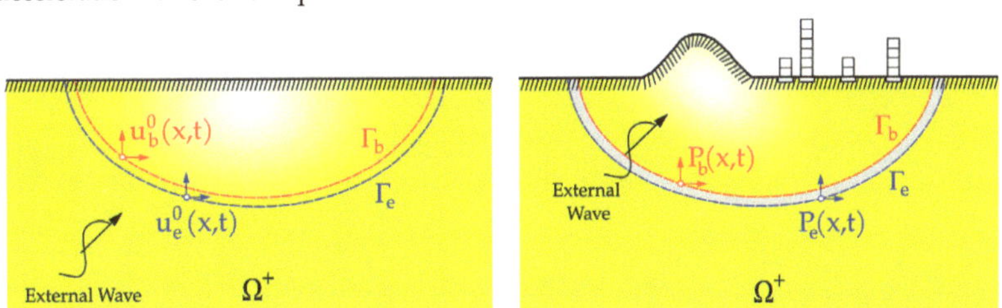

(**a**) Free-field wave propagation (**b**) Effective forces applied to the near field

Figure 4. The domain reduction method schematic representation.

The effective input forces $\mathbf{P}^{\text{eff}}$ vector acting within the layer of elements is

$$\mathbf{P}^{\text{eff}} = \begin{bmatrix} \mathbf{P}_{\text{i}}^{\text{eff}} \\ \mathbf{P}_{\text{b}}^{\text{eff}} \\ \mathbf{P}_{\text{e}}^{\text{eff}} \end{bmatrix} = \begin{bmatrix} \mathbf{0} \\ -\mathbf{M}_{\text{be}}^{\Omega^+}\ddot{\mathbf{u}}_{\text{e}}^{0} - \mathbf{C}_{be}^{\Omega^+}\dot{\mathbf{u}}_{\text{e}}^{0} - \mathbf{K}_{\text{be}}^{\Omega^+}\mathbf{u}_{\text{e}}^{0} \\ \mathbf{M}_{\text{eb}}^{\Omega^+}\ddot{\mathbf{u}}_{\text{b}}^{0} + \mathbf{C}_{\text{eb}}^{\Omega^+}\dot{\mathbf{u}}_{\text{b}}^{0} + \mathbf{K}_{\text{eb}}^{\Omega^+}\mathbf{u}_{\text{b}}^{0} \end{bmatrix}, \tag{4}$$

where the subscripts i, b, and e denote the regions corresponding to the interior of the designated domain, the boundary, and the area outside the DRM layer. The matrices $\mathbf{M}^{\Omega^+}$, $\mathbf{C}^{\Omega^+}$, and $\mathbf{K}^{\Omega^+}$ represent the portions of the mass, damping, and stiffness matrices that are situated off the main diagonal. These matrices are constructed using the data from the DRM layer positioned between two boundaries denoted as Γ_{b} and Γ_{e}. Lastly, $\mathbf{u}^0$, $\dot{\mathbf{u}}^0$, and $\ddot{\mathbf{u}}^0$ are the free-field displacements, velocity, and acceleration of the background layered soil. These forces are computed internally at the element level using the `Element::ComputeDomainReductionForces()` member function, which returns the $\mathbf{P}^{\text{eff}} \in \mathbb{R}^{N_{\text{dof}}^{\text{e}}}$ force vector to be assembled.

The propagation of plane waves (P, SV, Rayleigh) in a 3D space is readily determined by recognizing that, at a specific moment in time, the spatial variation remains constant across a plane that is perpendicular to the direction of propagation. As illustrated in Figure 5, the displacement fields within any 3D coordinate system (x_1, x_2, x_3) are derived through a rotation matrix,

$$\mathbf{u}(x_1, x_2, x_3) = \begin{bmatrix} u \\ v \\ w \end{bmatrix} = \begin{bmatrix} \cos\varphi & \sin\varphi & 0 \\ -\sin\varphi & \cos\varphi & 0 \\ 0 & 0 & 1 \end{bmatrix} \begin{bmatrix} u_1 \\ 0 \\ u_2 \end{bmatrix}, \tag{5}$$

where φ is the azimuth angle, $\mathbf{u}(x_1, x_2) = (u_1, u_2)$ is the free-field motion in 2D, and $\mathbf{u}(x_1, x_2, x_3) = (u, v, w)$ is the free-field motion in 3D, respectively.

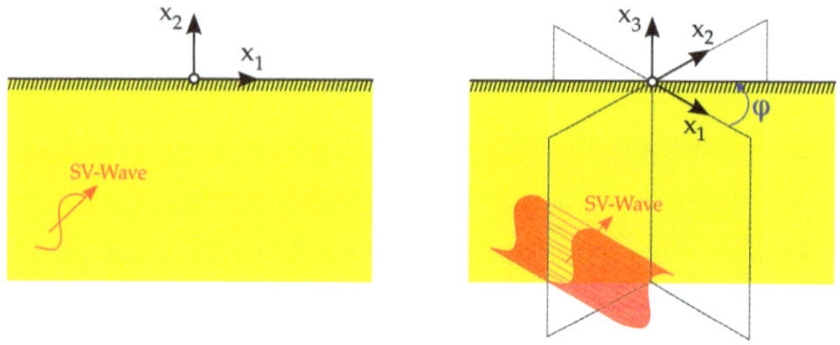

Figure 5. Displacement, velocity, and acceleration mapping from 2D to 3D coordinate systems.

2.2.2. Verification

The DRM implementation in `SVL` is demonstrated, and the solution is verified using solutions presented in [55,97,98].

A 3D soil domain with a horizontal length of 120×120 m^2 and a vertical length of 80 m is considered. Within this domain, isotropic linear elastic materials, characterized by a density of $\rho_s = 2000$ kg/m^3 and Poisson's ratio of $\nu_s = 0.25$, are employed. The DRM is used to transmit the ground motion generated by an in-plane SV wave propagating within the near field at an angle of 15° degrees. The incident ground motion is defined using a Ricker function similar to Equation (15). This numerical example considers a central frequency of $f_0 = 2.0$ Hz and shear wave velocity of $V_s = 120$ m/s. Three control points at coordinates $P_1 = (-40, -40, 0)$, $P_2 = (40, 40, -60)$ and $P_3 = (40, 40, 0)$ are selected for the purpose of comparing the time series with results presented in [55]. The model has 87,778 nodes, 25,635 restrains, and 100,335 elements divided into 73,728 3D linearized eight-node hexahedron elements (i.e., `lin3DHexa8`) used to discretized the linear and elastic soil domain, and 25,635 1D two-node zero-length elements (i.e., `ZeroLength1D`) placed along the boundary to absorb possible scatter waves. The simulation time is set to be $T_{sim} = 4.0$ s, with a temporal discretization of $\Delta t = 0.004$ s, leading to a number of $n_t = 1001$ time steps. The simulation is performed using three processors, and an execution time of 68 min is required to complete the simulation on a Lenovo laptop equipped with an Intel(R) Core(TM) i7-4720HQ CPU running at 2.60 GHz and x86_64 architecture.

Figure 6 displays the velocity time series comparison at the three control points. The results show a perfect agreement with the solution presented in [55,97,98] for each component. In addition, Figure 7 shows the velocity amplitude field at (a) $t = 2.0$ s, (b) $t = 2.5$ s, and (c) $t = 3.0$ s. Since the truncated soil domain, in this case, has no features that can generate scattering waves, the near-field response has to match the free-field conditions imposed at the DRM elements. This fact demonstrates the proper implementation of DRM in 3D settings in `SVL`. The reader should note that the DRM implementation is correct, since the wave field is fully contained in the DRM box. A wrong implementation will generate scatter waves outside the DRM layer of elements represented by the blue volume in Figure 7. In this regard, the lysmer dashpots will not be enough to absorb the scattered field efficiently due to the proximity of the wave field to the boundaries.

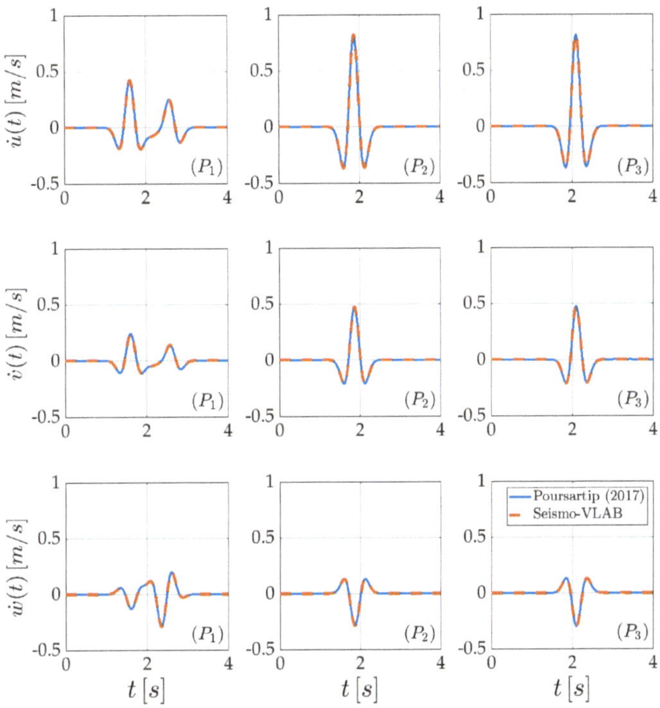

Figure 6. Timeseries of the 3D velocity vector field components u, v, and w computed using the DRM at the control points P_1, P_2, and P_3 for an inclined wave at an incident angle of 15° degrees in a homogeneous half-space.

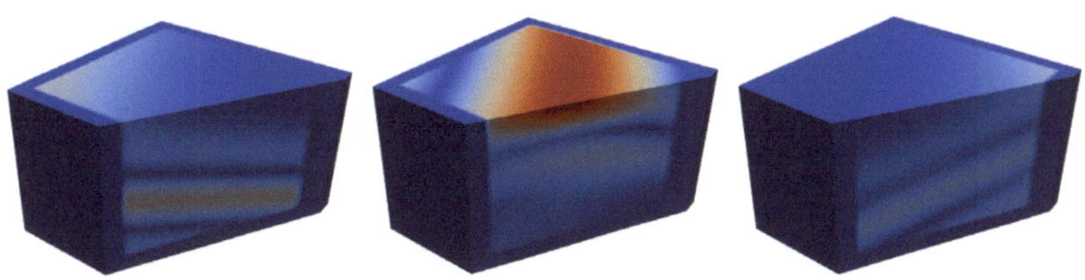

(**a**) (**b**) (**c**)

Figure 7. Snapshots of the 3D velocity amplitude field computed at time steps (**a**) $t = 2.0$ s, (**b**) $t = 2.5$ s, and (**c**) $t = 3.0$ s using the DRM load modeling for an inclined wave at an incident angle of 15° degrees in a homogeneous half-space. The red and blue colors represent a velocity magnitude of 1 m/s and 0 m/s, respectively.

2.3. Absorbing Boundary Conditions

`Seismo-VLAB` offers perfectly matched layer (PML) functionality for simulating semi-infinite half-spaces in both 2D and 3D simulations. Currently, the software includes implementations of various PML elements, such as 2D linearized four-node quadrilateral (`PML2DQuad4`), 2D linearized eight-node quadrilateral (`PML2DQuad8`), 3D linearized eight-node hexahedron (`PML3DHexa8`), and 3D linearized twenty-node hexahedron (`PML3DHexa20`).

These implementations are based on fully mixed symmetric formulations presented in [24,25,99] for plane-strain (2D) and 3D settings.

2.3.1. Implementation

The key idea in PML is the use of complex coordinate stretching. The complex coordinate stretching function in direction s, which can be x, y, or z directions in the Cartesian coordinate system, is defined as

$$\epsilon_s(s,\omega) = \alpha_s(s) + \frac{\beta_s(s)}{\mathrm{i}\omega}, \tag{6}$$

where i is the imaginary number, and α_s and β_s are scaling and attenuation functions, defined as

$$\alpha_s(s) = \begin{cases} 1 & 0 \le s \le s_0 \\ 1 + \frac{(m+1)b}{2\,\mathrm{L_{pml}}} \log \frac{1}{\mathrm{R}} \left[\frac{(s-s_0)n_s}{\mathrm{L_{pml}}}\right]^m & s_0 \le s \end{cases}, \tag{7}$$

$$\beta_s(s) = \begin{cases} 0 & 0 \le s \le s_0 \\ \frac{(m+1)\,\mathrm{V_{ref}}}{2\,\mathrm{L_{pml}}} \log \frac{1}{\mathrm{R}} \left[\frac{(s-s_0)n_s}{\mathrm{L_{pml}}}\right]^m & s_0 \le s \end{cases}, \tag{8}$$

where m is the user-defined degree of the stretching polynomial; n_s is the s-th component of the outward normal to the interface between the PML region and the regular (soil) domain (Figure 8); $\mathrm{L_{pml}}$ is the thickness of the PML region in the s direction (Figure 8); s_0 is the s-th component of the reference point where stretching is defined; b is a characteristic length, set to $\mathrm{L_{pml}}/10$; $\mathrm{V_{ref}}$ is a reference velocity, set to be the P wave velocity; and R is a user-defined reflection coefficient.

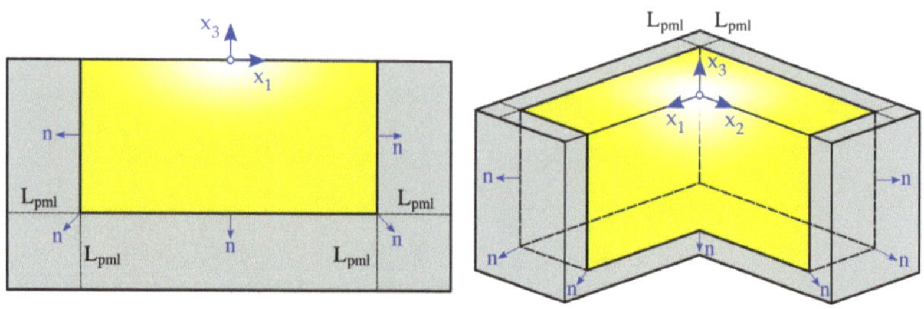

(**a**) 2D PML domain (**b**) 3D PML domain

Figure 8. Illustration of PML domain attached to the soil domain. The soil domain is represented in yellow, whereas the PML domain is represented in grey.

The weak form of the PML formulation presented in [24,99] yields a second- and a third-order ODE, respectively, for the governing equation of motion, with a mixed free variable $\mathbf{U}$ consisting of both displacement and stress fields. The second-order ODE arising in the plane-strain PML problems can be solved seamlessly using conventional numerical time integration methods such as the Newmark-beta method. For solving the third-order ODE of the 3D PML problems, i.e.,

$$\mathbf{M}\dddot{\mathbf{U}}_{n+1} + \mathbf{C}\ddot{\mathbf{U}}_{n+1} + \mathbf{K}\dot{\mathbf{U}}_{n+1} + \mathbf{G}\,\mathbf{U}_{n+1} = \dot{\mathbf{R}}^{(i)}_{n+1}. \tag{9}$$

Fathi et al. [99] suggested using the extended Newmark-beta method. This requires introducing an internal state variable $\overline{\mathbf{U}} = \int \mathbf{U}dt$ to reduce the order of the third-order

ODE, such that $\mathbf{M}\ddot{\mathbf{U}}_{n+1} + \mathbf{C}\dot{\mathbf{U}}_{n+1} + \mathbf{K}\mathbf{U}_{n+1} + \mathbf{G}\overline{\mathbf{U}}_{n+1} = \mathbf{R}^{(i)}_{n+1}$, and approximating the mixed response field and their derivatives as follows:

$$\overline{\mathbf{U}}_{n+1} = \overline{\mathbf{U}}_n + \Delta t\,\mathbf{U}_n + \frac{\Delta t^2}{2}\dot{\mathbf{U}}_n + \left(\frac{1}{6} - \beta\right)\Delta t^3\,\ddot{\mathbf{U}}_n + \beta\Delta t^3\,\ddot{\mathbf{U}}_{n+1}\,, \tag{10}$$

$$\mathbf{U}_{n+1} = \mathbf{U}_n + \Delta t\,\dot{\mathbf{U}}_n + \left(\frac{1}{2} - \gamma\right)\Delta t^2\,\ddot{\mathbf{U}}_n + \gamma\Delta t^2\,\ddot{\mathbf{U}}_{n+1}\,, \tag{11}$$

$$\dot{\mathbf{U}}_{n+1} = \dot{\mathbf{U}}_n + (1-\alpha)\Delta t\,\ddot{\mathbf{U}}_n + \alpha\Delta t\,\ddot{\mathbf{U}}_{n+1}\,. \tag{12}$$

This time integration scheme has been implemented in `SVL` for $(\beta,\gamma,\alpha) = (1/12, 1/4, 1/2)$, which results in solving $\mathbf{K}_{\text{eff}}\,\Delta\mathbf{U} = \mathbf{F}_{\text{eff}}$ with

$$\mathbf{K}_{\text{eff}} = \mathbf{K}^{(i-1)}_{n+1} + \frac{4}{\Delta t^2}\mathbf{M} + \frac{2}{\Delta t}\mathbf{C} + \frac{\Delta t}{3}\mathbf{G}\,, \tag{13}$$

$$\mathbf{F}_{\text{eff}} = \mathbf{R}^{(i)}_{n+1} - \mathbf{F}^{(i-1)}_{n+1} + \mathbf{M}\left(\frac{4}{\Delta t}\dot{\mathbf{U}}_n + \ddot{\mathbf{U}}_n\right) + \mathbf{C}\dot{\mathbf{U}}_n - \mathbf{G}\left(\overline{\mathbf{U}}_n + \Delta t\,\mathbf{U}_n + \frac{\Delta t^2}{6}\dot{\mathbf{U}}_n\right). \tag{14}$$

The matrix $\mathbf{G}$ is the PML history matrix, $\mathbf{R}^{(i)}_{n+1}$ is the external force vector, $\mathbf{F}^{(i-1)}_{n+1}$ is the internal force vector, and i is the nonlinear iteration step. The structures and explicit forms of the PML matrices are omitted, but they can be found in [24,25,99].

2.3.2. Verification

The PML implementation in `SVL` is demonstrated, and the solution is verified using enlarged domain solutions.

A 3D soil domain with a horizontal length of 150×150 m^2 and vertical length of 100 m is considered. Within this domain, isotropic linear elastic materials for the soil, characterized by a density of $\rho_s = 2000$ kg/m^3 and Poisson's ratio of $\nu_s = 0.25$, are considered. In addition, a PML zone of 20 m thickness is placed next to the truncated domain. A downward point load $F(t)$, applied at the center of the free surface, is prescribed as an effective force Ricker function, proportional to Equation (15):

$$F(t) = \left(1 - 2\,(\pi\,\mathrm{f}_0)^2(t-t_0)^2\right)\exp\left(-(\pi\,\mathrm{f}_0)^2(t-t_0)^2\right). \tag{15}$$

In this numerical example, a central frequency of $\mathrm{f}_0 = 2.0$ Hz and a soil shear wave velocity of $V_s = 200$ m/s are employed. The soil domain is now discretized using 13,500 3D linearized eight-node hexahedron (i.e., `lin3DHexa8`) elements, and the PML layer of 25 m is discretized using 18,500 3D linearized eight-node hexahedron perfectly matched layer (i.e., `PML3DHexa8`) elements. Three control points at coordinates $P_1 = (0,0,-40)$, $P_2 = (30,30,-40)$, and $P_3 = (30,30,0)$ are defined to compare the time series against results of an enlarged model with fixed boundaries. The simulation is performed using three processors, and the execution time of 16 min is reported using a Lenovo laptop using an Intel(R) Core(TM) i7-4720HQ CPU 2.60 GHz with eight cores and x86_64 architecture.

Figure 9 shows the velocity time series comparison at the three control points P_1, P_2, and P_3, respectively. The results show a perfect agreement with the enlarged model solution. In addition, in Figure 10, the velocity field amplitude for the truncated soil domain at (a) $t = 1.00$ s, (b) $t = 1.20$ s, and (c) $t = 1.75$ s are displayed, convincingly showing that there are no reflections generated from the boundary and demonstrating the proper implementation of PML in 3D settings in `SVL`. The reader should note that the PML implementation is correct since the wave field is fully absorbed in the boundaries. A wrong implementation will generate waves that bounce back from the boundaries, noticeable after 2 s in the time series provided.

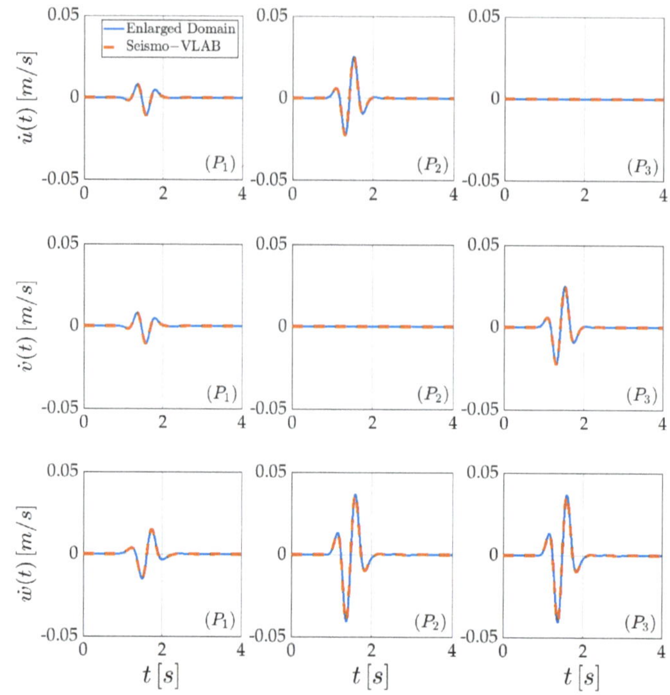

Figure 9. Time series of the 3D velocity vector field components u, v, and w computed using the truncated model using PML at the control points P_1, P_2, and P_3 in a homogeneous half-space.

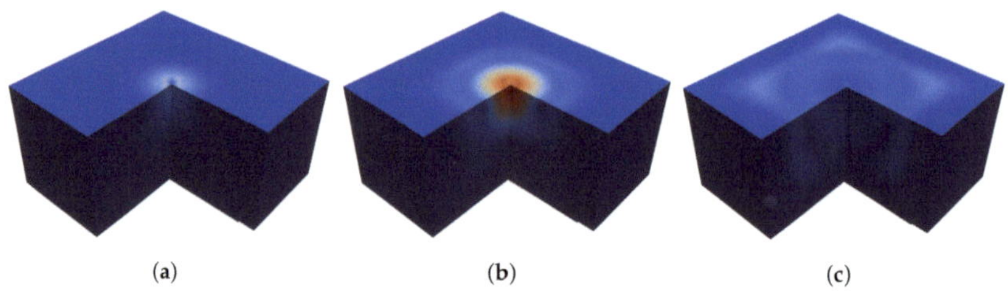

Figure 10. A snapshot of the velocity amplitude field in 3D under vertical loading at the surface of the domain at time steps (**a**) $t = 1.00$ s, (**b**) $t = 1.20$ s, and (**c**) $t = 1.75$ s. The red and blue colors represent a velocity magnitude of 0.05 m/s and 0 m/s, respectively.

3. Evaluation of the SSI Effects on a 3D Building Subjected to a Seismic Excitation for Different Attack Angles

In this application case, the model's dimension and the domain element's distribution are depicted in Figure 11. Because the model discretization rendered a large number of elements, a parallel execution for which the same domain's partition is represented in Figure 2 on the left is considered. For simplicity, and due to the small magnitude of the seismic excitation considered in this analysis, a linearized formulation for the elements and material is assumed. The main goal of this application case is threefold: (a) to showcase some of the relevant features encountered in SSI, (b) to verify that the coupled DRM–PML technique is necessary for accurately solving SSI problems, and (c) to demonstrate SVL's capacity to model real-world earthquake responses in structural engineering due to directionality effects.

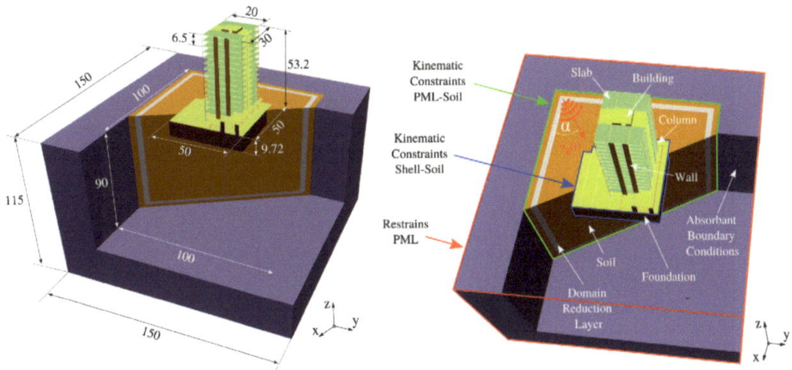

(**a**) Finite element model's dimensions (m) (**b**) Finite element domain distribution

Figure 11. Finite element model considered for the evaluation of the SSI effects on a 3D building subjected to a *sv* seismic excitation. The purple, orange, red, and green volumes represent the PML, soil, foundation, and building domains, respectively. The green, blue, and red line interfaces represent areas where the PML-Soil constraints, Foundation-Soil constraints, and PML restraints are applied, respectively.

The soil domain is a square prism with horizontal lengths of 100×100 m^2 and vertical lengths of 90 m. Standard 3D linearized eight-node hexahedron elements (i.e., `lin3DHexa8`) are employed to discretize the domain. Linear elastic material with properties of $\rho_s = 2000$ kg/m^3, $\nu_s = 0.30$, and $V_s = 150$ m/s are considered to describe the soil behavior. A PML zone discretized using a perfectly matched layer of eight-node hexahedron elements (i.e., `PML3DHexa8`) of 25 m thickness is placed next to the boundaries to emulate the half-space condition. On the other hand, the reinforced concrete main tower (superstructure) has sixteen floors with a total height of 53.2 m. The basement (substructure) has three floors designed for parking and is buried -9.72 m below the ground level. The substructure surface area is approximately 2100 m^2, while the superstructure surface area is approximately 750 m^2. A core of walls is provided around the elevator to control the horizontal deformations. The reinforced concrete elasticity modulus varies between 20–26 GPa depending on the element, with a density of $\rho_c = 2500$ kg/m^3 and Poisson's ratio of $\nu_c = 0.20$. Slabs in the main tower (i.e., from floors 1 through 16) are considered to behave as a rigid diaphragm. The building model is discretized using 3D linearized two-node beam elements (i.e., `lin3DFrame2`) for beams and columns, and 3D linearized four-node shell elements (i.e., `lin3DShell4`) for walls and slabs. As solid elements (i.e., soil) and structural elements (i.e., beams, columns, and shells) have different numbers of degrees of freedom per node, it becomes necessary to establish an indirect coupling between them. To ensure a clean and numerically stable approach, kinematic constraints following the recommendations of [3,100,101] at the contact interface, as illustrated in the blue interface in Figure 11b, are used. In this method, the connections are established by linking the nodes of frame and shell elements with nodes of solid elements solely for translational degrees of freedom (three for each node). Meanwhile, the rotational degrees of freedom (three for each) from beam, column, and shell elements are left unconnected. This sort of connection imposes identical displacements on the soil nodes at the soil–foundation interface; however, some localized deformations in the surrounding soil may be induced using this approach. Therefore, columns at the bottom, as well as the foundation elements, are not in direct contact with the soil (see, Figure 11a interface between the red and orange domain). The same coupling between soil and PML elements is achieved through kinematic constraints on the displacement degree of freedom (see, Figure 11b represented by the green interface). Finally, the rigid diaphragm behavior of the floors is imposed by adding an auxiliary node with three degrees of freedom (i.e., diaphragm node) and then imposing kinematic constraints on all nodes at the floor level.

The domain reduction method (DRM, represented in Figure 11b by the white layer of soil elements) is used in order to transmit an SV wave ground motion. The input signal is propagated upwards at different angles with respect to the horizontal x-axis. In particular, the angles $\alpha = 0^\circ$, 30°, 60°, and 90° degrees are considered. The incident ground motion velocity $\dot{u}_g(t)$ is a Ricker pulse, expressed as

$$\dot{u}_g(t) = \dot{u}_P\left(1 - 2\gamma(t - t_0)^2\right)\exp\left(-\gamma(t - t_0)^2\right), \tag{16}$$

where $\dot{u}_P$ is the characteristic value of the pulse velocity, $\gamma = (\pi f_0)^2$, f_0 is the characteristic frequency, and t_0 is the time position where the velocity attains its maximum. In all simulations, a characteristic value of $\dot{u}_P = 10$ cm/s, characteristic frequency of $f_0 = 2.0$ Hz, and a peak velocity time of $t_0 = 1.0$ s are considered. The characteristic frequency f_0 is selected to generate an input signal with frequency content ranging between 0–7.5 Hz, which emulates most real earthquake signals. The simulation time is $T_s = 10.0$ s with a temporal discretization of $\Delta t = 0.002$ s, leading to a time step number of $n_t = 5001$ for the entire simulation. All simulations were carried out in a server with an Intel(R) Xeon(R) CPU E5-2687W v3 3.10 GHz, x86_64 architecture, and 40 CPU cores. Overall, the simulation took 520 min using five partitions (i.e., using only five processors), and employed 35.9 GB in evolving 5001 time steps.

In Figure 12, the first three fixed-base mode shapes for the building are represented. The figure displays the deformed configuration in solid colors, whereas black lines represent the undeformed configuration. In particular, Figure 12a displays a decoupled translational mode shape along the y-direction generated at a fundamental frequency of 0.75 s. On the other hand, Figure 12b shows a coupled translational and rotational mode shape along the x-direction. Note that the coupling is a result of a concrete reinforcement wall on one side, which creates a misalignment between the center of mass and the structural stiffness. The second fixed-base mode shape is obtained at a fundamental frequency of 0.68 s. Finally, Figure 12c illustrates the third fixed-base mode shape, which is purely torsional, vibrating at a frequency of 0.47 s.

In Figure 13, both the velocity field amplitude and deformed configuration at time (a) $t = 1.20$ s, (b) $t = 1.60$ s, (c) $t = 2.32$ s, (d) $t = 3.52$ s, (e) $t = 5.20$ s, and (f) $t = 8.00$ s for $\alpha = 30^\circ$ degrees are displayed. Note how in Figure 13a,b, inside the DRM (near-field) domain, the SV wave propagating upwards is successfully generated. However, because of the building, a scattered field is generated outside the DRM (far-field) domain in Figure 13c–e. In particular, at time $t = 3.52$ s, the wavefront generated by the building due to the so-called inertial interaction is shown. Inertial interaction refers to the displacements and rotations occurring at the foundation level of a structure as a consequence of inertial forces that emerge during the motion. These displacements and rotations can represent a significant source of energy dissipation within the soil–structure system. In practice, inertial interaction induces two distinct effects: (a) it leads to a period elongation because of the deformable soil underneath, and (b) it alters the damping characteristics of the structure, primarily due to the contributions from the hysteresis damping of the surrounding soil and radiation of energy in the form of stress waves transmitted from the foundation to the soil half-space, known as radiation damping. Similarly, comparing time $t = 1.20$ and 1.60 s shows how the foundation barely deforms, averaging the velocity at the interface due to the so-called kinematic interaction. Kinematic interaction arises due to the presence of rigid foundation elements within or on the soil, causing movements at the foundation level to differ from those in the free field. One cause of these deviations is base-slab averaging, which occurs because the stiffness of the foundation system leads to the averaging of ground motion variations within the foundation's footprint, causing deviations from the free-field motions. Another cause of such deviation is embedment effects, which occur as a result of a reduction in foundation-level motions due to the attenuation of ground motion as depth increases beneath the free surface. This demonstrates that the coupled DRM–PML system can adequately reproduce the half-space conditions and SSI effects.

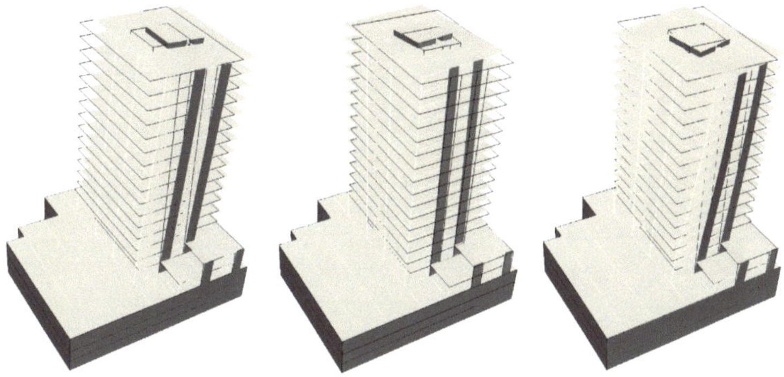

(**a**) $T_1 = 0.75$ s (**b**) $T_2 = 0.68$ s (**c**) $T_3 = 0.47$ s

Figure 12. Fixed-base modal shape for the first three modes. The first mode exhibits pure translational behavior, while the second and third modes display rotational behavior. The 3D visualization depicts the deformed configuration in solid white (slabs) and grey (walls) colors, whereas black lines represent the undeformed configuration.

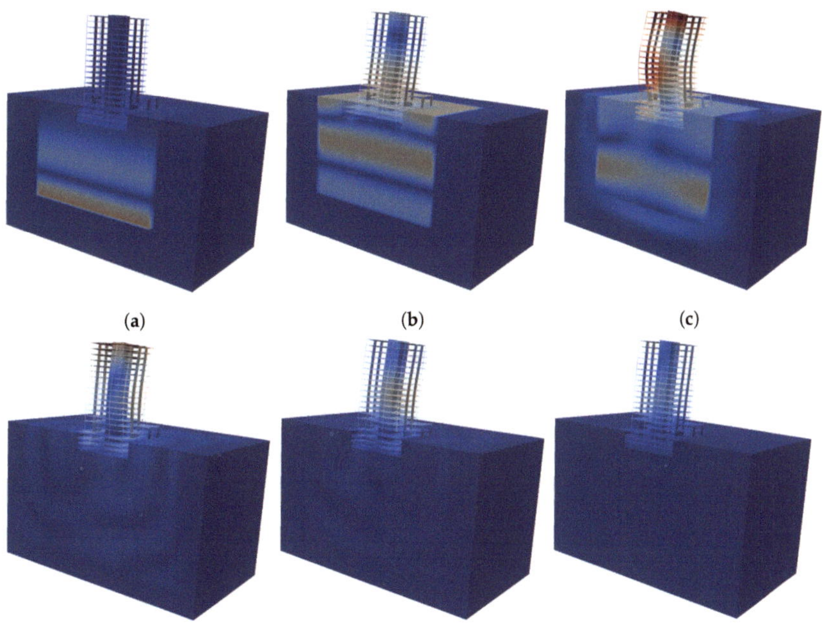

(**a**) (**b**) (**c**)

(**d**) (**e**) (**f**)

Figure 13. Velocity field amplitude and deformed configuration at time (**a**) $t = 1.20$ s, (**b**) $t = 1.60$ s, (**c**) $t = 2.32$ s, (**d**) $t = 3.52$ s, (**e**) $t = 5.20$ s, and (**f**) $t = 8.00$ s for the problem. The blue color represents a velocity amplitude of 0.0 m/s, while the red color represents a velocity amplitude of 0.2 m/s.

3.1. SSI Effects on Site Response

It is of interest to study the influence of the vibration of the building over the surrounding areas. In order to evaluate the radiated wavefields generated by the building, the perturbed displacement field is calculated as

$$\mathbf{u}_{\mathrm{P}}(\mathbf{x},t) = \mathbf{u}_{\mathrm{SSI}}(\mathbf{x},t) - \mathbf{u}_{\mathrm{FFM}}(\mathbf{x},t)\,, \tag{17}$$

where $\mathbf{u}_{\mathrm{P}}(\mathbf{x},t), \mathbf{u}_{\mathrm{SSI}}(\mathbf{x},t), \mathbf{u}_{\mathrm{FFM}}(\mathbf{x},t) : \mathbb{R}^3 \times \mathbb{R}^+ \rightarrow \mathbb{R}^3$ are the perturbation displacement field, the displacement field due to the presence of the building, and the displacement field at the far field (or motion on the soil surface in absence of the building), respectively. These fields are evaluated at coordinate $\mathbf{x} \in \mathbb{R}^3$ on the soil surface at time $t \in \mathbb{R}^+$. The perturbed velocity field $\mathbf{v}_{\mathrm{P}}(\mathbf{x},t)$ as well as the perturbed acceleration field $\mathbf{a}_{\mathrm{P}}(\mathbf{x},t)$ can be obtained in a similar manner, as in Equation (17).

The SSI effects on site response are thus defined in the following manner:

(a) The peak ground displacement ($\mathcal{PGD} : \mathbb{R}^3 \rightarrow \mathbb{R}^+$) of the perturbed displacement field,

$$\mathcal{PGD}(\mathbf{x}) = \max_{t \in [0,\mathrm{T_s}]} \left\|\mathbf{u}_{\mathrm{P}}(\mathbf{x},t)\right\|_2, \tag{18}$$

where $\mathrm{T_s}$ the simulation time, and $\|\cdot\|_2 : \mathbb{R} \rightarrow \mathbb{R}^+$ is the Euclidean or ℓ^2 vector norm.

(b) The pseudo-spectral acceleration ($\mathcal{PSA} : \mathbb{R}^3 \times \mathbb{R}^+ \rightarrow \mathbb{R}^+$) of the perturbed acceleration field,

$$\mathcal{PSA}(\mathbf{x},\omega) = \omega^2 \max_{t \in [0,\mathrm{T_s}]} \left|\mathbf{u}_{\mathrm{sdof}}(\mathbf{x},t)\right|, \tag{19}$$

where $\mathbf{u}_{\mathrm{sdof}}(\mathbf{x},t)$ is the displacement response evaluated at $\mathbf{x} \in \mathbb{R}^3$ on the soil surface for a single-degree-of-freedom system when $\mathbf{a}_{\mathrm{P}}(\mathbf{x},t)$ is employed as the input, ω is the angular frequency of a single-degree-of-freedom system, and $|\cdot| : \mathbb{R} \rightarrow \mathbb{R}^+$ is the absolute value function.

Figure 14 shows the $\mathcal{PGD}$ distribution on the soil surface generated by the vibration of the building for different angles of incidence. This figure shows traces of two important SSI phenomena. First, an outward-propagating wavefield is qualitatively similar regardless of incident angle. Second, significant perturbations are generated in the sharp corners of the foundation layout. In particular, a maximum $\mathcal{PGD}$ of 4.5 mm is reached when $\alpha = 30°$, while a minimum $\mathcal{PGD}$ of 0.8 mm is reached when $\alpha = 90°$. Overall, a minimum displacement wavefield of magnitude 1 mm is developed by the building in the surrounding areas. In essence, the soil compliance allows the rocking of the building to generate outgoing waves, as if the vibration building was a source force acting on a half-space. The geometrical complexity of the foundation gives rise to a complex pattern of outgoing waves that may affect other structures near the building, and that can be captured and scrutinized using our 3D FE model.

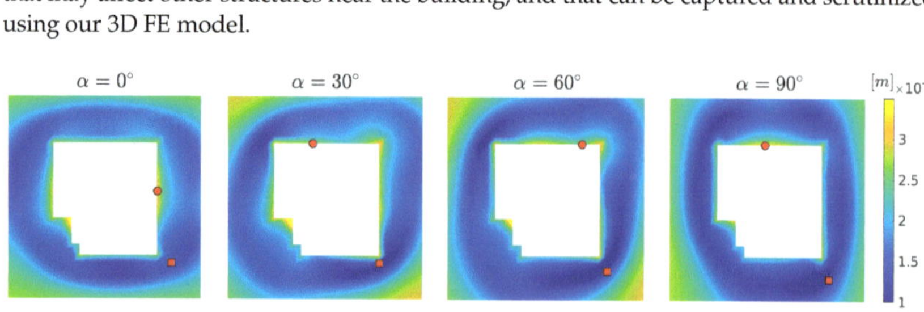

Figure 14. The peak ground displacement ($\mathcal{PGD}$) distribution on the soil surface generated by the vibration of the building for different angles of incidence. The red solid circle and red solid square represent the location where the maximum and minimum $\mathcal{PSA}$ are attained.

In a similar fashion, Figure 15 shows the pseudo-spectral acceleration ($\mathcal{PSA}$) for different angles of incidence. This output corresponds to the maximum basal shear experienced by an SDOF system whose fundamental mode has a certain period [102]. In this figure, the grey lines represent the $\mathcal{PSA}$ for all points on the soil surface; the black line is the average of all cases; and the red and blue lines correspond to the maximum and minimum $\mathcal{PSA}$, respectively, whose locations are displayed in Figure 14 as a red solid circle and square, respectively. Maxima of $\mathcal{PSA} = 5.6\ \mathrm{m/s^2}$ when $\alpha = 0°$, $\mathcal{PSA} = 4.5\ \mathrm{m/s^2}$ when $\alpha = 30°$, $\mathcal{PSA} = 6.3\ \mathrm{m/s^2}$ when $\alpha = 60°$, and $\mathcal{PSA} = 7.3\ \mathrm{m/s^2}$ when $\alpha = 90°$ are obtained. Note that the vibration of the building triggers amplification in hypothetical SDOF between 0.20–0.40 s, which suggests that most of the frequency content of the soil deformation induced by the scattered wavefield stays in that range. It is worth mentioning that this range contains periods substantially shorter than that of the building (the fixed-base period of the building was computed to be 0.75 s using modal analysis, so one would expect the elongated period due to SSI effects to be larger). The prior numbers can be interpreted in terms of geometrical considerations: the shape of the foundation defines the perturbance introduced to the soil at each portion of the interface between the two, the superposition of the different contributions at one point rendering the unique deformation time history of each ground surface location and, by extension, a unique spectrum. Such a spectrum describes a supplementary potential base shake to be felt by surrounding structures. Thus, the simulation allows one to conclude that the building–soil deformation can induce vibrations that may affect structures with very different typologies when compared to the building acting as a source: the level of amplification due to SSI can increase in seismic demand on secondary structures in surrounding areas. In particular, structures such as footbridges, low-rise structures, or social events areas could be potentially affected.

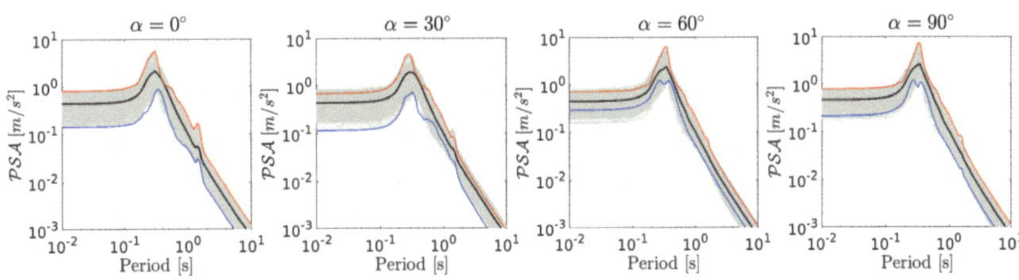

Figure 15. The pseudo-spectral acceleration ($\mathcal{PSA}$) generated by the vibration of the building for different angles of incidence. The grey lines represent the $\mathcal{PSA}$ for all points on the soil surface, the black line represents its average, and the red and blue lines are the maximum and minimum $\mathcal{PSA}$.

Finally, Figure 16 shows the vertical component for the perturbed velocity field $\mathbf{v}_{\mathrm{p}}(\mathbf{x}, t)$ considering different angles of incidence. In this figure, the maximum vertical response magnitude is attained at $t^* = 1.20$ s for the four angles. In particular, a maximum value of $\mathbf{v}_{\mathrm{p}}^{z}(\mathbf{x}, t^*) = -0.063$ and 0.050 m/s at the southwest (square marker) and east (circle marker) foundation sectors when $\alpha = 0°$, a maximum value of $\mathbf{v}_{\mathrm{p}}^{z}(\mathbf{x}, t^*) = -0.075$ and 0.046 m/s at the southwest and east foundation sectors when $\alpha = 30°$, a maximum value of $\mathbf{v}_{\mathrm{p}}^{z}(\mathbf{x}, t^*) = -0.068$ and 0.046 m/s at the southwest and north foundation sectors when $\alpha = 60°$, and a maximum value of $\mathbf{v}_{\mathrm{p}}^{z}(\mathbf{x}, t^*) = -0.042$ and 0.051 m/s at the southwest and north foundation sectors when $\alpha = 0°$, are obtained. Note that, once again, these maximum values are attained at these places as a consequence of the perfect bonding between the foundation and the soil that is imposed through kinematic constraints.

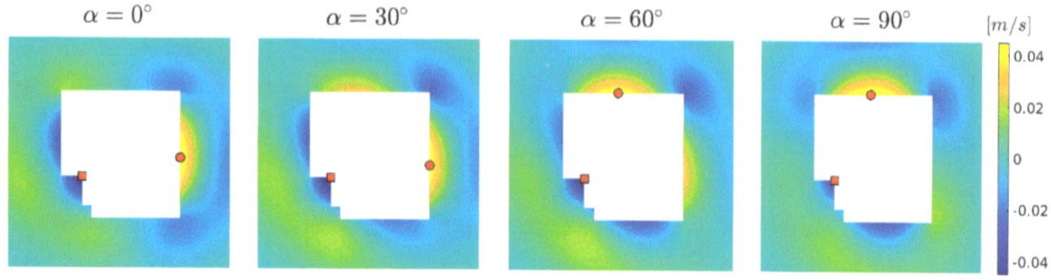

Figure 16. The vertical velocity component for the perturbed velocity field $\mathbf{v}_p(\mathbf{x}, t)$ generated by the vibration of the building for different angles of incidence. The positions where the maximum positive and negative velocity magnitudes occur are indicated with a red solid circle and square, respectively.

3.2. SSI Effects on Structural Response

Let $\mathbf{x} \in \mathbb{R}^3$ be the coordinate of the center of the rigid diaphragm, H be the inter-storey height, T_s be the simulation time, and $|\cdot| : \mathbb{R} \to \mathbb{R}^+$ be the absolute value function. Then, the following structural response quantities can be defined.

(a) The maximum inter-storey drift ratio ($\mathcal{ISD} : \mathbb{R}^3 \to \mathbb{R}^+$) along a certain direction at i-th storey:

$$\mathcal{ISD}(\mathbf{x}) = \frac{1}{\mathrm{H}} \max_{t \in [0, \mathrm{T_s}]} |\mathbf{u}_{\mathrm{i}}(\mathbf{x}, t) - \mathbf{u}_{\mathrm{i\text{-}1}}(\mathbf{x}, t)|, \tag{20}$$

where $\mathbf{u}_{\mathrm{i}}(\mathbf{x}, t)$ is the displacement component along the said direction at the diaphragm center of the i-th floor.

(b) The maximum inter-storey rotation ($\mathcal{ISR} : \mathbb{R}^3 \to \mathbb{R}^+$) at the i-th storey:

$$\mathcal{ISR}(\mathbf{x}) = \frac{1}{\mathrm{H}} \max_{t \in [0, \mathrm{T_s}]} |\theta_{\mathrm{i}}(\mathbf{x}, t) - \theta_{\mathrm{i\text{-}1}}(\mathbf{x}, t)|, \tag{21}$$

where $\theta_{\mathrm{i}}(\mathbf{x}, t)$ is the rotation along the z-axis of the diaphragm.

(c) The maximum relative storey acceleration ($\mathcal{MSA} : \mathbb{R}^3 \to \mathbb{R}^+$) at the i-th storey:

$$\mathcal{MSA}(\mathbf{x}) = \max_{t \in [0, \mathrm{T_s}]} |\mathbf{a}_{\mathrm{i}}(\mathbf{x}, t) - \mathbf{a}_{\mathrm{g}}(\mathbf{x}, t)|, \tag{22}$$

where $\mathbf{a}_{\mathrm{i}}(\mathbf{x}, t)$ is the acceleration response evaluated at the center of the rigid diaphragm, and $\mathbf{a}_{\mathrm{g}}(\mathbf{x}, t)$ is the acceleration evaluated at the ground level.

Figure 17 shows how the drift changes as the angle of incidence of the impinging wave increases. See how when $\alpha = 0$ degrees (the shake is aligned with the x-direction), the maximum drift occurs along the same direction, and, likewise, a similar result happens for $\alpha = 90$ degrees and the y-direction. In these two limit scenarios, the drift is concentrated along one of the two orthogonal directions, which in turn can also be identified with the main axes of inertia: the x-direction corresponds to the stiffest direction, while the y-direction corresponds to the least stiff direction. Therefore, it is logical that the maximum drift, among all the possibilities, corresponds to the y-direction when $\alpha = 90$ degrees, as it can be acknowledged immediately by comparing the first and second panels in Figure 17.

The two intermediate cases, $\alpha = 30$, 60 degrees, display drift along both orthogonal directions simultaneously, with magnitudes bounded by those of the two limit cases. It is also worth remarking on how the drift increases from the base to the first floor, then decreases, and then increases again until it almost reaches the top, with a slight decrease at the very top. This behavior belongs to the reinforcement of intermediate floors, which prompts some intermediate floors to move together with less differential deflections among them. The third panel in Figure 17 shows inter-storey rotation, i.e., the differential torsion between consecutive floors, going from bottom to top. It can be observed from this output that the maximum rotations happen in the case of $\alpha = 0$ degrees, and the minimum occur when $\alpha = 90$ degrees. The building layout explains this behavior: there is a significant stiffness asymmetry due to a concrete reinforcement wall on one of the flanks that produces a misalignment between the center of mass of the structure and its main axis of inertia, which in turn leads to induced torsion as the building bends. However, such asymmetry is not so acute when considering the orthogonal axis. Hence, the induced torsions are much weaker and more uniform when loading along the y-direction, so the $\mathcal{ISR}$ remains substantially smaller. The simulations allow us to quantify these numerically in case of seismic events.

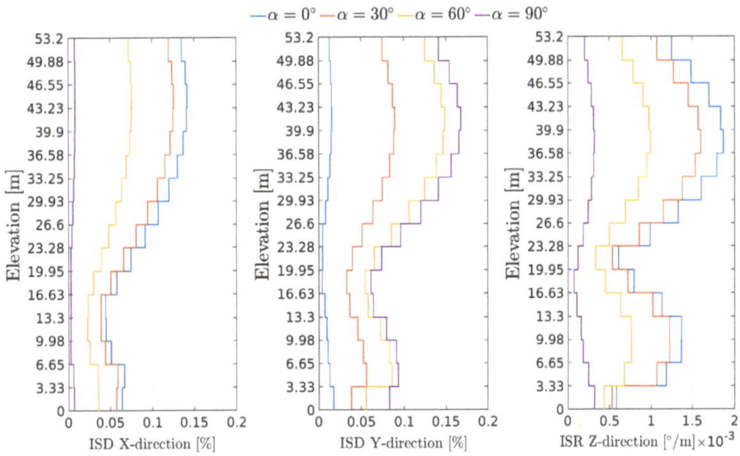

Figure 17. Inter-storey drifts ($\mathcal{ISD}$) along each direction as a function of the angle.

Inter-storey drift and rotation, measuring the differential deformation between consecutive floors, are thus directly correlated with the internal forces that develop within the columns that connect consecutive levels. To account for inertial forces at the different floors, the maximum storey acceleration (with respect to the ground-level acceleration) $\mathcal{MSA}$ is introduced. This output indicates the sudden jerk that people and equipment will experience during the seismic event. Therefore, it is an important variable to consider when it comes to utility design and the comfort and safety of occupants (serviceability limit states). The $\mathcal{MSA}$ results are represented in Figure 18. Unsurprisingly, the maximum accelerations are experienced at the top floors, and are aligned again with the direction of loading in all four cases. Conversely, it is interesting to note how the stiffening of the intermediate floors also translates into a non-monotonic evolution of the acceleration; this result suggests that the building deforms predominately following a modal shape that is more complex than a simple cantilever beam simplified model.

Lastly, the reader may consider that nonlinear materials and large deformation can also be specified for more accurate analysis in `Seismo-VLAB`. Introducing nonlinear soil behavior opens the door to energy dissipation mechanisms that can reduce building vibrations. However, this can also lead to increased deformation, potentially caused by substantial displacements and rotations developing at the soil–foundation interface. Additionally, introducing geometric nonlinearity into the structural system, primarily driven by significant displacements, may trigger effects such as P-delta, plastic hinges within the beam and column elements, and yield lines within slab elements. The former mechanism introduces an extra source of dissipation within the structural system. Although incorporating a nonlinear analysis may capture a more accurate response, the execution time increases drastically. It is essential to underscore that while these considerations hold significant relevance in structural engineering, their detailed exploration lies outside the scope of this particular example. More technical details regarding this illustrative example can be found in the performance cases `H01` provided with the `SVL` software package.

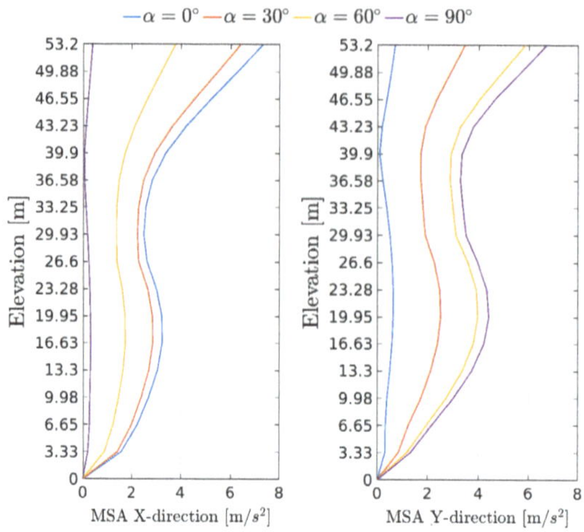

Figure 18. Maximum storey acceleration ($\mathcal{MSA}$) along each direction as a function of the angle.

4. Discussion and Conclusions

`Seismo-VLAB` represents a remarkable advancement in the field of soil–structure interaction (SSI) analysis. Its innovative open-source approach, combining state-of-the-art techniques, advanced parallel computing capabilities, and user-friendly implementation, makes it a pioneering tool for engineers and researchers. By addressing critical limitations in existing software, such as modeling wave propagation in half-spaces and facilitating code customization, `SVL` empowers users to explore complex SSI scenarios with efficiency and precision. Its versatility and applicability to various SSI problems make it an indispensable resource for the seismic engineering community. `SVL` not only fills a vital gap, but also propels the field forward, contributing to the analysis for safer and more resilient structures in the face of seismic events.

Building upon its innovative open-source approach and versatile capabilities, `Seismo-VLAB`'s methodology employs state-of-the-art methods for appropriately emulating truncated half-space. A detailed procedure for the validation of DRM and PML for 3D settings is described. The PML implementation includes (1) a recent symmetric hybrid formulation suitable for existing FE codes and (2) a compatible version of DRM for inclined plane incident P, SV, and Rayleigh waves. The DRM and PML implementation is verified using a set of verification cases through problems involving vertical and inclined incident SV waves for inhomogeneous 3D soil. Additionally, a practical application for assessing the SSI effects on the site and structural response for a real 3D building when a vertical SV wave of small amplitude is applied. In particular, the latter application case not only showcases `SVL`'s current modeling and parallel computing capabilities, but also demonstrates its capacity to model real-world earthquake responses in structural engineering.

Furthermore, the coupled DRM–PML technique proves to be a key factor for solving SSI problems. Therefore, the `Seismo-VLAB` project will be disseminated for broader use, since the already-implemented features will allow enthusiastic developers and users to explore other research fields. Some fields where `SVL` can be useful are (1) the modeling of spatial variability of soil properties for uncertainty quantification in linear and nonlinear models of engineering structures, (2) inverse problems for parameter estimation as well as reliability-based performance analysis in nonlinear finite element models of engineering structures, and (3) site response analysis for the study of amplification or deamplification of seismic waves considering topographic and basin effects. `SVL` has already proved its suitability to analyze the seismic response of structural systems. The `Seismo-VLAB` project can be downloaded at https://github.com/SeismoVLAB/SVL (accessed on 2 May 2023), and the documentation is available at http://www.seismovlab.com/ (accessed on 2 May 2023) for more specific details.

Author Contributions: Conceptualization, D.S.K., E.E.S. and D.A.; methodology, D.S.K., E.E.S. and D.A.; software, D.S.K., K.T.N. and E.E.S.; validation, D.S.K., E.E.S., P.A., K.T.N. and J.G.-S.; formal analysis, D.S.K., P.A., K.T.N. and J.G.-S.; investigation, D.S.K., E.E.S. and D.A.; resources, D.A. and A.R.K.; writing—original draft preparation, D.S.K., E.E.S., P.A., K.T.N., J.G.-S., A.R.K. and D.A.; writing—review and editing, D.S.K., E.E.S., P.A., K.T.N., J.G.-S., A.R.K. and D.A.; visualization, D.S.K., K.T.N. and J.G.-S.; supervision, A.R.K. and D.A.; project administration, A.R.K. and D.A.; funding acquisition, A.R.K. and D.A. All authors have read and agreed to the published version of the manuscript.

Funding: This research was possible thanks to the external funding provided by the Pacific Gas and Electric Company (PG&E).

Data Availability Statement: The data presented in this study are available on request from the corresponding author. Examples and verification case used in this manuscript are freely available in the https://github.com/SeismoVLAB/SVL/03-Validations/02-Performance (accessed on 2 May 2023) folder.

Acknowledgments: The authors would like to acknowledge the financial support of PG&E that made the development of this code possible.

Conflicts of Interest: The authors declare no conflict of interest. The funders played no part in shaping the study's design, data collection, analysis, or interpretation, nor did they contribute to the manuscript's preparation or the decision to publish the findings.

References

1. Strang, G.; Fix, G.J. *An Analysis of the Finite Element Method*; Prentice-Hall: Englewood Cliffs, NJ, USA, 1973; Volume 212.
2. Quarteroni, A.; Sacco, R.; Saleri, F. *Numerical Mathematics (Texts in Applied Mathematics)*; Springer: Berlin/Heidelberg, Germany, 2006.
3. Bathe, K. *Finite Element Procedures*; Prentice Hall: Upper Saddle River, NJ, USA, 2006.
4. Hughes, T. *The Finite Element Method: Linear Static and Dynamic Finite Element Analysis*; Dover Civil and Mechanical Engineering; Dover Publications: Mineola, NY, USA, 2012.
5. McKenna, F. OpenSees: A Framework for Earthquake Engineering Simulation. *Comput. Sci. Eng.* **2011**, *13*, 58–66. [CrossRef]
6. Taucer, F.; Spacone, E.; Filippou, F.C. *A Fiber Beam-Column Element for Seismic Response Analysis of Reinforced Concrete Structures*; University of California at Berkeley: Berkeley, CA, USA, 1991.
7. Spacone, E.; Filippou, F.C.; Taucer, F.F. Fibre Beam–Column Model for Non-Linear Analysis of R/C Frames: Part II. Applications. *Earthq. Eng. Struct. Dyn.* **1996**, *25*, 727–742. [CrossRef]
8. Scott, M.H.; Fenves, G.L. Plastic hinge integration methods for force-based beam–column elements. *J. Struct. Eng.* **2006**, *132*, 244–252. [CrossRef]
9. Meo, M.; Zumpano, G. On the optimal sensor placement techniques for a bridge structure. *Eng. Struct.* **2005**, *27*, 1488–1497. [CrossRef]
10. Van der Linden, G.W.; Emami-Naeini, A.; Kosut, R.L.; Sedarat, H.; Lynch, J.P. Optimal sensor placement for health monitoring of civil structures. In Proceedings of the 2011 American Control Conference, San Francisco, CA, USA, 29 June–1 July 2011; pp. 3116–3121. [CrossRef]
11. Chang, M.; Pakzad, S.N. Optimal Sensor Placement for Modal Identification of Bridge Systems Considering Number of Sensing Nodes. *J. Bridge Eng.* **2014**, *19*, 04014019. [CrossRef]
12. McCormick, C.W. *MSC/NASTRAN User's Manual*; MSR-39; The MacNeal Schwendler Corporation: Los Angeles, CA, USA, 1981.
13. DeSalvo, G.; Gorman, R.W. *ANSYS Engineering Analysis System User's Manual: For ANSYS Revision 4.4*; Swanson Analysis Systems: Canonsburg, PA, USA, 1989.
14. Hibbitt; Karlsson; Sorensen. *ABAQUS/Standard: User's Manual*; Hibbitt, Karlsson & Sorensen: Pawtucket, RI, USA, 1998; Volume 1.
15. Hallquist, J.O. *LS-DYNA User's Manual*; LS-DYNA, Livermore Software Technology Corporation: Livermore, CA, USA, 1976; Volume 4.
16. *ETABS: Extended Three Analysis of Building System*; Computers and Structures Inc.: Walnut Creek, CA, USA, 2023.
17. *PERFORM3D: Nonlinear Analysis and Performance Assesment for 3D Structures*; Computers and Structures Inc.: Walnut Creek, CA, USA, 2023.
18. *SAP2000: Integrated Software for Structural Analysis and Design*; Computers and Structures Inc.: Walnut Creek, CA, USA, 2023.
19. *FLAC2D/3D: Continuum Modeling for Geomechanics*; Itasca Software: Minneapolis, MN, USA, 2023.

20. Bielak, J.; Christiano, P. On the effective seismic input for non-linear soil-structure interaction systems. *Earthq. Eng. Struct. Dyn.* **1984**, *12*, 107–119. [CrossRef]
21. Bielak, J.; Loukakis, K.; Hisada, Y.; Yoshimura, C. Domain Reduction Method for Three-Dimensional Earthquake Modeling in Localized Regions, Part I: Theory. *Bull. Seismol. Soc. Am.* **2003**, *93*, 817–824. [CrossRef]
22. Yoshimura, C.; Bielak, J.; Hisada, Y.; Fernández, A. Domain Reduction Method for Three-Dimensional Earthquake Modeling in Localized Regions, Part II: Verification and Applications. *Bull. Seismol. Soc. Am.* **2003**, *93*, 825–841. [CrossRef]
23. Basu, U.; Chopra, A.K. Perfectly matched layers for time-harmonic elastodynamics of unbounded domains: Theory and finite-element implementation. *Comput. Methods Appl. Mech. Eng.* **2003**, *192*, 1337–1375. [CrossRef]
24. Kucukcoban, S.; Kallivokas, L. Mixed perfectly-matched-layers for direct transient analysis in 2D elastic heterogeneous media. *Comput. Methods Appl. Mech. Eng.* **2011**, *200*, 57–76. [CrossRef]
25. Fathi, A.; Poursartip, B.; Kallivokas, L.F. Time-domain hybrid formulations for wave simulations in three-dimensional PML-truncated heterogeneous media. *Int. J. Numer. Methods Eng.* **2015**, *101*, 165–198. [CrossRef]
26. *MASTODON: Multi-Hazard Analysis for STOchastic Time-DOmaiN Phenomena*; Facility Risk Group at the Idaho National Laboratory: Idaho Falls, ID, USA, 2023.
27. de France, E. Finite Element *code_aster*, Analysis of Structures and Thermomechanics for Studies and Research 1989–2017. Available online: www.code-aster.org (accessed on 2 May 2023).
28. Lysmer, J.; Tabatabaie-Raissi, M.; Tajirian, F.; Vahdani, S.; Ostadan, F. *SASSI: A System for Analysis of Soil-Structure Interaction*; University of California: Berkeley, CA, USA, 1981.
29. Jeremić, B.; Jie, G.; Cheng, Z.; Tafazzoli, N.; Tasiopoulou, P.; Pisanó, F.; Abell, J.A.; Watanabe, K.; Feng, Y.; Sinha, S.K.; et al. The Real-ESSI Simulator System. 1988–2020. Available online: http://real-essi.us/ (accessed on 2 May 2023).
30. McKenna, F.; Fenves, G.L.; Scott, M.H.; Jeremic, B. *Open System for Earthquake Engineering Simulation*; University of California: Berkeley, CA, USA, 2000.
31. Kusanovic, D.S. Improving Reduced Order Models of Soil-Structure Interaction Using an Ensemble Kalman Inversion Finite Element Model Updating Framework. Ph.D. Thesis, The California Institute of Technology, Mechanical and Civil Engineering Department, Pasadena, CA, USA, 2020.
32. Kusanovic, D.S.; Seylabi, E.; Asimaki, D. Seismo-VLAB: An open-source finite element software for seismic meso-scale simulations. *SoftwareX* **2023**, *21*, 101300. [CrossRef]
33. Guennebaud, G.; Jacob, B.; Niesen, J.; Mierle, K. Eigen v3. 2010. Available online: http://eigen.tuxfamily.org (accessed on 2 May 2023).
34. Kucukcoban, S.; Kallivokas, L. A symmetric hybrid formulation for transient wave simulations in PML-truncated heterogeneous media. *Wave Motion* **2013**, *50*, 57–79. [CrossRef]
35. Karypis, G.; Kumar, V. *METIS—Unstructured Graph Partitioning and Sparse Matrix Ordering System, Version 2.0*; Technical Report; University of Minnesota, Department of Computer Science & Engineering: Minneapolis, MN, USA, 1995.
36. Borja, R.I.; Amies, A.P. Multiaxial Cyclic Plasticity Model for Clays. *J. Geotech. Eng.* **1994**, *120*, 1051–1070. [CrossRef]
37. Simo, J.; Hughes, T. *Computational Inelasticity*; Springer: New York, NY, USA, 1998; pp. 240–275. [CrossRef]
38. Borja, R. *Plasticity: Modeling & Computation*; Springer: Berlin/Heidelberg, Germany, 2013.
39. Clarke, L.; Glendinning, I.; Hempel, R. The MPI Message Passing Interface Standard. In *Programming Environments for Massively Parallel Distributed Systems*; Decker, K.M., Rehmann, R.M., Eds.; Monte Verità. Birkhäuser: Basel, Switzerland, 1994; pp. 213–218.
40. Dagum, L.; Menon, R. OpenMP: An Industry-Standard API for Shared-Memory Programming. *IEEE Comput. Sci. Eng.* **1998**, *5*, 46–55. [CrossRef]
41. Assimaki, D.; Pecker, A.; Popescu, R.; Prevost, J. Effects of spatial variability of soil properties on surface ground motion. *J. Earthq. Eng.* **2003**, *7*, 1–44. [CrossRef]
42. Popescu, R.; Deodatis, G.; Nobahar, A. Effects of random heterogeneity of soil properties on bearing capacity. *Probabilistic Eng. Mech.* **2005**, *20*, 324–341. [CrossRef]
43. Stefanou, G. The stochastic finite element method: Past, present and future. *Comput. Methods Appl. Mech. Eng.* **2009**, *198*, 1031–1051. [CrossRef]
44. El Haber, E.; Cornou, C.; Jongmans, D.; Youssef Abdelmassih, D.; Lopez-Caballero, F.; AL-Bittar, T. Influence of 2D heterogeneous elastic soil properties on surface ground motion spatial variability. *Soil Dyn. Earthq. Eng.* **2019**, *123*, 75–90. [CrossRef]
45. Pieczyńska-Kozłowska, J.; Bagińska, I.; Kawa, M. The Identification of the Uncertainty in Soil Strength Parameters Based on CPTu Measurements and Random Fields. *Sensors* **2021**, *21*, 5393. [CrossRef]
46. Savvides, A.A.; Papadrakakis, M. Uncertainty Quantification of Failure of Shallow Foundation on Clayey Soils with a Modified Cam-Clay Yield Criterion and Stochastic FEM. *Geotechnics* **2022**, *2*, 348–384. [CrossRef]
47. Jensen, H.; Valdebenito, M.; Schuëller, G.; Kusanovic, D. Reliability-based optimization of stochastic systems using line search. *Comput. Methods Appl. Mech. Eng.* **2009**, *198*, 3915–3924. [CrossRef]
48. Jensen, H.A.; Kusanovic, D.S.; Valdebenito, M.A.; Schuëller, G.I. Reliability-Based Design Optimization of Uncertain Stochastic Systems: Gradient-Based Scheme. *J. Eng. Mech.* **2012**, *138*, 60–70. [CrossRef]
49. Jensen, H.; Kusanovic, D. On the effect of near-field excitations on the reliability-based performance and design of base-isolated structures. *Probab. Eng. Mech.* **2014**, *36*, 28–44. [CrossRef]

50. Jensen, H.; Millas, E.; Kusanovic, D.; Papadimitriou, C. Model-reduction techniques for Bayesian finite element model updating using dynamic response data. *Comput. Methods Appl. Mech. Eng.* **2014**, *279*, 301–324. [CrossRef]
51. Astroza, R. Vibration-Based Health Monitoring and Mechanics-Based Nonlinear Finite Element Model Updating of Civil Structures. Ph.D. Thesis, University of California San Diego, Departament of Civil and Environmental Engineering, San Diego, CA, USA, 2015.
52. Ebrahimian, H. Nonlinear Finite Element Model Updating for Nonlinear System and Damage Identification of Civil Structures. Ph.D. Thesis, University of California San Diego, Departament of Civil and Environmental Engineering, San Diego, CA, USA, 2015.
53. Kerfriden, P.; Kundu, A.; Claus, S. Adaptivity in Bayesian Inverse Finite Element Problems: Learning and Simultaneous Control of Discretisation and Sampling Errors. *Materials* **2019**, *12*, 642. [CrossRef]
54. Mohammadi, K. Geometry and Stratigraphy Parameterization of Topography Effects: From the Infinite Wedge to 3D Convex Features. Ph.D. Thesis, The Georgia Institute of Technology, Georgia Tech Library, Atlanta, GA, USA, 2015.
55. Poursartip, B. Topographic Amplification of Seismic Motion. Ph.D. Thesis, University of Texas at Austin, Austin, TX, USA, 2017.
56. Mohammadi, K.; Asimaki, D. Topography Effects Are Not Dominated by Ground Surface Geometry: A Site Effects Paradox. In *Geotechnical Frontiers 2017*; ASCE Library: Lawrence, KS, USA, 2017; pp. 171–181. [CrossRef]
57. Asimaki, D.; Mohammadi, K. On the complexity of seismic waves trapped in irregular topographies. *Soil Dyn. Earthq. Eng.* **2018**, *114*, 424–437. [CrossRef]
58. Ayoubi, P.; Asimaki, D.; Mohammdi, K. Basin Effects in Strong Ground Motion: A Case Study from the 2015 Gorkha, Nepal, Earthquake. In *Geotechnical Earthquake Engineering and Soil Dynamics V*; ASCE Library: Lawrence, KS, USA, 2018; pp. 288–296. [CrossRef]
59. Asimaki, D.; Mohammadi, K.; Ayoubi, P.; Mayoral, J.M.; Montalva, G. Investigating the spatial variability of ground motions during the 2017 Mw 7.1 Puebla-Mexico City earthquake via idealized simulations of basin effects. *Soil Dyn. Earthq. Eng.* **2020**, *132*, 106073. [CrossRef]
60. Ayoubi, P.; Mohammadi, K.; Asimaki, D. A systematic analysis of basin effects on surface ground motion. *Soil Dyn. Earthq. Eng.* **2021**, *141*, 106490. [CrossRef]
61. Nguyen, V.Q.; Aaqib, M.; Nguyen, D.D.; Luat, N.V.; Park, D. A Site-Specific Response Analysis: A Case Study in Hanoi, Vietnam. *Appl. Sci.* **2020**, *10*, 3972. [CrossRef]
62. Hu, Y.; Khatiwada, P.; Tsang, H.H.; Menegon, S. Site-Specific Response Spectra and Accelerograms on Bedrock and Soil Surface. *CivilEng* **2023**, *4*, 311–332. [CrossRef]
63. Li, J.; Chen, M.; Li, Z. Improved soil—Structure interaction model considering time-lag effect. *Comput. Geotech.* **2022**, *148*, 104835. [CrossRef]
64. Wu, M.; Ba, Z.; Liang, J. A procedure for 3D simulation of seismic wave propagation considering source-path-site effects: Theory, verification and application. *Earthq. Eng. Struct. Dyn.* **2022**, *51*, 2925–2955. [CrossRef]
65. Wang, W.; Li, D.Q.; Tang, X.S.; Du, W. Seismic fragility and demand hazard analyses for earth slopes incorporating soil property variability. *Soil Dyn. Earthq. Eng.* **2023**, *173*, 108088. [CrossRef]
66. Li, J.; Liu, Y.; Lin, G. Implementation of a coupled FEM-SBFEM for soil-structure interaction analysis of large-scale 3D base-isolated nuclear structures. *Comput. Geotech.* **2023**, *162*, 105669. [CrossRef]
67. Naserkhaki, S.; Aziz, F.N.A.A.; Pourmohammad, H. Earthquake induced pounding between adjacent buildings considering soil-structure interaction. *Earthq. Eng. Eng. Vib.* **2012**, *11*, 343–358. [CrossRef]
68. Kusanovic, D.S.; Seylabi, E.; Asimaki, D. Optimization of frequency domain impedances for time-domain response analyses of building structures with rigid shallow foundations. *Earthq. Spectra* **2021**, *37*, 1955–1979. [CrossRef]
69. Nguyen, K.T.; Kusanovic, D.S.; Asimaki, D. Three-dimensional nonlinear soil—Structure interaction for Rayleigh wave incidence in layered soils. *Earthq. Eng. Struct. Dyn.* **2022**, *51*, 2752–2770. [CrossRef]
70. Nguyen, K.T.; Kusanovic, D.S.; Asimaki, D. Dynamic soil impedance functions for cylindrical structures buried in elastic half-space. *Soil Dyn. Earthq. Eng.* **2022**, *162*, 107431. [CrossRef]
71. Donnellan, A.; Garcia-Suarez, J.; McPhillips, D.; Asimaki, D.; Goulet, C.; Meng, X.; Devine, S.; Lyzenga, G. Toppling of a Trona Pinnacles Spire following the Mw 5.5 Ridgecrest Aftershock of June 2020. *Seismol. Res. Lett.* **2022**, *93*, 1768–1776. [CrossRef]
72. Kusanovic, D.S.; Taborda, R.; Asimaki, D. Soil–Structure Interaction Effects on a Regional Scale through Ground-Motion Simulations and Reduced Order Models: A Case Study from the 2008 Mw 5.4 Chino Hills Mainshock. *Bull. Seismol. Soc. Am.* **2023**. [CrossRef]
73. Crisfield, M.A. *Non-Linear Finite Element Analysis of Solids and Structures: Essentials*; John Wiley & Sons, Inc.: Hoboken, NJ, USA, 1991.
74. Tadmor, E.B.; Miller, R.E.; Elliott, R.S. *Continuum Mechanics and Thermodynamics: From Fundamental Concepts to Governing Equations*; Cambridge University Press: Cambridge, UK, 2011. [CrossRef]
75. Böhme, D. Characterizing Load and Communication Imbalance in Parallel Applications. Ph.D. Dissertation, RWTH Aachen University, Aachen, Germany, 2014. [CrossRef]
76. Chevalier, C.; Pellegrini, F. PT-Scotch: A Tool for Efficient Parallel Graph Ordering. *Parallel Comput.* **2008**, *34*, 318–331. [CrossRef]
77. Devine, K.; Boman, E.; Riesen, L.; Catalyurek, U.; Chevalier, C. Getting Started with Zoltan: A Short Tutorial. In Proceedings of the 2009 Dagstuhl Seminar on Combinatorial Scientific Computing, Istanbul, Turkey, 12–15 March 2009; Sandia National Labs Tech Report SAND2009-0578C.

78. Berge, C. *Graphs and Hypergraphs*; Elsevier Science Ltd.: Amsterdam, The Netherlands, 1985.
79. Karypis, G.; Kumar, V. Multilevel k-Way Hypergraph Partitioning. In Proceedings of the 36th Annual ACM/IEEE Design Automation Conference, DAC '99, New York, NY, USA, 21–25 June 1999; pp. 343–348. [CrossRef]
80. Gabriel, E.; Fagg, G.E.; Bosilca, G.; Angskun, T.; Dongarra, J.J.; Squyres, J.M.; Sahay, V.; Kambadur, P.; Barrett, B.; Lumsdaine, A.; et al. Open MPI: Goals, Concept, and Design of a Next Generation MPI Implementation. In Proceedings of the 11th European PVM/MPI Users' Group Meeting, Budapest, Hungary, 19–22 September 2004; pp. 97–104.
81. Broquedis, F.; Clet Ortega, J.; Moreaud, S.; Furmento, N.; Goglin, B.; Mercier, G.; Thibault, S.; Namyst, R. hwloc: A Generic Framework for Managing Hardware Affinities in HPC Applications. In Proceedings of the PDP 2010—The 18th Euromicro International Conference on Parallel, Distributed and Network-Based Computing, Pisa, Italy, 17 February 2010.
82. Hursey, J.; Mallove, E.; Squyres, J.M.; Lumsdaine, A. An Extensible Framework for Distributed Testing of MPI Implementations. In Proceedings of the Euro PVM/MPI, Paris, France, 30 September–3 October 2007.
83. Balay, S.; Gropp, W.D.; McInnes, L.C.; Smith, B.F. Efficient Management of Parallelism in Object Oriented Numerical Software Libraries. In *Modern Software Tools in Scientific Computing*; Arge, E., Bruaset, A.M., Langtangen, H.P., Eds.; Birkhäuser Press: Basel, Switzerland, 1997; pp. 163–202.
84. Balay, S.; Abhyankar, S.; Adams, M.F.; Brown, J.; Brune, P.; Buschelman, K.; Dalcin, L.; Dener, A.; Eijkhout, V.; Gropp, W.D.; et al. *PETSc Users Manual*; Technical Report ANL-95/11—Revision 3.12; Argonne National Laboratory: Lemont, IL, USA, 2019.
85. Balay, S.; Abhyankar, S.; Adams, M.F.; Brown, J.; Brune, P.; Buschelman, K.; Dalcin, L.; Dener, A.; Eijkhout, V.; Gropp, W.D.; et al. PETSc Web Page. 2019. Available online: https://www.mcs.anl.gov/petsc (accessed on 2 May 2023).
86. Amestoy, P.R.; Duff, I.S.; L'Excellent, J.Y.; Koster, J. A Fully Asynchronous Multifrontal Solver Using Distributed Dynamic Scheduling. *SIAM J. Matrix Anal. Appl.* **2001**, *23*, 15–41. [CrossRef]
87. Amestoy, P.R.; Guermouche, A.; L'Excellent, J.Y.; Pralet, S. Hybrid scheduling for the parallel solution of linear systems. *Parallel Comput.* **2006**, *32*, 136–156. [CrossRef]
88. Kawase, H. Time-domain response of a semi-circular canyon for incident SV, P, and Rayleigh waves calculated by the discrete wavenumber boundary element method. *Bull. Seismol. Soc. Am.* **1988**, *78*, 1415–1437. [CrossRef]
89. Kawase, H.; Aki, K. A study on the response of a soft basin for incident S, P, and Rayleigh waves with special reference to the long duration observed in Mexico City. *Bull. Seismol. Soc. Am.* **1989**, *79*, 1361–1382.
90. Sánchez-Sesma, F.J.; Ramos-Martinez, J.; Campillo, M. An indirect boundary element method applied to simulate the seismic response of alluvial valleys for incident P, S and Rayleigh waves. *Earthq. Eng. Struct. Dyn.* **1993**, *22*, 279–295. [CrossRef]
91. Sánchez-Sesma, F.J.; Luzon, F. Seismic response of three-dimensional alluvial valleys for incident P, S, and Rayleigh waves. *Bull. Seismol. Soc. Am.* **1995**, *85*, 269–284.
92. Todorovska, M.I. Effects of the wave passage and the embedment depth for in-plane building-soil interaction. *Soil Dyn. Earthq. Eng.* **1993**, *12*, 343–355. [CrossRef]
93. Zhang, Y.; Yang, Z.; Bielak, J.; Conte, J.; Elgamal, A. Treatment of seismic input and boundary conditions in nonlinear seismic analysis of a bridge ground system. In Proceedings of the 16th ASCE Engineering Mechanics Conference, University of Washington, Seattle, WA, USA, 16–18 July 2003; pp. 16–18.
94. Jeremić, B.; Kunnath, S.; Xiong, F. Influence of soil–foundation–structure interaction on seismic response of the I-880 viaduct. *Eng. Struct.* **2004**, *26*, 391–402. [CrossRef]
95. Kausel, E.; Roësset, J.M. Stiffness matrices for layered soils. *Bull. Seismol. Soc. Am.* **1981**, *71*, 1743–1761. [CrossRef]
96. Ancheta, T.D.; Darragh, R.B.; Stewart, J.P.; Seyhan, E.; Silva, W.J.; Chiou, B.S.J.; Wooddell, K.E.; Graves, R.W.; Kottke, A.R.; Boore, D.M.; et al. NGA-West2 Database. *Earthq. Spectra* **2014**, *30*, 989–1005. [CrossRef]
97. Zhang, W.; Seylabi, E.E.; Taciroglu, E. An ABAQUS toolbox for soil-structure interaction analysis. *Comput. Geotech.* **2019**, *114*, 103143. [CrossRef]
98. Zhang, W.; Taciroglu, E. 3D time-domain nonlinear analysis of soil-structure systems subjected to obliquely incident SV waves in layered soil media. *Earthq. Eng. Struct. Dyn.* **2021**, *50*, 2156–2173. [CrossRef]
99. Fathi, A.; Kallivokas, L.F.; Poursartip, B. Full-waveform inversion in three-dimensional PML-truncated elastic media. *Comput. Methods Appl. Mech. Eng.* **2015**, *296*, 39–72. [CrossRef]
100. Cook, R.D.; Malkus, D.S.; Plesha, M.E.; Witt, R.J. *Concepts and Applications of Finite Element Analysis*; John Wiley & Sons Inc.: Hoboken, NJ, USA, 2007.
101. Jeremić, B.; Jie, G.; Preisig, M.; Tafazzoli, N. Time domain simulation of soil–foundation–structure interaction in non-uniform soils. *Earthq. Eng. Struct. Dyn.* **2009**, *38*, 699–718. [CrossRef]
102. Clough, R.; Penzien, J. *Dynamics of Structures*; McGraw-Hill: New York, NY, USA, 1994.

mathematics

MDPI

Article

A p-Refinement Method Based on a Library of Transition Elements for 3D Finite Element Applications

Adnan Shahriar * and Ahmed Jenan Mostafa

Department of Mechanical Engineering, The University of Texas at San Antonio, San Antonio, TX 78249, USA; ahmed.m@purple.com
* Correspondence: adnan.shahriar@utsa.edu; Tel.: +1-210-803-5230

Abstract: Wave propagation or acoustic emission waves caused by impact load can be simulated using the finite element (FE) method with a refined high-fidelity mesh near the impact location. This paper presents a method to refine a 3D finite element mesh by increasing the polynomial order near the impact location. Transition elements are required for such a refinement operation. Three protocols are defined to implement the transition elements within the low-order FE mesh. Due to the difficulty of formulating shape functions and verification, there are no transition elements beyond order two in the current literature for 3D elements. This paper develops a complete set of transition elements that facilitate the transition from first- to fourth-order Lagrangian elements, which facilitates mesh refinement following the protocols. The shape functions are computed and verified, and the interelement compatibility conditions are checked for each element case. The integration quadratures and shape function derivative matrices are also computed and made readily available for FE users. Finally, two examples are presented to illustrate the applicability of this method.

Keywords: p-refinement; 3D transition element; fourth-order transition element; Lagrangian; Gauss–Lobatto quadrature

MSC: 74S05

Citation: Shahriar, A.; Mostafa, A.J. A p-Refinement Method Based on a Library of Transition Elements for 3D Finite Element Applications. *Mathematics* **2023**, *11*, 4954. https://doi.org/10.3390/math11244954

Academic Editors: Joaquim Infante Barbosa and José Alberto Rodrigues

Received: 12 November 2023
Revised: 6 December 2023
Accepted: 12 December 2023
Published: 14 December 2023

1. Introduction

Interest in space activities, including satellite launches, space tourism, deep-space exploration, and space colonization, has increased in recent years. The development of long-term deep-space habitats is of interest to the engineering community. These structures will be exposed to harsh environmental loading conditions, including hypervelocity impact (HVI) caused by meteoroids or debris. The finite element method (FEM) is a widely used numerical approach for solving partial differential equations (PDEs) in mathematics and engineering, especially in the field of structural dynamics [1–3]. However, the solutions of wave propagation problems cannot be effectively replicated through a standard FEM. In the case of harmonic wave solutions, it is well known that the accuracy of numerical solutions rapidly degrades as the wave number increases [4,5]. Novel techniques based on higher-order discontinuous Galerkin methods exist to mitigate this issue [6,7]. In the field of FEM, there are two methods of reducing error and improving the ability of the basis functions to represent the variation of the unknown function over the local domain: (1) increasing the number of the elements, or h-refinement, and (2) increasing the polynomial order, or p-refinement. H-refinement techniques have been used widely in conjunction with low-order vector basis functions. However, very fine meshes are necessary to find reasonable solutions for problems with short waves—so fine that the numerical solution effort may be prohibitive. The spectral element approach offers a great solution for resolving this issue [8–12]. In this case, high-order Lagrangian-based finite elements are employed in conjunction with particular nodal positions and integration algorithms. In comparison to typical finite element methods, this method has low numerical dispersion and can be particularly effective in explicit time integration. While implementing a high-order element in a lower-order mesh, p-refinement is needed [13]. However, due to the relatively recent emergence of higher-order hierarchical vector basis functions, p-refinement approaches have not been widely researched to date [14–16].

The advantage of p-refinement is that it eliminates the time-consuming mesh regeneration procedure associated with h-refinement. The process must be adaptable to benefit fully from either type of refinement technique. Adaptive refinement uses the error estimate from a numerical solution at a particular level of refinement to forecast which areas of the computational domain will most require more degrees of freedom. After that, the process remedies the issue by allocating more degrees within certain zones. Since they enable most of the equations in the FEM system to stay constant across refinement levels, hierarchical vector basis functions are virtually always used for adaptive refinement. Conversely, interpolatory vector basis functions would necessitate the replacement of all equations in the regions that are being refined. Furthermore, unique transition elements are needed in an interpolatory expansion in order to link regions with varying polynomial degrees [14].

In a three-dimensional finite element application, hexahedron transition elements are extensively used for p-mesh refinement [17]. When implementing a transition element in a multi-element mesh, the hanging node problem arises. This violates the interelement compatibility conditions. Hence, several strategies to circumvent the hanging node problem have been developed. For two-dimensional applications, variable-node elements for 1-irregular/balanced meshes have been constructed by Gupta, while Morton et al. published an extension for three dimensions [18]. These elements utilize piecewise linear shape functions on their boundaries, so two smaller finite elements can be coupled conformally to a larger transition element [1]. Gordon and co-workers developed a transfinite interpolation or blending function method [19], where the functions are identical in certain parts but not over the whole domain [20]. Scholz developed two- and three-dimensional transition elements with piecewise linear and quadratic shape functions for mesh refinement purposes [21], where 1-irregular meshes can be generated without introducing hanging nodes. Developing higher-order transition elements is a challenge. Unconventional elements, such as the xNy-element concept [14,16], are developed by utilizing linear blending functions and projection operators to tackle this issue. However, there is still the problem of efficient mesh generation for these transition elements, especially for three-dimensional models, as this procedure is very cumbersome [22].

Transition elements are also employed in contact problems [23]. Buczkowski [24] developed 22- and 21-node elements, and Smith et al. [25] developed 14-node hexahedral isoparametric elements to analyze contact problems by modifying the reference 8- and 20-node hexahedral elements. The modification of the shape functions of the reference element needs to be carried out by hand and is very laborious for a 3D element. In addition to lower-order transition elements, there is also a need for higher-order transition elements, as they offer higher accuracy when calculating Lagrangian solid dynamics. For instance, the spectral finite element method [9] uses the interpolation function of high-order Lagrange polynomials to capture high-frequency wave propagation that benefits fields such as structural health monitoring [10–12,26] and seismology [8]. Employing transition elements can reduce the degrees of freedom and computation effort for such applications.

A library of transition elements can mitigate these issues. However, creating a library is very labor-intensive when higher-order elements are considered. The shape functions of higher-order elements are numerous and lengthy, so it is extremely difficult to modify and verify them to form a higher-order transition element. In summary, there is no methodology for formulating arbitrary hexahedron elements and implementing multi-element mesh that is programmatically available. Hence, there is no transition element beyond order 2 in the literature.

This paper develops a method to perform p-refinement that involves three protocols. The implementation of these protocols is based on a library of transition elements. Six 3D transition elements of an order up to four are developed to act as a library that can facilitate the p-refinement procedure. The development procedure utilizes the GUI developed in [16]. First, the reference element, the Lagrangian [27] or Serendipity [28] element that represents a transition element closely in terms of element order, is formulated following methods available in the literature. The formulation includes the nodal coordinates and the monomial basis functions of the interpolation function. Next, the generated nodal coordinates and the monomial basis functions are modified to replicate the transition element. The nodal coordinates and interpolation function consist of the monomial basis functions that will be used to formulate the shape functions. The modification of the monomial basis functions is extremely simple compared to the modification of the shape functions. However, the method for determining the shape functions is very laborious and can be carried out by hand for one-dimensional and lower-order two-dimensional elements [29]. For this reason, the computer algorithm was implemented to automate this task instead [16]. Finally, the element is verified in terms of local support and interelement compatibility conditions [29].

The remainder of this paper is organized as follows: Section 2 presents the methodology for p-refinement and generating element properties, while Section 3 showcases the implementation and results for the formulated transition elements. The developed p-refinement method is verified for an FE mesh that contains all six transition elements developed in this paper through a patch test [30]. Subsequently, this method is implemented in two 3D FE meshes and, finally, Section 4 concludes this paper with some final remarks.

2. Materials and Methods

In this section, a procedure is developed to perform p-refinement for the given refined element. First, the protocol to refine a single element is presented. Then the method based on the protocol to refine all the elements in the mesh is illustrated.

2.1. p-Refinement Procedure

Assume that element e_i is refined as order n, and another adjacent element, e_j, needs to be refined so that it can (1) act as a transition element from order n to order $n-1$, and (2) satisfy the interelement boundary conditions. Due to this dependency of element e_j on e_i, the elements e_i and e_j are termed as master and slave elements, respectively. Three protocols have been developed to refine element e_j, shown as a linear eight-node brick element, with node numbers ranging from 1 to 8 at the local coordinate [2].

Protocol 1: Only one edge has the highest order. Assume element e_i shares an edge with element e_j, where the order of the edge is n, as presented in Figure 1. In this case, the transition element will have order n only at the edge and order $n-1$ everywhere else. This paper defines the edge by nodes 7–8 in local coordinates.

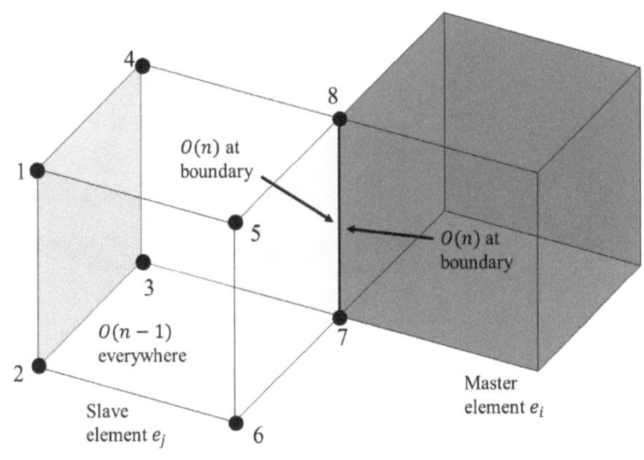

Figure 1. Case 1 schematic. Numbers 1–8 indicates the node number for a 8 node brick element.

Protocol 2: Four edges have the highest order, and that forms the face of the element. If four edges form an interelement surface, the order at the surface will be n and $n-1$ everywhere else. A schematic of this case is presented in Figure 2, where the nodes 5–8 define the interelement surface.

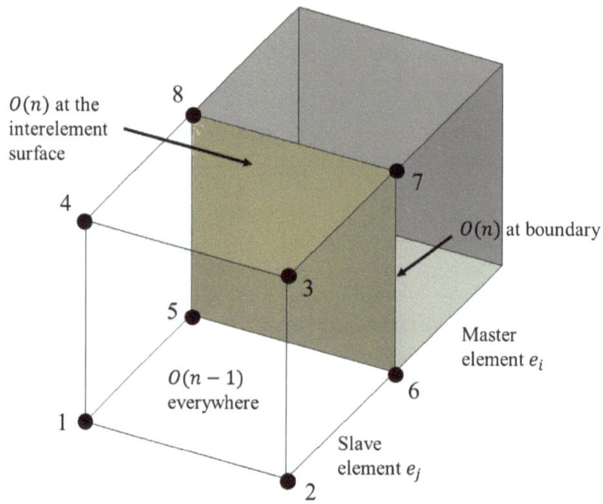

Figure 2. Case 2 schematic. Numbers 1–8 indicates the node number for a 8 node brick element.

Protocol 3: More than four edges have order n. For protocol 3, there will be several master elements that form an interelement boundary with the element to be refined (e_j). If there are more than four edges, the order will be n throughout the element space. Two cases with more than four edges at the interface are presented in Figure 3, where the dark elements are of order n; hence, the order of the element e_j will be n.

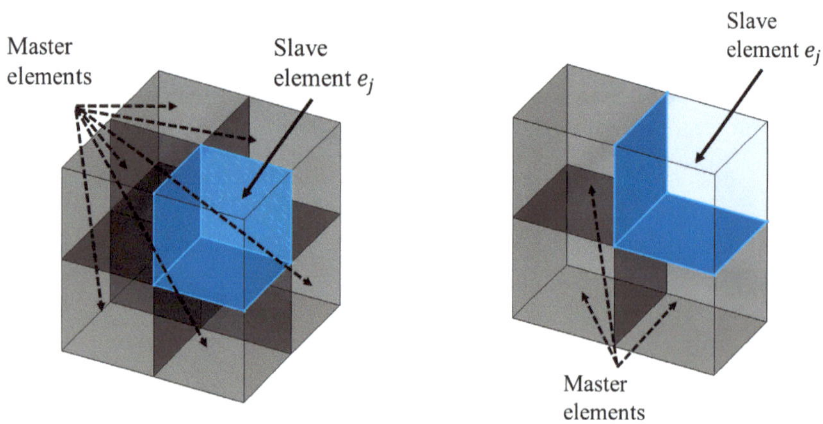

Figure 3. Case 3 schematic.

The p-refinement utilizes one transition element for each protocol that follows the node number presented above. The formulation of these elements is presented in the next subsection. The shared boundary between elements e_j and e_j does not necessarily match the node numbering sequence (7–8 for protocol 1) in local coordinates. Hence, while implementing the transition elements, the node number of element e_j needs to be renamed to match the transition element with no number. The refinement is followed by the refinement of element e_j, carried out element by element from the lowest to the highest distance from the element centroids with respect to e_i. The transition of element order decreases by one as the refinement continues. For 8-noded elements, the distance follows

$$d_{ij} = \left\| \left(\frac{\sum_{k=1}^{8} [x_k \quad y_k \quad z_k]}{8} \right)_{e_i} - \left(\frac{\sum_{k=1}^{8} [x_k \quad y_k \quad z_k]}{8} \right)_{e_j} \right\| \tag{1}$$

where $[x_i \quad y_i \quad z_i]$ is the nodal coordinate of node i and $\|.\|$ indicates the second norm. A 2D overview is presented for a four-element case in Figure 4, where $d_{ij} < d_{il} < d_{ik}$. Hence, the refinement procedure is carried out on element j first, then element l, and finally k. The refinement for the whole mesh involves:

1. Creating a set of d_{ij} following Equation (1), and sorting from lowest to the highest;
2. For each element associated with the sorted d_{ij}, e_j:
   i. determining all the adjacent elements for e_j;
   ii. For each adjacent element, obtaining the interelement boundary order;
   iii. If the order of the element boundary > the order of e_j:
      a. Renaming the node number of e_j to match the interelement boundary;
      b. Refining the element following the protocol.

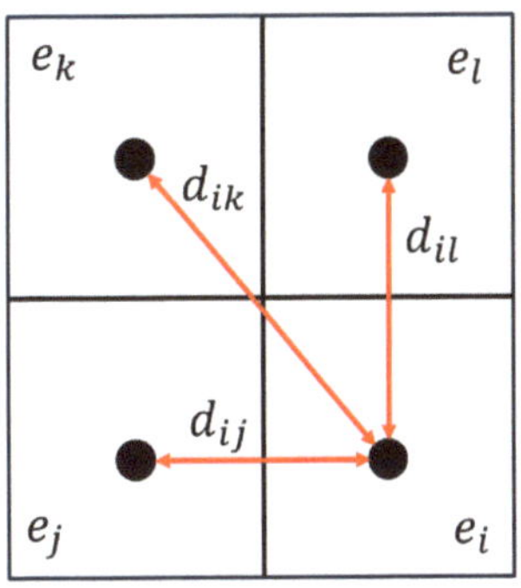

Figure 4. Renimenet sequence.

2.2. Formulation of Transition Elements

This section illustrates the procedure to formulate and implement a transition element within a multi-element FE mesh, as presented in Figure 5. First, the nodal coordinates and the monomial basis function of the reference element are computed. The reference element is the element that closely resembles the arbitrary element in terms of element order and type (Lagrangian or Serendipity).

Next, the nodal coordinates and the monomial basis functions are updated to replicate the arbitrary element. The shape functions for these two inputs are then determined through computer implementation [3]. If the shape functions can be determined, verification of the local support conditions will be carried out. Next, the element can be incorporated into a multi-element mesh if the interelement compatibility is satisfied between the adjacent elements of different types. If the element is compatible, the formulation is complete and ready to be implemented for FE applications.

For this purpose, methodology and the toolbox, ShapeGen3D v.1, developed by [16] is utilized. Here, the element is subdivided into a 3D grid, and the value of the shape functions is determined for each point. The results are plotted, with the void where the value of the shape function is 0. Hence, if a surface does not contain a node i, and there is a void throughout for the value of shape function i, the element satisfies the local support condition for that shape function. The interelement compatibility conditions are also checked and satisfied following the procedure described in [16]. In addition to the shape function value, the integration points and weights for the Gauss–Lobatto [27] quadrature was obtained.

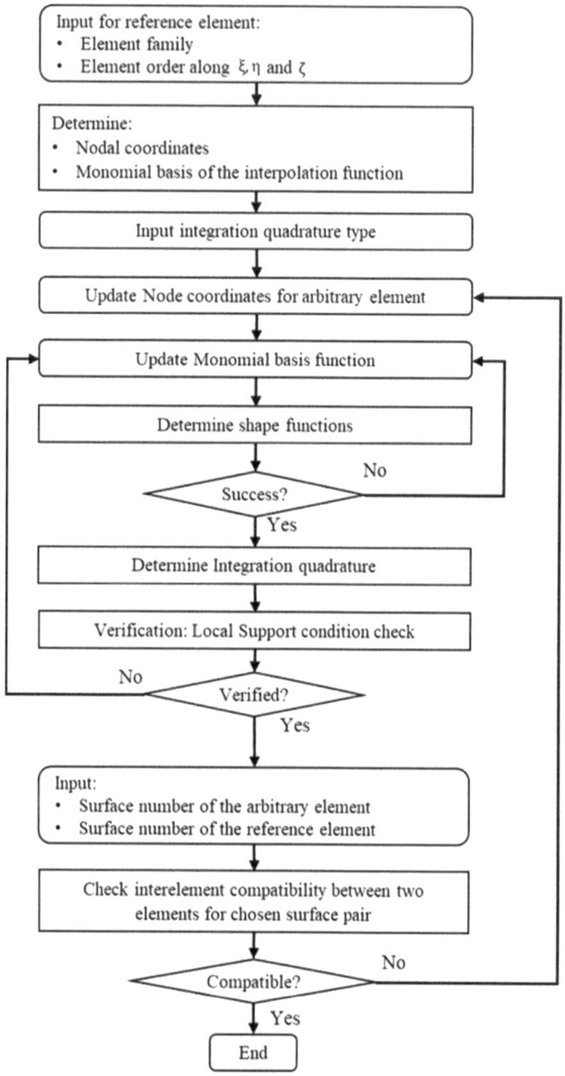

Figure 5. Arbitrary element formulation procedure flowchart.

3. Results

3.1. Transition Elements

Six transition elements that enable the transition from the fourth- to first-order Lagrangian element were formulated. All the elements underwent an interelement compatibility check to make sure they could form a multi-element mesh. A second-to-first-order transition element for case 2 is presented in detail in Figure 6. Figure 6A shows the two elements assembled to form an interelement boundary. The red hollow diamond represents the nodes of the second order, whereas the black dots represent the nodes of the transition element. The interelement boundary is presented in Figure 6B, which shows that the nodes coincide and shape function profiles corresponding to the node of these two elements match each other. As all the shape functions corresponding to the common nodes matched, the $\zeta = 1$ surface of the transition element was compatible with the second-order element.

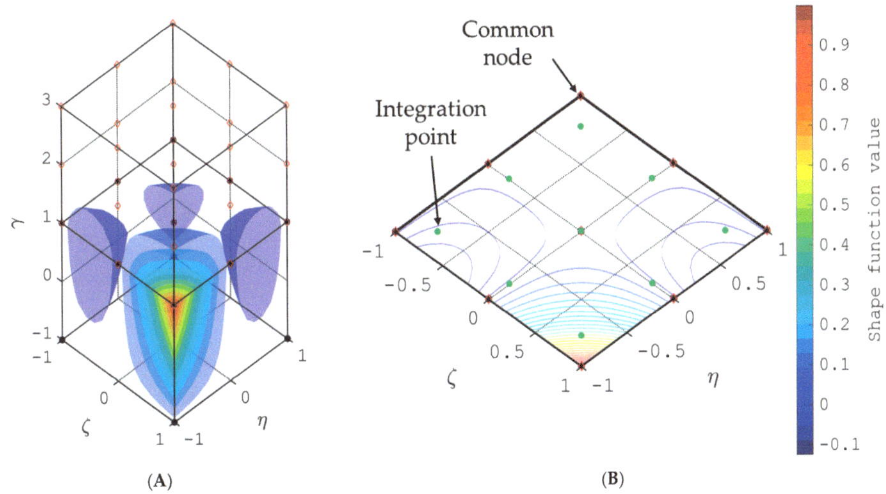

Figure 6. Interelement compatibility check between second-order and second-to-first-order transition elements (case 2). (**A**) Two elements assembled; (**B**) interelement surface.

The parameters obtained for each of the elements are

1. Nodal coordinates;
2. Shape functions;
3. Integration quadrature.

The parameters obtained for these transition elements are lengthy and difficult to describe in a paper. Hence, only the results for the transition element presented in Figure 6 are detailed in Appendix A. Tables A1–A3 present the nodal coordinates, shape functions, and integration quadrature, respectively. The coordinates are presented in terms of (x, y, z), which is equivalent to the (ξ, η, ζ) coordinate system used to define isoparametric elements. Online data containing all the information on the elements can be found as text files (Link: https://zenodo.org/records/10015183, accessed on 17 October 2023). This will enable other users to read this and implement the elements to perform p-refinement following the approach developed in this paper. The name of each dataset with respect to the element case is presented in Table 1 in the source file name column along with the corresponding element schematics presented in Figures 7–10.

Table 1. Element description and corresponding dataset name.

Element Description	Figure Number	Number of Nodes	Source File Name
Fourth-order element	Figure 7B	125	Fourth_order.txt
Fourth-to-third-order transition element for case 1	Figure 10A	65	Transition_4to3_Case1.txt
Fourth-to-third-order transition element for case 2	Figure 10B	73	Transition_4to3_Case2.txt
Third-order element	Figure 7A	64	Third_order.txt
Third-to-second-order transition element for case 1	Figure 9A	28	Transition_3to2_Case1.txt
Third-to-second-order transition element for case 2	Figure 9B	34	Transition_3to2_Case2.txt
Second-order element	Figure 6A	27	Second_order.txt
Second-to-first-order transition element for case 1	Figure 8A	9	Transition_2to1_Case1.txt
Second-to-first-order transition element for case 2	Figure 8B	13	Transition_2to1_Case2.txt

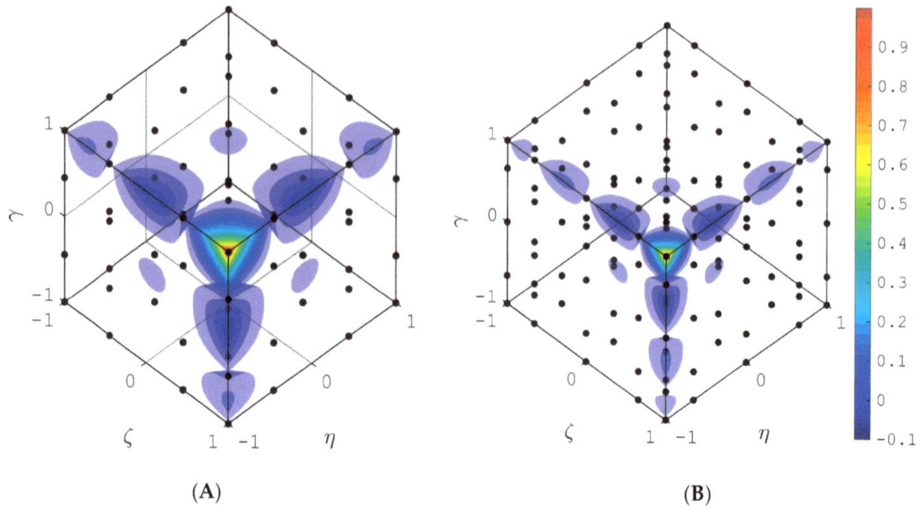

Figure 7. Full-order elements of order (**A**) 3 and (**B**) 4.

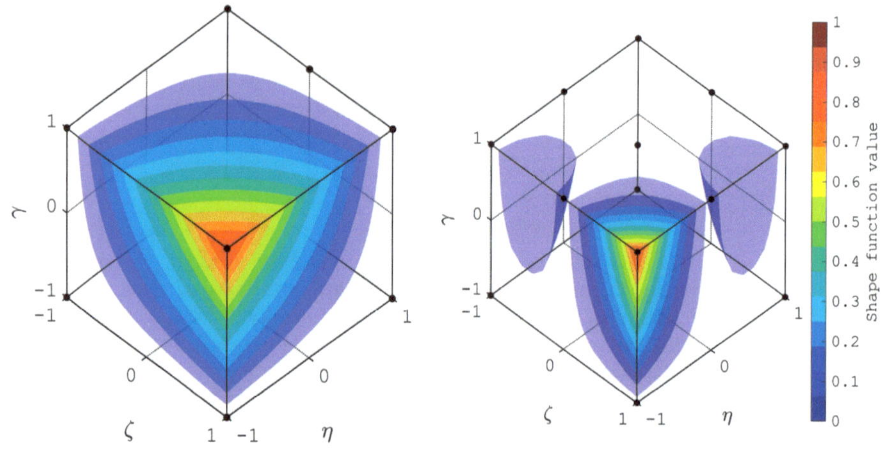

Figure 8. Transition elements from order 2 to 1; (**A**) Case 1; (**B**) Case 2.

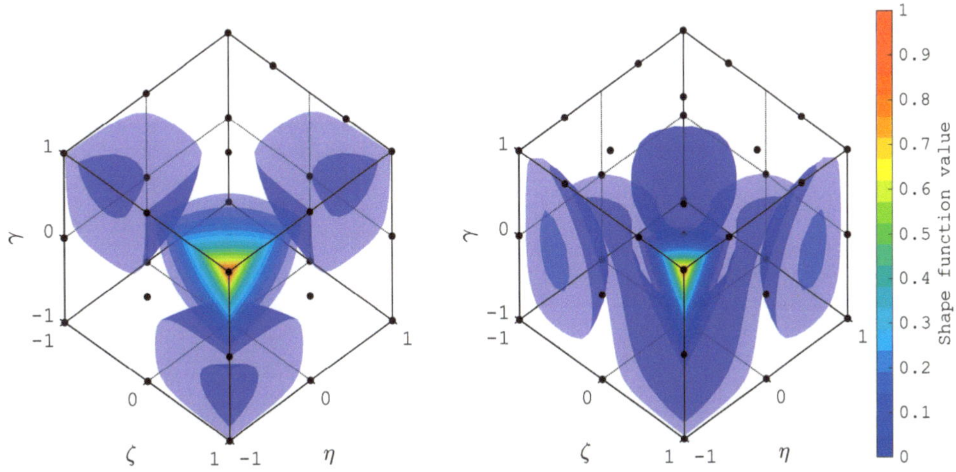

(A) (B)

Figure 9. Transition elements from order 3 to 2; (**A**) Case 1; (**B**) Case 2.

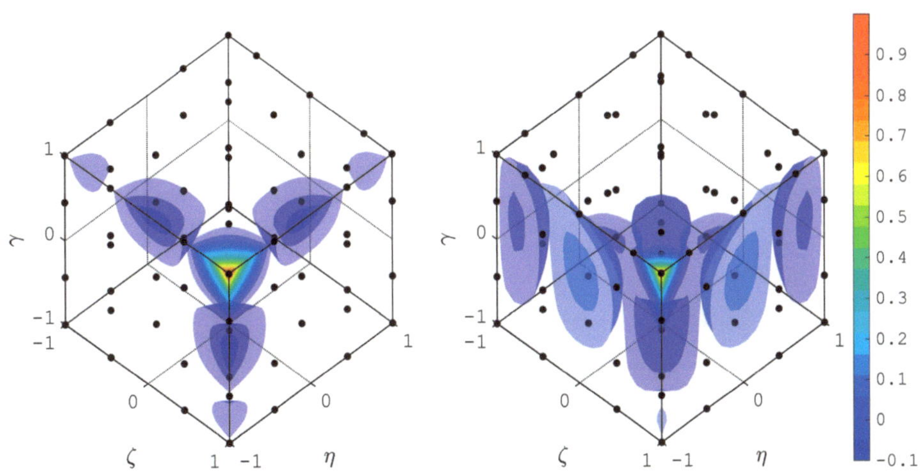

(A) (B)

Figure 10. Transition elements from order 4 to 3; (**A**) Case 1; (**B**) Case 2.

3.2. Verification

For verification, a specimen of dimension 10 m × 10 m × 5 m along the x, y, and z axes was modeled and discretized using 256 irregular-shaped linear elements. The element shapes were chosen to be irregular as the patch test would be performed [31]. The material property was chosen as concrete with a modulus of elasticity, density, and Poisson's ratio of 30 GPa, 3000 kg/m^3 and 0.3, respectively [32]. One of the elements marked as red in Figure 11A was refined to the fourth order, and the methodology developed in this paper was implemented to transition from the fourth to the first order, as presented in Figure 11B, which produces no hanging nodes. Next, the boundary conditions were applied to restrict the rigid body motions by enforcing displacement $u_x = u_y = u_z = 0$ at the $x = 0$, $y = 0$ and $z = 0$ surfaces, respectively, where u_x, u_y and u_z show this displacement along the x, y and

z axes, respectively. The patch test was performed, wherein a unit displacement $u_z = 1$ at all the nodes of the $z = 5$ surface was applied, and the static solution was obtained in terms of displacement. The obtained displacement along the z axis is presented in Figure 12A, which shows a linear profile along the z axis throughout the specimen. The displacement u_z was plotted along the $x = y = 0$ line, as shown in Figure 13, which shows a linear profile that confirms that the model passed the patch test. The obtained stress profile was also observed as being constant throughout the specimen, as shown in Figure 12B, which provides additional confidence in this method's capability to produce an accurate solution.

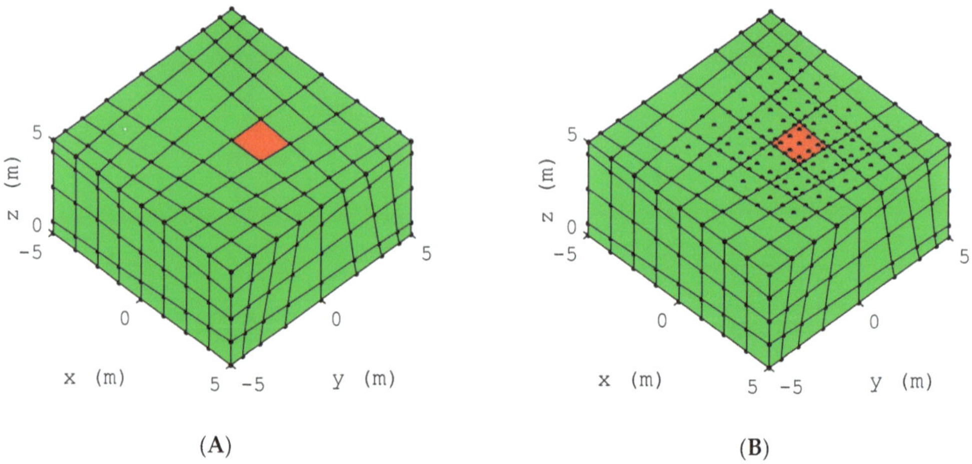

Figure 11. Mesh refinement: (**A**) original mesh; (**B**) refined mesh following refinement of red marked element to order four (isometric view). Dots represents the nodes.

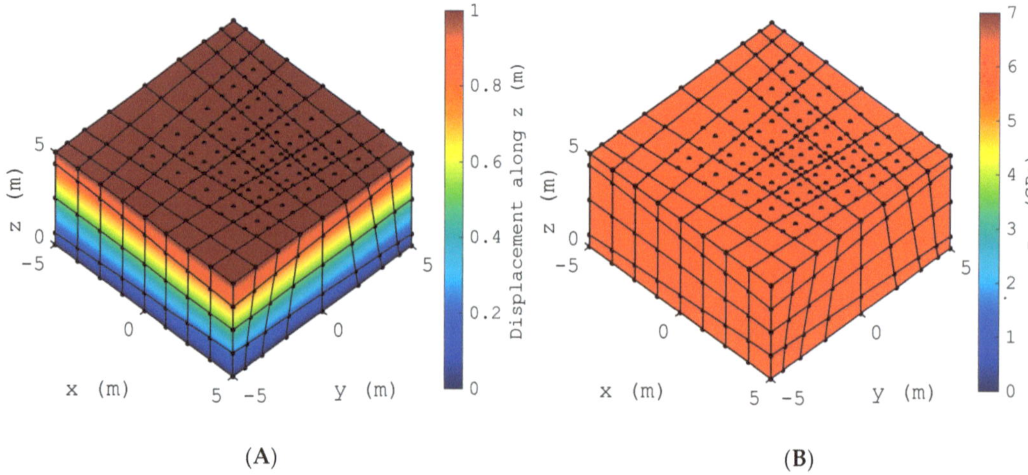

Figure 12. (**A**) Displacement and (**B**) σ_{33} stress profile for the patch test. Dots represents the nodes.

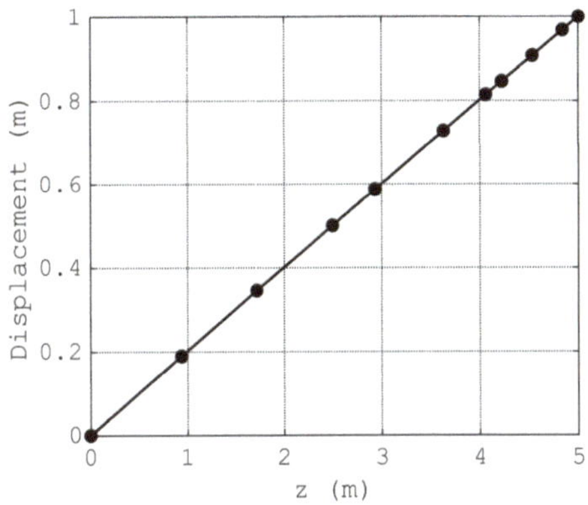

Figure 13. Displacement along the z axis profile on the $x = 0$, $y = 0$ line.

3.3. Implementation of 3D FE Meshes

Two examples are presented in this section. First, the model developed for the verification purpose was subjected to an impact load. Impact load can be replicated through elastic contact modeling [33]. For the sake of simplicity, instead of a contact model, a loading of $F = sin(2\pi 10,000t)e^{(-100,000t)}10^{10}$ along the z axis at the central node (T; marked as red in Figure 14) of the refined element was implemented. Such a loading profile can be observed during the cavity expansion at a hypervelocity impact event [34] as presented in Figure 15A. With a timestep [35] of 0.001 mili-s, following the central difference time-stepping algorithm, the displacement profile was obtained. The displacement profiles along z at two nodes (Nodes S and D of Figure 14) are presented in Figure 15B. The distance between nodes T and S is 0.551 m, whereas it is 0.1585 for Node D. It is obvious that, as the distance increases, the wave attenuates. A 3D profile for both displacement and pressure stress profiles is presented in Figure 16, which shows the propagation of the wave in a qualitative manner.

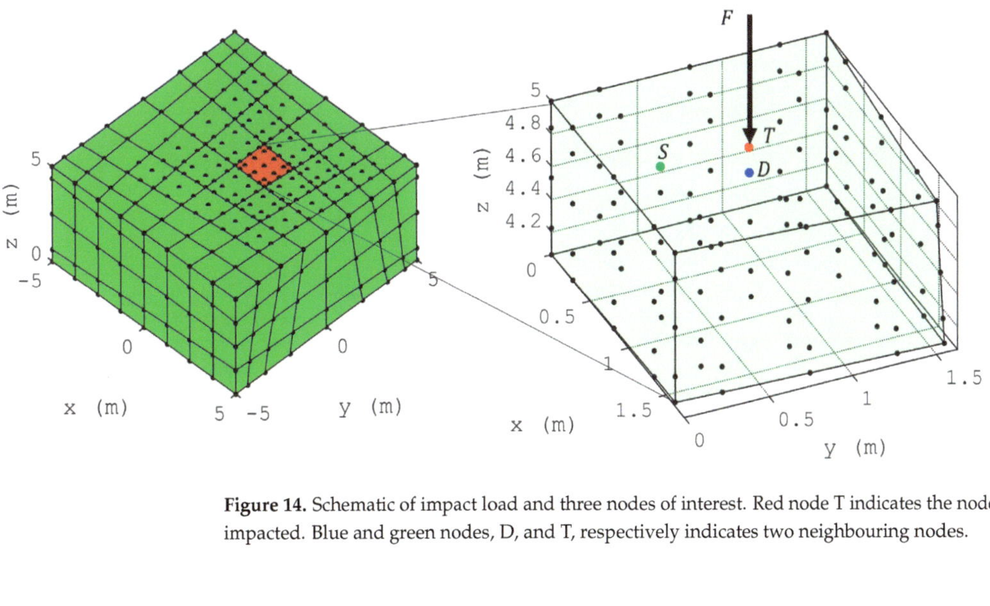

Figure 14. Schematic of impact load and three nodes of interest. Red node T indicates the node to be impacted. Blue and green nodes, D, and T, respectively indicates two neighbouring nodes.

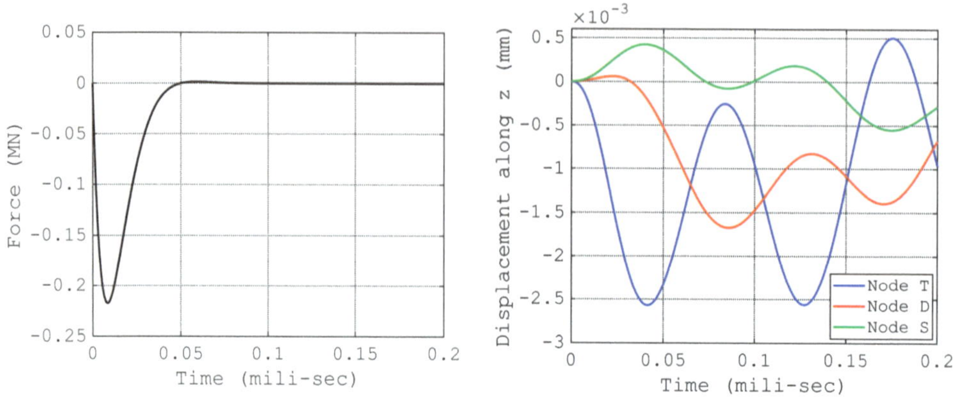

Figure 15. (**A**) Force profile and (**B**) displacement along the z axis at three different nodes.

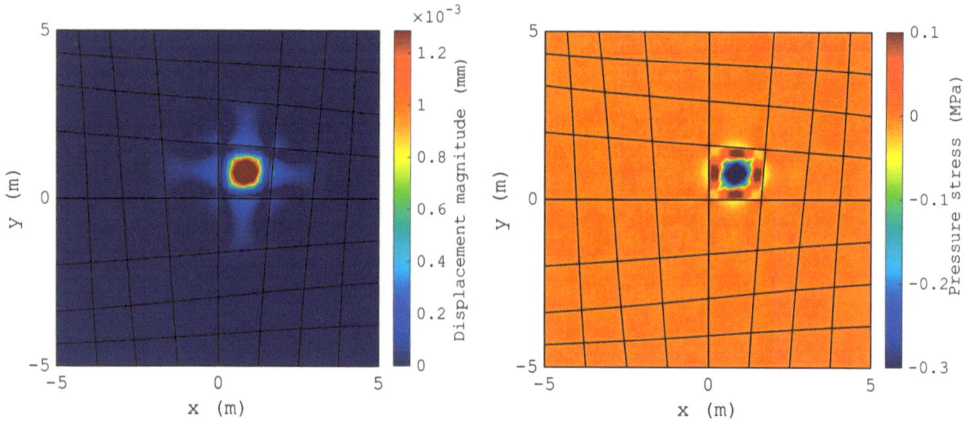

Figure 16. Top view of (**A**) Displacement norm and (**B**) pressure stress profile at 0.04 mili-sec of the refined mesh.

Next, a space habitat model with an outer radius of 2.9 m and an inner radius of 2.5 m is presented. The habitat was discretized into 64 linear elements, as presented in Figure 17A. Scenarios such as meteorite impact cause wave propagation that requires high-density mesh at the impact point. Such action requires re-meshing corresponding to the impact location. Instead of increasing mesh density, higher-order elements offer an excellent solution for simulation wave propagation [8,11,26]. Hence, one of the elements (red in Figure 17B of the model) was enriched to order four, and the procedure developed in this paper was implemented to refine all other elements of the model. The obtained mesh produced no hanging node and a positive definite stiffness matrix. An impact load similar to the previous case perpendicular to the central node of the refined element was implemented. The material property was chosen as aluminum with a modulus of elasticity, density, and Poisson's ratio of 68 GPa, 2703 kg/m^3 and 0.3, respectively. The results in terms of radial displacement are presented in Figure 18 for three different distances from the impact node, showing wave decay as distance increases. The nodes T, D, and S follow the same definition as Figure 14, with the distance from T to D and S being 0.0668m and 0.3202, respectively. The 3D profile for displacement norm and pressure stress is also presented in Figure 19A,B, respectively, to provide an overview of the implementation of this method.

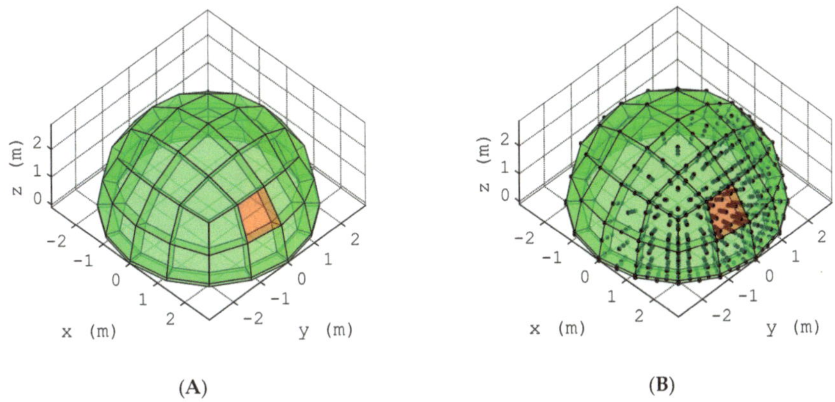

Figure 17. (**A**) Original mesh with 8 node brick element, (**B**) refined mesh followed by refinement of an element to the fourth order.

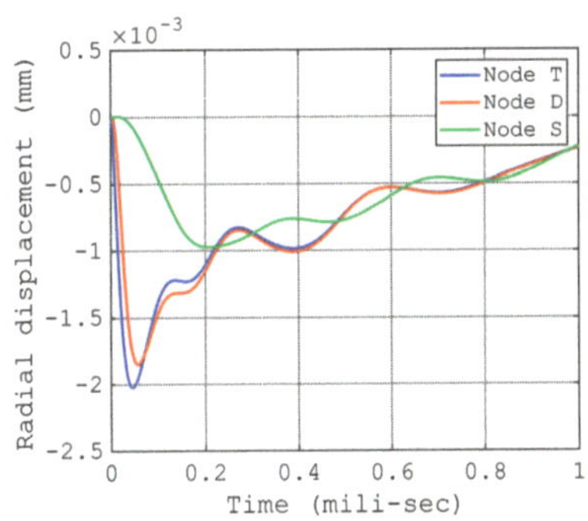

Figure 18. Radial displacement norm at three different nodes.

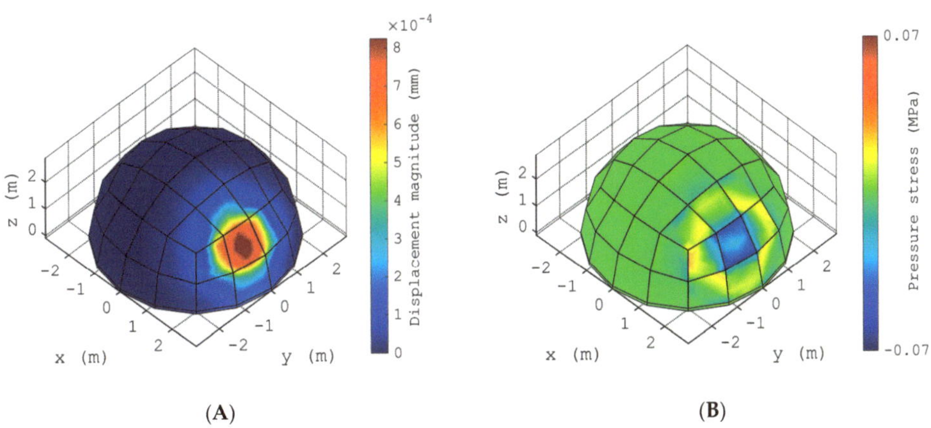

Figure 19. Isometric view of (**A**) Displacement norm and (**B**) pressure stress profile at 0.35 mili-sec of the refined mesh.

4. Conclusions

This paper developed a p-refinement method and a library of six three-dimensional transition elements with the highest order of four, in order to perform p-refinement that gradually decreases polynomial order, element by element, from a refined high-order element. The shape functions and the integration quadratures were computed for each of these elements. The local support and interelement compatibility conditions were checked for each of these elements to verify them. The element properties have been made readily available to FEM users. The p-refinement procedure was tested on irregular mesh, which showed no hanging nodes and passed the patch test. Such refinement is useful in simulating structural vibration due to impact loading, which is presented through two numerical implementations. This development makes local p-refinement possible in 3D finite element applications. The application of these research findings can be extended to the discontinuous Galerkin method applied to wave propagation [6,7], and can help provide competitive results compared to existing methods. Researchers in the field of FEA can benefit by refining only one element to reduce the degrees of freedom. Re-meshing corresponding to the h-refinement can also be avoided, saving computational time and resources.

Author Contributions: Conceptualization, A.S. and A.J.M.; methodology, A.S.; software, A.S.; validation, A.S. and A.J.M.; formal analysis, A.S.; investigation, A.S. and A.J.M.; resources, A.S.; data curation, A.S.; writing—original draft preparation, A.S.; writing—review and editing, A.S. and A.J.M.; visualization, A.S.; supervision, A.S.; project administration, A.S. All authors have read and agreed to the published version of the manuscript.

Funding: This material was based on work carried out under the Resilient Extra-Terrestrial Habitat Institute (RETHi) and supported by a Space Technology Research Institute grant (No.80NSSC19K1076) from NASA's Space Technology Research Grants Program. We also thank Arturo Montoya for his support and funding acquisitions that led to the publication of this work.

Data Availability Statement: The data presented in this study are openly available in https://zenodo.org/records/10015183, accessed on 17 October 2023.

Conflicts of Interest: The authors declare no conflict of interest.

Appendix A

Table A1. Node coordinates of the 13-node transition element.

Node No.	x	y	z
1	−1	−1	−1
2	1	−1	−1
3	1	1	−1
4	1	−1	−1
5	−1	−1	1
6	1	−1	1
7	1	1	1
8	1	−1	1
9	0	−1	1
10	1	0	1
11	0	1	1
12	−1	0	1
13	0	0	1

Table A2. Shape functions of the 13-node transition element.

N_i	Shape Functions in Terms of (x,y,z)
N_1	$\frac{xy}{8}-\frac{y}{8}-\frac{z}{8}-\frac{x}{8}+\frac{xz}{8}+\frac{yz}{8}-\frac{xyz}{8}+\frac{1}{8}$
N_2	$\frac{x}{8}-\frac{y}{8}-\frac{z}{8}-\frac{xy}{8}-\frac{xz}{8}+\frac{yz}{8}+\frac{xyz}{8}+\frac{1}{8}$
N_3	$\frac{x}{8}+\frac{y}{8}-\frac{z}{8}+\frac{xy}{8}-\frac{xz}{8}-\frac{yz}{8}-\frac{xyz}{8}+\frac{1}{8}$
N_4	$\frac{y}{8}-\frac{x}{8}-\frac{z}{8}-\frac{xy}{8}+\frac{xz}{8}-\frac{yz}{8}+\frac{xyz}{8}+\frac{1}{8}$
N_5	$\frac{xy}{8}-\frac{xy^2(z+1)}{8}-\frac{x^2y(z+1)}{8}+\frac{xyz}{8}+\frac{x^2y^2(z+1)}{8}$
N_6	$\frac{xy^2(z+1)}{8}-\frac{xy}{8}-\frac{x^2y(z+1)}{8}-\frac{xyz}{8}+\frac{x^2y^2(z+1)}{8}$
N_7	$\frac{xy}{8}+\frac{xy^2(z+1)}{8}+\frac{x^2y(z+1)}{8}+\frac{xyz}{8}+\frac{x^2y^2(z+1)}{8}$
N_8	$\frac{x^2y(z+1)}{8}-\frac{xy^2(z+1)}{8}-\frac{xy}{8}-\frac{xyz}{8}+\frac{x^2y^2(z+1)}{8}$
N_9	$\frac{y^2(z+1)}{4}-\frac{y}{4}-\frac{yz}{4}+\frac{x^2y(z+1)}{4}-\frac{x^2y^2(z+1)}{4}$
N_{10}	$\frac{x}{4}+\frac{x^2(z+1)}{4}+\frac{xz}{4}-\frac{xy^2(z+1)}{4}-\frac{x^2y^2(z+1)}{4}$
N_{11}	$\frac{y}{4}+\frac{y^2(z+1)}{4}+\frac{yz}{4}-\frac{x^2y(z+1)}{4}-\frac{x^2y^2(z+1)}{4}$
N_{12}	$\frac{x^2(z+1)}{4}-\frac{x}{4}-\frac{xz}{4}+\frac{xy^2(z+1)}{4}-\frac{x^2y^2(z+1)}{4}$
N_{13}	$\frac{z}{2}-\frac{x^2(z+1)}{2}-\frac{y^2(z+1)}{2}+\frac{x^2y^2(z+1)}{2}+\frac{1}{2}$

Table A3. Integration quadrature of the 13-node transition element.

Integration Point No.	x	y	z	Weight
1	−1	−1	−1	0.11111111
2	1	−1	−1	0.11111111
3	1	1	−1	0.11111111
4	−1	1	−1	0.11111111
5	−1	−1	1	0.11111111
6	1	−1	1	0.11111111
7	1	1	1	0.11111111
8	−1	1	1	0.11111111
9	0	−1	−1	0.44444444
10	1	0	−1	0.44444444
11	0	1	−1	0.44444444
12	−1	0	−1	0.44444444
13	0	−1	1	0.44444444
14	1	0	1	0.44444444
15	0	1	1	0.44444444
16	−1	0	1	0.44444444
17	0	0	1	1.77777778
18	0	0	−1	1.77777778

References

1. Zienkiewicz, O.C.; Taylor, R.L.; Zhu, J.Z. *The Finite Element Method: Its Basis and Fundamentals*; Butterworth Heinemann: Oxford, UK, 2013. [CrossRef]
2. Bunting, C.F. Introduction to the finite element method. In Proceedings of the 2008 IEEE International Symposium on Electromagnetic Compatibility—EMC 2008, Detroit, MI, USA, 18–22 August 2008; pp. 1–9.
3. Bathe, K.-J. *Discontinuous Finite Element Procedures*; Springer: London, UK, 2006; pp. 21–43. [CrossRef]
4. Ihlenburg, F.; Babuška, I. Finite element solution of the Helmholtz equation with high wave number part I: The h-version of the FEM. *Comput. Math. Appl.* **1995**, *30*, 9–37. [CrossRef]
5. Babuska, I.M.; Sauter, S.A. Is the pollution effect of the FEM avoidable for the Helmholtz equation considering high wave numbers? *SIAM J. Numer. Anal.* **1997**, *34*, 2392–2423. [CrossRef]
6. Baccouch, M.; Temimi, H. A high-order space–time ultra-weak discontinuous Galerkin method for the second-order wave equation in one space dimension. *J. Comput. Appl. Math.* **2021**, *389*, 113331. [CrossRef]
7. Shukla, K.; Chan, J.; de Hoop, M.V.; Jaiswal, P. A weight-adjusted discontinuous Galerkin method for the poroelastic wave equation: Penalty fluxes and micro-heterogeneities. *J. Comput. Phys.* **2020**, *403*, 109061. [CrossRef]
8. Komatitsch, D.; Tromp, J. Spectral-element simulations of global seismic wave propagation-I. Validation. *Geophys. J. Int.* **2002**, *149*, 390–412. [CrossRef]
9. Canuto, C.; Hussaini, M.Y.; Quarteroni, A.; Zang, T.A. Spectral Approximation. In *Spectral Methods in Fluid Dynamics*; Springer: Berlin/Heidelberg, Germany, 1988; pp. 31–75. [CrossRef]

10. Palacz, M.; Krawczuk, M.; Żak, A. Spectral Element Methods for Damage Detection and Condition Monitoring. In *Advances in Asset Management and Condition Monitoring*; Springer: Cham, Switzerland, 2020; pp. 549–558.
11. Ostachowicz, W.; Kudela, P.; Krawczuk, M.; Zak, A. *Guided Waves in Structures for SHM: The Time-Domain Spectral Element Method*; John Wiley & Sons, Ltd.: New York, NY, USA, 2012. [CrossRef]
12. Patera, A.T. A spectral element method for fluid dynamics: Laminar flow in a channel expansion. *J. Comput. Phys.* **1984**, *54*, 468–488. [CrossRef]
13. Ihlenburg, F.; Babuska, I. Finite element solution of the helmholtz equation with high wave number part II: The h-p version of the FEM. *SIAM J. Numer. Anal.* **1997**, *34*, 315–358. [CrossRef]
14. Park, G.-H. P-Refinement Techniques for Vector finite Elements in Electromagnetics. Ph.D. Thesis, Georgia Institute of Technology, Atlanta, GA, USA, 2005.
15. Salazar-Palma, M. *Iterative and Self-Adaptive Finite-Elements in Electromagnetic Modeling*; Artech House: Norwood, MA, USA, 1998.
16. Shahriar, A.; Majlesi, A.; Montoya, A. A General procedure to formulate 3D elements for finite element applications. *Computation* **2023**, *11*, 197. [CrossRef]
17. Staten, M.L.; Jones, N.L. Local refinement of three-dimensional finite element meshes. *Eng. Comput.* **1997**, *13*, 165–174. [CrossRef]
18. Morton, D.J.; Tyler, J.M.; Dorroh, J.R. A new 3D finite element for adaptive h-refinement in 1-irregular meshes. *Int. J. Numer. Methods Eng.* **1995**, *38*, 3989–4008. [CrossRef]
19. Gordon, W.J.; Hall, C.A. Transfinite element methods: Blending-function interpolation over arbitrary curved element domains. *Numer. Math.* **1973**, *21*, 109–129. [CrossRef]
20. Gordon, W.J. Blending-Function Methods of Bivariate and Multivariate Interpolation and Approximation. *SIAM J. Numer. Anal.* **1971**, *8*, 158–177. [CrossRef]
21. Altenbach, J.; Scholz, E. Ableitung von Formfunktionen für finite Standard-und Übergangselemente auf der Grundlage der gemischten Interpolation. *Tech. Mech. -Eur. J. Eng. Mech.* **1987**, *8*, 18–30.
22. Duczek, S.; Saputra, A.; Gravenkamp, H. High order transition elements: The xy-element concept—Part I: Statics. *Comput. Methods Appl. Mech. Eng.* **2020**, *362*, 112833. [CrossRef]
23. Kim, J.H.; Lim, J.H.; Lee, J.H.; Im, S. A new computational approach to contact mechanics using variable-node finite elements. *Int. J. Numer. Methods Eng.* **2008**, *73*, 1966–1988. [CrossRef]
24. Buczkowski, R. 21-node hexahedral isoparametric element for analysis of contact problems. *Commun. Numer. Methods Eng.* **1998**, *14*, 681–692. [CrossRef]
25. Smith, I.M.; Kidger, D.J. Elastoplastic analysis using the 14-node brick element family. *Int. J. Numer. Methods Eng.* **1992**, *35*, 1263–1275. [CrossRef]
26. Soman, R.; Kudela, P.; Balasubramaniam, K.; Singh, S.K.; Malinowski, P. A study of sensor placement optimization problem for guided wave-based damage detection. *Sensors* **2019**, *19*, 1856. [CrossRef]
27. von Winckel, G. *Legende-Gauss-Lobatto Nodes and Weights*; MathWorks: Natick, MA, USA, 2020; Volume 20.
28. Arnold, D.N.; Awanou, G. The serendipity family of finite elements. *Found. Comput. Math.* **2011**, *11*, 337–344. [CrossRef]
29. Chari, M.; Salon, S. *Numerical Methods in Electromagnetism*; Elsevier BV: Amsterdam, The Netherlands, 2000; ISBN 9780126157604.
30. Taylor, R.L.; Simo, J.C.; Zienkiewicz, O.C.; Chan, A.C.H. The patch test—A condition for assessing FEM convergence. *Int. J. Numer. Methods Eng.* **1986**, *22*, 39–62. [CrossRef]
31. Irons, B.M.; Razzaque, A. Experience with the patch test for convergence of finite elements. In *The Mathematical Foundations of the Finite Element Method with Applications to Partial Differential Equations*; Elsevier: Amsterdam, The Netherlands, 1972; pp. 557–587.
32. Rashid, M.A.; Mansur, M.A.; Paramasivam, P. Correlations between mechanical properties of high-strength concrete. *J. Mater. Civ. Eng.* **2002**, *14*, 230–238. [CrossRef]
33. Seok, S.; Shahriar, A.; Montoya, A.; Malla, R.B. A finite element approach for simplified 2D nonlinear dynamic contact/impact analysis. *Arch. Appl. Mech.* **2023**, *93*, 3511–3531. [CrossRef]
34. Sun, Y.; Shi, C.; Liu, Z.; Wen, D. Theoretical research progress in high-velocity/hypervelocity impact on semi-infinite targets. *Shock Vib.* **2015**, *2015*, 265321. [CrossRef]
35. Marfurt, K.J. Accuracy of finite-difference and finite-element modeling of the scalar and elastic wave equations. *Geophysics* **1984**, *49*, 533–549. [CrossRef]

mathematics

Article

Research on Auxetic Lattice Structure for Impact Absorption in Machines and Mechanisms

Levente Széles [1], Richárd Horváth [2] and Livija Cveticanin [3,*]

[1] Doctoral School on Materials Sciences and Technologies, Óbuda University, 1034 Budapest, Hungary
[2] Bánki Donát Faculty of Mechanical and Safety Engineering, Óbuda University, 1034 Budapest, Hungary; cpinter.livia@uni-obbuda.hu
[3] Faculty of Technical Sciences, University of Novi Sad, Trg D. Obratodica 6, 21000 Novi Sad, Serbia
* Correspondence: cveticanin@uns.ac.rs

Abstract: In this paper, a new type of filled doubly re-entrant auxetic lattice structure for application in damping and energy absorption devices is considered. The structure is modeled to give protection for machines and mechanisms of intensive impact. The suggested structure is the modified version of the auxetic one with silicone fillings. The unit of the structure is assumed as a re-entrant hexagon with four quadrangular absorbers. For the assumed model of unit, the deformation properties and the Poisson's ratio were computed. The obtained results were experimentally tested. Specimens of filled and unfilled structures were investigated under quasi-static compression. The measured results show that the energy dissipation is more than two times higher for filled structure than for unfilled ones. In the filled structure, the absorber's rigidity has the crucial role. If the rigidity is small, the absorber, inside the unit, continues to deform from rectangle into rhomboid. Otherwise, if the rigidity is high, units with absorbers form a beam-like structure that buckles and shows high energy absorption effect. The experimentally obtained results are in good agreement with the theoretical ones.

Keywords: auxetic lattice structure; doubly re-entrant auxetic unit; analytical modelling procedure; specific energy dissipation; elimination of the impact effect

MSC: 37M10

Citation: Széles, L.; Horváth, R.; Cveticanin, L. Research on Auxetic Lattice Structure for Impact Absorption in Machines and Mechanisms. *Mathematics* **2024**, *12*, 1983. https://doi.org/10.3390/math12131983

Academic Editors: Joaquim Infante Barbosa and José Alberto Rodrigues

Received: 6 June 2024
Revised: 21 June 2024
Accepted: 24 June 2024
Published: 27 June 2024

1. Introduction

Mechanisms and machine parts that work with impact, in addition to the standard requirements, are subject to requirements for increased strength, wear resistance and hardness of parts, as well as for impact energy absorption, noise and vibration reduction, etc. [1,2]. Honeycomb and lattice structures are found to be the best answer to the aforementioned demands [3,4]. The artificial porous periodical structures with light weight [5], called 'elastic metastructures', due to their energy absorption properties [6,7] and noise and vibration suppression [8], are appropriate to be applied in many industries including the automotive [9,10], aerospace [11], and military [12] ones, as well as in the sports equipment industry [13]. The utilized structures are manly produced by 3D printing [14]. To improve the structure, two main directions are evident: one to improve the structure material, and the second to reconstruct the geometry of the structure.

Based on the rule for buildings materials about their dependence of properties on material combination [15–18], the material combination method is developed for the metastructure production. Additional materials are mixed into the base material for printing [19,20]. The fiber-reinforced parts have undeniably better mechanical properties, but there remain the problems of anisotropy, porosity, and delamination, which have a negative impact on product use.

As an improvement, the combining metastructures are developed, inspired by the structure of the human tooth [21]. The conventional honeycomb lattice structure is combined of two materials. The lattices are printed with a hard material along the outside and inside of their perimeter, while the center of the perimeter is printed with a soft material. By varying the thickness ratio of the rigid and flexible regions, the mechanical properties of the structure (energy absorption and damping characteristics) can be tuned [22–25]. A wide spectrum of lightweight materials is used for filling lattices and other structures, such as polyurethane foams [26,27], syntactic foams [28], metallic foams [29,30], and agar gel [31]. Prajapati et al. [32,33] have created a 3D-printed hard outer layer specimen filled with soft polyurethane foam, giving the material significantly improved impact and fracture properties. Chapkin et al. [34] printed titanium alloy lattice specimens which were filled with compressible and non-compressible elastomers. Black et al. [31] have filled simple cubic lattices with agar gel. It was found that comparing to the unfilled control group, the lattices filled with gel demonstrated a 50% increase in the energy absorbed and a 55% increase in the displacement to failure. Their work perfectly illustrates that filling is relevant even in the case of simple geometries and manufacturing technologies.

The previously presented multi-material-based structures achieved more favorable energy-absorbing and vibration-damping capabilities than the one-material structures. However, to successfully merge certain properties of multiple materials, proper bonding is inevitable. Multi-material structures generally may fail at interfaces; the proper interface bond must be as strong as the strength of the weaker material. Otherwise, the structure is failed at lower stress, making the combination disadvantageous [35,36]. However, the main disadvantage of the previous structures is that the vibration and noise suppression is only for a certain frequency domain [37–40].

An improvement can be created by topologically optimal geometries of different materials (see [41,42]). In addition, to overcome the problem, the auxetic structures are introduced [43,44]. Namely, the energy absorption property of this structure is constant and independent of the ratio of the frequency of the external force and the structure's eigenfrequency. The suggested system is also a kind of lattice structure, with the elementary constitutive units having the negative Poisson's coefficient. This units are hexagonal.

Recently, the units are rearranged with the aim to improve the mechanical properties [45]. A novel doubly re-entrant auxetic honeycomb structure was introduced [46]. In this paper, a rearranged doubly re-entrant auxetic structure partially filled with a soft absorber material is considered. The aim of the research is to obtain the influence of the coupled combination of the basic structure and filling absorbers on the specific energy absorption. The investigation is done theoretically and experimentally. The result is that the structure with optimal energy absorption is obtained and suggested for application in devices for impact protection in machines and mechanisms.

The paper is divided into 4 sections. After the Introduction, in Section 2, the novel doubly re-entrant auxetic unit cell with and without filling is theoretically investigated. The deformation properties and conditions for auxetic behavior are considered. The absorber displacement and its deformation in the cell due to compression is determined. In addition, the buckling conditions in the structure are obtained. In Section 3, the fabrication of test specimens is presented. The force-displacement and absorbed energy-displacement curves are determined for the unfilled and filled structures with various geometric properties. An explanation of specific absorption energy based on the experimental and theoretical consideration is presented. The unfilled and filled specimens with various rigidity property are compared. The structure with the best energy absorption property is suggested. The result is proved by applying of the statistical T-method. The paper ends with Conclusions.

2. Models of Filled and Unfilled Structures

In Figure 1, the unfilled (Figure 1a) and partially filled (Figure 1b) doubly re-entrant honeycomb structures are shown. Namely, in the quadrilateral voids formed by neighboring unit cells, the filling, which represents the absorber, is settled. The aim of the section is to compare the deformation properties of the filled and unfilled structures. For this reason, independent parameters, which are related to the deformation i.e., shape and dimension variation, have to be introduced. These parameters are of geometrical type.

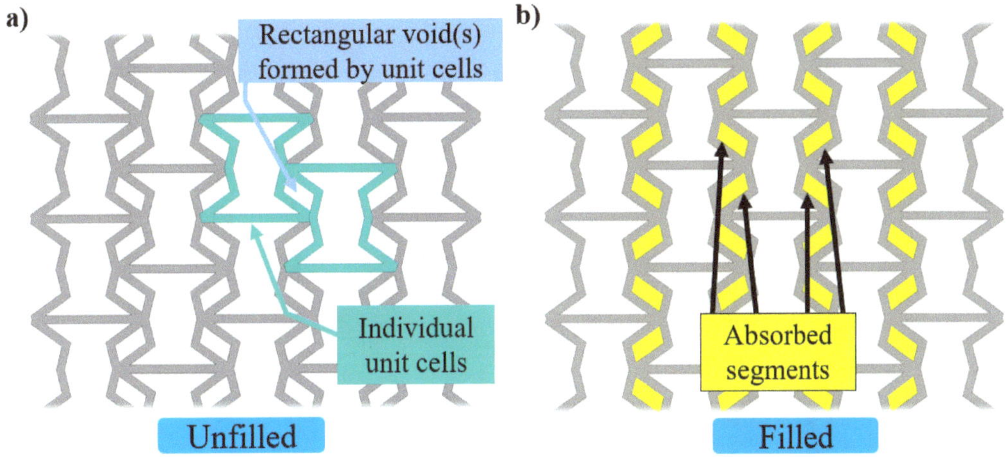

Figure 1. Doubly re-entrant honeycomb structures: (**a**) unfilled and (**b**) filled.

For structure analysis, the unit cell with four absorbers is separated (Figure 2). The constant unit cell dimensions are the width L, thickness t and out-of-plane thickness b, and for the absorber the dimensions are the length h and width w. Due to force action, the unit cell deforms and the inner width L_1 and the high H of the unit are varying.

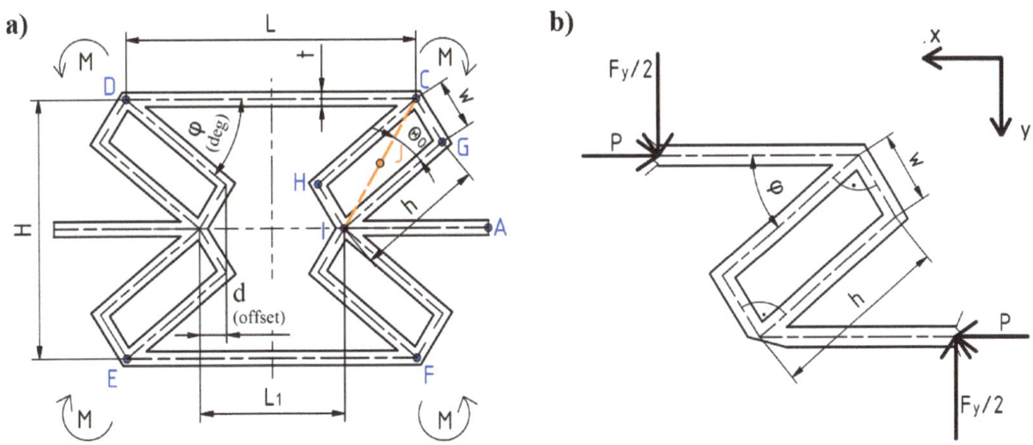

Figure 2. (**a**) Scheme of the unit cell with four absorbers and (**b**) loading of the quarter of unit section.

The dimensions variation is assumed as a function of two independent values: the angle φ between the horizontal and upper re-entrant edges (called *deg*) and the distance between the breakpoints d (called *offset*). Then, it is calculated as

$$H = 2hsin\varphi + 2\sqrt{w^2 - d^2}, \quad L_1 = L - 2hcos\varphi + 2d. \tag{1}$$

However, the geometric constraint of the unit is

$$\frac{L}{2} - hcos\varphi \geq 0. \tag{2}$$

In this section, the deformation properties of the filled structure are modelled. Two types of models are introduced: one with soft filling, and a second where the absorber is an almost rigid body.

2.1. Auxetic Deformation of the Structure

For far field stress in y-direction, the unit with four absorbers (Figure 2a) is loaded with the force F_y. Due to symmetry, let us analyze the upper quarter segment of the unit (Figure 2b). The cross-section A_b and the Young's modulus of elasticity of material E_b of the basic unit are constant. The elasticity of absorber material is E_a. For simplicity, it is assumed that the absorber is rectangular, with constant cross section A_a. In addition, it is supposed that the absorber dimensions satisfy the relation w << h. The segment of the unit (Figure 2b) is in equilibrium if the external moment is balanced with the moment of forces $\frac{F_y}{2}$. For computational reasons, in the segment, two opposite virtual forces P in x direction are introduced. The forces $\frac{F_y}{2}$ and P cause axial and bending deformation. The total strain energy for the unit-absorber section is the sum of bending and compression energies and is as follows:

$$U = \frac{1}{2E_bA_b}\int_0^{L/2} P^2ds + \left(\frac{1}{2E_bA_b} + \frac{1}{2E_aA_a}\right)\int_0^h \left(\frac{F_y}{2}sin\varphi - Pcos\varphi\right)^2 ds + \frac{1}{2E_bA_b}\int_0^w \left(\frac{F_y}{2}cos\varphi - Psin\varphi\right)^2 ds + \frac{1}{2E_bI_b}\int_0^{\frac{L}{2}} \left(\frac{F_y}{2}s\right)^2 ds + \left(\frac{1}{2E_bI_b} + \frac{1}{2E_aI_a}\right)\int_0^h \left(\frac{F_y}{2}\left(\frac{L}{2} - scos\varphi\right) - Pssin\varphi\right)^2 ds + \frac{1}{2E_bI_b}\int_0^h \left(\frac{F_y}{2}\left(\frac{L}{2} - hcos\varphi + ssin\varphi\right) - P(hsin\varphi + scos\varphi)\right)^2 ds \tag{3}$$

where

$$A_a = wb, \quad I_a = \frac{bw^3}{12}, \quad A_b = tb, \; I_b = \frac{tb^3}{12}. \tag{4}$$

According to the Castigliano theorem, the displacement u in x direction and v in y direction are derived as

$$u = \left(\frac{\partial U}{\partial(P)}\right)_{P=0} = -\left(\frac{F_y}{2}\right)\left(\left(\frac{1}{E_bA_b} + \frac{1}{E_aA_a}\right)\frac{h}{2}\sin(2\varphi) - \frac{w}{2E_bA_b}\sin(2\varphi) + \left(\frac{1}{E_bI_b} + \frac{1}{E_aI_a}\right)h^2sin\varphi\left(\frac{L}{2} - \frac{2h}{3}cos\varphi\right) + \frac{1}{E_bI_b}\left(\left(\frac{L}{2} - hcos\varphi\right)hwsin\varphi + h\frac{w^2}{2}sin^2\varphi + \frac{w^2}{2}\left(\frac{L}{2} - hcos\varphi\right)cos\varphi + \frac{w^3}{6}\sin(2\varphi)\right)\right), \tag{5}$$

$$v = \left(\frac{\partial U}{\partial(F_y/2)}\right)_{P=0} = \left(\frac{F_y}{2}\right)\left(\left(\frac{1}{E_bA_b} + \frac{1}{E_aA_a}\right)hsin^2\varphi + \frac{w}{E_bA_b}cos^2\varphi + \frac{1}{3E_bI_b}\left(\frac{L}{2}\right)^3 + \left(\frac{1}{E_bI_b} + \frac{1}{E_aI_a}\right)\left(\frac{L}{2}h\left(\frac{L}{2} - hcos\varphi\right) + \frac{h^3}{3}cos^2\varphi\right) + \frac{1}{E_bI_b}\left(w\left(\frac{L}{2} - hcos\varphi\right)^2 + w^2\left(\frac{L}{2} - hcos\varphi\right)sin\varphi + \frac{w^3}{3}sin^2\varphi\right)\right). \tag{6}$$

Analyzing (5) and (6), it is obtained that for the constraint (2), the displacement (5) in the x direction is negative, while in y direction (6) it is opposite, i.e., positive.

In the relations (1), the angle φ is varying in the interval $\varphi\epsilon[0, \varphi_0]$, where φ_0 is the initial deg angle. For $\varphi = \varphi_0$, according to (1), the initial inner width and initial height of the segment is as follows:

$$L_1/2 = \frac{L}{2} - hcos\varphi_0 + 2d_0, \quad H/2 = hsin\varphi_0 + \sqrt{w^2 + d_0^2} \tag{7}$$

where d_0 is the initial offset dimension. Comparing the displacements (5) and (6) with the initial inner width and height (7), the strains in x and y direction are as follows:

$$\varepsilon_x = \frac{u}{\frac{L}{2} - hcos\varphi_0 + 2d_0}, \qquad \varepsilon_y = \frac{v}{hsin\varphi_0 + 2\sqrt{w^2 + d_0^2}}. \tag{8}$$

Thus, based on (5), (6), and (8), the sign of the Poisson's ratio $\nu = \frac{\varepsilon_y}{\varepsilon_x}$ is negative. It proves that the filled structure is auxetic.

Analyzing relations (5) and (6), it is obvious that the value of the displacement is higher for the filled structure than for the unfilled one. The effect of absorber depends on the elasticity of the filling: The smaller the Young's modulus of elasticity E_a, the higher the terms with $E_a A_a$ and $E_a I_a$.

For $\varphi = 0$, the displacements (5) and (6) are

$$u = \left(\frac{F_y w}{2}\frac{w}{2E_b I_b}\right)\left(\frac{L}{2} - h\right), \quad v = \left(\frac{F_y}{2}\frac{1}{E_b A_b}\right)w \tag{9}$$

and the corresponding inner width and high (1) are

$$L_1 = 2\left(\frac{L}{2} - h\right), \quad H = 2w \tag{10}$$

when for the rectangular absorber, $d = w \sin 0° = 0$. The segment is deformed into a simple rectangle with width h in x-direction and height w in y-direction (Figure 3a). In addition, the units form a beam-like structure along the y-axis (Figure 3b). The length l of the beam depends on the number n of structure's units, i.e., $l = n\ (2w)$. The beam of units has a periodical variable rigidity EI. For simplification, the rigidity of the absorber $E_a I_a$, is assumed to be the dominant one.

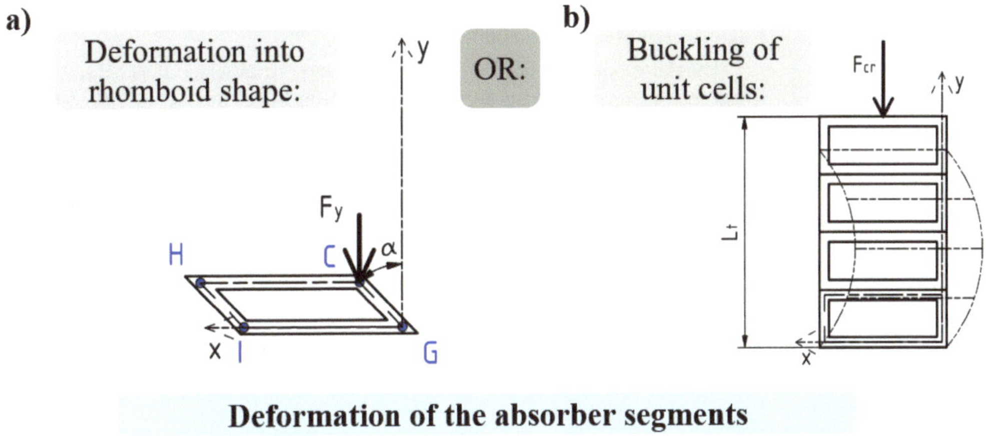

Figure 3. (**a**) Rectangular unit cell deformation into rhomboid shape and (**b**) beam-line absorber structure.

Deformation of the aforementioned unit and of the beam structure depend on the axial force F_y and its corresponding moment M.

2.2. *Shape Variation of the Absorber Unit and Buckling of the Beam-Like Structure*

Due to action of the axial force F_y, deformation of the rectangle shape into rhomboid one occurs (Figure 3a). Theoretically, the limit deformation is up to one line. In addition, the moment M, which is the result of the force F_y, causes bending of the beam-like structure (Figure 3b). The maximal deflection of the beam, caused by moment M, is

$$x_{max} = \frac{\sqrt{3}M(2nw)^2}{27E_a I_a,}. \tag{11}$$

The higher the number of units in y-direction and the softer the absorber material E_a, the higher the deformation.

Finally, the buckling of the beam-line structure occurs if the force that acts has the critical value F_{cr}:

$$F_{cr} = \pi^2 \frac{E_a I_a}{L_e^2} \tag{12}$$

where L_e is the effective length of the beam, which depends on the boundary conditions of the beam. In the suggested model, the beam is pin–pin supported and has the effective length $L_e = 2nw$. The critical force is

$$F_{cr} = \pi^2 \frac{E_a I_a}{(2nw)^2}. \tag{13}$$

The displacement due to buckling is affected by several factors, including the material properties, cross-sectional shape, and dimensions, but also the loading conditions. These factors determine the critical load (13) at which buckling occurs and the resulting displacement. However, the structure, in buckling, becomes unstable, and to model what happens after buckling requires a nonlinear analysis.

REMARK: The critical force (12) depends on the boundary conditions and the value of L_e. If the beam is fixed–free supported, the critical force is four times smaller than (13), as $L_e = 4nw$. If the beam is fixed–pin or fixed–fixed supported, the critical force is two times and even four times higher than (13) as $L_e = (nw)/\sqrt{2}$ and $L_e = (nw)$, respectively.

3. Experimental Research and Results

The deformation of the filled and unfilled structures was experimentally tested. The specimens were printed on an Anycubic Photon M3 printer via masked stratigraphy, which is a form of Masked Stereolithography Apparatus (MSLA) additive manufacturing technology. The free spaces in the honeycomb were manually filled with silicone. The overall dimensions of samples are shown in Figure 4. Two-unit cell parameters were varied: deg φ_0 and offset d_0. Deg had the values of 30, 35 and 40 degrees, while offset was 0.9 mm, 1.5 mm and 2.1 mm. In total, 18 specimens (9 unfilled and 9 filled) were considered.

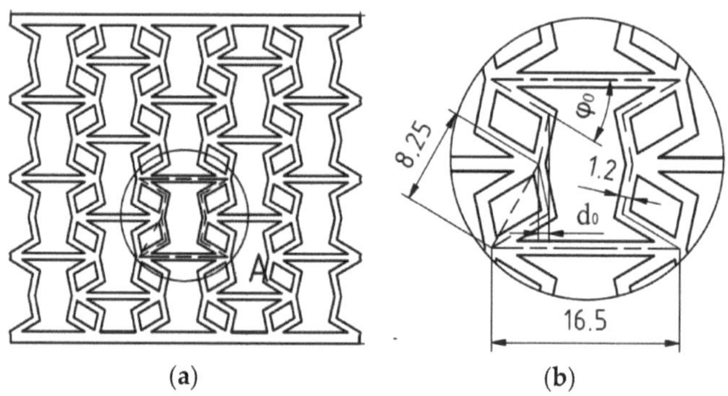

Figure 4. (**a**) Model of specimen and (**b**) dimensions of the unit cell with parameters.

The parameter combinations for specimens are shown in the Table 1.

Table 1. Parameter combinations and specimen designations.

d_0	0.9	0.9	0.9	1.5	1.5	1.5	2.1	2.1	2.1
φ_0	30	35	40	30	35	40	30	35	40
Unfilled	0930	0935	0940	1530	1535	1540	2130	2135	2140
Filled	0930SZ	0935SZ	0940SZ	1530SZ	1535SZ	1540SZ	2130SZ	2135SZ	2140SZ

The printing material was a unique resin mixture with high flexibility and firm properties. The resin mixture contained 75% Litliq FX60 Flexible rubber-like and 25% Litliq TH50 Tough resins. The printing parameters were as follows. The layer exposure time for 0.05 mm layer thickness was 4 s with 2 s wait time (off-time) between layers, enabling the high viscosity resin evenly to spread in the resin tank. Each specimen was printed at a 14-degree angle relative to the build platform. Specimens were washed for 3 min in 99.8% purity isopropyl alcohol, and then UV cured for 15 min. Anycubic Wash & Cure 2.0 25W resin curing machine was used. Specimens were filled with Soudal Polysiloxane based Trade sanitary silicone (silicone). We chose silicone for filling as is found to have substantially high impact resistance, good dimensional stability, and stability of physical and mechanical properties (does not end up losing the elasticity and has high load-bearing properties in compression and tension). Silicone is not chemically reactive and has excellent adhesion to smooth surfaces.

For the filling procedure, syringes with special tips were designed and manufactured (Figure 5). The tips have holes of the same form and size as the regions to be filled in specimens, allowing for homogeneous filling. The syringes were filled with silicone and then de-aerated. Specimens were filled under pressure, ensuring complete and homogeneous filling. Once the silicone cured, the excess was trimmed.

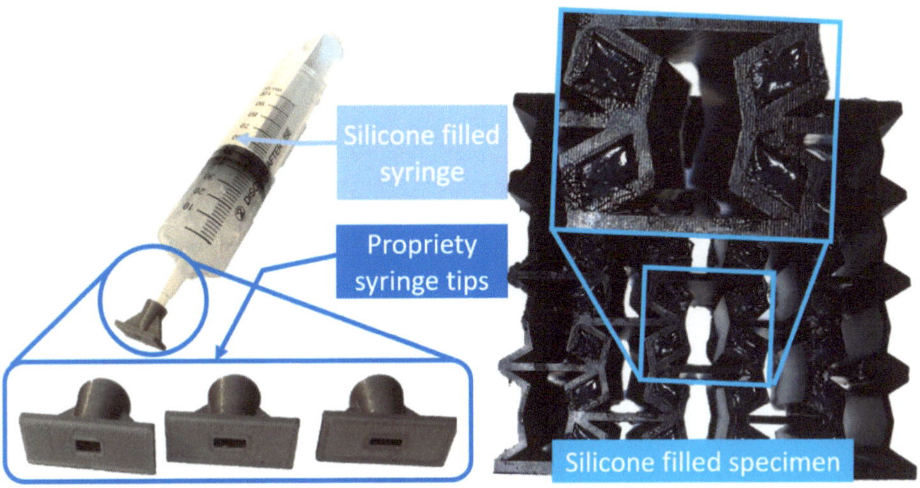

Figure 5. Specimen filling device.

Tensile testing of the structure was carried out according to EN ISO 527-2 [47], using a Zwick Z020 type tensile testing machine (Ulm, Germany) with a measuring limit of 20 kN. The measured stress–strain values are plotted in Figure 6. The stress–strain diagram shows that the relation is linear only for a small deformation range. The mean modulus of elasticity for the material is $E = 128.3$ MPa and the stress is $\sigma_p = 0.03$ MPa. At the other side, the modulus of elasticity of the Trade sanitary silicone, used for filling, is much lower (0.4 MPa [32]).

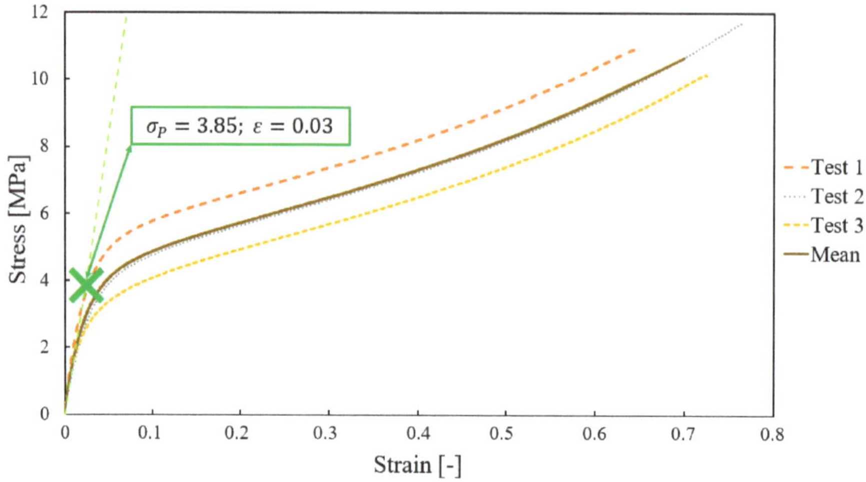

Figure 6. Stress–strain diagrams for 3 tensile tests and the corresponding mean diagram. The linear stress-strain relation is given with green dotted line.

3.1. Testing of Specimens on Compression: Force-Displacement Curves

Measuring on filled and unfilled specimens with offset $d_0 = 0.9$ mm, $d_0 = 1.5$ mm and $d_0 = 2.1$ mm, and deg angles $\varphi_0 = 30°$, $40°$, and $45°$ were done. During research, each specimen was subjected to compression testing at low speed of 5 mm/min, up to 30 mm/min on a Hegewald & Peschke 40-ton capacity machine.

In Figures 7–9, the force–displacement diagrams are plotted. Analyzing the plots, it is evident that for small deformations, the force-displacement diagrams are almost linear for all filled and unfilled specimens. It agrees with the theoretical result (6). The diagram of the force–displacement relation is nonlinear only for higher values of displacements.

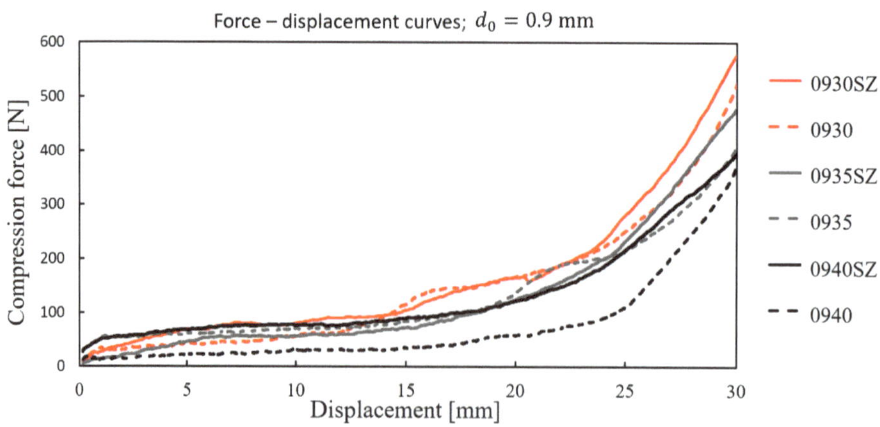

Figure 7. Force–displacement curves for filled and unfilled specimens, for $d_0 = 0.9$ mm.

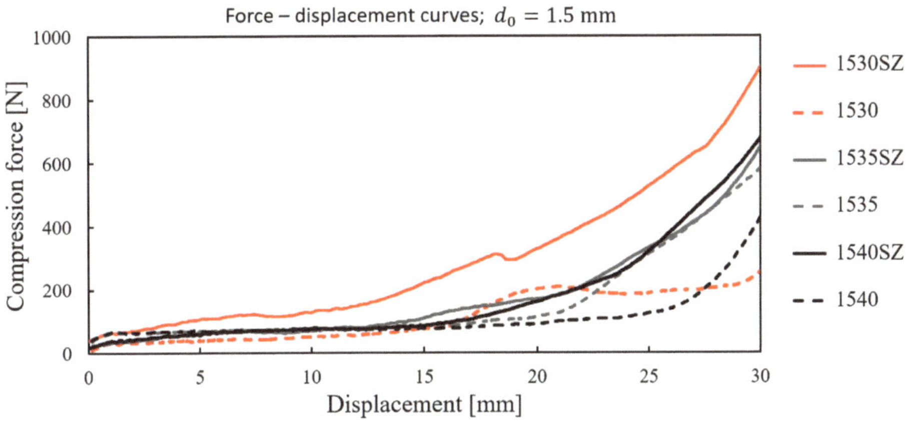

Figure 8. Force–displacement curves for filled and unfilled specimens, for $d_0 = 1.5$ mm.

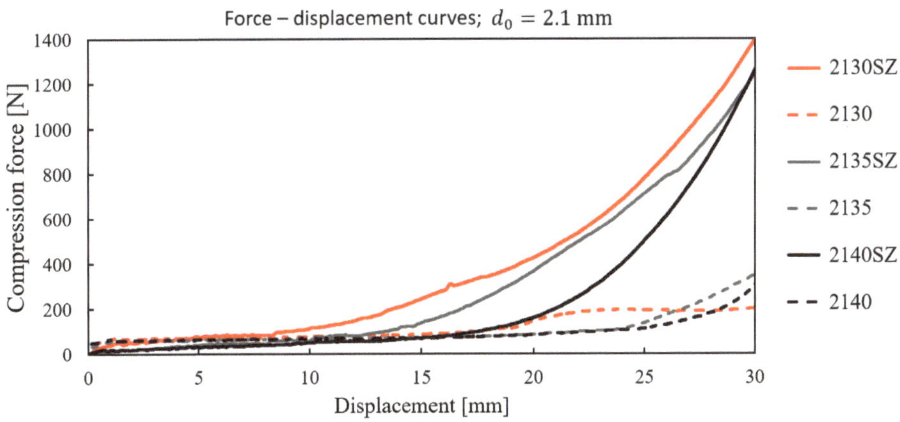

Figure 9. Force–displacement curves for filled and unfilled specimens, for $d_0 = 2.1$ mm.

In Figures 7–9, the force–displacement curves for filled specimens with corresponding unfilled ones are compared. It is obtained that the curve for filled specimen is above the corresponding unfilled one. Thus, the diagram for 0930SZ ($d_0 = 0.9$ mm, $\varphi_0 = 30°$, filled) is higher than the diagram for 0930 ($d_0 = 0.9$ mm, $\varphi_0 = 30°$, unfilled) in Figure 6. This conclusion is valid for all filled specimens in comparison to corresponding unfilled ones. However, the difference between filled and unfilled samples is smaller for small displacements and lower *offset* values.

For specimens with an equal value of the initial *offset*, the increase in the force versus displacement curve is higher for a smaller initial *deg* angle. Thus, for $d_0 = 0.9$ mm, the force–displacement diagram of 0930SZ with $\varphi_0 = 30°$ is above 0940SZ with $\varphi_0 = 40°$ and 0945SZ with $\varphi_0 = 45°$ (see Figure 7). The same conclusion is evident for specimens with $d_0 = 1.5$ mm (Figure 8) and $d_0 = 2.1$ mm (Figure 9).

In addition, in the samples with the same *deg* angle, the force is higher if the *offset* value is higher (see Figures 7–9). Comparing the force-displacement diagrams for different *offset* values (see in Figures 7–9, offset values 0.9 mm, 1.5 mm, and 2.1 mm) and a constant *deg* (for example 30 deg), it is obtained that the force increase is faster, and the maximum compressive force is higher for higher values of *offset* than for smaller ones. Thus, the force increase is the fastest for 2140SZ and the slowest for 0930SZ. For the same displacement and *deg* angle, the force in the sample is higher for offset $d_0 = 2.1$ mm than for 1.5 mm and 0.9 mm. Finally, the best force-deflection property is evident for 2130SZ.

3.2. Absorbed Energy-Displacement Curves

Using the force–displacement expression, the absorbed energy ($\mathfrak{J}$) is computed. The absorbed energy corresponds to the area under the experimentally recorded force–displacement curve and is given by:

$$\mathfrak{J} = \int_0^{v_{max}} F(v)dv \tag{14}$$

where $F(v)$ is the force distribution function, v is the displacement, and $v_{\max}$ is the maximal displacement. In Figures 10–12, the absorbed energy–displacement diagrams for filled and unfilled structures with *offset* values $d_0 = 0.9$ mm, $d_0 = 1.5$ mm, and $d_0 = 2.1$ mm and *deg* angles $\varphi_0 = 30°, 40°$, and $45°$ are plotted. Comparing these curves with those in Figures 7–9, the qualitative similarity is seen. Thus, the comments regarding the force–displacement curves apply to the absorbed energy–displacement curves, too.

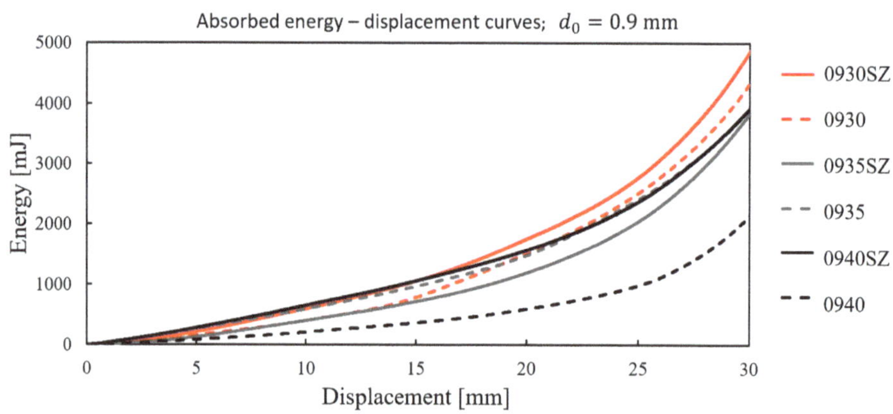

Figure 10. Absorbed energy–displacement curves for filled and unfilled, for $d_0 = 0.9$ mm.

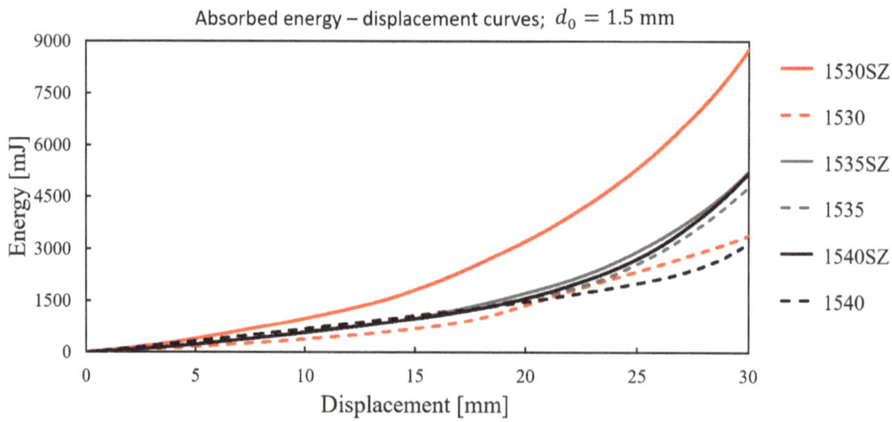

Figure 11. Absorbed energy–displacement curves for filled and unfilled, for $d_0 = 1.5$ mm.

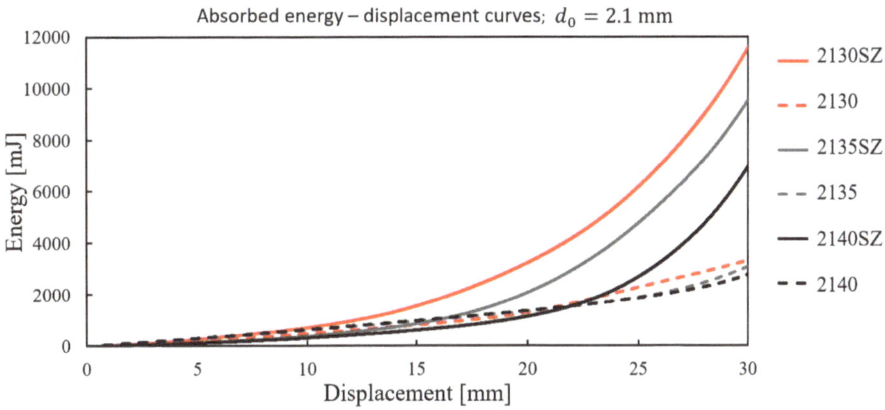

Figure 12. Absorbed energy–displacement curves for filled and unfilled, for $d_0 = 2.1$ mm.

3.3. Specific Absorbed Energy

As the filled and unfilled specimens differ in weight, for comparison of the energy absorption, the specific absorbed energy parameter [47] is introduced. Namely, dividing $\mathfrak{I}$ with the mass m of the specimen, the specific absorbed energy follows as

$$\mathfrak{I}_s = \frac{\mathfrak{I}}{m}. \tag{15}$$

The values of specific absorbed energy for all specimens are compared. The results of these calculations are presented in Figure 13.

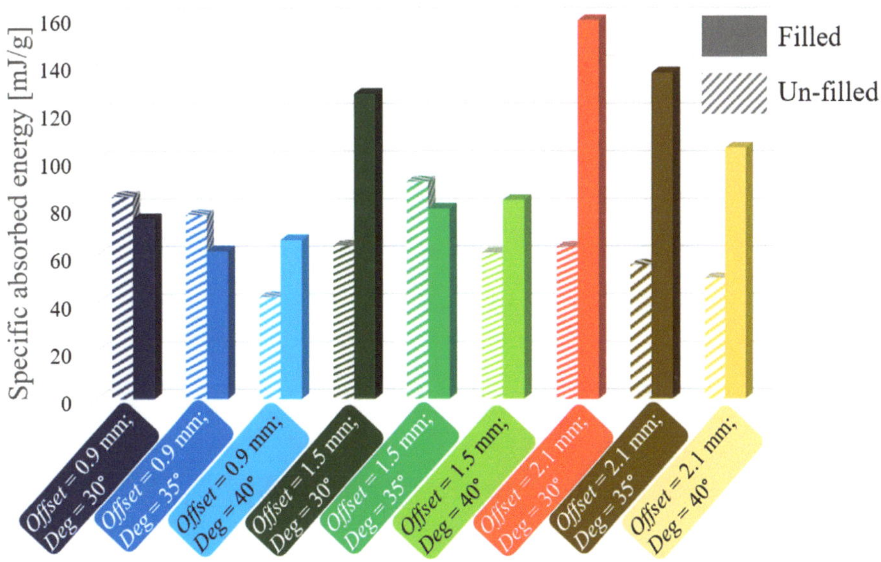

Figure 13. Specific absorbed energy values for various specimens.

It is obtained that the $\mathfrak{I}_s$ values for specimens 2130SZ, 2135SZ, 2140SZ, 1540SZ, 1530SZ and 0940SZ, which are filled with silicon, are higher compared to the corresponding 2130, 2135, 2140, 1540, 1530, and 0940 unfilled ones. However, the addition of the silicon absorbers results in a lower $\mathfrak{I}_s$ value for 0930SZ, 0935SZ, and 1535SZ than for the corresponding 0930,

0935, and 1535 unfilled ones. Overall, it can be stated that filling the specimens increased the absorbed energy amount.

The best results are obtained for specimens with *offset* values of 2.1 mm for all *deg* parameter values. For the filled 2130SZ lattice, the $\mathfrak{I}_s$ is 159 mJ/g and it is evident that the energy absorption is 2.5 times higher than in the unfilled one. In the filled sample 2135SZ, the $\mathfrak{I}_s$ value is 137 mJ/g, and is 2.4 times higher compared to the unfilled specimen. The unfilled lattice 1530 has $\mathfrak{I}_s$ of 60 mJ/g, which is half that of its silicon-filled pair.

Finally, it is seen that the geometric parameters such as the offset value and deg parameter have influence on the energy absorption. The *deg* parameter affects the specimen's energy absorption capability. The energy absorption capability increases with increasing the *deg* value: for 30 degrees, it is 1.7; for 40 degrees, it is 1.2; and for 45 degrees, it is 1.7. In addition, with increase of the *offset* value, the average absorbed energy ratio increases, too. Thus, for *offset* of 0.9, the average absorbed energy ratio is 1; for 1.5 mm, it is 1.3; and for 2.1 mm, it is 2.4.

Comparing specimens with the same *deg* parameter but with different *offset* values, the following statements can be made. The fastest increase of $\mathfrak{I}_s$ with an increase of the *offset* value is for filled specimens with initial *deg* angle of 30°. The same tendency of increase of $\mathfrak{I}_s$ with an increase of offset is observed for filled specimens with *deg* values of 35 and 40. The increase velocity of $\mathfrak{I}_s$ is greater for the smaller initial *deg* parameter specimens. These phenomena may be explained using the following theoretical consideration. Namely, according to Figure 2b, the length of the filling l_f orthogonal to compression force is approximately

$$l_f \approx hcos\varphi + d. \tag{16}$$

For constant *deg*, but higher deformation, i.e., higher offset d, the value of l_f is also higher and gives the larger absorption region of the filling. On the contrary, for the fixed offset d, the first term of the relation (16) is higher for smaller *deg* angle. Thus, the smaller is *deg* the l_f is longer, causing the absorption region and the velocity of absorption of the filling to increase.

3.4. Explanation of Energy Absorption

Compressed specimens exhibited either buckling or continuous auxetic deformation behavior. Due to loading, most of the unfilled specimens exhibit in-cell deformation. Deformation is unrestricted and no significant increase of energy absorption until compaction (around 20 mm deformation) is evident.

At the other side, at small deformations, the filled rectangular segments restrict in-cell deformation, resulting in buckling. As the deformation progresses, the absorber segments are progressively loaded and progressively increase the compressive resistance as well as the amount of the absorbed energy. Overall, the absorber segments, at first, allow great displacement at low compressive resistance, and then progressively become stiffer.

In Table 2. the experimentally observed deformation behaviors as the function of geometrical parameters i.e., *offset* and *deg* values, for filled and unfilled structures, are presented. In Table 2, it is shown that in unfilled structures 0930, 0940, 0945, and 1530, buckling occurs under influence of compression force, while the other unfilled structures, 1540, 1545, 2130, 2140, and 2145, show continuous auxetic deformation. The filled specimens 0930SZ, 0940SZ, 0945SZ, 1530SZ, 1540SZ, 1545SZ, and 2130SZ buckle during compression, while the 2140SZ and 2145SZ specimens exhibit continuous auxetic deformation.

To explain the effect of filling on deformation properties of the specimens, let us consider the two of them: 1540 and 1540SZ (Figure 14). Comparing the compression behavior of 1540 and 1540SZ, it is obvious that the unfilled sample exhibits continual auxetic deformation while the filled one exhibits buckling.

Table 2. The deformation behavior of specimens.

Deformation Behavior—In Function of Geometrical Parameters and Fill Status									
d_0 (mm)	0.9	0.9	0.9	1.5	1.5	1.5	2.1	2.1	2.1
φ_0 (°)	30	40	45	30	40	45	30	40	45
Unfilled Specimens									
Deformation behavior	Buckling	Buckling	Buckling	Buckling	Cont. aux	Cont. aux	Cont. aux	Cont. aux	Cont. aux
Filled Specimens									
Deformation behavior	Buckling	Buckling	Buckling	Buckling	Buckling	Buckling	Buckling	Cont. aux	Cont. aux

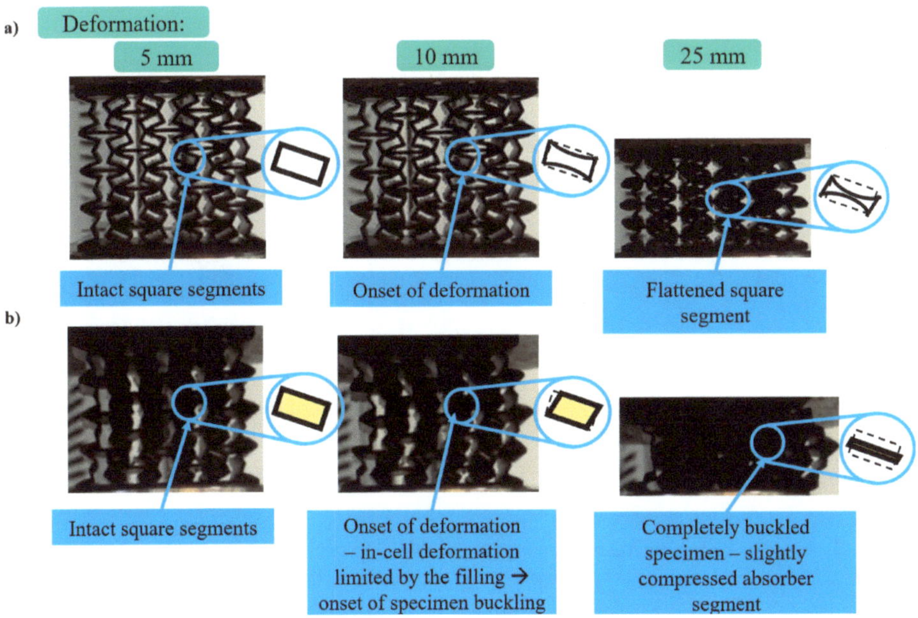

Figure 14. Comparison of deformation process of (**a**) unfilled 1540 and (**b**) filled 1540SZ samples ($d_0 = 1.5$ mm; $\varphi_0 = 40°$).

During compression, the 1540 specimen deforms—the voids are compacted and the edges come into contact with each other and basically eliminate the quadrangular segment (Figure 14a). During compression, the unfilled specimen 1540 deforms in an unrestricted manner, and no significant increase in absorbed energy for the specimen is evident.

On the other hand, in the filled sample 1540SZ (Figure 14b), the absorber segments are progressively loaded. First, the absorber shape variation occurs: The rectangle becomes a rhomboid. However, due to compressive resistance, the displacement of absorbers as rigid bodies occurs. The specimen become stiffer and, consequently, the deformation in the regions of absorbers is impossible. When the force reaches the critical value, the buckling of the specimen occurs (see Figure 14). The same result was previously proved mathematically in Section 2.

Namely, the compression force in the unfilled sample causes extensive deformation. The absorbed energy is used for the deformation of the auxetic structure according to expression (8). In the filled sample, the external energy is partly used for the motion of the units and partly applied for the deformation of structure. The rectangle units change their forms into rhomboids, and for the critical value of the force, the buckling of the beam-like structure occurs.

3.5. Statistical Indication of Significance of Deg and Offset Parameters

In this section, the main effect plots are shown for determination of the significance of parameters of structure on the force, specific force, absorbed energy, and specific absorbed energy. In Figure 15, the measured values as a function of the geometric parameters *deg* and *offset* for the displacement interval up to 30 mm are plotted.

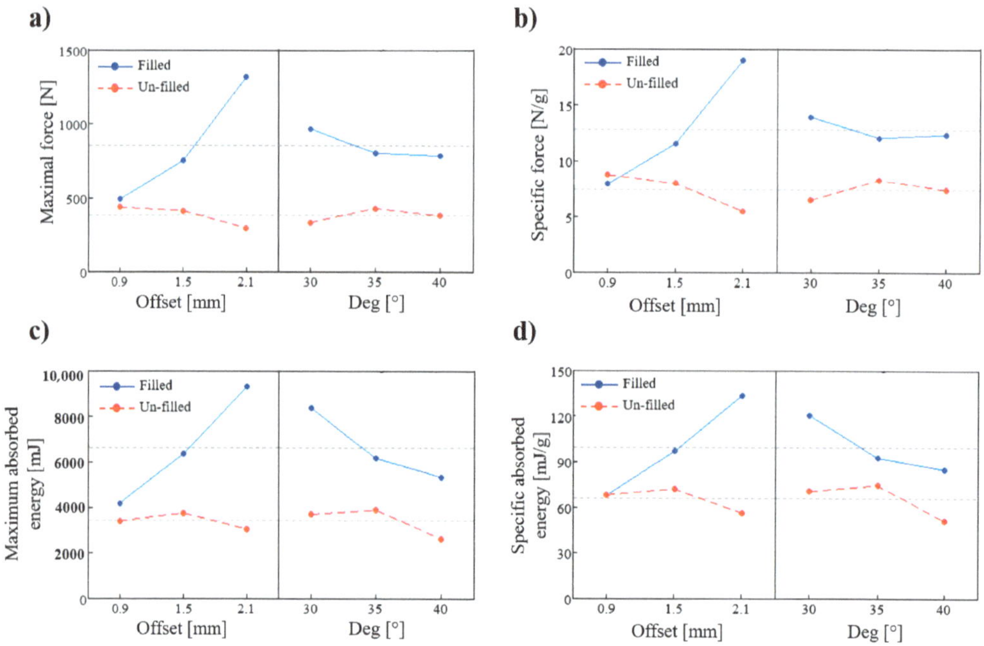

Figure 15. (**a**) Maximal force via offset and deg, (**b**) Maximal specific force via offset and deg, (**c**) Energy via offset and deg, and (**d**) Specific energy via offset and deg diagrams.

It is obtained that there is a significantly increase of compression force and specific compression force in filled structure when the *offset* parameter is increased (Figure 15a,b). The *deg* parameter has no significant effect on these properties. Filling has a similar effect on absorbed and specific absorbed energy (Figure 15c,d). Increasing the *offset* parameter leads to a large increase in absorbed and specific absorbed energy, while increasing the *deg* parameters lead to a decrease. In case of the unfilled specimens, geometric parameters have considerably less effect on the measured physical properties; they only affect the deformation behavior, i.e., the auxeticity.

Based on the aforementioned analysis, it is evident that the energy absorption capability varies significantly with changes in geometry and rigidity, indicating a need for precise control over these factors. The accuracy of controlling the geometry and rigidity of the proposed design is evaluated with the adequate printing of specimen. Namely, specimen accuracy is ensured by the applied additive manufacturing technology (MSLA) and the 3D printer itself, which has a 40-micron resolution. The mentioned print resolution gives a high accuracy in geometry and does not allow deviation. On the other hand, the base material is a unique resin mixture with constant rigidity. The control of rigidity of specimen is also connected with the printing parameters and the post-process ones.

4. Conclusions

In this paper, the novel doubly re-entrant auxetic honeycomb structure partially filled with a soft absorbed material is considered. For experimental reasons, specimens based on the novel doubly re-entrant auxetic unit cell were additively manufactured by 3D printing and filled with silicon. The specimens were tested under quasi-static compression. Based on our investigation, the following conclusions can be drawn:

1. Specimens exhibit two significantly different deformation behaviors: buckling and continuous auxetic (preferred). Filling has a negative effect on the deformation behavior: During deformation, the silicone filled voids limit the in-cell deformation (for d_0 = 0.9–1.5 mm) and this results in specimen buckling. However, for higher offset values ($d_0 = 2.1$ mm), compaction occurs more even throughout the geometry; thus, buckling will not occur even with filled structure.
2. Owing to the silicon filling, a new structure applicable for energy dissipation is obtained. The coupled combination aims to significantly improve the energy absorption capacity and to achieve a deformation-induced hardening characteristic. Compared to the unfilled control group, it was found that the filled structure demonstrates an increase in energy absorption. Silicone filled specimens can absorb up to 2.5 times more energy. The energy absorption depends on the geometry and rigidity of the structure.
3. The filled structure increases the rigidity of the specimens with the increase in the *offset* value. The absorbed energy ratio between filled and unfilled structures increases with the increase in the *offset* value. Thus, for *offset* of 0.9, the average absorbed energy ratio is 1; for 1.5 mm, it is 1.3; and for 2.1 mm, it is 2.4.
4. The *deg* parameter, used to characterize the geometrical modification, effects the specimen's energy absorption capability. The energy absorption capability decreases with a decreasing *deg* value. The ratio of energy absorption of filled to unfilled specimens varies with the angle value: for 30 degrees, it is 1.7; for 40 degrees, it is 1.2; and for 45 degrees, it is 1.7.
5. Based on the research, it is concluded that the filled specimen 2130SZ has the best energy absorption property. The complex behavioral mechanism of the 2130SZ specimen is very beneficial for impact protection. At the beginning of the impact process, the structure absorbs the energy with great deformation and slows down the displacement. After that, the impact energy is intensively absorbed. By achieving a deformation-induced hardening characteristic, the collision energy can be sufficiently absorbed. It makes the structure beneficially applicable for the protection against impact. However, certain applications may require easier compressibility and smaller energy absorption. Then, the specimens may have other properties that can be considered as optimal for that specific application.
6. Finally, the aforementioned researched filled structure is recommended to be applied in energy absorbing and damping devices in machines and mechanisms.

Author Contributions: Conceptualization, L.C.; Methodology, L.C.; Validation, L.S.; Formal analysis, R.H.; Investigation, L.S.; Writing—original draft, L.C.; Visualization, L.S.; Supervision, R.H. All authors have read and agreed to the published version of the manuscript.

Funding: This research was funded by the ÚNKP-23-3 New National Excellence Program of the Ministry for Culture and Innovation from the source of the National Research, Development and Innovation Fund.

Data Availability Statement: The original contributions presented in the study are included in the article, further inquiries can be directed to the corresponding author.

Conflicts of Interest: The authors declare no conflict of interest.

Nomenclature

A_a, A_b	[mm^2]	Cross section of absorber and of basic unit, respectively
b, t	[mm]	Thickness and width of the unit cell structure
d	[mm]	*Offset* value of the until cell
E_a, E_b	[MPa]	Modulus of elasticity of absorber and basic unit, respectively
$F(x)$	[−]	Force–displacement function
F_{cr}	[N]	Critical buckling force
F_y	[N]	Force in y direction
H, L, L_1	[mm]	Height, width, and inner width of the unit cell, respectively
h, w	[mm]	Height and width of the absorber segment, respectively
I_a, I_b	[mm^4]	Moment of inertia of the absorber and basic unit
$\mathfrak{I}$	[mJ]	Absorbed energy
$\mathfrak{I}_s$	[mJ/g]	Specific absorbed energy
l	[mm]	Total heigh of the beam-line series of absorbers
m	[g]	Mass of a specimen
M	[Nm]	Moment between unit cells
P	[N]	Virtual force
U	[J]	Total strain energy
u, v	[mm]	Displacement in x and y direction
x_{max}, y_{max}	[mm]	Maximal deflection in x and y direction
$\varepsilon_x, \varepsilon_y$	[−]	Average strain in x and y direction, respectively
ν	[−]	Effective Poisson's ratio of the unit cell
σ_x, σ_y	[MPa]	Far field stress in the x and y direction
φ	[°]	*deg* angle value of the unit cell

References

1. Jafari, M.H.A.; Zarastvand, M.R.; Zhou, J. Doubly curved truss core composite shell system for broadband diffuse acoustic insulation. *J. Vib. Control* **2023**, *2023*, 17. [CrossRef]
2. Nema, V.; Jakab, A.; Molnar, J.; Szabo, B.; Szoke-Trenyik, E.; Mihalko, J.; Szabo, B.P. Behaviour of flexible/elastic materials under quasi-static force. *Analecta Tech. Szeged.* **2023**, *17*, 9–15. [CrossRef]
3. Fleck, N.A.; Deshpande, V.S.; Ashby, M.F. Micro-architectured materials: Past, present and future. *Proc. R. Soc. A Math. Phys. Eng. Sci.* **2010**, *466*, 2495–2516. [CrossRef]
4. Barthelat, F. Architectured materials in engineering and biology: Fabrication, structure, mechanics and performance. *Int. Mater. Rev.* **2015**, *60*, 413–430. [CrossRef]
5. Yin, H.; Zhang, W.; Zhu, L.; Meng, F.; Liu, J.; Wen, G. Review on lattice structures for energy absorption properties. *Compos. Struct.* **2023**, *304*, 116397. [CrossRef]
6. Cho, H.; Seo, D.; Kim, D.N. Mechanics of auxetic materials. In *Handbook of Mechanics of Materials*; Springer: Singapore, 2019; pp. 733–757. [CrossRef]
7. Rad, M.S.; Hatami, H.; Alipouri, R.; Nejad, A.F.; Omidinasab, F. Determination of energy absorption in different cellular auxetic structures. *Mech. Ind.* **2019**, *20*, 302. [CrossRef]
8. Liu, J.; Chen, T.; Zhang, Y.; Wen, G.; Qing, Q.; Wang, H.; Sedaghati, R.; Xie, Y.M. On sound insulation of pyramidal lattice sandwich structure. *Compos. Struct.* **2019**, *208*, 385–394. [CrossRef]
9. Yin, S.; Chen, H.; Wu, Y.; Li, Y.; Xu, J. Introducing composite lattice core sandwich structure as an alternative proposal for engine hood. *Compos. Struct.* **2018**, *201*, 131–140. [CrossRef]
10. Wang, C.Y.; Li, Y.; Zhao, W.Z.; Zou, S.C.; Zhou, G.; Wang, Y.L. Structure design and multi-objective optimization of a novel crash box based on biomimetic structure. *Int. J. Mech. Sci.* **2018**, *138–139*, 489–501. [CrossRef]
11. Spadoni, A.; Ruzzene, M. Numerical and experimental analysis of the static compliance of chiral truss-core airfoils. *J. Mech. Mater. Struct.* **2007**, *2*, 965–981. [CrossRef]
12. Wu, S.; Sikdar, P.; Bhat, G.S. Recent progress in developing ballistic and anti-impact materials: Nanotechnology and main approaches. *J. Mod. Def. Technol.* **2023**, *21*, 33–61. [CrossRef]
13. Foster, L.; Peketi, P.; Allen, T.; Senior, T.; Duncan, O.; Alderson, A. Application of auxetic foam in sports helmets. *Appl. Sci.* **2018**, *8*, 354. [CrossRef]
14. Reddy, A.H.; Davuluri, S.; Boyina, D. 3D Printed Lattice Structures: A Brief Review. In Proceedings of the 2020 IEEE 10th International Conference Nanomaterials: Applications & Properties (NAP), Sumy, Ukraine, 9–13 November 2020; pp. 02SAMA10-1–02SAMA10-5. [CrossRef]
15. Chahar, A.S.; Pal, P. Study on various properties of reinforced concrete—A review. *Mater. Today Proc.* **2022**, *65*, 597–602. [CrossRef]

16. Yang, Z.-M.; Chen, J.; Wang, F.; Wang, J. Seismic performance of circular concrete-filled steel tube columns reinforced with inner latticed steel angles. *J. Constr. Steel Res.* **2023**, *205*, 107908. [CrossRef]
17. Liu, Y.-S.; Zhou, X.-H.; Wang, Y.-H.; Zhou, Y.; Lan, Y.-S.; Li, Q. Seismic behavior of prestressed concrete filled steel tubular lattice tower subjected to combined compression-bending-torsion. *J. Constr. Steel Res.* **2023**, *204*, 107883. [CrossRef]
18. Yang, L.; Fang, H.; Xie, H.; Li, B. Compressive behaviour of concrete-filled multi-cell GFRP pultruded square columns reinforced with lattice-webs. *Eng. Struct.* **2023**, *279*, 115584. [CrossRef]
19. Parandoush, P.; Lin, D. A review on additive manufacturing of polymer-fiber composites. *Compos. Struct.* **2017**, *182*, 36–53. [CrossRef]
20. Blok, L.G.; Longana, M.L.; Yu, H.; Woods, B.K.S. An investigation into 3D printing of fibre reinforced thermoplastic composites. *Addit. Manuf.* **2018**, *22*, 176–186. [CrossRef]
21. Yavas, D.; Liu, Q.; Zhang, Z.; Wu, D. Design and fabrication of architected multi-material lattices with tunable stiffness, strength, and energy absorption. *Mater. Des.* **2022**, *217*, 110613. [CrossRef]
22. Li, S.; Yang, J.S.; Schmidt, R.; Wu, L.Z.; Schröder, K.U. Compression and hysteresis responses of multilayer gradient composite lattice sandwich panels. *Mar. Struct.* **2021**, *75*, 102845. [CrossRef]
23. Ramirez, B.J.; Misra, U.; Gupta, V. Viscoelastic foam-filled lattice for high energy absorption. *Mech. Mater.* **2018**, *127*, 39–47. [CrossRef]
24. Taghipoor, H.; Eyvazian, A.; Musharavati, F.; Sebaey, T.A.; Ghiaskar, A. Experimental investigation of the three-point bending properties of sandwich beams with polyurethane foam-filled lattice cores. *Structures* **2020**, *28*, 424–432. [CrossRef]
25. Zhang, G.; Wang, B.; Ma, L.; Wu, L.; Pan, S.; Yang, J. Energy absorption and low velocity impact response of polyurethane foam filled pyramidal lattice core sandwich panels. *Compos. Struct.* **2014**, *108*, 304–310. [CrossRef]
26. Tomlinson, D.; Fam, A. Axial response of flax fibre reinforced polymer-skinned tubes with lightweight foam cores and bioresin blend. *Thin-Walled Struct.* **2020**, *155*, 106923. [CrossRef]
27. Wang, L.; Liu, W.; Fang, Y.; Wan, L.; Huo, R. Axial crush behavior and energy absorption capability of foam-filled GFRP tubes manufactured through vacuum assisted resin infusion process. *Thin-Walled Struct.* **2016**, *98*, 263–273. [CrossRef]
28. Gao, G.; Hu, Y.; Jia, H.; Liu, P.; Du, P.; Xu, D. Acoustic and dielectric properties of epoxy resin/hollow glass microsphere composite acoustic materials. *J. Phys. Chem. Solids* **2019**, *135*, 109105. [CrossRef]
29. Baroutaji, A.; Sajjia, M.; Olabi, A.G. On the crashworthiness performance of thin-walled energy absorbers: Recent advances and future developments. *Thin-Walled Struct.* **2017**, *118*, 137–163. [CrossRef]
30. Hussein, R.D.; Ruan, D.; Lu, G.; Sbarski, I. Axial crushing behaviour of honeycomb-filled square carbon fibre reinforced plastic (CFRP) tubes. *Compos. Struct.* **2016**, *140*, 166–179. [CrossRef]
31. Black, S.; Tzagiollari, A.; Mondal, S.; Dunne, N.; MacManus, D.B. Mechanical behaviour of gel-filled additively-manufactured lattice structures under quasi-static compressive loading. *Mater. Today Commun.* **2023**, *35*, 106164. [CrossRef]
32. Prajapati, M.J.; Kumar, A.; Lin, S.-C.; Jeng, J.-Y. Multi-material additive manufacturing with lightweight closed-cell foam-filled lattice structures for enhanced mechanical and functional properties. *Addit. Manuf.* **2022**, *54*, 102766. [CrossRef]
33. Prajapati, M.J.; Kumar, A.; Lin, S.-C.; Jeng, J.-Y. Reducing mechanical anisotropy in material extrusion process using bioinspired architectured lattice structures. *Addit. Manuf.* **2023**, *66*, 103480. [CrossRef]
34. Chapkin, W.A.; Simone, D.L.; Frank, G.J.; Baur, J.W. Mechanical behavior and energy dissipation of infilled, composite Ti-6Al-4V trusses. *Mater. Des.* **2021**, *203*, 109602. [CrossRef]
35. Bandyopadhyay, A.; Heer, B. Additive manufacturing of multi-material structures. *Mater. Sci. Eng. R Rep.* **2018**, *129*, 1–16. [CrossRef]
36. Lumpe, T.S.; Mueller, J.; Shea, K. Tensile properties of multi-material interfaces in 3D printed parts. *Mater. Des.* **2019**, *162*, 1–9. [CrossRef]
37. Cveticanin, L.; Zukovic, M. Negative effective mass in acoustic metamaterial with nonlinear mass-in-mass subsystems. *Commun. Nonlinear Sci. Numer. Simul.* **2017**, *51*, 89–104. [CrossRef]
38. Cveticanin, L.; Zukovic, M.; Cveticanin, D. Influence of nonlinear subunits on the resonance frequency band gaps of acoustic metamaterial. *Nonlinear Dyn.* **2018**, *93*, 1341–1354. [CrossRef]
39. Cveticanin, L.; Zukovic, M.; Cveticanin, D. On the elastic metamaterial with negative effective mass. *J. Sound Vib.* **2018**, *436*, 295–309. [CrossRef]
40. Cveticanin, L.; Zukovic, M.; Ninkov, I.; Mester, G. Nonlinear lightweight metastructure with effective negative stiffness. *Acta Mech.* **2022**, *233*, 4311–4325. [CrossRef]
41. Chan, Y.-C.; Shintani, K.; Chen, W. Robust topology optimization of multi-material lattice structures under material and load uncertainties. *Front. Mech. Eng.* **2019**, *14*, 141–152. [CrossRef]
42. Stanković, T.; Mueller, J.; Egan, P.; Shea, K. A generalized optimality criteria method for optimization of additively manufactured multimaterial lattice structures. *J. Mech. Des.* **2015**, *137*, 111405. [CrossRef]
43. Liu, Y.; Hu, H. A review on auxetic structures and polymeric materials. *Sci. Res. Essays* **2010**, *5*, 1052–1063.
44. Ren, X.; Das, R.; Tran, P.; Ngo, T.D.; Xie, Y.M. Auxetic metamaterials and structures: A review. *Smart Mater. Struct.* **2018**, *27*, 023001. [CrossRef]
45. Meena, K.; Singamneni, S. A new auxetic structure with significantly reduced stress concentration effects. *Mater. Des.* **2019**, *173*, 107779. [CrossRef]

46. Zhu, Y.; Luo, Y.; Gao, D.; Yu, C.; Ren, X.; Zhang, C. In-plane elastic properties of a novel re-entrant auxetic honeycomb with zigzag inclined ligaments. *Eng. Struct.* **2022**, *268*, 114788. [CrossRef]
47. *ISO 527-2:2012*; Determination of Tensile Properties—Part 2: Test Conditions for Moulding and Extrusion Plastics. International Organization for Standardization: Geneva, Switzerland, 2012. Available online: https://dl2phipa8wx75.cloudfront.net/danalim/produktinformation/uk/512.pdf (accessed on 1 January 2022).

mathematics

Article

Numerical Simulation of Shock Wave in Gas–Water Interaction Based on Nonlinear Shock Wave Velocity Curve

Zongduo Wu [1,†], Dapeng Zhang [1,*], Jin Yan [1,2], Jianhua Pang [3] and Yifang Sun [1]

1 Naval Architecture and Shipping College, Guangdong Ocean University, Zhanjiang 524091, China
2 Guangdong Provincial Key Laboratory of Intelligent Equipment for South China Sea Marine Ranching, Guangdong Ocean University, Zhanjiang 524091, China
3 Ocean Intelligence Technology Center, Shenzhen Institute of Guangdong Ocean University, Shenzhen 518055, China
* Correspondence: zhangdapeng@gdou.edu.cn; Tel.: +86-0759-2383007
† Current address: No. 5, Middle Haibin Road, Zhangjiang 524091, China.

Abstract: In a gas–water interaction problem, the nonlinear relationship between shock wave velocity is introduced into a Hugoniot curve, and a Mie–Grüneisen Equation of state (EOS) is established by setting the Hugoiot curve as the reference state. Unlike other simple EOS based on the thermodynamics laws of gas (such as the Tait EOS), the Mie–Grüneisen EOS uses reference states to cover an adiabatic impact relationship and considers the thermodynamics law separately. However, the expression of the EOS becomes complex, and it is not adaptive to many methods. A multicomponent Mie–Grüneisen mixture model is employed in this study to conquer the difficulty of the complex form of an EOS. In this model, some coefficients in the Mie–Grüneisen EOS are regarded as variables and solved using newly constructed equations. The performance of the Mie–Grüneisen mixture model in the gas–water problem is tested by low-compression cases and high-compression cases. According to these two tests, it is found that the numerical solutions of the shock wave under the Mie–Grüneisen EOS agrees with empirical data. When compared to other simple-form EOSs, it is seen that the Mie–Grüneisen EOS has slight advantages in the low-compression case, but it plays an important role in the high-compression case. The comparison results show that the solution of the simple-form EOS clearly disagrees with the empirical data. A further study shows that the gap between the Mie–Grüneisen EOS and other simple-form EOSs becomes larger as the initial pressure and particle velocity increase. The impact effects on the pressure, density and particle velocity are studied. Moreover, the gas–water interaction in a spherical coordinate plane and a two-dimensional coordinate is a significant part of our work.

Keywords: gas–water flow; shock wave; Riemann problem; Mie–Grüneisen mixture model; equation of state (EOS)

MSC: 37M10

Citation: Wu, Z.; Zhang, D.; Yan, J.; Pang, J.; Sun, Y. Numerical Simulation of Shock Wave in Gas–Water Interaction Based on Nonlinear Shock Wave Velocity Curve. *Mathematics* **2024**, *12*, 3268. https://doi.org/10.3390/math12203268

Academic Editors: Joaquim Infante Barbosa and José Alberto Rodrigues

Received: 31 August 2024
Revised: 7 October 2024
Accepted: 8 October 2024
Published: 18 October 2024

1. Introduction

The behavior of shock wave in gas–water flow is an interest of researchers of many fields, such as underwater explosion [1], bubble motion [2], liquid jets, cavitation [3], etc. As the shock wave occurs via an interaction of compressible flow [4], the process of this interaction is always studied using an Euler system. This gas–water problem becomes a so-called "Riemann problem" [5] due to its discontinuous solution. In calculating Riemann problems, the accuracy of the shock wave depends on the numerical method and the equation of state (EOS) [6]. The EOS plays an irreplaceable role in determining the property of materials in an Euler system.

For a gas–water Riemann problem, an ideal gas EOS, which is widely used in the modeling of various gaseous substances, is employed here. Otherwise, there are a number of different forms of EOSs for water. In the early stage, the EOS of water is expressed in a simple form. Tait EOS [7] is such a typical EOS with brief expression. It has a similar form as an ideal gas EOS and brings convenience to numerical calculation. Another popular EOS for water is stiffened gas EOS [8], which is also written in a simple function. This EOS can be easily coupled with many numerical methods in gas–water interaction, even in recent works [9–13]. The simple forms of an EOS are preferred by researchers because it is much easier to establish Riemann solvers with such an EOS. Nevertheless, some material properties are always ignored by these simple-form EOSs. A modified EOS, named the NASG (Noble Abel Stiffened Gas) EOS [14], is derived from a traditional stiffened gas EOS. The NASG EOS takes temperature into account and is used to describe the thermodynamic properties of water in a specific temperature range. The shock wave problem is based on a set of conservative laws about shock wave parameters [6], wherein the temperature is not a necessary parameter. These conservative laws in terms of shock wave parameters are called the "Hugoniot relationship" [15]. But this relationship is not taken seriously by many EOSs, such as stiffened gas EOS. In addition, the Hugoniot relationship needs to couple with another relationship between shock wave velocity and post-shock particle velocity, whereby the relationship between the two velocities is obtained with experiments. Several decades ago, the LASL (Los Alamos Scientific Laboratory) [16] accumulated a large amount of experimental data under impact and provided particular curves showing the the relationship between shock wave velocity and post-shock particle velocity. This relationship of shock wave and particle velocities is taken as a linear relationship by Miller [17] and introduced into the Mie–Grüneisen EOS. The Mie–Grüneisen EOS can set different reference states to adapt to different material properties [18], and is regarded as a type of general-form EOS, especially for solid and liquid materials. For the Mie–Grüneisen EOS based on the Hugoniot curves, Kerley [19] discussed the validity of the linearity. In this discussion, it is concluded that the expression of the Mie–Grüneisen EOS can be used in a wide variety of materials but it is not absolutely correct.

Water is a common medium, and many researchers study its behavior under impact. Nakayama [20] carried out a shock wave experiment with the help of a gas gun. In this experiment, a series of shock waves parameters are recorded, and the shock wave velocity is defined as a linear function of post-shock particle velocity. However, the ultimate pressure in this experiment is only a little more than 1 Gpa, the effectivity of this linear function under higher pressure is still unknown. LLNL (Lawrence Livermore National Laboratory) [21] provides another representative relationship between shock waves and post-shock particle velocities. This relationship is based on a detonation experiment in water, and a new EOS of water is deduced with the help of this relationship. The LLNL relationship of shock waves and post-shock particle velocities is written in a nonlinear form. However, when it is introduced into the Mie–Grüneisen EOS, the EOS becomes so complex that it is replaced by the stiffened gas EOS [22], even in the latest literature [23]. On the other hand, the EOS for gas also needs to be seriously considered in terms of its applications [24].

In the numerical calculation of the gas–water Riemann problem, it is very complicated to establish a non-oscillation solver for the Mie–Grüneisen EOS due to its complex expression of reference states. As the interface is located between the gas and water, its discontinuity property makes it difficult for researchers to provide an analytic solution for the gas and water [25]. Under this situation, the Mie–Grüneisen mixture model [18] is adaptive. It is considered a whole mixture, and the relative parameters for each phase are considered as a particular parameter of mixture. In the fluid mixture, the interface is identified by a color function, and other parameters are converted to a weighted sum of each fluid component [26]. Comparing with the popular five-equation model by Allaire [27], it is not necessary to consider both the mass fraction and volume fraction in the calculation. Unlike Saurel and Abgrall's multiphase model [28], the conservative laws for each phase do not need to be considered separately. Moreover, it can be well coupled with numerical techniques such as interface tracking [29], grid mapping [30] or some other limiters [31]. In the previous works, the Mie–Grüneisen mixture model is rarely applied in the study of shock waves. Many research works about shock waves are carried out with the help of commercial software. In this case, a supplement of numerical study becomes very significant. Moreover, the Mie–Grüneisen mixture model can help us to further investigate the performance of different EOSs.

This study seeks an efficient and effective way to simulate the gas-water shock wave problem. When water suffers from outside impact, the dynamic property can be expressed by a nonlinear relationship between the shock wave and particle velocities. Based on the nonlinear relationship, a complex but significant Mie–Grüneisen EOS is derived and used in the numerical calculation of the shock wave problem. The Mie–Grüneisen mixture model is employed here to adapt to such a gas-water two-phase problem. The numerical results are compared with other simple-form EOSs and the effect of the Mie–Grüneisen EOS is given special attention. Afterwards, the performance differences between the Mie–Grüneisen EOS and other EOSs are investigated further. Moreover, the Mie–Grüneisen physical model and numerical model are extended to spherical coordinates, as well as to the 2D problem. During this procedure, the accuracy of calculation is also seriously considered.

2. Basic Theory

2.1. Reference State in Shock Wave Problems

For shock wave problems, it is found in impact experiments that many materials share an approximate relationship between particle velocity u_m and shock wave velocity D [6,8,17,19]:

$$D = c_0 + s u_m \tag{1}$$

where c_0 is the speed of sound and s is a coefficient related to the isentropic bulk modules. For a wide range of materials, the linear relation (1) is enough, and the high-order items can be neglected [32]. Certainly, the linear $D - u_m$ relationship is also available for water. However, the linear relationship is not absolutely right, and sometimes, it needs more consideration [19]. To adapt to a strong shock problem (shock pressure more than 10^9 Pa), the relationship of water is described by a nonlinear $D - u_m$ curve given by the Lawrence Livermore National Laboratory (LLNL) [21]:

$$\frac{D - c_0}{u_m} = s_1\left(\frac{u_m}{D}\right) + s_2\left(\frac{u_m}{D}\right)^2 + s_3\left(\frac{u_m}{D}\right)^3 \tag{2}$$

where s_1, s_2 and s_3 are constant coefficients, which are deduced from experimental data. c_0 is the sound speed of static water. The values of s_1, s_2, s_3 and c_0 are given in Table 1. And the Rankine–Hugoniot jump conditions for the conservation of mass, momentum and energy are [17]

$$\begin{cases} \rho = \rho_0 D/(D - u_m) \\ p = p_0 + \rho_0 D u_m \\ e = e_0 + \dfrac{1}{2}(p + p_0)\left(\dfrac{1}{\rho_0} - \dfrac{1}{\rho}\right) \end{cases} \tag{3}$$

where p and e are the pressure and internal energy, respectively. And p_0 and e_0 stand for parameters of initial states. Sometimes, p_0 and e_0 are neglected in strong shock problems. By combining (2) and (3), the Hugoniot state for pressure and energy can be obtained as follows:

$$\begin{cases} p = \dfrac{\rho_0 c_0^2 \mu(1+\mu)}{[1 - (s_1 - 1)\mu - s_2\frac{\mu^2}{\mu+1} - s_3\frac{\mu^3}{(\mu+1)^2}]^2} = p_{ref} \\ e = \dfrac{c_0^2 \mu^2/2}{[1 - (s_1 - 1)\mu - s_2\frac{\mu^2}{\mu+1} - s_3\frac{\mu^3}{(\mu+1)^2}]^2} = e_{ref} \end{cases} \tag{4}$$

where $\mu = \rho/\rho_0 - 1$; p_{ref} and e_{ref} are the pressure and energy of the reference state, and the compression states are defined as points along the Hugoniot curve (as shown in Figure 1 [17]). However, for expansion states, it is hard to describe the reference state by Hugoniot curves due to the negative u_m in the following deduction:

$$\mu = \frac{\rho}{\rho_0} - 1 = \frac{D}{D - u_m} - 1 = \frac{u_m}{D - u_m} < 0$$

since the shock wave travels faster than the interface, so $D - u_m > 0$. As u_m is also a positive value, a conclusion $\mu > 0$ is deduced for the expansion state and this is not real. Therefore, the reference state as (4) is not valid in the expansion phase.

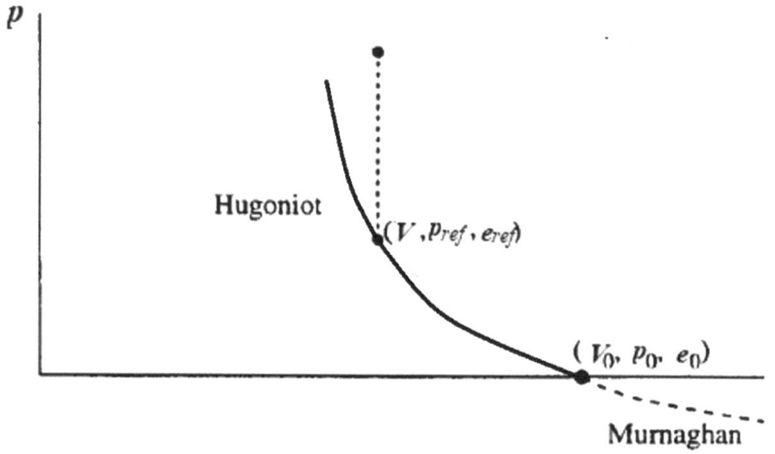

Figure 1. Hugoniot curves. Here, it is taken as the reference state for water.

For the expansion state $\mu < 0$, a Murnaghan isentropic EOS is used here. The compression and expansion states coexist in the same material but exhibit different physical behaviors:

$$\begin{cases} p_{ref} = \left(p_0 + \dfrac{\rho_0 c_0^2}{4s-1}\right)\left(\dfrac{\rho}{\rho_0}\right)^{4s-1} - \dfrac{\rho_0 c_0^2}{4s-1} \\ e_{ref} = e_0 + \displaystyle\int_{V_0}^{V} p_{ref} dV \end{cases} \tag{5}$$

where V denotes volume, and $V = 1/\rho$ [5]. The p_{ref} in (5) is always simplified in a first order of accuracy:

$$\begin{aligned} p_{ref} =& \left(p_0 + \frac{\rho_0 c_0^2}{4s-1}\right)(\mu+1)^{4s-1} - \frac{\rho_0 c_0^2}{4s-1} \\ =& \left(p_0 + \frac{\rho_0 c_0^2}{4s-1}\right)(1 + (4s-1)\mu + o(\mu)) - \frac{\rho_0 c_0^2}{4s-1} \\ =& \rho_0 c_0^2 \mu \end{aligned} \tag{6}$$

Except for cavitation flow, the expansion effect is very weak for liquid water and the variation in volume V can be neglected in the expansion phase, so it is approximately $V = V_0$ and the item $\int p_{ref} dV$ in (5) can be ignored. Thus, there are

$$e_{ref} = e_0 + \int_{V_0}^{V} p_{ref} dV = e_0 \tag{7}$$

Table 1. Parameters of the EOS for water.

C_0	S_1	S_2	S_3	γ_0	α	ρ_0
1480 m/s	2.56	−1.986	0.227	0.5	0	1000 kg/m^3

2.2. *Equation of State*

In the shock wave problem, the fluids are taken as compressible, and the conservative Euler equation is used to be the basic governing equation:

$$\frac{\partial U}{\partial t} + \frac{\partial F}{\partial x} = 0 \tag{8}$$

where U is a vector of conservative variables, and F represents the fluxes. They can be written as

$$U = \begin{bmatrix} \rho \\ \rho u \\ \rho E \end{bmatrix}, F = \begin{bmatrix} \rho u \\ \rho u^2 + p \\ (\rho E + p)u \end{bmatrix}$$

where E is the total energy and can be deduced by internal energy e and the kinetic energy:

$$E = e + \frac{1}{2}u^2$$

To complete the equation system, an EOS is needed here. For the shock wave problem, the EOS for water and gas must be seriously considered.

As the reference state is known, the EOS can be expressed in a general form:

$$p - p_{ref}(V) = \Gamma(V)(\rho e - \rho e_{ref}(V)) \tag{9}$$

where $V = 1/\rho$. Equation (9) is the Mie–Grüneisen EOS, and Γ is the Grüneisen parameter, which can be simply written as

$$\Gamma = \Gamma_0 \left(\frac{\rho}{\rho_0}\right)^{\alpha} \tag{10}$$

where Γ_0 and α depend on the property of the material. The reference state plays an important role in many physical problems. With the help of e_{ref}, the internal energy of a solid can be considered in two parts: one is a thermal vibrational energy, and another is a potential energy of cold contribution [33]:

$$e(V,T) = e_T(V,T) + e_{ref}(V) \tag{11}$$

the former part of internal energy $e(V,T)$ is in terms of temperature, which has little relationship with the Hugoniot curve. The latter part is defined as the reference state. By setting p_{ref} and e_{ref}, the proportional relationship between thermal pressure p_T and thermal internal energy e_T can be expressed more intuitively. In this case, the pressure can be expressed as

$$\begin{aligned} p(V,T) &= p_{ref}(V) + p_T(V,T) \\ p_T(V,T) &= \frac{\Gamma(V)}{V} e_T(V,T) \end{aligned} \tag{12}$$

Equations (11) and (12) are based on the thermodynamic behavior of crystals. Unlike the Mie–Grüneisen EOS, some other EOSs are derived from the thermodynamics law of gas and do not cover the cold contribution. The reference states provide a convenient way to take care of physical behavior that is not affected by thermodynamics.

Sometimes, the reference states are replaced by other conditions. For example, as an isentropic condition is considered, the internal energy can be written as [34]

$$e(V,S) = e_{ref}(V) + e_S(S) \tag{13}$$

where S is the specific entropy, and Equation (13) can also be used in a water-like substance. In this situation, the pressure p and temperature T satisfy

$$p(V,S) = \frac{\partial e}{\partial V}, T(S) = \frac{\partial e(V,S)}{\partial S} \tag{14}$$

and the derivates of S can be neglected under the constant entropy assumption. Therefore, p can be expressed in a function of ρ:

$$p = B\left[\left(\frac{\rho}{\bar{\rho}}\right)^{\gamma} - 1\right] \tag{15}$$

in which the coefficients for water are as follows: $\gamma = 7$, $B = 3268$ atm, and $\bar{\rho}$ is a constant whose value is 9.233×10^{-4} atm per ft/sec. Equation (15) is the Tait EOS. It can be also regarded as a Mie–Grüneisen EOS form with a constant reference state.

Inserting the reference expressions (4), (11) and (12) into (9), the EOS for water can be written in a piecewise function of p and ρe:

$$\begin{cases} p = \dfrac{\rho_0 c_0^2\left[\mu + (1 - \frac{1}{2}\gamma_0 - \frac{1}{2}a\mu)\mu^2)\right]}{[1 - (s_1 - 1)\mu - s_2\frac{\mu^2}{\mu+1} - s_3\frac{\mu^3}{(\mu+1)^2}]^2} + (\gamma_0 + a\mu)\rho e & \mu \geqslant 0 \\ p = \rho_0 c_0^2 \mu + (\gamma_0 + a\mu)\rho e & \mu < 0 \end{cases} \tag{16}$$

The EOS for gas is usually derived from the characteristics of ideal gas, which can be written as

$$p = (\gamma - 1)\rho e \tag{17}$$

where the parameter γ is 1.4 for common gas. For special explosive gaseous products with high pressure and temperature, the γ is 3.0 more or less [35].

Moreover, there is another form of EOS, named "stiffened gas EOS". It is derived from a similar behavior of ideal gas [36]:

$$p = (\gamma - 1)\rho e - \gamma p_\infty \tag{18}$$

in which the parameter p_∞ is calculated by the sound velocity c_0:

$$p_\infty = \frac{\rho_0 c_0^2}{\gamma} - p_0 \tag{19}$$

For water, $\gamma = 4.4$, $p_\infty = 6 \times 10^8$. The density ρ of (18) yields the following ratio:

$$\frac{\rho}{\rho_0} = \frac{(\gamma+1)(p + p_\infty) + (\gamma - 1)(p_0 + p_\infty)}{(\gamma+1)(p_0 + p_\infty) + (\gamma - 1)(p + p_\infty)} \tag{20}$$

Although written in a simple form, the determinations of γ and p_∞ are also based on Hugoniot curves. But the relationship $D - u_m$ of the stiffened gas EOS is in a different form (1):

$$D = \sqrt{c_0^2 + \left(\frac{\gamma+1}{4}u_m\right)^2} + \frac{\gamma+1}{4}u_m \tag{21}$$

2.3. Mie–Grüneisen Mixture Model

For such a gas–water problem with the Mie–Grüneisen EOS, a quasi-conservative model, which was proposed by Shyue [18], is employed here. This model is established with respect to the structure of the solution, which includes three characteristics: left wave, right wave and interface.

At the interface position, the structure of the solution shows that density, energy and other material-dependent coefficients are discontinuous across the interface. However, the pressure and particle velocity of each component remain continuous at the interface [8,37], as shown in Figure 2. Otherwise, entropy would be created as soon as the pressures or velocities are different for gas and water [38]. Here, we consider the energy conservative law of (8):

$$\frac{\partial \rho E}{\partial t}+\frac{\partial(\rho E u+pu)}{\partial x}=0 \tag{22}$$

Then, the EOS (9) can be introduced into (22):

$$\frac{\partial}{\partial t}\Big(\frac{p-p_{ref}}{\Gamma}+\rho e_{ref}\Big)+u\frac{\partial}{\partial x}\Big(\frac{p-p_{ref}}{\Gamma}+\rho e_{ref}\Big)=0$$

and we have

$$\Big[\frac{\partial}{\partial t}\Big(\frac{1}{\Gamma}\Big)+u\frac{\partial}{\partial x}\Big(\frac{1}{\Gamma}\Big)\Big]p+\Big[\frac{\partial}{\partial t}\Big(\frac{p_{ref}}{\Gamma}\Big)+u\frac{\partial}{\partial x}\Big(\frac{p_{ref}}{\Gamma}\Big)\Big]-\Big[\frac{\partial}{\partial t}\big(\rho e_{ref}\big)+u\frac{\partial}{\partial x}\big(\rho e_{ref}\big)\Big]=0 \tag{23}$$

Equation (23) is reconstructed using $\partial/\partial\rho$:

$$\Big[\frac{\partial\rho}{\partial t}+u\frac{\partial\rho}{\partial x}\Big]p\Big(\frac{1}{\Gamma}\Big)'+\Big[\frac{\partial\rho}{\partial t}+u\frac{\partial\rho}{\partial x}\Big]\Big(\frac{p_{ref}}{\Gamma}\Big)'-\Big[\frac{\partial\rho}{\partial t}+u\frac{\partial\rho}{\partial x}\Big]\big(\rho e_{ref}\big)'=0 \tag{24}$$

Equation (24) is satisfied under two conditions:

$$\frac{\partial\rho}{\partial t}+u\frac{\partial\rho}{\partial x}=0 \quad \text{or} \quad p\Big(\frac{1}{\Gamma}\Big)'+\Big(\frac{p_{ref}}{\Gamma}\Big)'-\big(\rho e_{ref}\big)'=0$$

The latter equation above is difficult to satisfy for general problems. It is thus clear that

$$\frac{\partial\rho}{\partial t}+u\frac{\partial\rho}{\partial x}=0 \tag{25}$$

Here, Equation (25) means that the discontinuous sections move with constant speed u at the interface. According to (25), Equation (23) can be split into three parts:

$$\begin{cases} \frac{\partial}{\partial t}\Big(\frac{1}{\Gamma}\Big)+u\frac{\partial}{\partial x}\Big(\frac{1}{\Gamma}\Big)=0 \\ \frac{\partial}{\partial t}\Big(\frac{p_{ref}}{\Gamma}\Big)+u\frac{\partial}{\partial x}\Big(\frac{p_{ref}}{\Gamma}\Big)=0 \\ \frac{\partial}{\partial t}\big(\rho e_{ref}\big)+u\frac{\partial}{\partial x}\big(\rho e_{ref}\big)=0 \end{cases} \tag{26}$$

Note that the deduction of (25) above is available only at the interface, and the relationship with the left or right wave still needs to be considered.

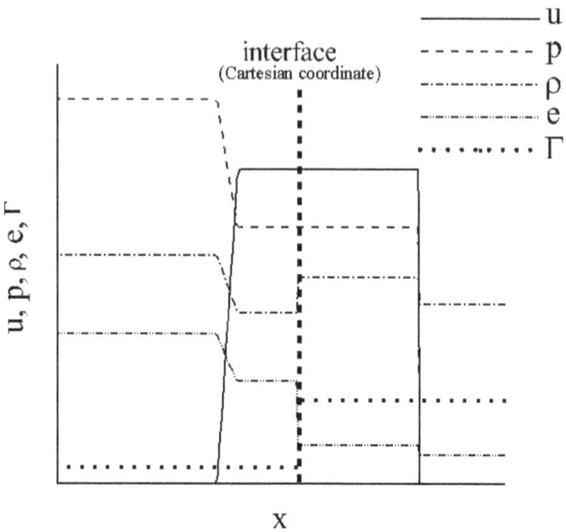

Figure 2. Discontinuous property in Cartesian coordinates. The pressure and velocity maintain equilibrium at the interface, while density and density-dependent parameters are discontinuous.

Meanwhile, at the left/right wave, the pressure and velocity are discontinuous, which means that there is no (25). Note that the left/right wave is separated from the interface and the wave is composed of a single form of fluid, as shown in Figure 3 (a total of five kinds of solutions). In Figure 3, the rarefaction wave corresponds to a weak discontinuity [39]. Thus, the following deduction can be made for $1/\Gamma$:

$$\begin{aligned}
\frac{\partial}{\partial t}\left(\frac{1}{\Gamma}\right)+u\frac{\partial}{\partial x}\left(\frac{1}{\Gamma}\right) &= \frac{\partial\rho}{\partial t}\frac{\partial}{\partial\rho}\left(\frac{1}{\Gamma}\right)+u\frac{\partial\rho}{\partial x}\frac{\partial}{\partial\rho}\left(\frac{1}{\Gamma}\right)\\
&= \frac{\partial\rho}{\partial t}\left(\frac{1}{\Gamma}\right)'+u\frac{\partial\rho}{\partial x}\left(\frac{1}{\Gamma}\right)'\\
&= \left(\frac{1}{\Gamma}\right)'\left(\frac{\partial\rho}{\partial t}+u\frac{\partial\rho}{\partial x}\right)\\
&= \left(\frac{1}{\Gamma}\right)'\left(\frac{\partial\rho}{\partial t}+u\frac{\partial\rho}{\partial x}+\rho\frac{\partial u}{\partial x}-\rho\frac{\partial u}{\partial x}\right)\\
&= \left(\frac{1}{\Gamma}\right)'\left(\frac{\partial\rho}{\partial t}+\frac{\partial(\rho u)}{\partial x}-\rho\frac{\partial u}{\partial x}\right)=-\left(\frac{1}{\Gamma}\right)'\rho\frac{\partial u}{\partial x}
\end{aligned}$$

Thus,

$$\frac{\partial}{\partial t}\left(\frac{1}{\Gamma}\right)+u\frac{\partial}{\partial x}\left(\frac{1}{\Gamma}\right)+\rho\frac{\partial u}{\partial x}\left(\frac{1}{\Gamma}\right)'=0 \tag{27}$$

as in (27)

$$\begin{aligned}
\frac{\partial}{\partial t}\left(\frac{p_{ref}}{\Gamma}\right)+u\frac{\partial}{\partial x}\left(\frac{p_{ref}}{\Gamma}\right)+\left(\frac{p_{ref}}{\Gamma}\right)'\rho\frac{\partial u}{\partial x}=0\\
\frac{\partial}{\partial t}\left(\rho e_{ref}\right)+u\frac{\partial}{\partial x}\left(\rho e_{ref}\right)+\left(\rho e_{ref}\right)'\rho\frac{\partial u}{\partial x}=0
\end{aligned} \tag{28}$$

Compared with Equation (26), Equations (27) and (28) are satisfied at the interface due to the constant u.

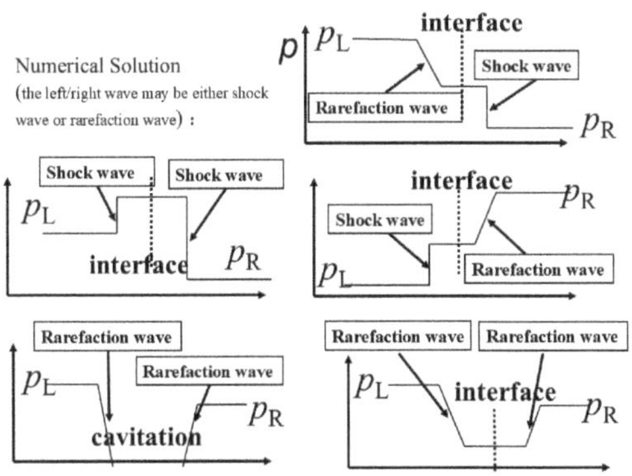

Figure 3. Discontinuous property of solutions.

To summarize (26)–(28), the equations for Γ, p_{ref} and e_{ref} can be written as

$$\begin{cases} \frac{\partial}{\partial t}(\frac{1}{\Gamma}) + u\frac{\partial}{\partial x}(\frac{1}{\Gamma}) + \rho[\frac{\partial}{\partial \rho}(\frac{1}{\Gamma})]\frac{\partial u}{\partial x} = 0 \\ \frac{\partial}{\partial t}(\frac{p_{ref}}{\Gamma}) + u\frac{\partial}{\partial x}(\frac{p_{ref}}{\Gamma}) + \rho[\frac{\partial}{\partial \rho}(\frac{p_{ref}}{\Gamma})]\frac{\partial u}{\partial x} = 0 \\ \frac{\partial}{\partial t}(\rho e_{ref}) + u\frac{\partial}{\partial x}(\rho e_{ref}) + \rho[\frac{\partial}{\partial \rho}(\rho e_{ref})]\frac{\partial u}{\partial x} = 0 \end{cases} \tag{29}$$

for some problems, the analytic forms of Γ, p_{ref} and e_{ref} are always in a complex form, the calculation of (29) can compute parameters Γ, p_{ref} and e_{ref} in an effective way and simplify the computation process.

For a single-component Mie–Grüneisen Riemann problem, the combination of the Euler Equation (8) and auxiliary Equation (29) is enough, while for the multi-phase problem, a transport equation is needed here. As y_g and y_w are used here to represent the mass fraction of gas and water, the transport equation in terms of y_g(or y_w) can be expressed as:

$$\frac{\partial \rho y_w}{\partial t} + \frac{\partial \rho y_w u}{\partial x} = 0 \tag{30}$$

Coupling (29) and (30) with the Euler formulation (8), a mixture model for the gas–water interaction problem can be obtained:

$$\begin{cases} \frac{\partial \rho}{\partial t} + \frac{\partial \rho u}{\partial x} = 0 \\ \frac{\partial \rho u}{\partial t} + \frac{\partial(\rho u^2 + p)}{\partial x} = 0 \\ \frac{\partial \rho E}{\partial t} + \frac{\partial(\rho E + p)u}{\partial x} = 0 \\ \frac{\partial}{\partial t}(\frac{1}{\Gamma}) + u\frac{\partial}{\partial x}(\frac{1}{\Gamma}) + \rho\phi\frac{\partial u}{\partial x} = 0 \\ \frac{\partial}{\partial t}(\frac{p_{ref}}{\Gamma}) + u\frac{\partial}{\partial x}(\frac{p_{ref}}{\Gamma}) + \rho\varphi\frac{\partial u}{\partial x} = 0 \\ \frac{\partial}{\partial t}(\rho e_{ref}) + u\frac{\partial}{\partial x}(\rho e_{ref}) + \rho\psi\frac{\partial u}{\partial x} = 0 \\ \frac{\partial(\rho y_w)}{\partial t} + \frac{\partial(\rho y_w u)}{\partial x} = 0 \end{cases} \tag{31}$$

where the symbols ϕ, φ and ψ denote the derivative functions of the split items $\partial(1/\Gamma)/\partial\rho$, $\partial(p_{ref}/\Gamma)/\partial\rho$ and $\partial(\rho e_{ref})/\partial\rho$, and they are functions in terms of ρ. The derivatives ϕ, φ and ψ are calculated as:

$$\begin{cases} \phi = z_g\left(\frac{1}{\Gamma}\right)'_g + z_w\left(\frac{1}{\Gamma}\right)'_w \\ \varphi = z_g\left(\frac{p_{ref}}{\Gamma}\right)'_g + z_w\left(\frac{p_{ref}}{\Gamma}\right)'_w \\ \psi = z_g\left(\rho e_{ref}\right)'_g + z_w\left(\rho e_{ref}\right)'_w \end{cases} \tag{32}$$

The pressure p is calculated by

$$p = \left(\frac{1}{\Gamma}\right)^{-1}\left[\rho E - \frac{\rho u^2}{2} + \frac{p_{ref}}{\Gamma} - \rho e_{ref}\right]$$

2.4. MUSCL Scheme with Roe Solver

The basic discrete equation in terms of time and space is

$$\frac{U_i^{n+1} - U_i^n}{\triangle t} + \frac{\overline{F}_{i+1/2} - \overline{F}_{i-1/2}}{\triangle x} = 0 \tag{33}$$

where $\triangle t$ and $\triangle x$ are the time step and grid size in x direction. U_i^{n+1} and U_i^n are vectors of conservative variables at the $(n+1)$th and nth time step, $\overline{F}_{i+1/2}$ is the flux between the i and $(i+1)$th cell along the x direction. For the time step $\triangle t$, it is defined as

$$\triangle t = CFL\frac{min(\triangle x)}{max(|u|_i + c_i)} \tag{34}$$

where c_i and u_i represent the particle velocity and sound velocity, respectively. In (34), the convergence conditions are satisfied when $CFL \leqslant 1$. The sound velocity is defined as

$$c^2 = \frac{\partial p}{\partial \rho} + \frac{p}{\rho}\frac{\partial p}{\partial \rho e} = \frac{E + p/\rho - (u^2/2) + p\phi - \varphi + \psi}{1/\Gamma} \tag{35}$$

In the discrete Equation (33), the variable vector U_i is the conservative variable which are listed as:

$$U_i = \left[\rho_i, \rho_i u_i, \rho_i E_i, \frac{1}{\Gamma_i}, \frac{p_{refi}}{\Gamma_i}, \rho_i e_{refi}, \rho_i y_{\mathbf{w}i}\right]^T$$

the fluxes are obtained here by an MUSCL (Monotone Upwind Scheme of Conservation Law)-TVD (Total Variation Diminishing) scheme; and for flux $\overline{F}_{i+1/2}$, there is

$$\begin{aligned} \overline{F}_{i+1/2} =& \frac{1}{2}[F(U_{Li+1/2}) + F(U_{Ri+1/2}) \\ &- \widehat{R}_{i+1/2}\left|\widehat{\Lambda}_{i+1/2}\right|\widehat{L}_{i+1/2}(U_{Ri+1/2} - U_{Li+1/2})] \end{aligned} \tag{36}$$

in which $U_{Li+1/2}$ and $U_{Ri+1/2}$ denote the vector of conservative variables of left and right states. The vectors $F_{Li+1/2}$ and $F_{Ri+1/2}$ can be obtained by

$$\begin{aligned} F_{Li+1/2} &= \left[\rho_{Li}, \rho_{L_i} u_{Li}, \rho_{L_i} E_{Li}, \frac{1}{\Gamma_{Li}}, \frac{p_{refL_i}}{\Gamma_{Li}}, \rho_{L_i} e_{refL_i}, \rho_{L_i} y_{\mathbf{w}L_i} u_{Li}\right]^T \\ &= U_i + \frac{1}{2}R_{i+1/2}\Phi_{Li+1/2} \\ F_{Ri+1/2} &= \left[\rho_{Ri}, \rho_{R_i} u_{Ri}, \rho_{R_i} E_{Ri}, \frac{1}{\Gamma_{Ri}}, \frac{p_{refR_i}}{\Gamma_{Ri}}, \rho_{R_i} e_{refR_i}, \rho_{R_i} y_{\mathbf{w}R_i} u_{Ri}\right]^T \\ &= U_{i+1} - \frac{1}{2}R_{i+1/2}\Phi_{Ri+1/2} \end{aligned} \tag{37}$$

where $R_{i+1/2}$ is the right eigenvector matrix of $\partial F/\partial U$, which can be expressed as

$$R_{i+1/2} = \begin{bmatrix} 1 & 1 & 1 & & & & \\ u_i - c_i & u_i & u_i + c_i & & & & \\ H_i - u_i c_i & u_i^2/2 & H_i + u_i c_i & p_i & -1 & 1 & \\ \phi_i & & \phi_i & 1 & & & \\ \varphi_i & & \varphi_i & & 1 & & \\ \psi_i & & \psi_i & & & 1 & \\ y_{\mathbf{w}i} & & y_{\mathbf{w}i} & & & & 1 \end{bmatrix} \tag{38}$$

And the items Φ_L and Φ_R in (37) are

$$\begin{aligned} \Phi_{Ri+1/2} &= (I - \frac{\triangle t}{\triangle x}\Lambda_{i+1/2})S_{i+1/2} \\ \Phi_{Li+1/2,j} &= (I + \frac{\triangle t}{\triangle x}\Lambda_{i+1/2})S_{i+1/2} \end{aligned} \tag{39}$$

where Λ is the diagonal matrix of the eigenvalue matrix and can be written as

$$\Lambda_{i+1/2} = \begin{bmatrix} u_i - c_i & & & & & & \\ & u_i & & & & & \\ & & u_i + c_i & & & & \\ & & & u_i & & & \\ & & & & u_i & & \\ & & & & & u_i & \\ & & & & & & u_i \end{bmatrix} \tag{40}$$

and $S_{i+1/2}$ is defined as

$$S_{i+1/2} = minmod\left[L_{i+1/2}DU_{i+1/2}, L_{i+3/2}DU_{i+3/2}\right]$$

where $L_{i+1/2}$ is the left eigenvector of $\partial F/\partial U$, and $DU_{i+1/2} = U_{i+1} - U_i$.

The matrix $L_{i+1/2}$ is

$$L_{i+1/2} = \frac{\Gamma_i}{2c_i^2} \cdot \begin{bmatrix} u_i c_i \xi_i + u_i^2/2 & -u_i - c_i\xi_i & 1 & -p_i & 1 & -1 & \\ -u_i^2 + 2\xi_i c_i^2 & 2u_i & -2 & 2p_i & -2 & 2 & \\ -u_i c_i \xi_i + u_i^2/2 & -u_i + c_i\xi_i & 1 & -p_i & 1 & -1 & \\ -\phi_i u_i^2 & 2\phi_i u_i & -2\phi_i & 2\phi_i p_i + 2c_i^2\xi_i & -2\phi_i & 2\phi_i & \\ -\varphi_i u_i^2 & 2\varphi_i u_i & -2\varphi_i & 2\varphi_i p_i & -2\varphi_i + 2c_i^2\xi_i & 2\varphi_i & \\ -\psi_i u_i^2 & 2\psi_i u_i & -2\psi_i & 2\psi_i p_i & -2\psi_i & 2\psi_i + 2c_i^2\xi_i & \\ -y_{\mathbf{w}i} u_i^2 & 2y_{\mathbf{w}i} u_i & -2y_{\mathbf{w}i} & 2y_{\mathbf{w}i} p_i & -2y_{\mathbf{w}i} & 2y_{\mathbf{w}i} & 2c_i^2\xi_i \end{bmatrix} \tag{41}$$

where $\xi = 1/\Gamma$.

In (36), the matrixes $\widehat{\Lambda}_{i+1/2}$, $\widehat{R}_{i+1/2}$ and $\widehat{L}_{i+1/2}$ are defined as the matrixes of the average value of the left and right states. Roe average [5] is a widely used style of average, which can be expressed as

$$\begin{cases} \widehat{u} = \dfrac{\sqrt{\rho_L}u_L + \sqrt{\rho_R}u_R}{\sqrt{\rho_L} + \sqrt{\rho_R}}, \ \widehat{H} = \dfrac{\sqrt{\rho_L}H_L + \sqrt{\rho_R}H_R}{\sqrt{\rho_L} + \sqrt{\rho_R}} \\ \widehat{\xi} = \dfrac{\sqrt{\rho_L}\xi_L + \sqrt{\rho_R}\xi_R}{\sqrt{\rho_L} + \sqrt{\rho_R}}, \ \widehat{\phi} = \dfrac{\sqrt{\rho_L}\phi_L + \sqrt{\rho_R}\phi_R}{\sqrt{\rho_L} + \sqrt{\rho_R}} \\ \widehat{\varphi} = \dfrac{\sqrt{\rho_L}\varphi_L + \sqrt{\rho_R}\varphi_R}{\sqrt{\rho_L} + \sqrt{\rho_R}}, \ \widehat{\psi} = \dfrac{\sqrt{\rho_L}\psi_L + \sqrt{\rho_R}\psi_R}{\sqrt{\rho_L} + \sqrt{\rho_R}} \\ \widehat{p} = \dfrac{1}{\widehat{\xi}} \dfrac{\sqrt{\rho_L}p_L\xi_L + \sqrt{\rho_R}p_R\xi_R}{\sqrt{\rho_L} + \sqrt{\rho_R}} \\ \widehat{c} = \sqrt{\dfrac{1}{\widehat{\xi}}\left[\widehat{H} - (\widehat{u}^2/2) + \widehat{p}\phi - \varphi + \psi\right]} \end{cases}$$

where the corner mark $_L$ and $_R$ represent the variables of left or right states, $H = E + p/\rho$. While for derivatives ϕ, φ and ψ, they have no partial differential items, so the values of $\widehat{\phi}$, $\widehat{\varphi}$ and $\widehat{\psi}$ are defined by the original data of the ith grid point:

$$\widehat{\phi} = \phi_i, \widehat{\varphi} = \varphi_i, \widehat{\psi} = \psi_i$$

A similar style is used to define the Roe average of mass fraction y_w:

$$\rho y_w = \frac{\sqrt{\rho_L}y_{wL} + \sqrt{\rho_R}y_{wR}}{\sqrt{\rho_L} + \sqrt{\rho_R}} \tag{42}$$

However, there is one that detail needs to be emphasized: the parameters of shock wave is affected by the path-conservative effects provided by Dal Maso [40]. There is a slight change, however, if the scheme is different. This property also exists in two-layer shallow water flows [41,42]. The path-conservative problem is analysized in Appendix A. The form of transport equation is also discussed in Appendix A.

3. Numerical Examples

3.1. Weak Shock Problem of Gas–Water Interaction

A simple 1D gas–water interaction problem, which is previously studied by Liu [43], is first considered. The initial states are constituted by gas in the left side, and water in the right side. Their physical parameters are:

$$(\rho, p, u) = \begin{cases} (1270\ \text{kg/m}^3, 8000\ \text{atm}, 0.0) & x \leq 0.0 \\ (1000\ \text{kg/m}^3, 1.0\ \text{atm}, 0.0) & x > 0.0 \end{cases}$$

When the time instant t = 0, the gas and water are both in a static state, and the water suffers from a weak impact of gas. Here, the water is described by the Tait EOS, which can provide an analytic solution for this gas–water problem.

In Liu's work, Tait EOS is employed to model the water and is reconstructed by a new form similar to (18): $p = (\gamma - 1)\rho e - \gamma B$. The coefficients of the Tait EOS are listed in Table 2. Our concern is the accuracy of solution when the Tait EOS of water is replaced by the Mie–Grüneisen EOS. On the other hand, the Mie–Grüneisen EOS is founded according to the nonlinear $D - u_m$ relationship as in (2).

Table 2. Initial states of gas and water in a weak shock problem. Both gas and water are initially static.

	p	ρ	EOS
Gas	8000 atm	1.27×10^3 kg/m^3	Ideal Gas EOS
Water	1 atm	1.0×10^3 kg/m^3	Tait EOS

Figure 4 exhibits the curves of density and pressure, as well as the shock velocity position records. From the comparison, it is noticed that the difference between the two kinds of EOSs is minimal. In the pressure curves shown in Figure 4b, the shock wave pressure of the Tait EOS is slightly higher than the Mie–Grüneisen EOS. It seems that the Tait EOS can also achieve excellent solutions even though it is in a simple form. Figure 4c provides the trace of shock sections, which corresponds to the discontinuous sections at the right side of Figure 4a,b. However, the analytic solutions can be easily obtained using the Tait EOS in calculation. Still, it is hard to deduce analytic solutions for the Mie–Grüneisen EOS. Therefore, some other referential data are needed here to check the solution of the Mie–Grüneisen EOS.

Here, the accuracy of shock wave parameters is examined by an empirical formula, which can be expressed as [6]

$$\begin{cases} p_{mx} = \rho_{mx} D u_{mx} \\ u_{mx} = \dfrac{D}{\gamma+1}\left[1 + \dfrac{2\gamma}{\gamma-1}\left(1 - (p_{mx}/p_{CJ})^{\frac{\gamma-1}{2\gamma}}\right)\right] \\ u_{mx} = \sqrt{(p_{mx} - p_0)(V_{mx} - V_0)}, \\ V_{mx} = 1/\rho_{mx} \end{cases}$$

Introducing the relationship (2) into the equation system above, one can obtain the values of p_m, ρ_m, u_m and D by a simple iteration. This approach is used to deduce an approximate solution for D, p_m and u_m, as shown in Table 3. As a reference, the $D - u_m$ relationships cover the experimental data of Nakayama (linear) and LLNL (nonlinear).

Table 3. The contrasts of the density, pressure and shock velocity with approximate solution.

	D (m/s)	p_m (Mpa)	ρ_m (kg/m^3)
Nakayama Linear $D - u_m$ *	1959	494	1146
LLNL Nonlinear $D - u_m$ *	1976	491	1146
Tait EOS	2080	534	1144
Mie–Grüneisen EOS	2084	517	1137

* Approximate iteration solution.

The results of the Mie–Grüneisen mixture model are also presented in Table 3. According to the contrast, it is found that our results are closer to the approximate iteration solutions. It is hard to obtain precise values for shock velocity because the shock section in the numerical results is not in a discontinuous shape, and so the position of the shock is challenging to locate due to the dispersion effects. In our work, the position of the shock is defined by the 200 Mpa pressure level. It is noticed that the density of the shock is only about 1140 kg/m^3, so the compression is not very high in this problem. In this problem, the variation in entropy is nearly unaffected by the compression [34]. A simple-form Tait equation is adequate here based on an isentropic condition.

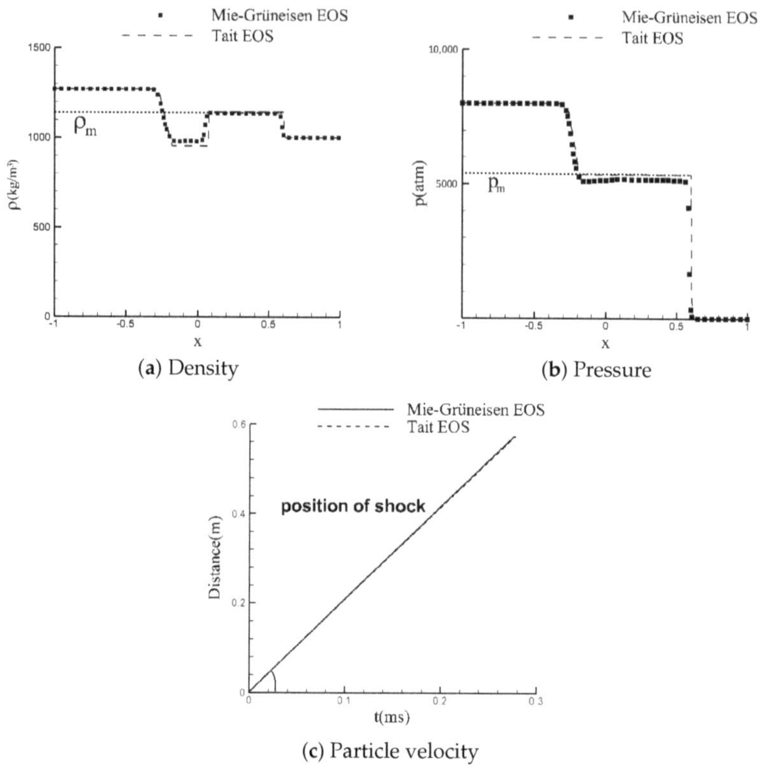

Figure 4. The curves of the density, pressure and shock position in the weak shock problem. The shock wave parameters p_m and u_m are analytic solutions of the Tait EOS. The contrast data of Tait are Liu's numerical solutions. The curves include the following: (**a**) Density. (**b**) Pressure. (**c**) Shock velocity.

3.2. Strong Shock Problem of Gas–Water Interaction

Then, a detonation shock tube problem is used here to test the adaptability of the EOS in a strong shock problem. At $t = 0$, the gaseous detonation product with a C-J (Chapman-Jouguet) state is distributed on the left side. The physical parameters of C-J states are defined as follows [35]:

$$\rho_{\text{C-J}} = \frac{\gamma+1}{\gamma}\rho_0, u_{\text{C-J}} = \frac{\gamma+1}{\gamma}D, p_{\text{C-J}} = \frac{1}{\gamma+1}\rho_0 D^2$$

where $\rho_0 = 1630\ \text{kg/m}^3$, $\gamma = 2.727$ and $D = 6950\ \text{m/s}$ [35]. According to the parameters of C-J states, it can be noticed that the pressure exceeds 10 Gpa (Nakayama's linear data are limited below 1 Gpa) and the gaseous product has an astonishing initial velocity. The EOS group in this example includes the Mie–Grüneisen EOS, Tait EOS, and another stiffened gas EOS of Abgrall. On the other hand, the EOS of gas is also an ideal gas EOS but with a renewed γ.

As three different forms of EOS simulate the gas–water interaction, the empirical values in the first example are used again here. The results of three EOSs are shown in Figure 5. The discontinuous shape of shock waves can be clearly seen in the figure. Nevertheless, significant difference can be found from a comparison of the empirical data. The shock wave parameter calculated by the Tait EOS does not agree well with the empirical data, especially the density ρ. The results indicate that the high-compression problem is complicated to model with the Tait EOS. The Tait EOS is constructed by the property of constant entropy. This property adapts to gas behavior, but it is hard to cover the Hugoniot relationship under impact. Comparing with the Tait EOS, the adapbility of the stiffened gas EOS is much better in a high-compression problem because the Hugoniot curve is embedded into the foundation of the stiffened gas EOS. However, limited by the simple form of the EOS, the Hugoniot curve is not taken as a reference state; thus, the expressions (18) and (19) only provide a reference state based on initial condition. As there is no condition to set separation as in (11) and (12), the parameters of the shock waves are still not so reliable for the stiffened gas EOS. Both Tait EOS and stiffened gas EOS are affected by the expression form, in which the coefficients cannot contain the compression functions. Thanks to the coefficients p_{ref} and e_{ref}, the Mie–Grüneisen EOS can set a particular ρ function according to detonation experimental curves. In this case, the results of the Mie–Grüneisen EOS are reasonable and close to the empirical data. Due to the complex form of the Mie–Grüneisen EOS, there are slight oscillations at the starting point of the rarefaction waves.

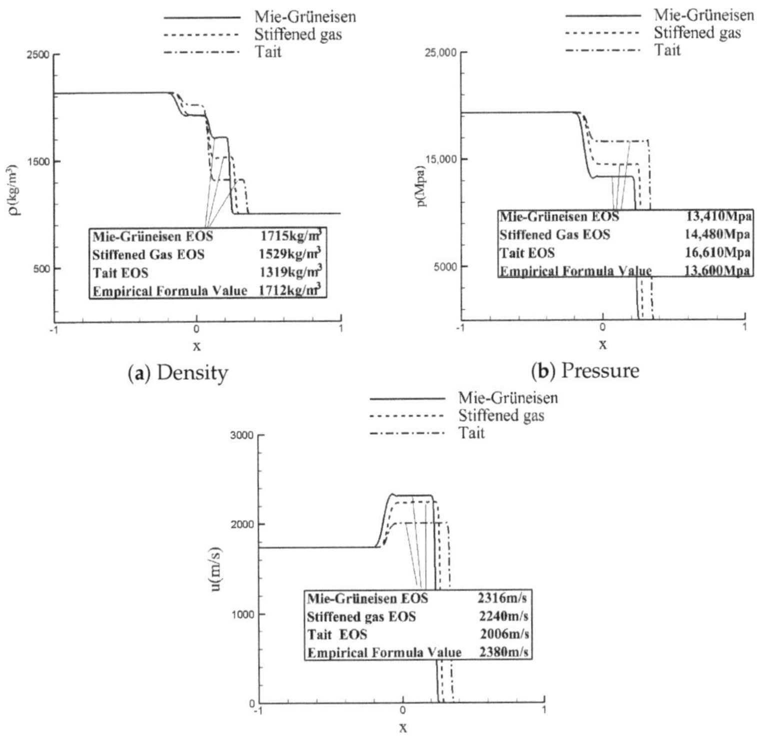

(**a**) Density (**b**) Pressure

(**c**) Particle velocity

Figure 5. The performances of different EOSs in a strong shock problem. The empirical data are evaluated by the coupling D-u_m curve with C-J parameters. The curves of relative shock parameters are as follows: (**a**) Density. (**b**) Pressure. (**c**) Particle velocity.

3.3. An Investigation of EOS Affection in Gas–Water Interaction

As Tait EOS and stiffened gas EOS are both simple-form equations in which the reference states of Hugoniot curves are not considered, a further study of their performance is carried out here. Here the initial conditions are set to be different to test the adaptability of the Tait EOS and stiffened gas EOS. The difference between the Tait EOS and Mie–Grüneisen EOS and between the stiffened gas EOS and Mie–Grüneisen EOS are presented here. As an extension of the first example, we considered the parameters exhibited in

Figure 5, which include shock density ρ_m, shock pressure p_m and the particle velocity of post shock u_m.

Initially, our attention is paid to the pressure in the initial condition. Two initial densities, 1200 kg/m^3 and 1500 kg/m^3, typical low-compression and high-compression cases, are considered here. The influence of pressure has an effect on the shock parameters, and the variations in ρ_m, p_m and u_m are shown in Figure 6. It can be found that the difference in p_m is the lowest parameter, no matter what EOS is used. The reason is that the EOS expression is always written as a function of pressure. Thus, the pressure is a benchmark parameter and the fitting curves of p are always taken seriously. Conversely, the compression state is represented by the density ρ, but it is not regarded as an essential parameter. There is evidence that the expression of the Tait EOS and stiffened gas EOS only take ρe as a variable and ignore the density ρ. Although the form of EOS is simplified, the density becomes an irrelevant parameter in the expression of EOS. This mistake is very weak when the density variation is small. However, it is amplified when the density becomes large and leads to a depression of impact effects. The results show that the difference among all three parameters maintains an upward trend as the pressure rises. The depression of impact effects cause this phenomenon. As the impact effects are strengthened by the increase in pressure, the compression state is not well described by the Tait EOS and stiffened gas EOS. Comparing with the Tait EOS, the stiffened gas EOS results in less of a difference because it is based on the Hugoniot curve, but the expression form is simplified. Thus, the differences in ρ_m and u_m are both controlled.

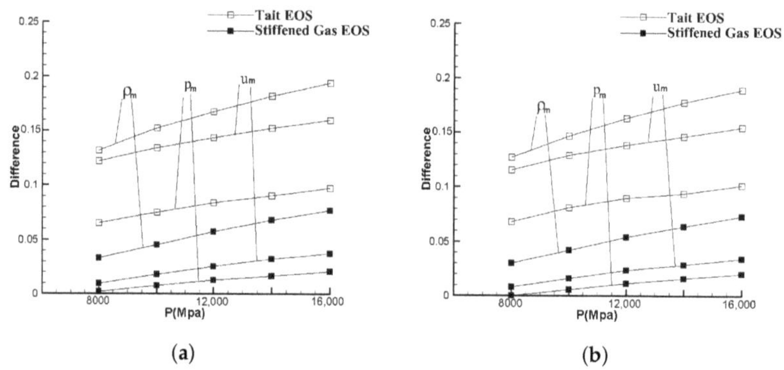

Figure 6. The influence of initial pressure. The difference between the Mie–Grüneisen EOS and Tait EOS and the difference between the Mie–Grüneisen EOS and stiffened gas EOS are distinctly plotted. The initial density of gas is set as follows: (**a**) ρ = 1200 kg/m^3. (**b**) ρ = 1500 kg/m^3.

Next, our attention is transferred to the mechanism of difference when initial velocity ranges from 0 to 1000 m/s. The difference curves are plotted in Figure 7. It is found that the trends of ρ_m, p_m and u_m curves are similar to those in Figure 6. Among the three parameters, the difference in ρ_m is the biggest, while u_m is a little better than ρ_m, p_m has the smallest difference. As u_m increases, the impact effects become larger, and thus the compression of water is enhanced and produces a similar mechanism to that mentioned above. Compared to Figure 6, a gentle slope can be seen in Figure 7. This is because the impact effects that resulting from the variation of u_0 are not strong enough for compression. In Figure 6, the addition of pressure is up to 8000 Mpa. While in Figure 7, by considering that $p = p_0 + \rho_0 D u_m$, the momentum amplification caused by u_0 = 1000 m/s is much lesser than 8000 Mpa (the value of u_m is slightly less than u_0).

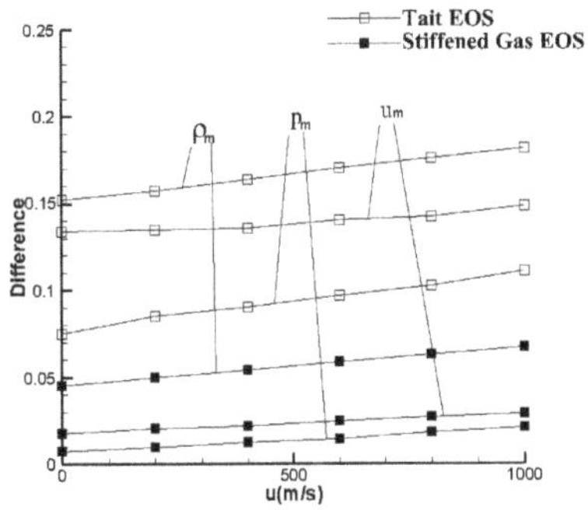

Figure 7. The influence of initial density. The difference between the Mie–Grüneisen EOS and Tait EOS and the difference between the Mie–Grüneisen EOS and stiffened gas EOS are distinctly plotted.

Then, the difference caused by the variation in ρ_0 is considered. Figure 8 presents the difference of ρ_m, p_m and u_m. Unlike p_0 and u_0, the variation in ρ_0 has little relationship with the impact effects when u_0 = 0 m/s. In this case, the changes in parameters ρ_m, p_m and u_m are very small, whereby even ρ_0 is up to 1600 kg/m^3 high in value. In addition, the differences in p_m nearly remain constant as the compression increases due to the weak impact. The values of ρ_m and u_m decline slightly. Moreover, the former order of difference ($\rho_m > u_m > p_m$) is also adapted here.

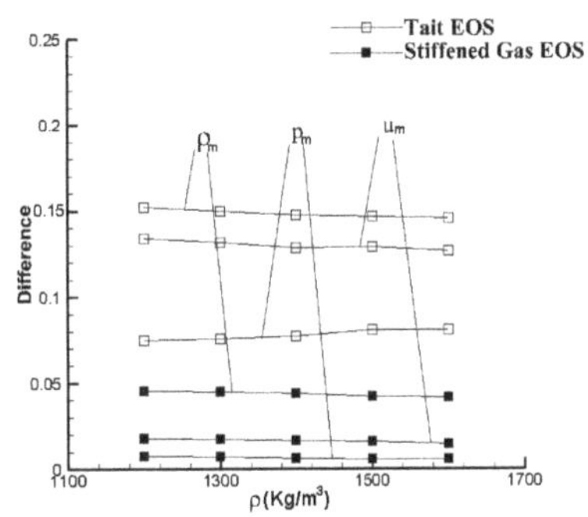

Figure 8. The influence of initial particle velocity. The difference between the Mie–Grüneisen EOS and Tait EOS and the difference between the Mie–Grüneisen EOS and stiffened gas EOS are distinctly plotted.

The results ($\rho_m > u_m > p_m$) in Figures 6–8 are closely related to the structure of real solution. Here, we consider a simple gas–water problem with exact solutions, as in Figure 3. At the interface, the values of p_m and u_m satisfy a characteristic system as follows:

$$\begin{cases} \dfrac{p_m - p_L}{W_L(p_m, p_L, \rho_L)} + (u_m - u_L) = 0 \\ \dfrac{p_m - p_R}{W_R(p_m, p_R, \rho_R)} - (u_m - u_R) = 0 \end{cases}$$

where the function W_L and W_R denote for the left and right waves, respectively. These two functions are determined by the EOS and wave characteristics (shock wave or rarefaction wave), and they have analytic forms when the EOS is either ideal gas EOS or stiffened gas EOS. Such an equation system implies that the p_m can be obtained by an iteration. Then, the value of u_m can be obtained using either equation above. While density is discontinuous at the interface, thus ρ_m can be calculated by a mass conservative law. The relationship among ρ_m, u_m and p_m indicates that ρ_m is affected by D and u_m but ρ_m itself causes no effects to either p_m or u_m. Furthermore, the u_m is affected by p_m, but p_m does not affect u_m.

Therefore, the difference in p_m raises the difference in u_m, then the difference in u_m raises the difference in ρ_m.

3.4. Gas–Water Shock Wave in Spherical System

In this case, a bubble experiment by the LLNL is concerned here [21]. The bubble is generated by the detonation product of 2.1 kg NM (nitromethane) spherical charge, with an initial density of 1.128 g/cm^3. As the charge explodes, a bubble of gaseous product diffuses quickly in water. The computational domain ranges from 0 to 20 $R0$, with 2000 uniform grids in it. $R0$ is the initial radius of the charge.

The numerical calculation is carried out under a spherical coordinate system. The governing equation for the spherical system is reconstructed as [44]

$$\frac{\partial \widetilde{U}}{\partial t} + \frac{\partial F(\widetilde{U})}{\partial r} = S(\widetilde{U})$$
$$\widetilde{U} = r^2 \cdot U,\ F(\widetilde{U}) = r^2 \cdot F,\ S(\widetilde{U}) = \begin{bmatrix} 0 \\ 2rp \\ 0 \\ 0 \\ 0 \\ 0 \\ 0 \end{bmatrix} \tag{43}$$

where r denotes the radius. In the new equation system (43), the center point is a singular point because there is no space to construct a discrete equation as (33) and the parameter at the singular point is difficult to evaluate. For the sake of convenience, the parameters at the singularity are defined as the same as the grid point nearby except for the particle velocity. In the center, it is defined as $u = 0$ and other parameters are not affected by any waves.

The movement of the main shock, which is represented by δS, is recorded by camera in this experiment. The shape of the bubble is also investigated in this experiment, and the experimental data contain a record of the radius change δR. The time evolution curves for δS and δR are shown in Figure 9. Compared with the experimental results of δS and δR, it is found that the calculated values become higher as time increases. The reason for the overvalued δS and δR lies in the nonequilibrium of u and p at the interface. As the spherical system is a diffusion system, there is a negative slope rate for real values of p and u at the interface. The sketch of the p and u solution is shown in Figure 10. As a result, the overall decline in u and p ultimately affects the accuracy and increases the strength of the shock wave. Eventually, the values of δS and δR become higher than real, the overvaluation of u and p and becomes larger and larger as distance increases.

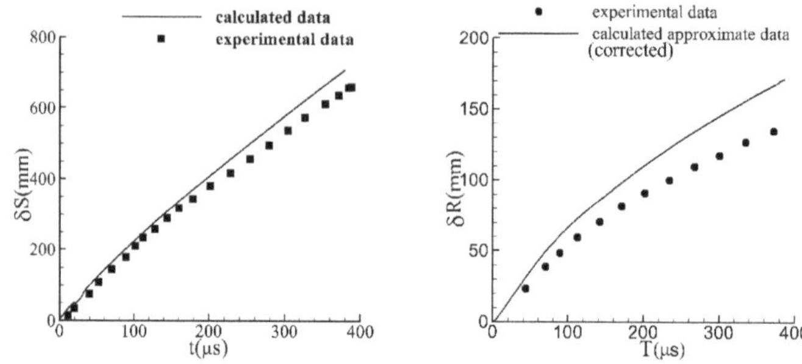

(**a**) Shock wave trace (**b**) Interface trace

Figure 9. The motion of shock and interface in spherical gas–water interaction problem. (**a**) The trace of a shock wave and (**b**) the trace of the interface.

In addition, the disagreement of δR in Figure 9 is slightly larger than δS. This is because the interface of the Mie–Grüneisen mixture model is taken as a diffused interface with thickness, so the exact position of the interface is hard to be defined by such an interface model. The errors of the interface location amplifies as time increases.

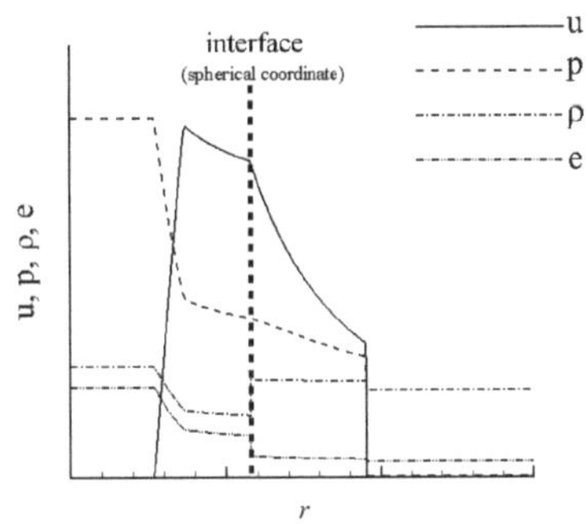

Figure 10. The discontinuous property in spherical coordinates.

In Figure 11, the curves of water density and pressure at instants $t = 200$ and 500 μs are posted. The profiles show the states when the main shock wave travels a long distant. In the beginning, the main shock wave spreads outside. On the other hand, a rarefaction wave moves backwards to the center. The cumulated rarefaction wave then becomes the second shock wave. Afterwards, yielding to the same mechanism, the third shock wave is generated. However, the shock wave generated at the second stage is much lower than the main shock wave, as shown in Figure 11. Regardless, compared with discontinuous parameters such as ρ, ρe, Γ, the velocity and pressure are not constant but are still kept continuous. So, the Mie–Grüneisen mixture model still make sense here.

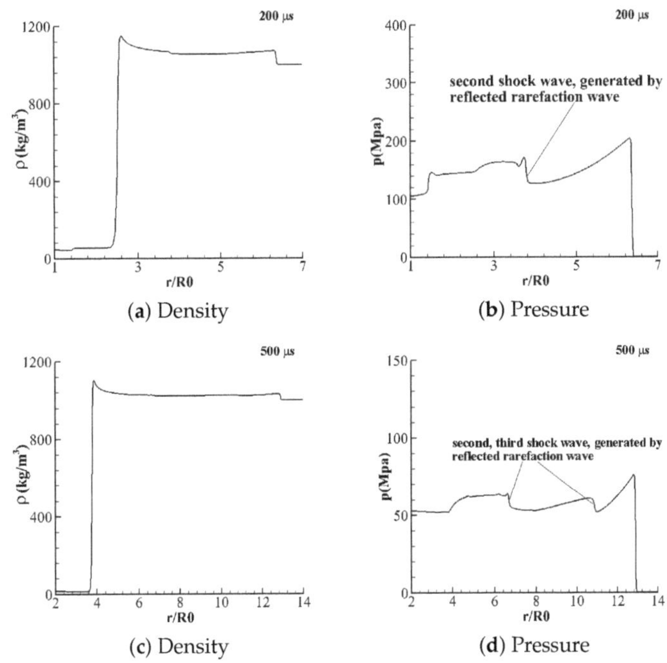

Figure 11. The profiles of density and pressure, respectively: (**a**,**b**) 0.2 ms; (**c**,**d**) 0.5 ms.

3.5. An Extension to the 2D Problem with Three Phases

As the Mie–Grüneisen EOS can adapt to a wide range of materials by setting the expressions of p_{ref} and e_{ref}, it is applied to a 2D problem with three phases. In this example, an underwater explosion phenomenon occurs on the sand bed [45]. So, the shock wave from the explosion not only spreads in water but also penetrates into the sand bed. The explosion charge is in a square shape with a size of 0.15 m. The sand bed is 0.5 m thick, with Mie–Grüneisen coefficients as: $\rho_0 = 1950\ \mathrm{kg/m^3}$, $\gamma = 1.28$, s=1.86 and $c_0 = 2450\ \mathrm{m/s}$ [46]. The bottom of the sand bed is set as a rigid wall. Under the impact, the sand could also be modeled by the Mie–Grüneisen EOS. Here, a linear $D - u_m$ relationship (2) is applied on the sand with coefficients.

Although the gas–water interaction and gas–sand interaction are coupled with each other and the whole interaction becomes complex, it is effective to take the three-phase field as a fluid mixture and use the Mie–Grüneisen mixture model to simulate the interaction process. The pressure contours of this three-phase interaction are given in Figure 12. In contrast, the work of Yao is used here to be a reference [45]. It can be observed that our results are approximate to Yao's results. The discontinuous sections of shock waves in water and in sand are both clearly seen in the contours. The drawback of our results lie in the interface, which is not as distinct as Yao's. This is because the interface is automatically captured and not modified by another procedure.

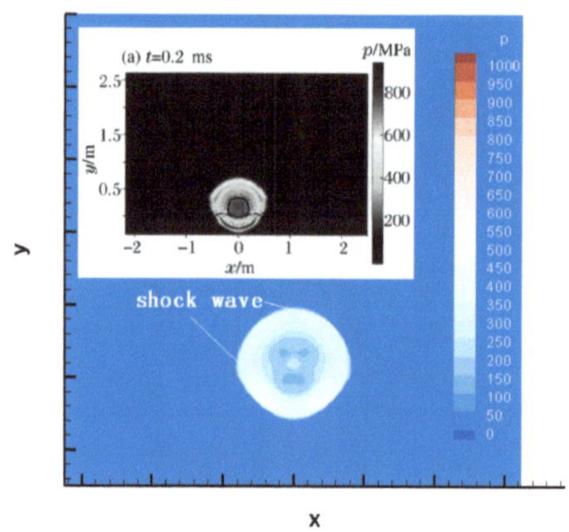

(**a**) 0.2 ms

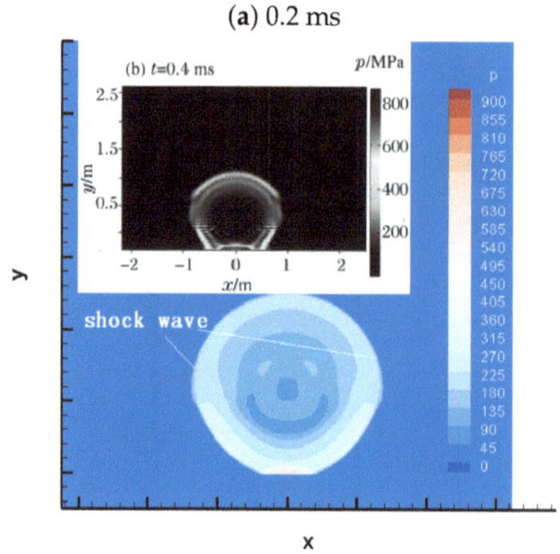

(**b**) 0.4 ms

Figure 12. The comparison of pressure contours in a 2D problem. The contrast contours are copied from Yao's SPH simulation: (**a**) 0.2 ms; (**b**) 0.4 ms.

Figure 13 shows the density distribution contours. It can be seen that the upper parts of the shock wave above the bed spreads freely in the water. On the other hand, another part of the shock wave moves downward and forms reflected shock waves in the sand. The shock wave in the sand is reflected immediately by the rigid wall below the sand. In the center, there is still some gaseous medium left.

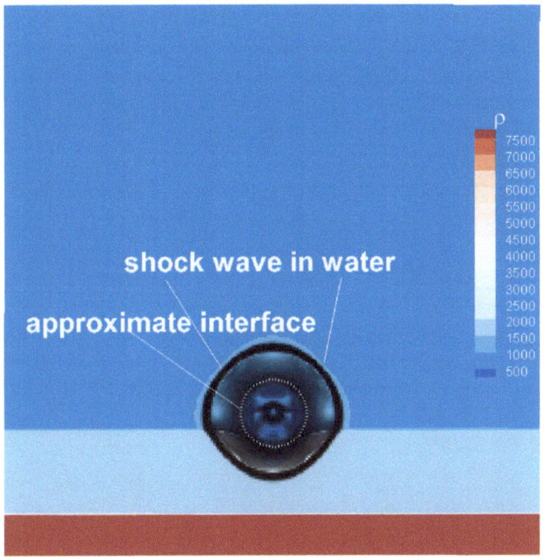

(**a**) 0.2 ms

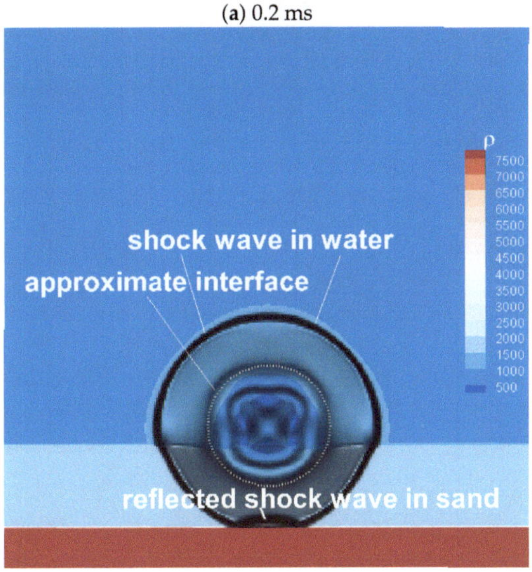

(**b**) 0.4 ms

Figure 13. The density distribution of shock waves in sand: (**a**) 0.2 ms; (**b**) 0.4 ms.

4. Conclusions

According to the calculation of the gas–water shock wave above, some conclusions are summarized as follows:

1. The Mie–Grüneisen mixture model can be applied well in a gas–water interaction and some other multi-phase Riemann problems. The Mie–Grüneisen EOS can rationally

describe the impact effects with the help of the Hugoniot reference state, and achieve precise results that agree well with empirical data.
2. For gas–water problems with low compression, the Mie–Grüneisen EOS does not have any advantage than other simple-form EOSs such as Tait EOS, because the problem can be approximately taken as under an isentropic condition, and a simple-form Tait EOS with a constant reference state is adequate.
3. For gas–water problems with high compression, the results of the Mie–Grüneisen EOS is much better than other simple-form EOSs. With the help of setting reference states as a Hugoniot curve, reliable parameters of shock waves are obtained by the Mie–Grüneisen EOS. The lack of reasonable reference states causes the Tait EOS and stiffened gas EOS to be out of range.
4. The difference between the Mie–Grüneisen EOS and other simple-form EOSs is enlarged by the impact effects of initial conditions. As the initial value of pressure or particle velocity increases, the EOS which is based on a simple isentropic condition (such as Tait EOS) encounters difficulty in describing the impact effects. Other EOSs based on the Hugoniot curve but expressed in a simple form (such as stiffened gas EOS) have some advantages but are still far from the empirical data.
5. Affected by the fundamental theory of an EOS, the deviations of shock wave parameters are different. The order is $\rho_m > u_m > p_m$ from high to low. The reason lies in the calculation process of the three parameters: p_m depends on the medium itself, as well as the initial density and pressure; u_m is affected by p_m according to a couple of characteristic formulas; and lastly, there is ρ_m.
6. The Mie–Grüneisen mixture model can be efficiently applied in a 2D problem, as well as a simple 3D spherical system.

The Mie–Grüneisen mixture model is used to model fluid interaction. It can be extended to fluid–structure interaction by coupling with the finite element method. The calculation of external load can be provided by the Mie–Grüneisen mixture model. On the other hand, this model can be applied to the detonation or combustion phenomena by using the Mie–Grüneisen mixture EOS to model unreacted and reacted substances.

Author Contributions: Conceptualization, Z.W.; methodology, Z.W.; validation, Z.W.; formal analysis, D.Z.; investigation, D.Z.; writing—original draft preparation, Z.W.; writing—review and editing, Z.W. and J.P.; visualization, J.P.; supervision, Y.S.; project administration, J.Y.; funding acquisition, J.Y. All authors have read and agreed to the published version of the manuscript.

Funding: This research was funded by Guangdong Basic and Applied Basic Research (2022A1515011562, 2024A1515012815), Guangdong Provincial Special Fund for promoting high-quality economic development (GDNRC[2021]56, [2021]161), and the National Natural Science Foundation of China (grant number 11702066).

Data Availability Statement: The original contributions presented in the study are included in the article, further inquiries can be directed to the corresponding author.

Conflicts of Interest: The authors declare no conflicts of interest.

Appendix A

Here, we add an appendix to provide an additional numerical test for the Mie–Grüneisen mixture model.

Initially, a mixture shock tube problem with different complex EOSs is considered here. Gaseous explosive and solid copper are placed at the left and right of the shock tube, respectively. The explosive is modeled by the JWL EOS, which can be written in the Mie–Grüneisen form as

$$\begin{cases} \Gamma = \Gamma_0 \\ p_{ref} = \dfrac{A_1}{R_1\rho_0}\exp\Big(-\dfrac{R_1\rho_0}{\rho}\Big) + \dfrac{A_2}{R_2\rho_0}\exp\Big(-\dfrac{R_2\rho_0}{\rho}\Big) \\ e_{ref} = A_1\exp\Big(-\dfrac{R_1\rho_0}{\rho}\Big) + A_2\exp\Big(-\dfrac{R_2\rho_0}{\rho}\Big) \end{cases}$$

$$\rho_0 = 1840\,\text{kg/m}^3, \Gamma_0 = 0.25, A_1 = 845.5\,\text{Gpa}, A_2 = 20.5\,\text{Gpa}, R_1 = 4.6, R_2 = 1.35$$

The copper is modeled by the C-C EOS:

$$\begin{cases} \Gamma = \Gamma_0 \\ p_{ref} = B_1\Big(\dfrac{\rho_0}{\rho}\Big)^{\varepsilon_1} - B_2\Big(\dfrac{\rho_0}{\rho}\Big)^{\varepsilon_2} \\ e_{ref} = -\dfrac{B_1}{\rho_0(1-\varepsilon_1)}\Big[\Big(\dfrac{\rho_0}{\rho}\Big)^{\varepsilon_1-1} - 1\Big] + \dfrac{B_2}{\rho_0(1-\varepsilon_2)}\Big[\Big(\dfrac{\rho_0}{\rho}\Big)^{\varepsilon_2-1} - 1\Big] \end{cases}$$

$$\rho_0 = 8900\,\text{kg/m}^3, \Gamma_0 = 2.00, B_1 = 145.67\,\text{Gpa}, B_2 = 147.75\,\text{Gpa}, \varepsilon_1 = 2.99, \varepsilon_2 = 1.99$$

The initial state of the two materials are

$$\begin{cases} \text{explosive} : \rho = 2485.37\,\text{kg/m}^3, p = 37\,\text{Gpa}, u = 0, e = 8149.158\,\text{kJ/kg} \\ \text{copper} : \rho = 8900\,\text{kg/m}^3, p = 1\,\text{atm}, u = 0, e = 117.900\,\text{kJ/kg} \end{cases}$$

Then, the problem is calculated by the Mie–Grüneisen mixture model.

Here, we use different transport equations. One is (30), another is in terms of volume fraction:

$$\frac{\partial z_g}{\partial t} + u\frac{\partial z_g}{\partial x} = 0$$

Taking the different transport equations into account, solutions obtained by conservative and non-conservative transport equations are presented here, as shown in Figure A1. It can be seen that the two results are all very close to the exact solution. No matter whether the transport equations are conservative or not, both of the two results satisfy our needs. In this case, the Mie–Grüneisen mixture model can prevent numerical oscillations and produce accuracy solutions and the interface can be clearly identified by both mass fraction and volume fraction. In Figure A1, the impact of copper generates a leftward rarefaction wave and a rightward shock wave.

In order to explain the path-conservative effects, we take the shock problem of G.M. Ward as an example [31]. The Riemann problem is a single-component impact problem. Initially, the left side of computational zone is the aluminum with compressed state: ρ_L = 4000 kg/m^3, u_L = 2000 m/s, p_L = 7.98 Gpa. The right side is the aluminum with reference state: ρ_R = 2785 kg/m^3, u_R = 0 m/s, $p_R = 0$. The aluminum is modeled by a traditional Mie–Grüneisen EOS with linear relationship (1), in which $\rho_0 = 2785$, c_0 = 5328 m/s, $s = 1.338$, $\gamma_0 = 2.8$, p_0 and e_0 are all set as 0. As the Mie–Grüneisen is used here, the transport equation in terms of y_i can be neglected. We show the influence of the discretization method on the solution, namely using Roe's and Rusanov' schemes. According to the results, it can be found that the two results are absolutely not the same. So, it is known that the parameters can be slightly affected by the schemes. The explanation is that the entropy creation mechanism depends on the schemes. Considering that the approximation effect has a close relation with the path, two different paths are used here. In this case, the numerical solution has a path-conservative property, and different paths would generate different outcomes. The fact is that the schemes converge to different solutions because a discontinuity exists.

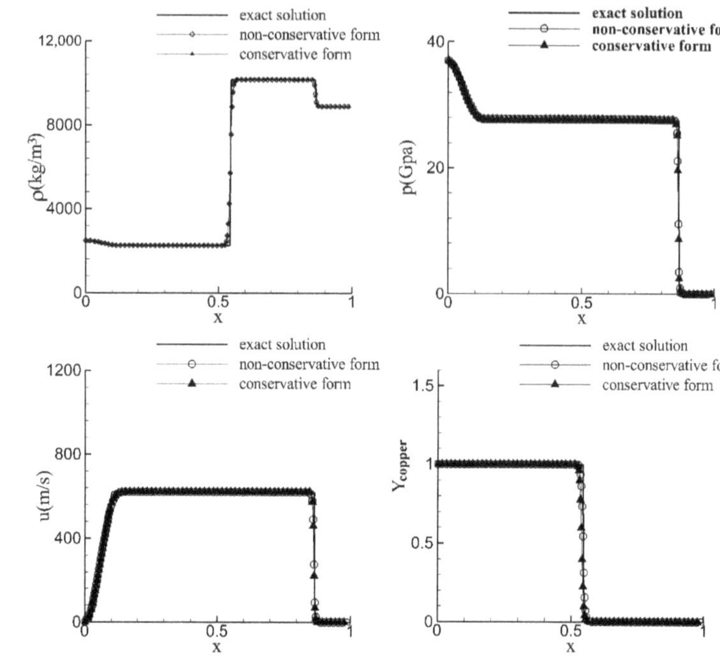

Figure A1. The distribution of mixture density, pressure, velocity and mass fraction (or volume fraction) for an explosive copper shock tube case.

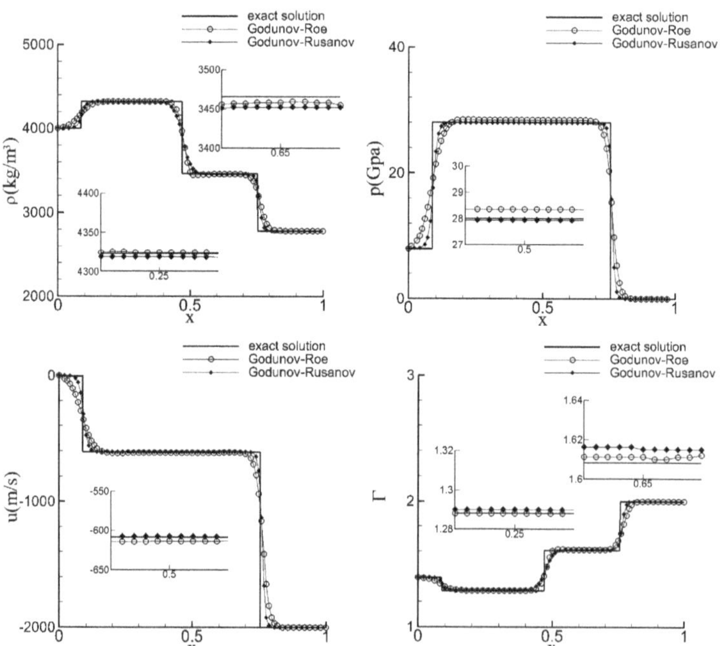

Figure A2. Numerical solution for the aluminum impact problem, including density, pressure, velocity and Γ.

References

1. Cole, R.H. *Underwater Explosion*; Princeton University: Princeton, NJ, USA, 1948.
2. Gilmore, F.R. The collapse and growth of a spherical bubble in a viscous compressible liquid. In *Hydrodynamics Laboratory Report No. 26-4*; California Institute of Technology: Pasadena, CA, USA, 1952.
3. Dellanoy, Y.; Kueny, J.L. Two phase flow approach in unsteady cavitation modeling. In Proceedings of the Cavitation and Multiphase Flow Forum, Toronto, ON, Canada, 4–7 June 1990; p. 98
4. Ren, Y.X. *Basic of Computational Fluid Dynamics*, 1st.; Tsinghua University Press: Beijing, China, 2006; pp. 111–144.
5. Toro, E.F. *Riemann Solvers and Numerical Methods for Fluid Dynamics*, 3rd ed.; University of Trento: Trento, Italy, 2009; pp. 1–24. 115–151. 345–354.
6. Zhang, B.P.; Zhang, Q.M.; Huang, F.L. *Detonation Physics*, 1st.; Weapon Industrial Press: Beijing, China, 2006; pp. 11–28. 336–345
7. Dymond, J.H.; Malhotra, R. The Tait Equation: 100 Years On. *Int. J. Thermophys.* **1988**, *9*, 941–951 [CrossRef]
8. Saurel, R.; Abgrall, R. A simple method for compressible multifluid flows. *SIAM J. Sci. Comput.* **1999**, *21*, 1115–1145. [CrossRef]
9. Yoo, Y.L.; Sung, H.G. Numerical investigation of an interaction between shock waves and bubble in a compressible multiphase flow using a diffuse interface method. *Int. J. Heat Mass Transf.* **2018**, *127*, 210–221. [CrossRef]
10. De Lorenzo, M.; Pelanti, M.; Lafon, P. HLLC-type and path-conservative schemes for a single-velocity six-equation two-phase flow model: A comparative study. *Appl. Math. Comput.* **2018**, *333*, 95–117. [CrossRef]
11. Carmouze, Q.; Saurel, R.; Chiapolino, A.; Lapebie, E. Riemann solver with internal reconstruction (RSIR) for compressible single-phase and non-equilibrium two-phase flows. *J. Comput. Phys.* **2020**, *408*, 109176. [CrossRef]
12. Carmouze, Q.; Fraysse, F.; Saurel, R.; Nkonga, B. Coupling rigid bodies motion with single phase and two-phase compressible flows on unstructured meshes. *J. Comput. Phys.* **2018**, *375*, 1314–1338. [CrossRef]
13. Bai, X.; Li, M. A conservative sharp-interface numerical method for two-dimensional compressible two-phase flows. *J. Sci. Comput.* **2023**, *97*, 30. [CrossRef]
14. Chandran, J.; Salih, A. A modified equation of state for water for a wide range of pressure and the concept of water shock tube. *Fluid Phase Equilibria* **2019**, *483*, 182–188. [CrossRef]
15. Shock Hugoniot. Available online: http://militzer.berkeley.edu/diss/node53.html (accessed on 15 January 2003).
16. Marsh, S.P. *LASL Shock Hugoniot Data*; University of California: Berkeley, CA, USA, 1980.
17. Miller, G.H.; Puckett, E.G. A high-order Godunov method for multiple condensed phases. *J. Comput. Phys.* **1996**, *128*, 110–136. [CrossRef]
18. Shyue, K.M. A Fluid-Mixture Type Algorithm for Compressible Multicomponent Flow with Mie-Gruneisen Equation of State. *J. Comput. Phys.* **2001**, *171*, 678–707. [CrossRef]
19. Kerley, G.I. *The Linear Us-Up Relation in Shock-Wave Physics*; Kerley Technical Services: Appomattox, VA,USA, 2006.
20. Nagayama, K.; Mori, Y.; Shimada, K.; Nakahara, M. Shock Hugoniot compression curve for water up to 1 Gpa by using a compressed gas gun. *J. Appl. Phys.* **2002**, *91*, 476–482. [CrossRef]
21. Steinberg, D.J. Spherical explosion and the equation of state of water. In *Lawrence Livermore National Laboratory Report*; University of California: Livermore, CA, USA, 1987.
22. Hennessey, M.; Kapila, A.K.; Schwendeman, D.W. An HLLC-type Riemann solver and high-resolution Godunov method for a two-phase model of reactive flow with general equations of state. *J. Comput. Phys.* **2020**, *405*, 109180. [CrossRef]
23. Li, Q.; Lv, Y.; Fu, L. A high-order diffuse-interface method with TENO-THINC scheme for compressible multiphase flows. *Int. J. Multiph. Flow* **2024**, *173*, 104732. [CrossRef]
24. Rodio, M.G.; Congedo, P.M.; Abgrall, R. Two-phase flow numerical simulation with real-gas effects and occurrence of rarefaction shock waves. *Eur. J. Mech. B/Fluids* **2014**, *45*, 20–35. [CrossRef]
25. El Idrissi, A.Q. Exact Riemann solver for a nonlinear hyperbolic system of equations modeling a compressible two-phase flow in pipes. *J. Math. Anal. Appl.* **2022**, *505*, 125580. [CrossRef]
26. Saurel, R.; Pantano, C. Diffuse-interface capturing methods for compressible two-phase flows. *Annu. Rev. Fluid Mech.* **2018**, *50*, 105–130. [CrossRef]
27. Saurel, R.; Abgrall, R. A multiphase Godunov method for compressible multifluid and multiphase flows. *J. Comput. Phys.* **1999**, *150*, 425–467. [CrossRef]
28. Allaire, G.; Clerc, S.; Kokh, S. A five-equation model for the Simulation of interfaces between compressible fluids. *J. Comput. Phys.* **2002**, *181*, 577–616. [CrossRef]
29. Shyue, K.M. A wave-propagation based volume tracking method for compressible multicomponent flow in two space dimensions. *J. Comput. Phys.* **2006**, *215*, 219–244. [CrossRef]
30. Shyue, K.M. A high-resolution mapped grid algorithm for compressible multiphase flow problems. *J. Comput. Phys.* **2010**, *229*, 8780–8801. [CrossRef]
31. Ward, G.M.; Pullin, D.I. A hybrid, center-difference, limiter method for simulations of compressible multicomponent flows with Mie-Gruneisen equation of state. *J. Comput. Phys.* **2010**, *229*, 2999–3018. [CrossRef]
32. Ruoff, A.L. Linear Shock-Velocity-Particle-Velocity Relationship. *J. Appl. Phys.* **1967**, *38*, 4976–4980. [CrossRef]
33. Heuzé, O. General form of the Mie-Gruneisen equation of state. *Comptes Rendus Mec.* **2012**, *340*, 679–687. [CrossRef]
34. Flores, J.; Holt, M. Glimm's method applied to underwater explosions. *J. Comput. Phys.* **1981**, *44*, 377–387. [CrossRef]

35. Lee, E.; Finger, M.; Collins, W. JWL equation of states coefficients for high explosives. In *Lawrence Livermore National Laboratory Report*; University of California: Livermore, CA, USA, 1973.
36. Cocchi, J.P.; Saurel, R.; Loraud, J.C. Treatment of interface problems with Godunov-type schemes. *Shock. Waves* **1996**, *5*, 347–357. [CrossRef]
37. Abgrall, R. How to prevent pressure oscillations in multicomponent flow calculations: A Quasi Conservative Approach. *J. Comput. Phys.* **1996**, *125*, 150–160. [CrossRef]
38. Qian, J.; Wang, Y.; Zhang, Y.; Wang, P. An entropy consistent and symmetric seven-equation model for compressible two-phase flows. *J. Comput. Phys.* **2003**, *489*, 112271. [CrossRef]
39. Pandey, M.; Sharma, V.D. Interaction of a characteristic shock with a weak discontinuity in a non-ideal gas. *Wave Motion* **2007**, *44*, 346–354. [CrossRef]
40. Dal Maso, G.; Le Floch, P.; Murat, F. Definition and weak stability of nonconservative products. *J. Math. Pures Appl.* **1995**, *74*, 483–548.
41. Abgrall, R.; Karni, S. Two-layer shallow water system: A relaxation approach. *SIAM J. Sci. Comput.* **2009**, *31*, 1603–1627. [CrossRef]
42. Shah, S.; Hernández-Dueñas, G. Weakly Compressible Two-Layer Shallow-Water Flows Along Channels. *J. Sci. Comput.* **2024**, *100*, 61. [CrossRef]
43. Liu, T.G.; Khoo, B.C.; Yeo, K.S. The simulation of compressible multi-medium flow. I. A new methodology with test applications to 1D gas–gas and gas–water cases. *Comput. Fluids* **2001**, *30*, 291–314. [CrossRef]
44. Liu, T.G.; Khoo, B.C.; Yeo, K.S. The numerical simulations of explosion and implosion in air: Use of a modified Harten's TVD scheme. *Int. J. Numer. Methods Fluids* **1999**, *31*, 661–680. [CrossRef]
45. Yao, X.L.; Yang, W.S.; Chen, J. Numerical calculation of explosion power of mines lying on seabed. *Explos. Shock. Waves* **2011**, *31*, 661–680.
46. Gao, F.; Qiu, Y.Y.; Wang, M.Y. Shock-hugoniot relationships of sand considering porosity evolution. *J. Vib. Shock.* **2017**, *36*, 134–140.

mathematics

Review

Review of Experimental, Theoretical and Numerical Advances in Multi-Crack Fracture Mechanics

Zhao-Wei Wang [1,*], D. M. Li [1,2,*], Yi-Fan Zhong [1], Yi-Kung Liu [1] and Yu-Nong Shao [1]

1 School of Civil Engineering and Architecture, Wuhan University of Technology, Wuhan 430070, China; soder@whut.edu.cn (Y.-F.Z.); wutlyk_.123@whut.edu.cn (Y.-K.L.); syn_7863135-@whut.edu.cn (Y.-N.S.)
2 Sanya Science and Education Innovation Park, Wuhan University of Technology, Sanya 572000, China
* Correspondence: tjwzw@whut.edu.cn (Z.-W.W.); dongmli2-c@my.cityu.edu.hk or domili@whut.edu.cn (D.M.L.)

Abstract: In engineering fracture problems, cracks tend to interact with each other rather than exist singly. In recent years, the phenomenon of multi-cracking has received attention from both academia and industry. This article firstly emphasizes the importance and research trends of crack interactions. The article then discusses the experimental observation and theoretical modeling of the multi-crack problem and compares the different numerical methods in detail. Finally, this paper offers a comprehensive summary and in-depth analysis of the advancements in multi-crack fracture mechanics, aiming to provide reliable support for solving the multi-crack problem in engineering.

Keywords: multi-crack; crack interactions; fracture mechanics; crack propagation; numerical methods

MSC: 74R99

Citation: Wang, Z.-W.; Li, D.M.; Zhong, Y.-F.; Liu, Y.-K.; Shao, Y.-N. Review of Experimental, Theoretical and Numerical Advances in Multi-Crack Fracture Mechanics. *Mathematics* **2024**, *12*, 3881. https://doi.org/10.3390/math12243881

Academic Editors: Joaquim Infante Barbosa and José Alberto Rodrigues

Received: 6 November 2024
Revised: 28 November 2024
Accepted: 4 December 2024
Published: 10 December 2024

1. Introduction

Many cracks exist in high-strength and brittle materials applied in engineering, such as rocks, concretes, alloys, composites, etc. These cracks may rapidly grow from micro-scale to macro-scale under external loads or harsh environments, leading to structural damage once they reach a critical size. The presence of multiple cracks complicates the assessment compared to a single crack, as each crack is affected by the others. It is difficult to assess the stress intensity factor (SIF) at the crack tip and the direction of crack initiation accurately with conventional methods. The complexity of the multi-crack problem increases the risk of structural failure and places higher demands on engineering design and materials. Therefore, assessing the fracture behavior of cracks and their interactions quantitatively has become an important topic that needs to be addressed in fracture mechanics.

In practical engineering, scholars are concerned with the real-time monitoring and prediction of crack propagation in structures under external effects such as static, cyclic and temperature loads. These multi-crack interactions are prevalent in a variety of structures, and crack development significantly affects material strength, which directly influences the overall structural service life. Secondly, with the wide application of functional materials in civil engineering and geotechnical, aerospace, automotive, and other industries, the study of multi-crack fracture behavior in composites and heterogeneous materials has become crucial, with different properties of the materials determining different crack propagation laws. Due to the limitations of experimental and theoretical research, computer numerical simulations such as the extended finite element method (XFEM), the boundary element method (BEM), and the meshfree method (MM) have become the mainstream methods and are suitable for modeling complex interactions of cracks.

This paper serves as a review article focusing on the multi-crack problem, which is an important topic in fracture mechanics. Currently, there are many review articles in the field of fracture mechanics that summarize the development of multiscale analysis [1,2], fractures of layered materials [3], fatigue fractures [4,5], composite fractures [6–8], and various numerical methods [9–12]. Nevertheless, the fracture problem remains a common challenge in engineering practice, as cracks often do not exist in isolation. The interactions of multiple cracks increase the complexity of the problem. Although multi-crack problems are common in fracture mechanics, there is a lack of systematic review papers to discuss this topic. In this paper, we provide a comprehensive overview and summary of the multi-crack propagation problem, mainly from three aspects: experimental observations in different media, theoretical studies, and numerical methods. The composition of research on multi-crack fracture mechanics is shown as Figure 1.

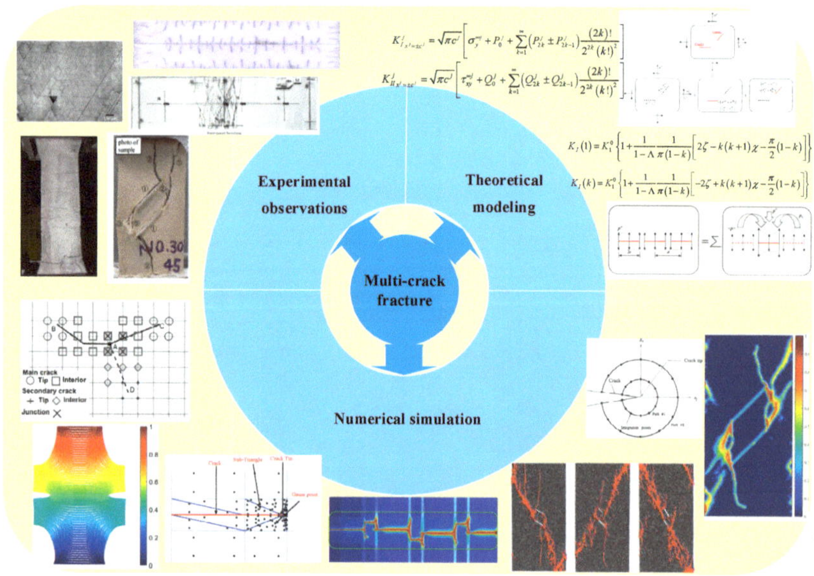

Figure 1. Composition of research on multi-crack fracture mechanics.

2. Experimental Observations

Multi-crack phenomena are very common in engineering, but the crack propagation modes show significant variability due to the diversity of physical properties of the materials and external loading modes. For example, in fiber composites, cracks tend to grow along the main direction of the fibers, showing a strong directionality, whereas in more brittle materials such as rock and concrete, cracks tend to branch and aggregate. In addition, when multiple cracks develop in the same material, the interactions between the cracks often cause significant changes in the crack paths, increasing the difficulty of predicting and controlling the cracking behavior. In recent years, many researchers have delved into the fracture behavior of multiple cracks through experimental studies, which are the basis for the study of fracture problems.

2.1. Rocks

The problem of multi-crack fractures in rock is widespread in industries such as mining, civil engineering, petroleum engineering, and geohazard assessment. Significant progress has been made in theory, experimentation, simulation, and engineering applications. Thermal cycling, freezing, thawing, magmatism, and creep of rocks in geology can cause cracking phenomena in rocks [13–16].

In the fracture test of rocks, researchers mainly focus on a series of fracture mechanisms such as crack initiation, propagation, branching, and aggregation. Unlike general elastomers, due to non-homogeneity and internal defects, cracks in rocks are difficult to explain with traditional elastic fracture mechanics, but have more variable fracture modes under different external loads, which are usually accompanied by cracks of different genesis, such as wing (tensile) cracks and horsetail (shear) cracks [17–21], as shown in Figure 2a. Damage and fractures of rocks are closely related to external loads [22], and the way cracks grow and interconnect in rocks depends on internal defects such as air cavities, microcracks, and impurities. Prefabricated cracks are a common experimental approach to study fracture problems, and a large number of studies have been carried out by researchers on two or more parallel cracks in different rock bodies and under different external loading conditions [20,23–26]. Ma and Yang et al. [21,23] observed the fracture pattern of multi-directional propagation of crack tips in rocks, as shown in Figure 2b. Shen et al. [24] performed uniaxial compression tests using a red sandstone cube specimen with three parallel cracks, as shown in Figure 2b. Haeri et al. [25,27] investigated the effect of the fracture behavior between two prefabricated L-shaped cracks in the sample, as shown in Figure 2d.

Cracks are usually observed in the laboratory using rock samples or synthetic materials that simulate rock properties with the help of techniques such as the digital image correlation (DIC) method [28,29], X-ray computed tomography [30,31], and acoustic emission monitoring [27,32], and the related processes or instruments are shown in Figure 2e–g. However, these techniques provide convenience while having problems, respectively, such as difficulty in dealing with off-surface displacement, inability to observe the dynamic crack propagation process directly, and uncertainty in the localization of cracks. Liu et al. [33] investigated the multi-crack cracking behavior of rocks under cyclic compressive loading. And Ghamsogar et al. [34] compared the crack propagation patterns of rocks under cyclic loading and static loading.

2.2. Concretes

Concrete is a man-made material widely used in civil engineering and hydraulic engineering. The development of cracks is the main reason for structural damage. By studying the law of multi-crack propagation in concrete, the growth of cracks can be monitored and controlled to ensure the safety and functionality of the structure.

Due to the casting process for concrete, the interior contains a large number of air holes, and these holes are the places where cracks are generated. Zhang et al. [35] established an intrinsic relationship for concrete coupling with air and verified it with uniaxial compression experiments, and the concrete slices were observed with a microscope, as shown in Figure 3a. Concrete is usually functioned in engineering as a reinforced concrete composite structure with steel reinforcement. Durand et al. [36] proposed an FEM considering the interactions of steel reinforcement with various structures of concrete, which was compared to the fracture experiments of reinforced concrete beams by Rabczuk et al. [37–39], as shown in Figure 3b. In civil engineering tests, multi-cracking of concrete is very common in impact tests [40] and three-point bending tests [41,42], which are used for assessing the strength and fracture toughness of concrete.

Reinforcement of concrete structures with fiber-reinforced composites is a concerning topic [43,44]. Pan et al. [45] found that the presence of multiple cracks on spans of reinforced concrete beams leads to the debonding of the FRP, as shown in Figure 3c. Cho et al. [46] observed multi-crack fractures of high-performance fiber-reinforced cementitious composites (HPFRCs) in the plastic hinge zone of reinforced concrete columns, as shown in Figure 3d.

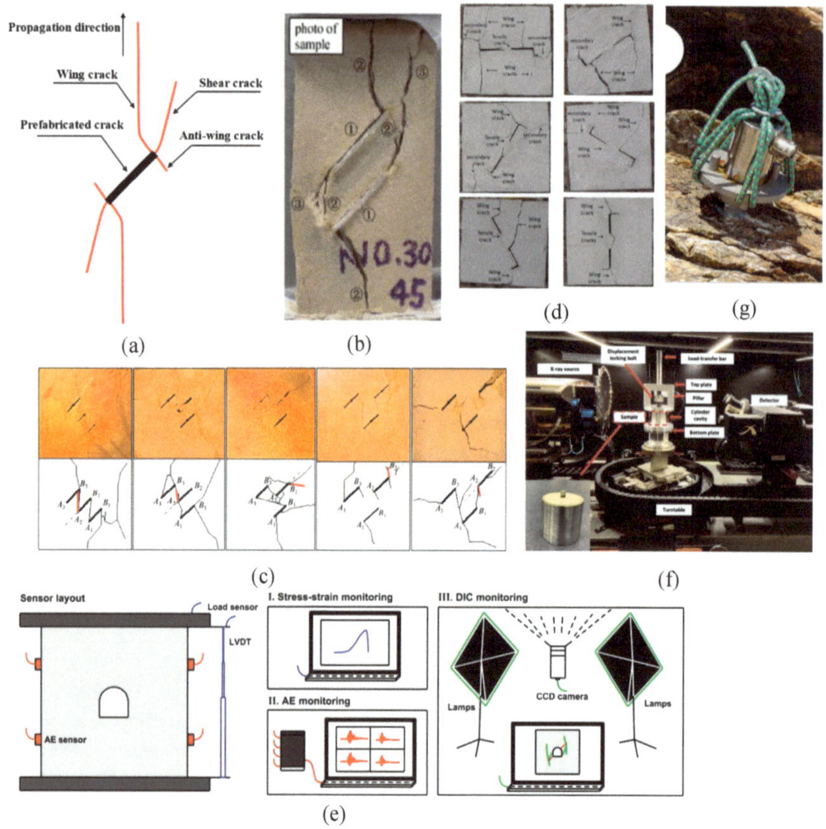

Figure 2. (**a**) Secondary cracks in a rock [21]. (**b**) Multi-crack propagation patterns in experiments [21]. (**c**) Fracture of red sandstone specimens [24]. (**d**) Damage patterns for L-shaped cracks [25]. (**e**) Procedure for analyzing the fracture problem in DIC [29]. (**f**) X-ray computed tomography scanning instrumentation [30]. (**g**) Acoustic emission transducer [13].

Fatigue damage is an important cause of deterioration in concrete structures, and under fatigue loading, crack propagation becomes more complex, so investigating the development of multiple cracks in this case is vital to understand the behavior of materials under cyclic loading, to predict the durability and safety of the structure [47,48]. Elshazli et al. [49] used several fiber-reinforced polymers to strengthen concrete beams under cyclic loading, and significant multi-crack development was observed. Figure 3e depicts the crack propagation in fatigue test of concrete columns from the experiment of Li et al. [50].

The techniques mentioned in the previous study, such as DIC, acoustic emission, and X-ray computed tomography, can also be used for the concrete fracture problem [51–54]. However, cracks in rock and concrete have poor experimental reproducibility and are difficult to be explained by theoretical models due to the heterogeneity and intrinsic defects of the material, and more computerized methods are currently used for the study of concrete structure fracture problems [55,56].

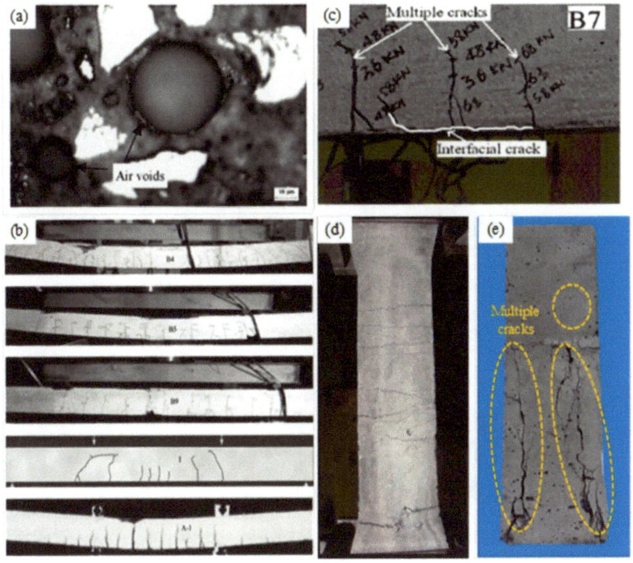

Figure 3. (**a**) Air voids in concrete slice [35]. (**b**) Multi-crack fracture of reinforced concrete beams [36]. (**c**) Cracks in FRP-reinforced concrete beam [45]. (**d**) Multi-crack in HPFRC column [46]. (**e**) Crack propagation in concrete columns in fatigue tests [50].

2.3. Fiber-Reinforced Composites

Fiber-reinforced composites are widely used in various engineering fields due to their excellent specific strength and designability; however, their fracture study is an active and complex field because of their material inhomogeneity, orientation, and heterogeneity. X-ray computed tomography [57–60] and DIC [61–63] methods are widely used in the research of fiber-reinforced composites.

In fiber-reinforced composites, the fracture of the member includes the pull-off of the fibers and the fracture of the matrix, and it is difficult to explain the fracture behavior of composites with the traditional fracture mechanics theory. Test methods for the fracture of fiber-reinforced composites are mainly divided into tensile and compression tests. The earliest experimental studies related to fiber-reinforced composites date back to the 1960s, when Rosen et al. [64] conducted a series of experiments on the destruction of fiber-reinforced composite samples. Li et al. [57] studied the fracture failure process in laminates by an over-height compact tension test combined with X-ray computed tomography. The experimental procedure is shown in Figure 4a. Zobeiry et al. [61] measured the fracture damage properties of laminated composites by combining over-height compact tension and compact compression tests. The fiber breakage and matrix cracking are shown in Figure 4b. Sadowski et al. [63] analyzed the propagation and interactions of parallel cracks in polymer matrix composites. The process of the tensile experiment and DIC results are shown by Figure 4c,d. As shown in Figure 4e, Nguyen et al. [62] used DIC to observe the tensile damage of double cross laminates.

Fatigue tests and indentation tests are also common methods to study the multi-crack fractures of composites. Garcea et al. [58] surveyed the fatigue damage cracking phenomenon of carbon fiber-reinforced epoxy specimens by computed tomography. Sommer et al. [65] observed microscopic damage in fatigue experiments on composite laminates with multiple off-axis plies. In composite laminates, multi-crack fracture problems are accompanied by delamination [57,66–68]. The phenomenon of delamination and fractures of laminates with different indenter displacements in the quasi-static indentation experiments of Wagih et al. [67] is shown in Figure 4f.

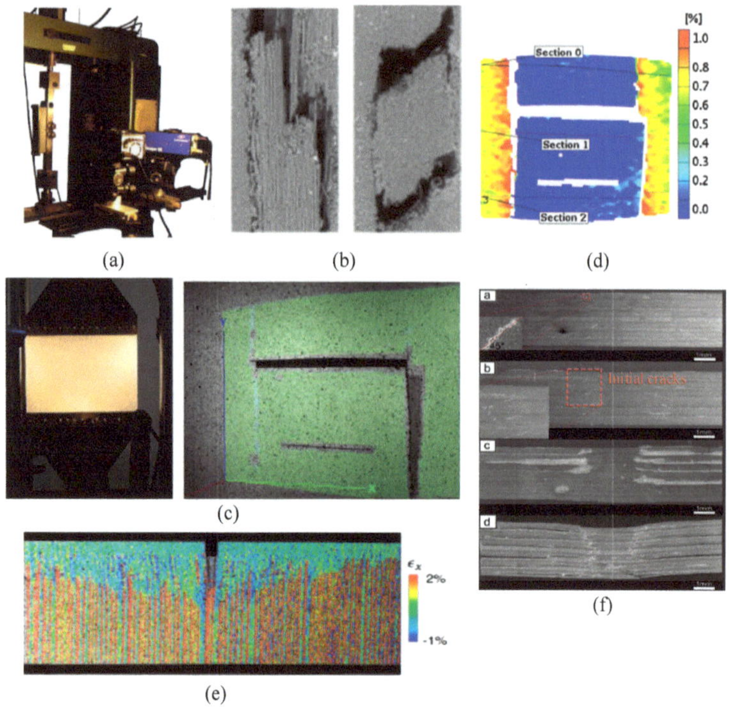

Figure 4. (**a**) Tension test combined with X-ray computed tomography [57]. (**b**) Fiber breakage and matrix cracking under tension [61]. (**c**) Parallel unequal crack propagation in polymer matrix composites [63]. (**d**) Plane strain data obtained by the DIC technique [63]. (**e**) Fatigue fracture damage of carbon fiber-reinforced epoxy specimens [62]. (**f**) Pressure fracture of laminates [67].

2.4. Compound Coating

A compound coating is defined here as a thin layer of a compound or a mixture that forms a double layer with another material as a substrate, and the structure is usually formed due to the reaction of the metal with an active gas or a spraying process in engineering. In this model, the top layer will fracture before the substrate because it is more brittle and thinner relative to the substrate. When multiple cracks are produced in the top layer, the fracture is easily observed due to the bonding of the substrate to the top layer.

Under uniaxial tension, the fracture of the top coating on the substrate takes the form of a parallel crack fracture. Thouless et al. [69] explored the relationship between the spacing of brittle film cracks on an elastic substrate and the film stress, thickness, and fracture toughness, and obtained TEM micrographs of oxides cracking in parallel on the substrate. Beuth, Hutchinson, and Suo et al. [70–72] investigated the phenomena of elastic fractures in laminar structures and deduced the case of multiple cracks, revealing the law of interactions between cracks in the top coating of the substrate and laying the foundation for subsequent studies of cracking in this problem. Chen et al. [73] developed an elastic-plastic fracture model combined with uniaxial tensile tests to investigate the multi-crack fractures of an alumina coating when it is fully bonded to an aluminum substrate under large tensile deformation, as shown in Figure 5a. Cheikh et al. [74] used a microscope to observe the multi-crack cracking pattern of a ZnO coating deposited on an ethylene-terafluoroethlene substrate by magnetron sputtering, as shown in Figure 5b. Shenoy et al. [75] observed a fracture pattern in a GaN top coating on a Si substrate, as shown in Figure 5c. Andersons et al. [76] analyzed the cracking patterns of a 100 nm thick silicon oxide coating on polyethylene terephthalate, polypropylene, and polyamide films, as shown in Figure 5d. Vellinga et al. [77] observed fracture, delamination, and buckling of an amorphous carbon-hydroxide coating on an Al substrate under tensile load.

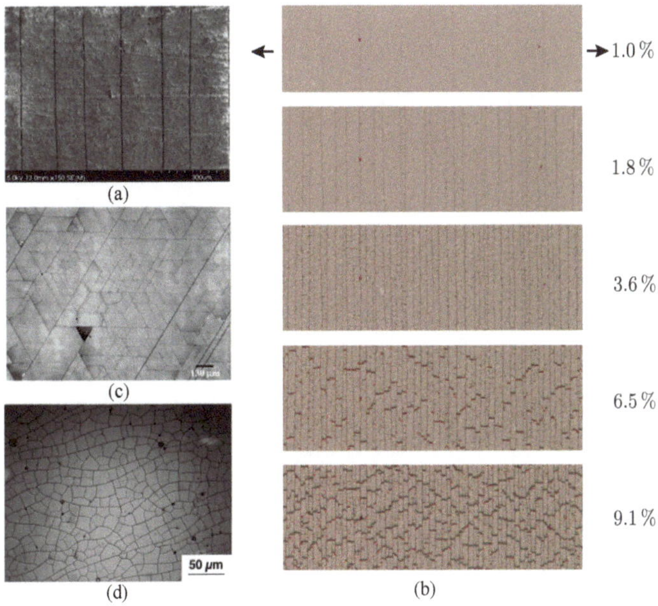

Figure 5. (**a**) Cracking of GaN coatings under tensile loading [73]. (**b**) Cracking of ZnO coatings under different substrate strains [74]. (**c**) Cracking of GaN coatings under residual stresses [75]. (**d**) Cracking of polypropylene coatings under biaxial stress [76].

2.5. Other Materials

Glass, ceramics and some polymer materials are known for their excellent physical and chemical properties. However, the brittleness of these materials makes them susceptible to cracking, which results in fractures when subjected to stress. Therefore, the study of multi-crack fracture behavior of such materials is not only crucial but also challenging.

Glass materials tend to fracture under external loading due to their high brittleness and poor ductility, and the cracks will split open, leading to extensive fractures [78]. Fineberg et al. [79] observed the phenomenon of typical microcrack branching in their study of fractures in glass polymers. When glass materials are subjected to single-point impact loading [80], a spider net of cracks is produced, as shown in Figure 6a,b. The fracture pattern of glass members in four-point bending tests [81] is shown in Figure 6c. Glass materials tend to chip on the surface or scratch during processing, which is often the cause of cracking and damage to the structure under external loads [82,83]. A fracture of glass with prefabricated scratches is shown in Figure 6d. Scratches [84] and fatigue [85] that produce fractures are also present in ceramic or composite ceramic bases; the cracks near the scratches are shown in Figure 7a, and a multi-crack fracture of the ceramic matrix in a composite under fatigue loading is shown in Figure 7b,c. Additionally, ceramic materials produce a large number of thermal shock cracks [86,87] during quenching experiments, as shown in Figure 7d.

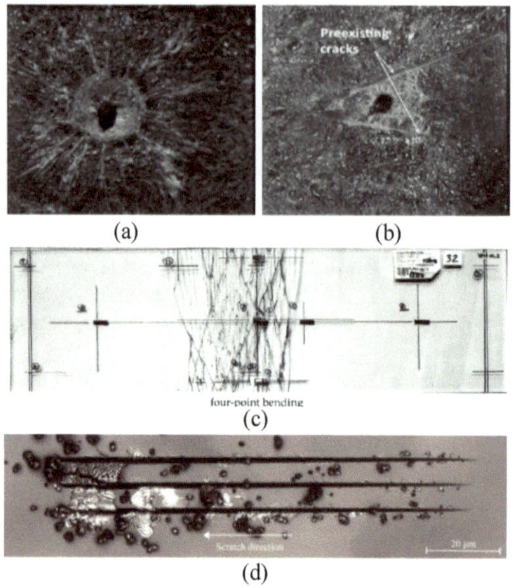

Figure 6. Fractures in glass. (**a**) Glass fracture under single-point impact [80]. (**b**) Glass fracture under single-point impact with preexisting cracks [80]. (**c**) Fracture behavior in four-point bending test [81]. (**d**) Fracture between scratches [82].

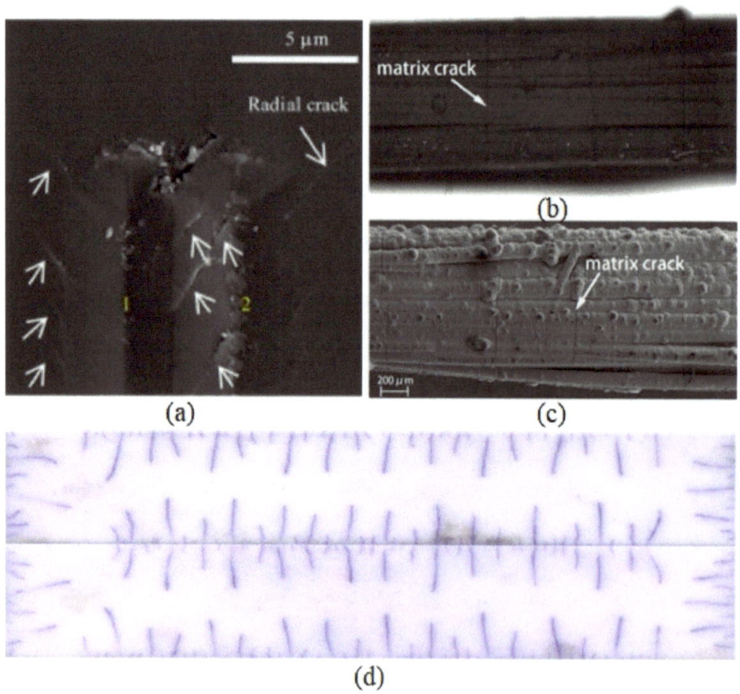

Figure 7. Fractures in ceramics. (**a**) Propagation of cracks around the scratches [84]. (**b**) Cracking of ceramic matrix [85]. (**c**) SEM image of cracks in ceramics [85]. (**d**) Ceramic cracks under thermal shock [86].

In addition to the typically brittle materials such as glass and ceramics, it has been observed that multi-crack fractures also occur in non-metallic materials such as polymer fluids [88], water-soluble gels [89], polymers [90,91], and crystals [92]. The gelatin material used by Fender et al. [89] and the PC material used by Belova et al. [90] both have good linear elasticity and photoelasticity, which can correspond well to the theory of linear elastic fracture. The tensile test procedure for gelatin is shown in Figure 8a–f, and the photoelasticity phenomenon is shown in Figure 8g,h. The photoelasticity test of a PC plane containing two cracks is shown in Figure 8i, and the stress distribution can be clearly observed. Goehring et al. observed the cracking process of colloidal film during drying, as shown in Figure 8j,k.

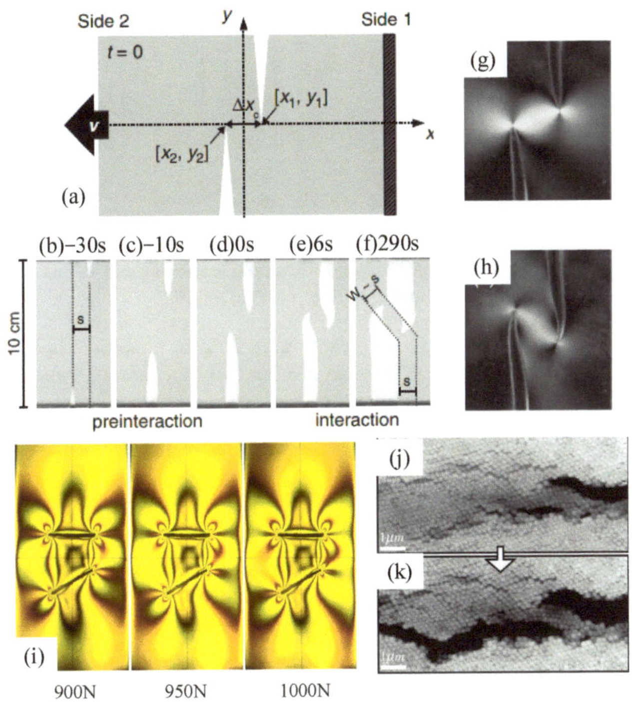

Figure 8. (**a**) Tensile test of gelatin material [89]. (**b–f**) Crack propagation process in gelatin sheet [89]. (**g,h**) Photoelasticity experiment of two-crack propagation in gelatin [89]. (**i**) Stress distribution of PC plane containing two cracks under different tensile forces in photoelastic experiment [90]. (**j,k**) Cracking process in colloidal film during drying [91].

Fractures of plastic materials, such as metals, are quite different from those of brittle materials in that they undergo significant plastic deformation as the material absorbs a large amount of energy during cracking and destruction. A plastic fracture usually has a large necking region; therefore, the phenomenon of multi-crack fractures is not common in plastic materials. Alloy materials represented by steels play an important role in engineering, and these materials are usually subject to multiple cracking and fatigue damage due to low-cycle fatigue and thermomechanical fatigue effects during service [93–96], as shown in Figure 9a, which represents the multiple cracking of austenitic stainless steels under low-cycle fatigue at 72% of its service life [97]. Figure 9b shows the path of crack propagation in fatigue tests [94]. In addition, stress corrosion causes steel to become less plastic, and brittle fractures occur below the yield strength [98,99]. Figure 9c–f illustrate the phenomenon of multi-crack propagation at macroscopic and microscopic scales in steel under stress corrosion [99].

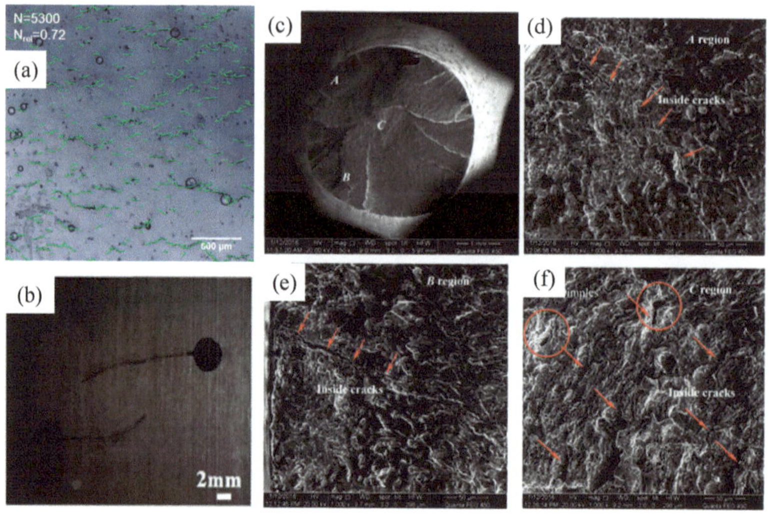

Figure 9. (**a**) Multiple cracks in austenitic stainless steels subjected to low-cycle fatigue [97]. (**b**) Crack propagation paths in steel during fatigue tests. (**c**) Cracks on the steel surface [94]. (**d–f**) Microscopic cracks corresponding to A, B, and C in (**c**) [99].

Compared to plastic materials, the materials of rocks, concrete, composites, and compounds are of interest in fracture mechanics because of their brittleness. The fracture process in these materials is sudden and lacks plastic deformation as a warning signal, which makes their fracture behavior unpredictable, so we need to study the multi-crack fracture problem as a challenge in engineering.

3. Theoretical Modeling

Fracture phenomena are common in brittle materials. The fundamental theory of fracture mechanics based on linear elasticity was developed by pioneers such as Griffiths and Owen, who introduced concepts like the stress intensity factor (SIF) and energy release rate. The current analytical solutions of single-crack fracture problems in linear elastic materials are usually dominated by the field functions containing SIF in polar coordinates proposed by Williams et al. [100] and the complex variable field functions by Sih et al. [101]. In multi-crack problems, the development of analytical methods is limited due to uncertainty in the locations of cracks.

For the analytical study of multiple cracks, there were many early exploratory works. In 1953, Muskhelishvili [102] proposed a complex function solution of the planar elasticity problem by two stress functions, $\Phi(z)$ and $\Omega(z)$, which provided the conditions for the theory of linear elastic fractures. The stress equation is

$$\sigma_x + \sigma_y = 2\left[\Phi(z) + \overline{\Phi(z)}\right] \tag{1}$$

$$\sigma_y - i\tau_{xy} = \Phi(z) + \Omega(\overline{z}) + (z - \overline{z})\overline{\Phi'(z)} \tag{2}$$

where the coordinate $z = x + iy$.

Some scholars [103,104] have solved problems involving colinear or parallel multiple cracks based on the analytical method of Muskhelishvili's complex function. The work of Koiter et al. [103] is the most representative, in which the stress functions $\Phi(z)$ and $\Omega(z)$ are revised to solve the model for colinear equidistant multiple cracks under the same boundary conditions, as shown in Figure 10. The strain energy increment for each crack under far-field stresses is

$$\Delta A = -\frac{8c^2}{\pi}\left(\frac{\tau_{xy}{}^2}{E} + \frac{\sigma_y{}^2}{E}\right)\log\cos\frac{\pi}{2}\frac{b}{c} \tag{3}$$

where E is the modulus of elasticity of the material, the crack length is $2c$, and the crack spacing is $2b$.

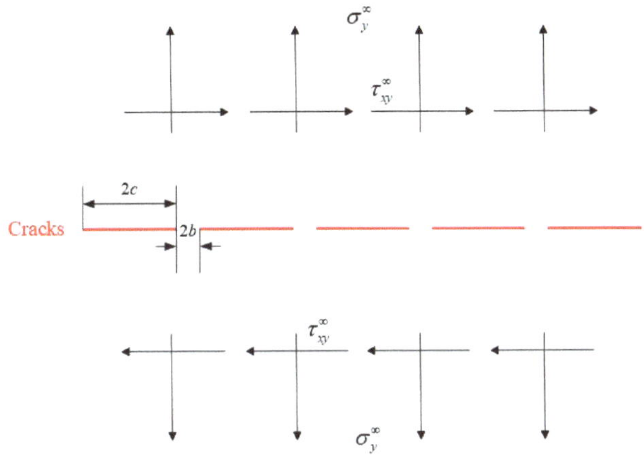

Figure 10. Multiple colinear equidistant cracks.

Horii et al. [105,106] proposed a method of pseudotractions to solve the problems of two arbitrary relative cracks, colinear cracks, and parallel cracks in a linear elastic solid. The problem of two arbitrarily located cracks is decomposed as shown in Figure 11, and the SIF is

$$K^j_{I\,x^j=\pm c^j} = \sqrt{\pi c^j}\left[\sigma_y^{\infty j} + P_0^j + \sum_{k=1}^{\infty}\left(P_{2k}^j \pm P_{2k-1}^j\right)\frac{(2k)!}{2^{2k}(k!)^2}\right] \tag{4}$$

$$K^j_{II\,x^j=\pm c^j} = \sqrt{\pi c^j}\left[\tau_{xy}^{\infty j} + Q_0^j + \sum_{k=1}^{\infty}\left(Q_{2k}^j \pm Q_{2k-1}^j\right)\frac{(2k)!}{2^{2k}(k!)^2}\right] \tag{5}$$

where the crack numbers j = 1,2, and P and Q are the coefficients of each term after Taylor expansion of Equation (2).

For the cases of colinear and parallel cracks, as shown in Figure 12, the SIFs are

Colinear cracks:

$$K_I = \sqrt{\pi c}\Big/\left[1 - \frac{\pi^2}{6}\left(\frac{c}{d}\right)^2\right]\sigma_y^{\infty} \tag{6}$$

$$K_{II} = \sqrt{\pi c}\Big/\left[1 - \frac{\pi^2}{6}\left(\frac{c}{d}\right)^2\right]\tau_{xy}^{\infty} \tag{7}$$

Parallel cracks:

$$K_I = \sqrt{\pi c}\,\sigma_y^{\infty}\Big/\left[1 + \frac{\pi^2}{2}\left(\frac{c}{d}\right)^2\right] \tag{8}$$

$$K_{II} = \sqrt{\pi c}\,\tau_{xy}^{\infty}\Big/\left[1 - \frac{\pi^2}{6}\left(\frac{c}{d}\right)^2\right] \tag{9}$$

where the crack length is $2c$ and the spacing between crack centers is d.

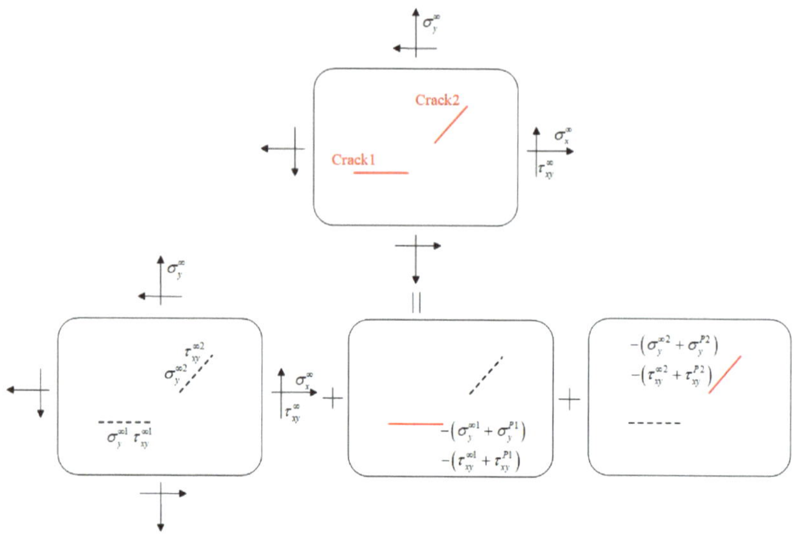

Figure 11. Decomposition of the fracture problem with two arbitrary cracks.

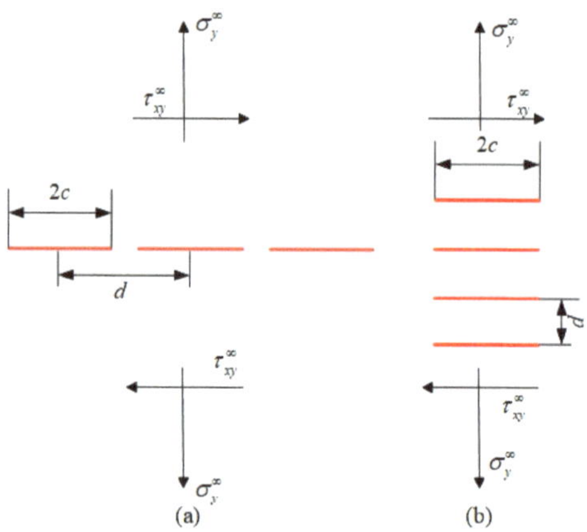

Figure 12. (**a**) Colinear cracks. (**b**) Parallel cracks.

Kachanov [107,108] proposed a simple method for stress analysis in elastic solids containing many cracks. As shown in Figure 13, p^{∞} is the crack surface traction, and p_k is considered to be generated by the uniform average traction <p> acting on the kth crack. By assuming that the traction force in each crack can be expressed as the sum of uniform and non-uniform components, the interactions between cracks are only caused by the uniform component, and the average stress ideology is used to solve the problem of adjacent cracks. Respectively, the SIFs of the outer and inner crack tips are

$$K_I(1) = K_1^0 \left\{ 1 + \frac{1}{1-\Lambda} \frac{1}{\pi(1-k)} \left[2\zeta - k(k+1)\chi - \frac{\pi}{2}(1-k) \right] \right\} \tag{10}$$

$$K_I(k) = K_1^0 \left\{ 1 + \frac{1}{1-\Lambda} \frac{1}{\pi(1-k)} \left[-2\zeta + k(k+1)\chi - \frac{\pi}{2}(1-k) \right] \right\} \tag{11}$$

where Λ is the traction attenuation factor, the positive and negative of k represent the crack number to the left and right of the corresponding crack, and ζ and χ are the complete elliptic integrals of $k' = \sqrt{1-k^2}$.

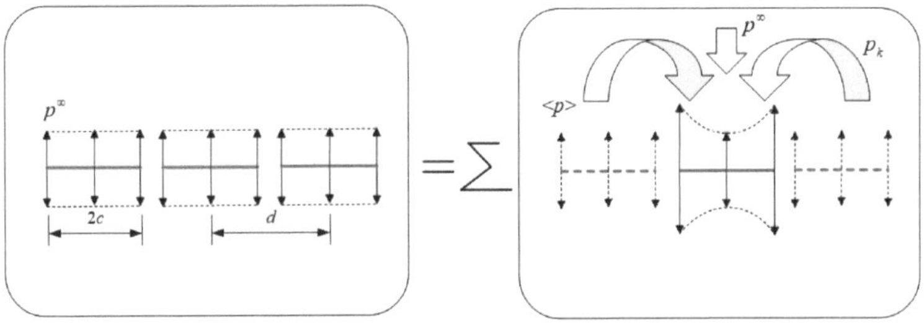

Figure 13. Superposition of periodic crack rows.

Li et al. [109] improved Kachanov's method and applied it to parallel and tilted cracks. Qing et al. [110] proposed a new method for solving the tight crack problem and plastic zone assessment based on Kachanov's method and alternating iteration technique. Recent analytical methods based on Muskhelishvili's complex function and superposition principle also remain in the modeling of colinear cracks [111,112], which are too poor to serve practical engineering.

It has been found that complex crack distributions are difficult to be solved by traditional analytical methods and that singular integral equations (SIE) can solve the problem of complex crack interactions [113]. Chen [114] found that the multi-crack problem can be easily transformed into a system of Fredholm integral equations to compute the SIF. Lam et al. [115] used the SIE to explore the effect on SIF by the interactions of the cracks. Cheung et al. [116] combined the Fredholm integral equation used for the infinite plate crack problem with a weighted residual method to solve the multi-crack problem. Yavuz et al. [117] analyzed the interactions of cracks in an infinite plate and determined the overall stress field and SIF. Chen [118,119] provided a review of the integral equations for the planar elastic cracking problem and split the plate into two edge value problems for the integral solution. Shen et al. [24] computed the SIF of the inclined-parallel cracks with different relative positions for a combination of the complex function method and the integral method. Denda et al. [120] enhanced the accuracy of the traditional integration method by incorporating a continuous distribution of dislocation dipoles. Doubly periodic cracking is a problem in which the crack arrangement is characterized by periodicity, as shown in Figure 14. Shi et al. [121–125] used SIE for a series of doubly periodic arrays of cracks to explore the interaction problem in periodic cracks. Ayatollahi et al. [126–128] used distributed dislocation in conjunction with Cauchy's singular equation to solve the problem of linear multi-crack interactions in bonded, functionally gradient, and electro-elastic materials. SIE is useful in solving the problems of nematic as well as magneto-electro-elastic materials [129,130], where it plays a crucial role in solving multi-field coupling problems with multiple cracks.

However, the implementation of singular integration techniques usually needs to be realized with the help of numerical methods [131], such as boundary integral equations (BIE) [132–134]. The boundary element method (BEM), which is a numerical implementation of the BIE, allows the construction of a system of equations to solve the problem by dividing the boundary into a finite number of elements and the boundary integral equations.

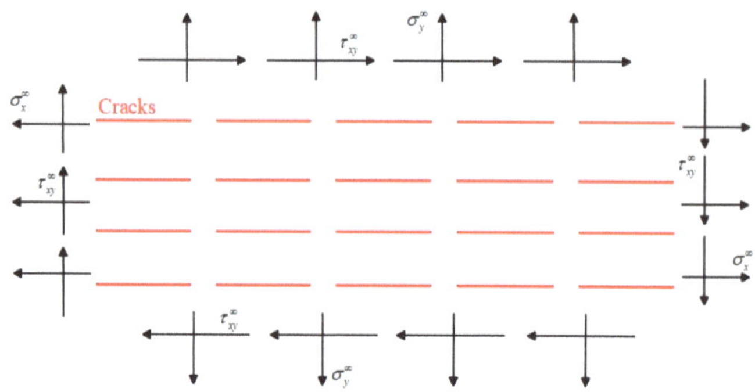

Figure 14. Doubly periodic cracking.

4. Numerical Simulation

The study of multi-crack models reveals the complexity of the fracture behavior, where the interactions between cracks and the interactions of stress fields constitute a complex system that introduces unpredictable variables into the crack propagation path and velocity. With the advancement of computer technology, numerical methods have become a key tool for solving fracture problems due to their flexibility, low cost, and ease of multiscale analysis and multi-physics field coupling.

Nowadays, several efficient and accurate simulation techniques, including the finite element method (FEM), the meshfree method (MM) and the boundary element method (BEM), have emerged. These techniques have enhanced our ability to understand and predict complex crack behavior. It is worth noting that these numerical methods enlist completely different mechanisms in solving crack propagation paths due to their own different principles. For example, extended finite element methods (XFEM), extended isogeometric analysis (XIGA), and boundary element methods (BEM) are based on continuum mechanics and use crack propagation criteria such as the maximum tangential stress criterion to determine the cracking, and the phase field method (PFM) is usually combined with continuum mechanics, which does not need to track the crack surface. The above methods usually assume that the material is homogeneous, continuous, and linear-elastic or elasto-plastic in modeling. On the contrary, the discrete element method (DEM) and peridynamics (PD) do not belong to continuum medium mechanics and naturally satisfy the conditions of random crack propagation through the contact and bond connection of discrete bodies, which gives these two methods a natural advantage in the study of multi-crack propagation problems in non-homogeneous, discrete media.

This section will focus on the application of numerical methods to multi-crack problems, demonstrating how they can provide strong support for deepening theoretical research and innovation in engineering practice.

4.1. Extended Finite Element Method

The FEM is one of the most representative numerical analysis tools due to its excellent applicability and flexibility. However, FEM depends on mesh and is difficult to apply to unknown crack paths and crack tip singularities. Although it has been reported in the literature that FEM can be improved or combined with other numerical methods to solve some multi-crack problems [135–137], difficulties limit the scope of application of FEM in complex fracture problems. To overcome these difficulties, the extended finite element method (XFEM), which demonstrates significant advantages with its efficiency and accuracy in dealing with multi-crack fracture problems, has emerged. XFEM effectively captures the singularity of the crack tip by introducing an enrichment function and tracing crack surfaces by techniques such as the level set method, without the need to predefine the crack path.

XFEM is vital in the study of fracture problems, and the analysis of multi-crack models has been developed. In 2000, Daux et al. [138] pioneered the use of XFEM to study the phenomena of arbitrary branched and intersecting cracks. The meshing principles for XFEM are different from those for FEM. The FEM approximation of displacement associated with Figure 15a is

$$\mathbf{u}^h(\mathbf{x}) = \sum_{i\in I} \mathbf{u}_i\phi_i(\mathbf{x}),\ I = \{1,\ldots,17\} \tag{12}$$

where $\mathbf{u}_i$ is the displacement at node i and ϕ_i is the bilinear shape function corresponding to node i. The approximated displacement by XFEM associated with Figure 15b is

$$\begin{aligned}\mathbf{u}^h = \ & \sum_{i=1}^{5} \mathbf{u}_i\phi_i(\mathbf{x}) + \boldsymbol{\alpha}_8 H_{II}(\mathbf{x})(\phi_6+\phi_7) \\ & +\boldsymbol{\alpha}_{12}(\phi_9+\phi_{10}+\phi_{11}) + \boldsymbol{\beta}_{12}H_I(\mathbf{x})(\phi_9+\phi_{10}+\phi_{11}) \\ & +\boldsymbol{\gamma}_{12}J(\mathbf{x})(\phi_9+\phi_{10}) \\ & +\boldsymbol{\alpha}_{15}(\phi_{13}+\phi_{14}) + \boldsymbol{\beta}_{15}H_I(\mathbf{x})(\phi_{13}+\phi_{14}) \\ & +\boldsymbol{\alpha}_{18}(\phi_{16}+\phi_{17}) + \boldsymbol{\beta}_{18}H_I(\mathbf{x})(\phi_{16}+\phi_{17})\end{aligned} \tag{13}$$

where $\boldsymbol{\alpha}$, $\boldsymbol{\beta}$, $\boldsymbol{\gamma}$ are the corresponding nodal vector variables, and the enrichment functions $H_I(\mathbf{x})$, $H_{II}(\mathbf{x})$, and $J(\mathbf{x})$ are defined as in Figure 15b. As shown in Figure 15c, the enrichment process of the main crack (solid line) branched cracks (dashed line) is carried out by the finite element shape function of the support point near the junction A. If we consider a main crack, which is connected to several other cracks, the approximated displacement is

$$\begin{aligned}\mathbf{u}^h(\mathbf{x}) = \ & \sum_{i\in I} \mathbf{u}_i\phi_i(\mathbf{x}) + \sum_{j=1}^{N_c}\sum_{i\in L_j} \mathbf{a}_{i,j}\phi_i(\mathbf{x})H_j(\mathbf{x}) + \sum_{j=1}^{N_t}\sum_{i\in K_j}\phi_i(\mathbf{x})\left(\sum_{l=1}^{4}\mathbf{b}_{i,j}^l F_j^l(\mathbf{x})\right) \\ & +\sum_{j=1}^{N_x}\sum_{i\in J_j} \mathbf{c}_{i,j}\phi_i(\mathbf{x})J_j(\mathbf{x})\end{aligned} \tag{14}$$

where N_c is the total number of cracks, N_t is the number of crack tips, and N_x is the number of nodes.

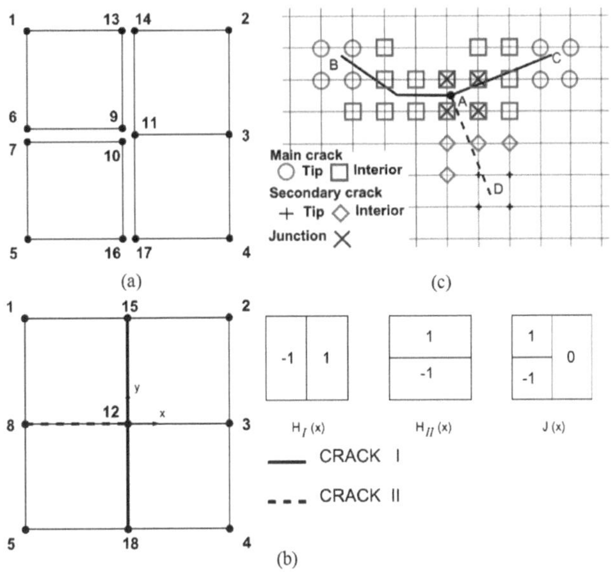

Figure 15. (**a**) FEM mesh. (**b**) XFEM mesh and definition of the discontinuous enrichment function. (**c**) Enrichment for branched cracks [138].

Belytschko et al. [139] modeled the discontinuity of arbitrary defects in the XFEM. Budyn et al. [140] introduced a crack-length control scheme to model arbitrary multi-cracks. Mousavi et al. [141] proposed a treatment of intersecting and branched cracks by harmonic enrichment functions. Richardson et al. [142] proposed a new geometric cutting algorithm to simulate crack propagation in complex geometries. Xu et al. [143] extended the junction enrichment in XFEM to simulate branched dynamic cracks. Sutula et al. [144–146] developed a minimum energy method for multiple cracks propagation. Agathos et al. [147] proposed a new algorithm in 3D structures for the multi-crack problem. Chen et al. [148] applied the phantom node method proposed by Song et al. [149] to solve multiple crack problems by the mesh-cutting technique. Ding et al. [150,151] developed a variable node XFEM with local mesh refinement. As shown in Figure 16a,b, Wen and Wang et al. [152,153] developed an improved XFEM that introduces the enrichment of crack tip singularities, which solves the problems of combining the level sets and the disorder of the global stiffness matrix in multi-crack problems. Its simulated crack propagation for double-crack and multi-crack problems is shown in Figure 16c,d. In numerical methods based on continuum mechanics, materials are usually assumed to be homogeneous and linear elastic. Ideal elastic-plastic intrinsics, segmented linear models, or the Ramberg–Osgood model are used for elasto-plastic modeling as an approximation of the material properties. Gajjar et al. [154,155] simulated multi-crack problems in plastic materials with XFEM. Fatigue problems usually accompany plastic materials; XFEM can effectively simulate multi-crack propagation under fatigue loading [34,156–158], and the work of Singh et al. [157] demonstrated that XFEM can effectively simulate fatigue propagation containing multiple discontinuities (holes, micro cracks and inclusions). Zhu et al. [159] used XFEM to simulate fatigue fractures in steel under stress corrosion. Currently, scholars have successfully implemented XFEM in commercial finite element software such as ABAQUS [160] and COMSOL [161], bringing this advanced technology into wider engineering applications.

4.2. Extended Isogeometric Analysis

Extended isogeometric analysis (XIGA) introduces a crack tip enrichment function to capture the singular stress field, which provides high efficiency and accuracy when dealing with multi-crack fracture problems. XIGA uses non-uniform rational B-splines (NURBS) as the basis function, allowing direct conversion from CAD models to numerical analysis without the need for remeshing. XIGA uses higher-order elements to obtain higher accuracy and local refinement compared to traditional FEM, making it suitable for simulating more complex geometries. In XIGA, the control node $\mathbf{x} = (x, y)$ corresponds to the node $\boldsymbol{\xi} = (\xi, \eta)$ in parametric coordinates with an approximate displacement of [162]

$$\mathbf{u}^h(\xi) = \overbrace{\sum_{i=1}^{n_{en}} \mathbf{R}_i(\xi)\mathbf{u}_i}^{\text{Standard isogemetric approximation}} + \text{enrichment terms} \tag{15}$$

where $\mathbf{R}_i$ is the NURBS basis function and $\mathbf{u}_i$ is the standard DOF associated with the control node i. In fracture problems, XIGA is usually combined with the Heaviside function to characterize the cracks and uses the maximum tangential stress criterion to determine the direction of crack propagation. The approximations of transverse displacement and rotational components for cracks are [163]

$$\omega^h(\xi) = \sum_{i=1}^{n_{en}} \chi_i(\xi)\omega_i + \sum_{j=1}^{n_{cf}} \chi_j(\xi)H(\xi)a_j + \sum_{k=1}^{n_{ct}} \chi_k(\xi)\left(\sum_{\alpha=1}^{4} \beta_\alpha(\xi)b_k^\omega\right) \tag{16}$$

$$\psi^h(\xi) = \sum_{i=1}^{n_{en}} \chi_i(\xi)\psi_i + \sum_{j=1}^{n_{cf}} \chi_j(\xi)H(\xi)a_j^\psi + \sum_{k=1}^{n_{ct}} \chi_k(\xi)\left(\sum_{\alpha=1}^{4} F_\alpha(\xi)b_k^\psi\right) \tag{17}$$

where $H(\xi)$ is the Heaviside function, β_α and F_α are the translational and rotational enrichment functions of the crack tip, a and b are the additional DOFs of the crack tip, n_{en} is the number of control points, and n_{cf} and n_{ct} are the number of control nodes for the Heaviside function and the crack tip enrichment function. Bhardwaj et al. [163] used XIGA against XFEM to calculate the SIF, and applied it to a plate with two cracks. The discretization of the cracking plate and sub-triangular dissections of the elements at the crack tip are shown in Figure 17.

Singh et al. [162,164] combined XIGA with higher-order shear deformation theory to calculate the SIF of crack tips in bilaterally cracked plates under two types of out-of-plane loads and multi-cracks in functional gradient plates. Gu et al. [165–167] proposed an adaptive XIGA based on LR B-splines, which can be used for curved surface cracks, multi-cracks, and a variety of complex structures with cracks in isotropic and anisotropic media. The adaptive XIGA element segmentation during crack propagation is shown in Figure 18. Yu et al. [168] proposed an error-controlled adaptive XIGA method for evaluating the multi-crack fracture behavior in Mindlin–Reissner plates. The XIGA method has been further applied by scholars to the multi-crack fracture problem in anisotropic piezoelectric materials [169,170]. In a recent study, Jiang et al. [171] used the B++ spline for the linear elastic single-crack and multi-crack fracture problems in XIGA.

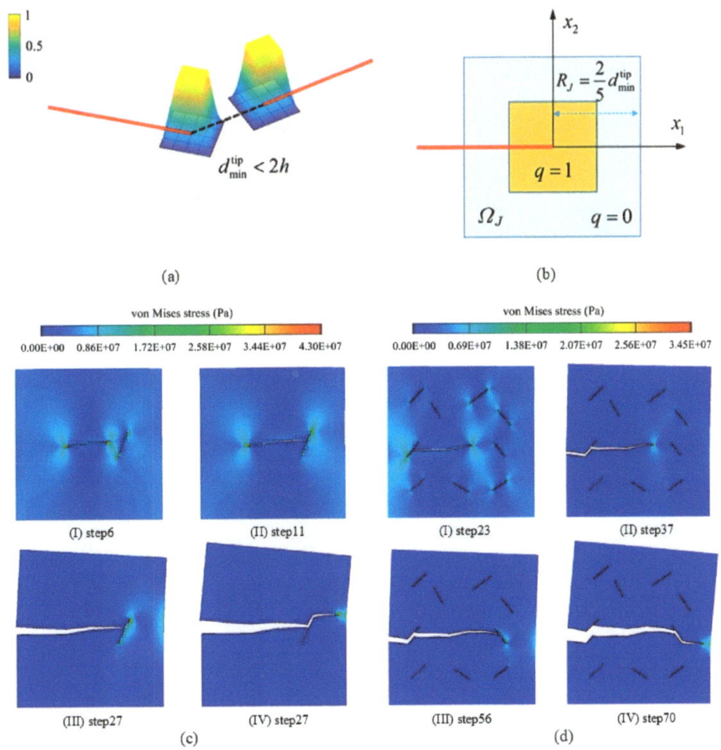

Figure 16. (**a**) Distribution of smooth functions in the coupled domain (Red lines indicate cracks, same below). (**b**) Size of the integral and coupled domains. (**c**) Simulation results for two cracks. (**d**) Simulation results for multiple cracks [153].

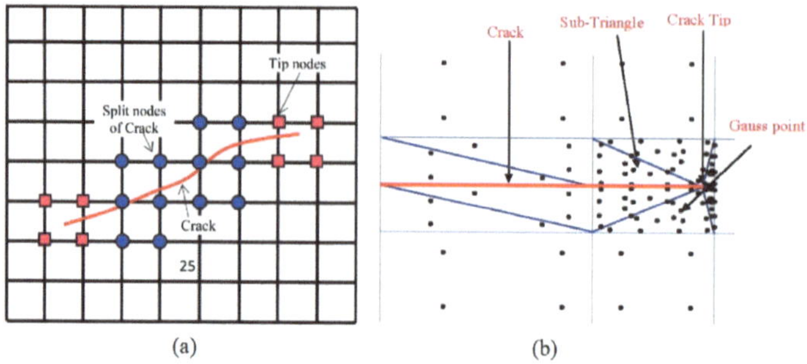

Figure 17. (**a**) Discretization of the cracking plate. (**b**) Sub-triangular element segmentation at the crack tip [163].

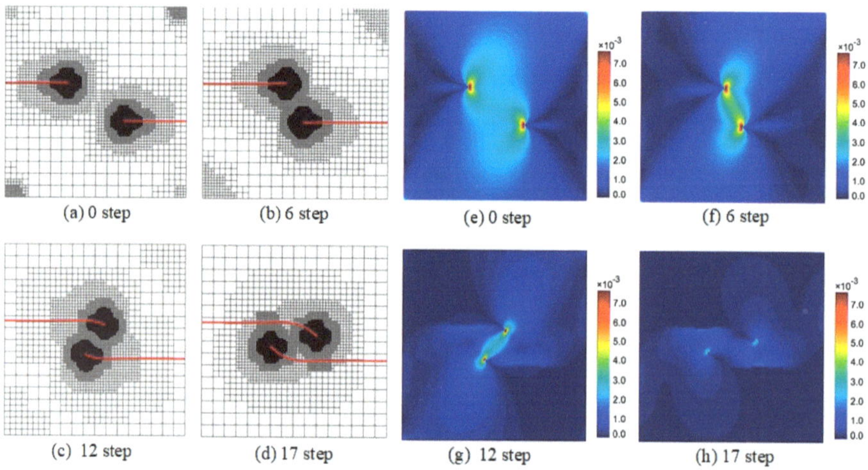

Figure 18. (**a–d**) Adaptive XIGA element segmentation during crack propagation (Red lines indicate cracks). (**e–h**) Contour of Von Mises stress during cracking [167].

4.3. Boundary Element Method

The elastic boundary element method (BEM) based on the boundary integral equation (BIE) has been applied to solve fracture problems for many years. In BEM, the integral terms in the boundary integral equation are approximated by numerical integration, and then the resulting system of equations is solved to obtain the value of the unknown function on the boundary. Assuming that the displacement at the boundary point $\mathbf{x}'$ is continuous, the boundary integral of its displacement u_i is [172]

$$\begin{aligned} C_{ij}(\mathbf{x}')u_j(\mathbf{x}') + \text{V.P.}\int_\Gamma T_{ij}(\mathbf{x}',\mathbf{x})u_j(\mathbf{x})d\Gamma = \\ \int_\Gamma U_{ij}(\mathbf{x}',\mathbf{x})t_j(\mathbf{x})d\Gamma + \int_\Omega U_{ij}(\mathbf{x}',\mathbf{X})t_j(\mathbf{X})d\Omega \quad \mathbf{x} \in \Gamma, \mathbf{X} \in \Omega \end{aligned} \tag{18}$$

T_{ij} and U_{ij} denote the traction and displacement at the boundary point $\mathbf{x}$, V.P. denotes the Cauchy principal value integral, the problem domain is Ω, and the boundary is denoted as

$$\Gamma = S + \sum_{k=1}^{K} \Gamma_+^k + \sum_{k=1}^{K} \Gamma_-^k \tag{19}$$

where K is the total number of cracks, S is the problem domain boundary, and Γ_-^k and Γ_+^k are the two crack surfaces of the kth crack. The calculation of the boundary element method for the multi-crack problem can be simplified to multiple single-crack problems by giving crack partitions, or it can be calculated by correcting the traction force t_j for each crack element by considering the other cracks [120]. The two-dimensional fracture problem and the element arrangement of the crack tip are shown in Figure 19 [173].

A proprietary program is needed to calculate the integrals on the problem domain boundaries and crack boundaries [174–176]. BEM has developed many variants in solving the multi-crack fracture problem, and the interaction integrals are usually used in calculation of the SIF. Denda et al. [120,177,178] developed a dislocation and point force approach to BEM for multi-cracks in isotropic and anisotropic media, which solves a series of fracture models in Figure 20. Wang et al. [179] proposed a new BIE and BEM for planar elastomers containing multiple cracks and holes with finite and infinite boundaries. Gray [180] et al. proposed the modified quarter-point crack tip elements for 2D boundary integral fracture analysis. Sutradhar et al. [173] proposed an interaction integration method for evaluating T-stress and SIF for 2D cracking problems by a symmetric Galerkin boundary element method. Saez et al. [181] proposed a 2D BEM based on displacement and traction BIE to analyze multi-crack fractures of piezoelectric solids. Guo et al. [182] proposed a fast multipole BEM for solving the 2D multi-crack problem in linear elastic fracture mechanics. Wu et al. [183] proposed a new BEM formulation to simulate cracks at micrometer scale. Liu et al. [184] proposed a fast multipole BEM for simulating crack propagation in 2D linear elastic solids. Hwu et al. [185] designed a meshless element along the boundary of holes or cracks to deal with the 2D anisotropic elastic solid problem. Cong et al. [186] proposed a method to simulate the crack propagation paths of multi-cracks in structures by coupling the crack tip characterization with the extended BEM.

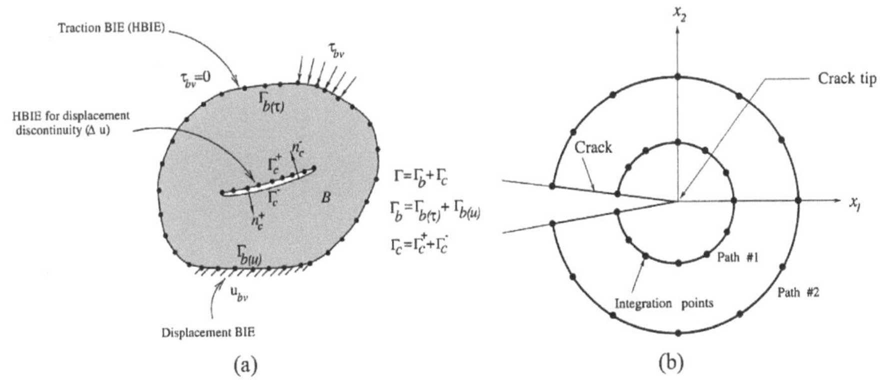

Figure 19. (**a**) Two-dimensional fracture problem. (**b**) Element arrangement of the crack tip [173].

4.4. Discrete Element Method

The discrete element method (DEM) is a numerical method used to simulate discontinuous media, and is particularly suitable for fracture and damage problems in materials such as particles, rocks, concrete, etc. The DEM does not require a mesh; the material is considered to consist of discrete particles, and the interactions between the particles are described by Newton's second law and the contact force model. Therefore, DEM is not dependent on mesh or the fracture criterion and is naturally suitable for simulating large deformations and multi-crack propagation in discrete bodies with complex shapes. However, DEM suffers from large errors and high computational costs in solving continuous problem in linear elastic and elasto-plastic media that are the specialties of methods such as XFEM. In the DEM, the general form of particle distribution is shown in Figure 21a–d [187], and the forms of cracks between particles are shown in Figure 21e,f [188].

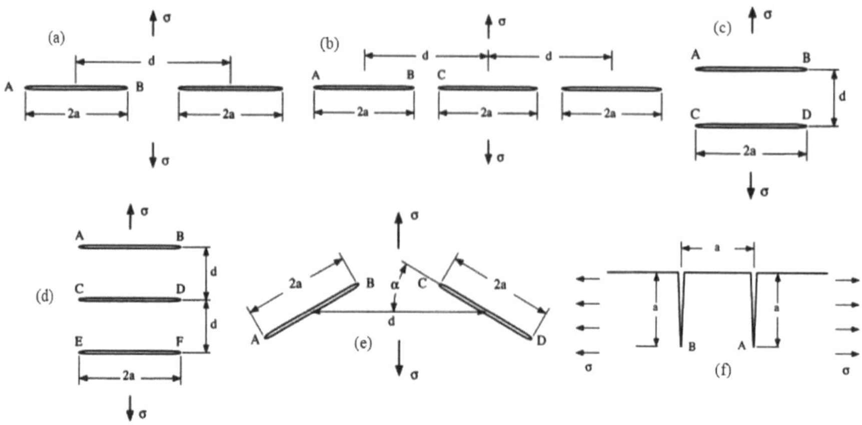

Figure 20. Some typical fracture problems in tension solved by Denda et al. [178]. (**a**) Two colinear cracks. (**b**) Three colinear cracks. (**c**) Two parallel cracks. (**d**) Three parallel cracks. (**e**) Two inclined cracks. (**f**) Two edged cracks in a semi-infinite plate.

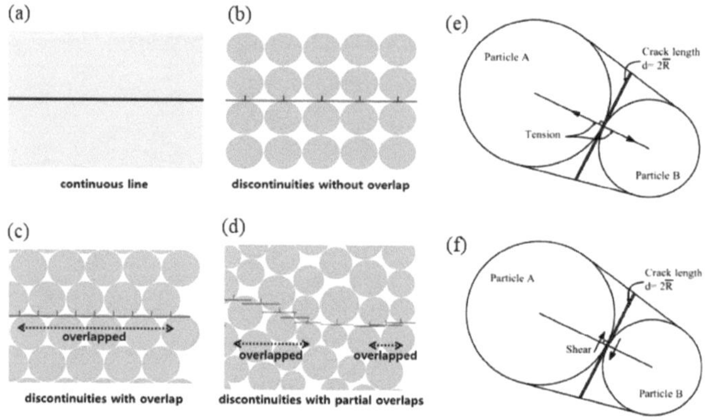

Figure 21. (**a**) Analytical model. (**b**) Rectangular array model. (**c**) Hexagonal array model. (**d**) Arbitrary array model [187]. (**e**) Tensile crack between particles. (**f**) Shear crack between particles [188].

DEM is mainly used in the analysis of fracture behavior of rocks. Especially in the last few years, the development and application of the method has shown a significant boom trend and a focus on the multi-crack problem. Fractures of prefabricated cracks are a common object for fracture problems. Li et al. [189] analyzed a cement mortar member with parallel cracks under uniaxial compression based on DEM, and the crack propagations are shown in Figure 22a–c. Wang et al. [190] conducted a series of DEM numerical uniaxial compression tests on 3D-printed rock specimens to investigate the mechanical behavior and fracture modes. Sun et al. [191] used DEM to study the effect of size on the strength and cracking pattern of crystalline rocks with artificial defects. DEM can also capture the fracture phenomena of rocks that have holes, joints and stratum [192,193]. Zhong et al. [188] reconstructed a DEM that can reflect the rock mechanical properties and damage modes of shale specimens. The fracturing of shale layers at different deflection angles is shown in Figure 22d–g. DEM can accurately construct fluid solid coupling models to simulate rock cracking under fluid pressure [194,195]. Hofmann et al. [196,197] studied the diffusion of cracks during hydraulic fracturing in rocks. The multi-crack propagation under fluid injection in a rock is shown in Figure 22h. Papachristos et al. [198] developed a fully coupled DEM hydrodynamic model. Lee et al. [199] investigated the fracture interactions of semicircular bending members of shale under complex hydraulic loading. Liu et al. [200] proposed an improved fluid flow model for fractured porous media based on the coupled DEM model of bonding.

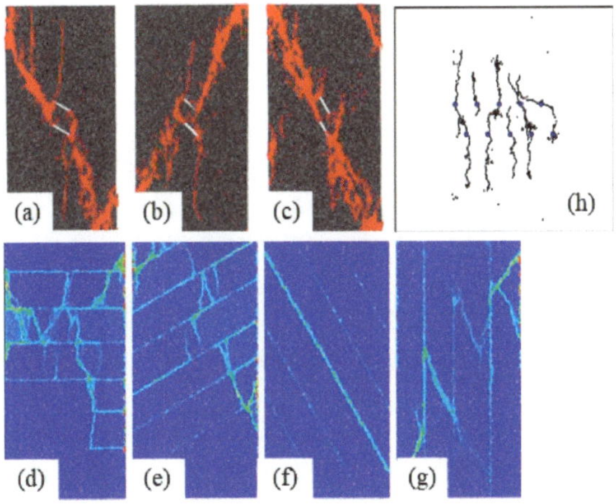

Figure 22. Crack propagation at deflection angle (**a**) α = 30°, (**b**) α = 45°, and (**c**) α = 60° for parallel prefabricated cracks [189], and at deflection angle (**d**) β = 0°, (**e**) β = 30°, (**f**) β = 60°, and (**g**) β = 90° for shale layers under uniaxial compression [188]. (**h**) Crack propagation in water-injected rock [196].

DEM can also be combined with other numerical methods to solve the multi-crack problem. Shao et al. [201] coupled FEM and spheropolyhedral-based DEM to predict the propagation of multiple cracks in concrete beams. Jiao et al. [202] combined the lattice Boltzmann method, DEM, and the theory of damage development in rocks to investigate the thermal–hydraulic–mechanical coupling for branched crack propagation. In addition to fractures in rocks, DEM has been applied to multi-crack fracture problems in polymers [203] and soils [204].

4.5. Meshfree Methods

Meshfree methods (MMs) are a type of numerical method that does not require traditional meshing. Belytschko et al. [205] applied the least squares approximation to a set of equations from Galerkin's weak formulas to formulate the element-free Galerkin method (EFGM), where the problem domain consists of a set of nodes, and numerical integration is carried out with the help of a background mesh for numerical integration. The moving least squares interpolation function in EFGM is [206]

$$u_{\alpha}^{h}(\mathbf{x}) = \mathbf{p}^{T}(\mathbf{x})\mathbf{a}_{\alpha}(\mathbf{x}) + \sum_{j+1}^{n_c}\left[k_1^j Q_{1\alpha}^j(\mathbf{x}) + k_2^j Q_{2\alpha}^j(\mathbf{x})\right], \quad \alpha = 1,2 \tag{20}$$

where $\mathbf{a}_{\alpha}(\mathbf{x})$ is the vector of coefficients to be solved, n_c is the number of cracks, k_1^j and k_2^j are the unknown coefficients of jth crack, $Q_{1\alpha}^j$ and $Q_{2\alpha}^j$ form the singularity of crack tips, $\mathbf{p}(\mathbf{x})$ is the basis function, and the 2D linear basis function is

$$\mathbf{p}^{T}(\mathbf{x}) = [1, x, y] \tag{21}$$

To capture the stress singularity at the crack tips, it is effective to add enrichment terms after the regular term of the basis function. Li et al. proposed a complex variable enrichment basis to reduce the computational effort [207–209]. EFGM has significant advantages in dealing with problems with complex geometries, large deformations, contact problems, fractures, and crack propagation, while the traditional methods need to be improved in multi-crack problems. For example, node refinement is needed for areas with high stress singularity, as shown in Figure 23a,b [210], or special treatment of the weight function in regions of multiple crack tips, as shown in Figure 23c–e [211].

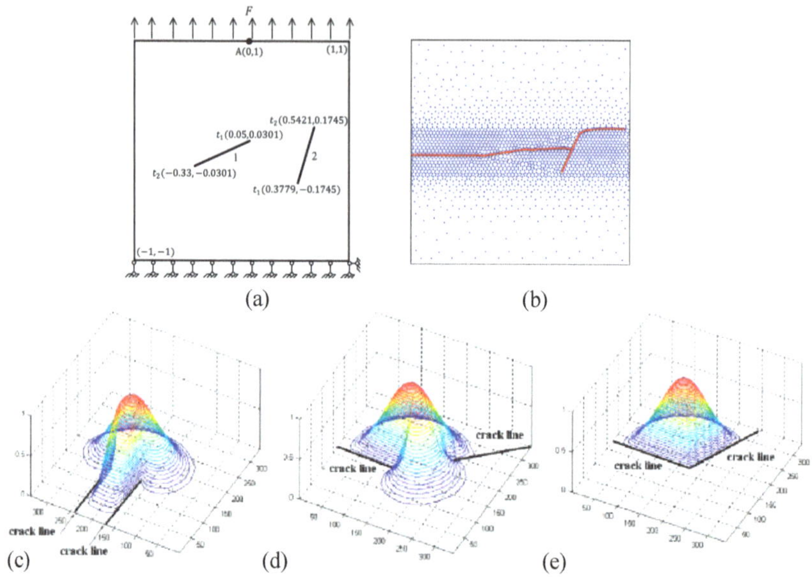

Figure 23. (**a**) Two-crack fracture model. (**b**) Node refinement of crack propagation [210]. Diffraction method spline weight function (λ = 2) corrected by the MCW method. (**c**) Two parallel cracks, (**d**) double corner and spacer cracks, and (**e**) two corner connected cracks [211].

Duflot et al. [212,213] analyze the fracture problem and characterize the crack propagation with triangular fragments. A meshfree analysis was carried out for 2D and 3D double crack propagation. Muravin et al. [211] proposed a multiple crack weights method to solve interacting crack problems by a meshfree numerical method. Singh et al. [214–216] conducted a systematic study of MM for the multi-crack problem, and proposed simulating the interacting cracks with an intrinsic enriched EFGM, The node stiffness matrix is weighted for the local coordinates of different crack tips as

$$[K_{ij}]_{total} = \sum_{i=1}^{n_c} [K_{ij}]_i \times R_i \quad (22)$$

where n_c is the total number of crack tips and R_i is the proportion of the effect of each crack tip on the computed node stiffness matrix, which is related to the distance between them. Barbieri et al. [217,218] also proposed intrinsic enrichment of the weight function for the numerical treatment of multiple arbitrary cracks. Zhu et al. [210] investigated the simulation of complex crack propagation by the independent cover meshfree method. Ai et al. [219,220] combined the weak MM and the cracking particle method for 2D brittle multi-crack propagation in thermo-mechanical coupling. Memari et al. [221] investigated the efficiency of the Petrov–Galerkin method and the linear test-function approximation method for complex crack propagation problems. Zhao et al. [222], based on the EFGM, developed a hydraulic crack propagation model to study multiple cracks. In addition to simulating linear elastic materials, the meshless method can easily be adapted to simulate large deformation problems of hyperelastic materials, as it is not restricted by the connection between the mesh and the nodes. Nguyen et al. [223] performed a meshfree analysis of multiple crack propagation in hyperelastic solids. Ahe member that has two cracks is shown in Figure 24a, and the nodal displacement contour of crack propagation is shown in Figure 24b.

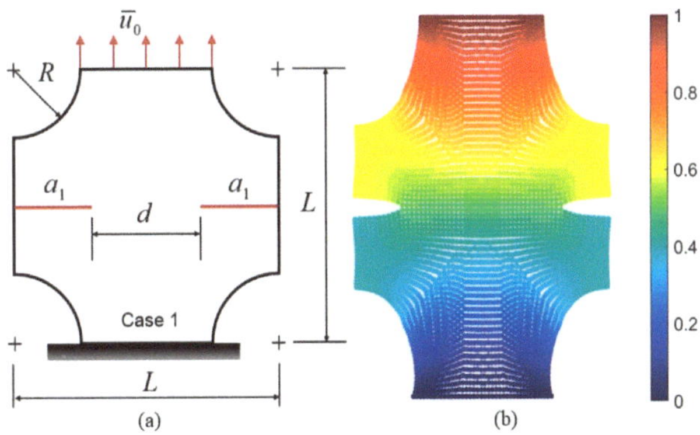

Figure 24. (**a**) Member with two cracks. (**b**) Contour of nodal displacement [223].

Meshfree methods are now widely used to deal with nonlinear problems [224–227]. Except for EFGM, smooth particle hydrodynamics (SPH) is a meshfree, pure Lagrangian particle method that describes material behavior through interactions between particles. SPH was initially used for fluid simulations. It has simulated the fracture damage in rocks [228–230] and the multi-crack dynamic fracture problem of brittle polymers [231] successfully.

4.6. Peridynamics

Peridynamics (PD) is a numerical method for simulating material damage and crack propagation. It does not belong to the class of method based on continuous mechanics like DEM and is suitable for modeling granular materials. The problem domain is discretized into several material points, and the whole model is simulated by considering the interactions between the material points. The PD equation based on the parameter position x and time t is [232]

$$\rho(x)\ddot{\mathbf{u}}(x,t) = \int_{H_x} \mathbf{f}(x',x,u,u',t)dV + \mathbf{b}(x,t) \tag{23}$$

where ρ is the mass density, $\ddot{\mathbf{u}}(x,t)$ is the acceleration, H_x is the domain of integration, δ is the radius of H_x, x' is the interaction point of x, ξ is the initial distance between x and x', η is the relative displacement at deformation, $\mathbf{f}(x',x,u,u',t)$ is the peridynamic force of non-local interaction, and $\mathbf{b}(x,t)$ is the body force. PD does not rely on mesh, and a large number of material points are connected to each other by bonds. The broken bonds form the cracks that are propagating, branching and aggregating. The scalar function that controls bond breakage between material points is

$$\mu = \begin{cases} 1\,, & s < s_0 \\ 0\,, & \text{others} \end{cases} \tag{24}$$

where s is the elongation and s_0 is the critical elongation, the bond is intact when η = 1, otherwise the bond is considered to be broken. The interaction between the material points before and after deformation in the PD is shown in Figure 25 [21].

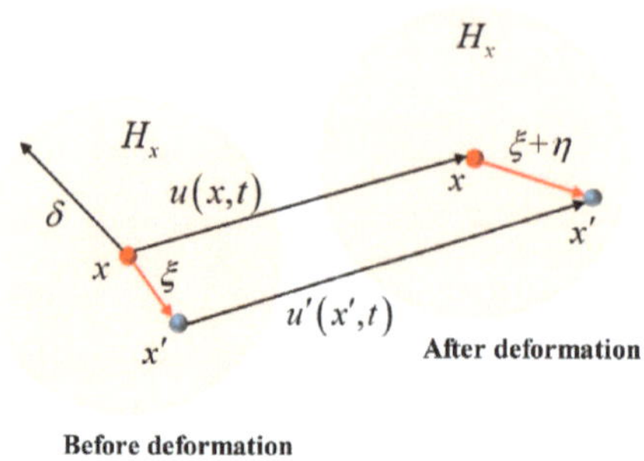

Figure 25. Interaction of material points [21].

PD does not belong to the scope of continuum mechanics and is naturally suited to solving multi-crack fracture problems in concrete, rock and some silicate inclusions due to its particle characteristic [233–235]. Madenci et al. [232,236] applied PD to the problem of crack propagation in glass plate and compared it with experiments as well as other numerical methods. Bobaru et al. [237–239] investigated the dynamic branched crack propagation in brittle materials by PD. Zhou et al. [240,241] developed an extended non-ordinary state-based PD for simulating the process of crack initiation, propagation, and coalescence in concrete and rock subjected to quasi-static and dynamic loading. Dai et al. [242] proposed a dual-horizon peridynamics model to simulate multi-crack propagation in concrete. Shojaei et al. [243] proposed a hybrid meshfree discretization to enhance the efficiency of PD in dealing with interacting cracks. Ma et al. [21] introduced a strain energy density softening criterion in PD to reflect the damage characteristics of rock materials. The PD simulation results for parallel cracks in concrete under compression are shown in Figure 26a. Wang et al. [244] developed a two-parameter extended bond-based PD model. Zhou et al. [245] proposed a Cosserat continuum-based PD model to predict rock fracture modes.

Nowadays, scholars have studied PD in enough depth to make it applicable to all kinds of homogeneous and non-homogeneous materials in multi-crack fractures [246,247]. Stress distributions in the tension of brittle plates containing doubly periodic rectangular arrays of cracks and diamond-shaped arrays of cracks simulated by Zhou et al. are shown in Figure 26b,c [241]. Bie et al. [248] proposed a fully coupled thermo-mechanical dual-horizon peridynamic model to solve problems involving branched cracks and kinked cracks in both homogeneous and inhomogeneous materials. The crack propagation patterns of ceramic thin plates under thermal shock are shown in Figure 26d–i. Chu et al. [249] used PD to simulate a variety of fracture modes in a thin-film substrate system. PD can also be coupled with FEM to perform multiscale multi-crack fracture simulations from the microscopic to macroscopic scale [250,251].

4.7. Phase Field Method

The phase field method (PFM) is a computational method for modeling crack propagation and phase transitions in materials. It describes the crack interface through a continuous phase transition process and uses phase field variables to characterize the internal structure of the material and the cracks. PFM is based on the minimization of energy, which regards fractures as a competition between elastic and surface energy. The equation of the energy minimization problem is [252]

$$E(\mathbf{u},\Gamma)=\underbrace{\int_{\Omega/\Gamma}\psi(\varepsilon(\mathbf{u}))\mathrm{d}V}_{\text{Elastic strain energy}}-\underbrace{\left(\int_{\Omega}\mathbf{b}^{\mathrm{T}}\mathbf{u}\mathrm{d}V+\int_{\partial\Omega_t}\bar{\mathbf{t}}^{\mathrm{T}}\mathbf{u}\mathrm{d}A\right)}_{\text{External work}}+\underbrace{G_c\int_{\Gamma}d\Gamma}_{\text{Fracture surface energy}} \tag{25}$$

where $\Psi(\varepsilon(\mathbf{u}))$ is the elastic strain energy density, the external work is determined by the body force $\mathbf{b}$ and the traction force $\bar{\mathbf{t}}$, G_c is the critical energy release rate, and Γ is the surface of cracks. Introducing the phase field s, regularizing the line integral in Equation (25), and transforming the line integral into a volume fraction, the representation of the surface cracks become diffuse, and the equation for crack propagation, branching, and aggregation can be solved as

$$\begin{aligned} E(\mathbf{u},\Gamma) = \; & \int_\Omega (1-s)^2 \psi(\varepsilon(\mathbf{u}))\mathrm{d}V - \left(\int_\Omega \mathbf{b}^T \mathbf{u} \mathrm{d}V + \int_{\partial\Omega} \bar{\mathbf{t}}^{\mathrm{T}} \mathbf{u} \mathrm{d}A\right) \\ & + \int_\Omega \frac{G_c}{4l}(s^2 + 4l^2 \Delta s)\mathrm{d}V \end{aligned} \tag{26}$$

where l is the crack width parameter $s = 1$ at complete damage to the structure and $s = 0$ at intact structure, as shown in Figure 27 [253].

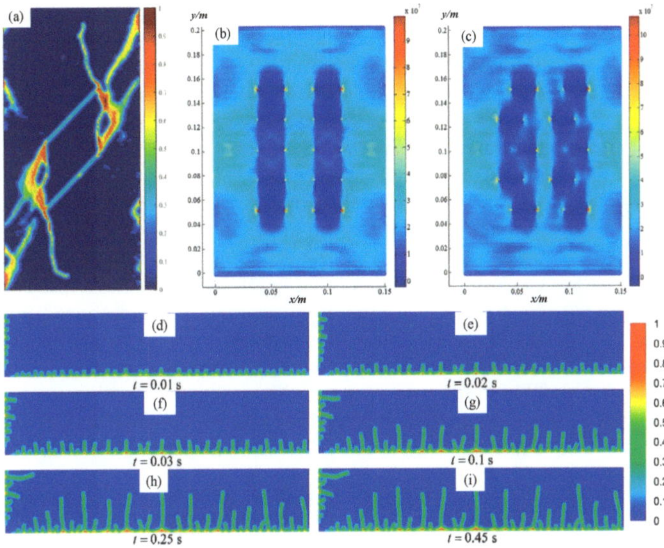

Figure 26. (**a**) Parallel cracks in concrete under compression [21]. Stress distributions of doubly (**b**) periodic rectangular array of cracks and (**c**) diamond-shaped array of cracks [241], (**d–i**) crack propagation modes of ceramic thin plates under thermal shock [248].

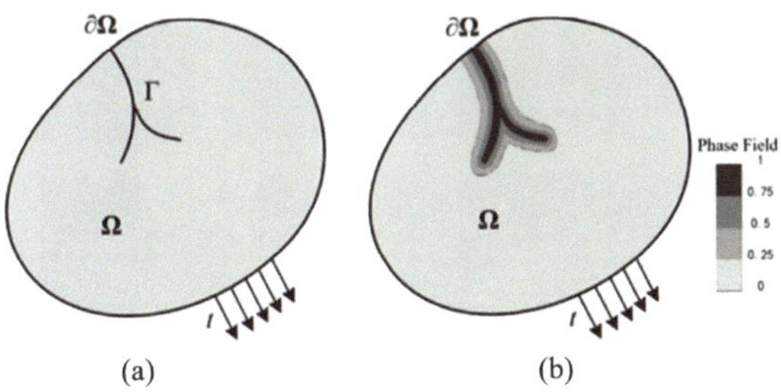

Figure 27. (**a**) A brittle solid with cracks. (**b**) Representation of branching cracks with phase field [253].

The advantage of PFM is the ability to deal with complex and 3D crack paths without the need for predefined crack paths, which makes it suitable for simulating the process of crack initiation, propagation and branching. Schänzel et al. [254] overcame the shortcomings of the crack propagation model by introducing a fracture phase field and modeled the two-crack propagation of rubber under large deformations, as shown in Figure 28a. Hou et al. [255] proposed a PFM to model crack interactions of asphalt binder. Mikelic et al. [256,257] extended the PFM to a fluid-driven crack problem. The cracking process of porous elastic plate is shown in Figure 28b. Ziaei-Rad et al. [258] proposed a variational splitting method for multiple and branched cracks to identify crack paths from PFM. Patil et al. [259] proposed a multiscale PFM for modeling crack propagation in composites. The cracking in the vertical fiber direction is shown in Figure 28c. Heider et al. [260] simulated subcritical crack propagation in porous solids under liquid pressure based on a PFM. You et al. [261] proposed a phase field damage model to capture the geotechnical materials with branching and propagation of cracks. Zhang et al. [262] introduced a fatigue history strain parameter in the phase field framework to capture the characteristics of cracks in fatigue fractures.

PFM also demonstrates its advantages in modeling multi-crack problems in rocks, which have complex crack path paths, anisotropy, multi-physical field coupling and multi-scale effects. Zhuang et al. [263] simulated both single-crack and multi-crack phenomena in rock deformation and damage by improved PFM. Fei and Yu et al. [264,265] proposed a double-phase-field formulation, which employs two different phase fields to describe cohesive tensile fractures and frictional shear fractures of rocks. Huang et al. [266] used PFM to simulate semi-circular bend tests to investigate the effect of two parallel veins on the fracture behavior of shale. Li et al. [267] proposed a PFM based on the unified crack propagation criterion.

With the advancement of computer technology, PFM has been combined with other numerical techniques for applications in multiscale simulation and fracture mechanics. Sun et al. [253] proposed a finite element meshfree model-phase field for multi-crack fracture problems. Zhang et al. [268] combined XFEM and PFM to simulate hydraulic crack propagation in unconventional shale formations with frictional and cemented natural cracks. Zhou et al. [269] proposed a smoothed particle hydrodynamics coupled PFM to simulate crack propagation and coalescence in rocks. Xu et al. [270] proposed an improved PFM to simulate mixed-mode cracking in rocks. Wang et al. [271] combined PFM and FEM to solve partial differential equations. The simulated crack propagation in rock is shown in Figure 28d.

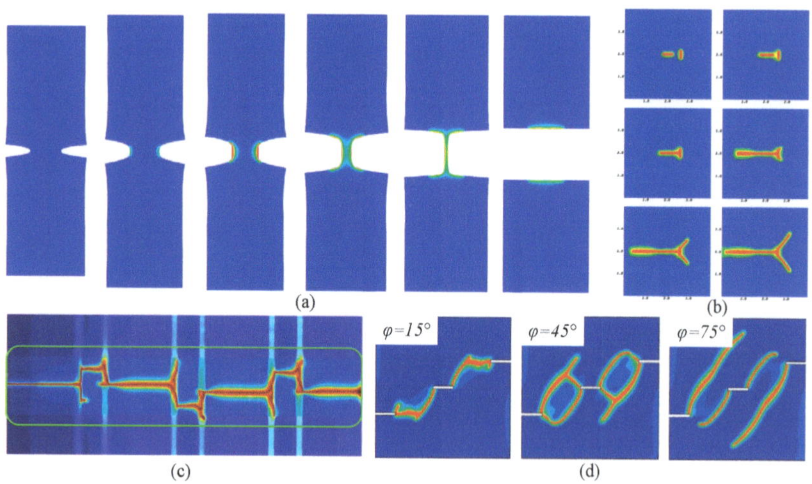

Figure 28. (**a**) Crack propagation process in rubbery polymers [254]. (**b**) Fluid-driven fracture process in porous elastic plate [257]. (**c**) Cracking in the vertical fiber direction in fiber composites [259]. (**d**) Crack propagation in rocks at different shear loading angles φ [271].

4.8. Other Numerical Methods

In the study of multi-crack interactions or crack propagation in materials, advanced numerical methods are essential to provide accurate predictions and insights into complex fracture mechanics. In addition to the mainstream numerical methods mentioned above, the numerical manifold method (NMM), displacement discontinuity method (DDM), hybrid displacement discontinuity method (HDDM), etc., are also useful in dealing with multi-crack fracture.

NMM is known for its simplified meshing and efficient ability in handling complex crack patterns. Because of the concepts of mathematical coverage and physical coverage, it allows cracks to grow naturally without the need for mesh reconfiguration [272,273]. NMM unifies the analysis of continuous and discontinuous media and provides an approach to analyze complex shapes with discontinuities, and it allows accurate simulation of multiple cracks in gradient-functional materials [274], viscoelastic materials [275], and rocky materials [276] under fluid pressure [277–279]. DDM simulates cracks by introducing displacement discontinuities on the crack face, which can guarantee the singularity of the crack tips, and is suitable for multi-crack fracture problems in rock mechanics [280–282]. HDDM combines DDM and meshfree methods to deal with complex discontinuities, and is suitable for the analysis of multi-hole and multi-crack interaction problems in planar elastic media [283,284].

In summary, all numerical methods have their own advantages and drawbacks in the study of multi-crack fracture mechanics, and together, they have contributed to the people's understanding of complex fracture phenomena, making it possible to predict and control the fracture behavior of materials more accurately and providing a powerful tool for engineering and scientific research. It is necessary to choose the appropriate numerical methods for different fracture problems.

5. Discussion

Multi-crack fracture mechanics is an important research area in the field of material science and engineering, aiming to reveal the complex dynamics of crack initiation, propagation and interaction. In recent years, the field has made significant progress in experimental and theoretical research and numerical simulations. However, there are still challenges and room for improvement. A summary of present multi-crack research is as follows:

(1) Experimental observation

Experiments are the basis for understanding the fracture behavior of materials. In experiments, researchers can observe the whole process of cracks, from initiation to propagation until fracture. However, the propagation of multiple cracks in experiments is affected by external loads, intrinsic material defects, and interactions of multiple cracks, which reduces the repeatability of the experiments. Currently, there is a lack of experimental standards related to multiple cracks, and most of the studies are only designed to observe the fracture phenomena and fail to analyze the fracture parameters. In the future, experimental studies will incorporate advanced imaging techniques and real-time monitoring systems to capture multi-crack fracture behavior more accurately.

(2) Theoretical modeling

Theoretical modeling helps in understanding fracture phenomena. By developing new theoretical models, researchers can predict the fracture behavior. However, theoretical studies are often limited by mathematical capabilities and are confined to dealing with simple problems, leaving a gap with practical applications. In addition, most theories are based on the assumptions of homogeneity, linear elasticity, and ideal elasto-plasticity, which are not satisfied by most materials in reality, making it difficult for theories to explain the fracture behavior of many materials at the macro level. Future theoretical studies may consider simulating the random distribution of cracks and the fracture problems of complex materials that contain defects.

(3) Numerical simulation

Nowadays, numerical simulation is the main tool for the investigation of multi-crack problems and provided analytical and predictive tools for engineering applications. However, numerical methods face challenges such as model assumptions, computational costs, multi-physical field coupling and numerical stability. For example, XFEM, XIGA, and BEM are based on the theories of continuous homogeneity, linear elasticity, and ideal elasto-plasticity in solving multi-crack fracture problems, but are not suitable for simulating granular and hyperelastic media due to the limitation in the mesh. Conversely, DEM and PD are based on the modeling of particles and material points and are suitable for simulating granular materials, but not for the continuous medium. Although they can simulate the large deformation problems of hyperelastic materials, MM and PFM present the problem of complicated pre-processing. Most explorations on numerical methods are still based on ideal linear elasticity, and there is a lack of research on the basis of plasticity, hyperelasticity, and other complex constitutive models in applied to the problem of multi-crack fractures. Currently, many of the methods have not yet produced software tools that require researchers to program. In the future, numerical simulation in multi-crack problems will improve the computational efficiency by focusing on multi-scale modeling and multi-physical field coupling analysis, and by expanding the simulation of fracture problems with more complex constitutive models. Table 1 summarizes the scope of applicable objects, advantages, and limits of the various methods in detail.

Table 1. Summary of various methods.

Method	Applicable Objects	Advantages	Limits
Experiments	Rock and concrete, with a variety of composites, compound facings, glass, polymers, etc.	Great visualization High reference value Verification	Poor repeatability Lack of relevant standards High cost Limited scalability
Theoretical modeling	Ideal linear elastic or plastic materials (isotropic/anisotropic)	Predictive Deeper understanding Simplified complexity Guiding experiments and numerical simulations	Idealization Mathematical complexity Difficulty of experimental verification Application limitations
XFEM	Rocks, composites, metals, ceramics, plastics, etc.	Arbitrary crack paths No remeshing required Multi-physics coupling	High computational costs Numerical stability Complex pre-processing
XIGA	Rocks, composites, functional gradient materials, etc.	High-order accuracy No mesh required Multi-physics coupling Multiscale simulation	High computational costs Complex technical implementation Software limitations
BEM	Rock, concrete, metals, alloys, ceramics, glass, composites, etc.	Precise boundary condition handling Application to infinite domain problems Low computational cost Stress singularity treatment	Complex integration Complex geometric challenges Multi-crack interaction handling Software limitations
DEM	Granular materials such as sand, soil, rock, composite materials, etc.	Dynamic crack propagation No mesh required Complex boundary adaptation Multiscale problems	High computational cost High parameter requirements Dynamic loading challenges Complex post-processing
MM	Rock, concrete, metals, alloys, composites, etc.	No mesh required High order accuracy Dynamic crack paths Localized refinement capability	Technical implementation complexity Stability considerations Software limitations
PD	Rock, concrete, composites, etc.	Non-localized Arbitrary crack paths No remeshing required Dynamic fracture simulation Internal interactions	High computational cost Numerical stability challenges Parameter calibration
PFM	Rock, concrete, metals, alloys, composites, etc.	Natural crack path Complex crack processing Multi-field coupling Continuous description Multiscale simulation	High computational costs Parameter calibration Numerical stability Software limitations

6. Conclusions

Cracks in engineering often do not exist singly, but rather in interactions with each other. Multi-crack fracture mechanics focuses on understanding and predicting the effects of the initiation, propagation, and interaction of multiple cracks in different materials. This area of research is critical to improving the safety and reliability of engineering structures. Experiments, theoretical models, and numerical simulations are complementary to each other. However, the research space for the study of multi-crack fracture problems is still vast. For practical engineering, the appropriate research method should be chosen to address the multi-crack fracture problem, with the aim of solving it accurately and efficiently.

Funding: The authors are thankful for the supports of the National Natural Science Foundation of China (12002247), the Fundamental Research Fund for the Central Universities of China (WUT: 2021IVB013) and the National Training Program of Innovation and Entrepreneurship for Undergraduates of China (20240100123).

Data Availability Statement: Data sharing is not applicable.

Conflicts of Interest: The authors declare no conflict of interest.

References

1. Budarapu, P.R.; Rabczuk, T. Multiscale Methods for Fracture: A Review. *J. Indian Inst. Sci.* **2017**, *97*, 339–376. [CrossRef]
2. Wu, J.; Sigmund, O.; Groen, J.P. Topology optimization of multi-scale structures: A review. *Struct. Multidiscip. Optim.* **2021**, *63*, 1455–1480. [CrossRef]
3. Zhang, S.; Zhang, X. Toughness evaluation of hard coatings and thin films. *Thin Solid Film.* **2012**, *520*, 2375–2389. [CrossRef]
4. Correia, J.A.F.O.; Zhu, S.P.; Berto, F. Fatigue in Advanced Materials: Advanced Methods and Applications. *J. Mater. Res. Technol.* **2023**, *26*, 4902–4905. [CrossRef]
5. Li, P.; Li, W.; Li, B.; Yang, S.; Shen, Y.; Wang, Q.; Zhou, K. A review on phase field models for fracture and fatigue. *Eng. Fract. Mech.* **2023**, *289*, 109419. [CrossRef]
6. Cheng, Z.Q.; Liu, H.; Tan, W. Advanced computational modelling of composite materials. *Eng. Fract. Mech.* **2024**, *305*, 110120. [CrossRef]
7. Zimmermann, N.; Wang, P.H. A review of failure modes and fracture analysis of aircraft composite materials. *Eng. Fail. Anal.* **2020**, *115*, 104692. [CrossRef]
8. Siddique, A.; Abid, S.; Shafiq, F.; Nawab, Y.; Wang, H.; Shi, B.; Saleemi, S.; Sun, B. Mode I fracture toughness of fiber-reinforced polymer composites: A review. *J. Ind. Text.* **2021**, *50*, 1165–1192. [CrossRef]
9. Cervera, M.; Barbat, G.B.; Chiumenti, M.; Wu, J.Y. A comparative review of XFEM, mixed FEM and phase-field models for quasi-brittle cracking. *Arch. Comput. Methods Eng.* **2022**, *29*, 1009–1083. [CrossRef]
10. Zhang, M.; Abidin, A.R.Z.; Tan, C.S. State-of-the-art review on Meshless methods in the application of crack problems. *Theor. Appl. Fract. Mech.* **2024**, *131*, 104348. [CrossRef]
11. Ambati, M.; Gerasimov, T.; De Lorenzis, L. A review on phase-field models of brittle fracture and a new fast hybrid formulation. *Comput. Mech.* **2015**, *55*, 383–405. [CrossRef]
12. Ural, A. Advanced modeling methods—Applications to bone fracture mechanics. *Curr. Osteoporos. Rep.* **2020**, *18*, 568–576. [CrossRef] [PubMed]
13. Amitrano, D.; Gruber, S.; Girard, L. Evidence of frost-cracking inferred from acoustic emissions in a high-alpine rock-wall. *Earth Planet. Sci. Lett.* **2012**, *341*, 86–93. [CrossRef]
14. Benson, P.M.; Heap, M.J.; Lavallée, Y.; Flaws, A.; Hess, K.-U.; Selvadurai, A.; Dingwell, D.B.; Schillinger, B. Laboratory simulations of tensile fracture development in a volcanic conduit via cyclic magma pressurisation. *Earth Planet. Sci. Lett.* **2012**, *349*, 231–239. [CrossRef]
15. Le Corvec, N.; Menand, T.; Lindsay, J. Interaction of ascending magma with pre-existing crustal fractures in monogenetic basaltic volcanism: An experimental approach. *J. Geophys. Res. Solid Earth* **2013**, *118*, 968–984. [CrossRef]
16. Brantut, N.; Heap, M.; Meredith, P.; Baud, P. Time-dependent cracking and brittle creep in crustal rocks: A review. *J. Struct. Geol.* **2013**, *52*, 17–43. [CrossRef]
17. Tenthorey, E.; Cox, S.F.; Todd, H.F. Evolution of strength recovery and permeability during fluid–rock reaction in experimental fault zones. *Earth Planet. Sci. Lett.* **2003**, *206*, 161–172. [CrossRef]
18. Li, Y.P.; Chen, L.Z.; Wang, Y.H. Experimental research on pre-cracked marble under compression. *Int. J. Solids Struct.* **2005**, *42*, 2505–2516. [CrossRef]
19. Lee, J.; Hong, J.W.; Jung, J.W. The mechanism of fracture coalescence in pre-cracked rock-type material with three flaws. *Eng. Geol.* **2017**, *223*, 31–47. [CrossRef]
20. Li, H.; Shen, R.; Li, D.; Jia, H.; Li, T.; Chen, T.; Hou, Z. Acoustic emission multi-parameter analysis of dry and saturated sandstone with cracks under uniaxial compression. *Energies* **2019**, *12*, 1959. [CrossRef]

21. Ma, P.; Li, S.; Wang, X.; Yuan, C.; Li, J.; Zhang, F. Numerical simulation of crack propagation and coalescence in rock materials by the peridynamic method based on strain energy density theory. *Comput. Geosci.* **2022**, *26*, 1379–1396. [CrossRef]
22. Yang, S.Q.; Yang, J.; Mu, Z.L.; Liu, G.J.; Huang, M.; Li, K.S.; Huang, Y.H. Experimental Study on Mechanical Behavior, Fracture Characteristics, and Acoustic Emission Damage Characteristics of Sandstone Under Triaxial Multistage Stress Disturbance. *Rock Mech. Rock Eng.* **2024**, *57*, 8633–8655. [CrossRef]
23. Yang, L.; Jiang, Y.; Li, B.; Li, S.; Gao, Y. Application of the expanded distinct element method for the study of crack growth in rock-like materials under uniaxial compression. *Front. Struct. Civ. Eng.* **2012**, *6*, 121–131. [CrossRef]
24. Shen, Q.-Q.; Rao, Q.-H.; Li, Z.; Yi, W.; Sun, D.-L. Interacting mechanism and initiation prediction of multiple cracks. *Trans. Nonferrous Met. Soc. China* **2021**, *31*, 779–791.12. [CrossRef]
25. Haeri, H. Propagation mechanism of neighboring cracks in rock-like cylindrical specimens under uniaxial compression. *J. Min. Sci.* **2015**, *51*, 487–496. [CrossRef]
26. Sun, L.; Tao, S.; Liu, Q. Frost crack propagation and interaction in fissured rocks subjected to freeze–thaw cycles: Experimental and numerical studies. *Rock Mech. Rock Eng.* **2023**, *56*, 1077–1097. [CrossRef]
27. Haeri, H.; Sarfarazi, V.; Marji, M.F. Experimental and numerical investigation of uniaxial compression failure in rock-like specimens with L-shaped nonpersistent cracks. *Iran. J. Sci. Technol. Trans. Civ. Eng.* **2021**, *45*, 2555–2575. [CrossRef]
28. Li, X.; Wang, S.; Xia, K.; Tong, T. Dynamic tensile response of a microwave damaged granitic rock. *Exp. Mech.* **2021**, *61*, 461–468. [CrossRef]
29. Xu, H.; Li, S.; Xu, D.; Liu, X.; Huang, X.; Zheng, M.; Zhang, S. Investigation on the failure mechanism of hard rock cavern subjected to adjacent structural plane based on physical model experiments. *Theor. Appl. Fract. Mech.* **2024**, *131*, 104447. [CrossRef]
30. Xu, J.; Haque, A.; Gong, W.; Gamage, R.P.; Dai, G.; Zhang, Q.; Xu, F. Experimental study on the bearing mechanisms of rock-socketed piles in soft rock based on micro X-ray CT analysis. *Rock Mech. Rock Eng.* **2020**, *53*, 3395–3416. [CrossRef]
31. Ma, Z.; Wang, Y.; Zheng, Y. In situ dynamic X-ray imaging of fluid-rock interactions inside tight sandstone during hydraulic fracturing: Fluid flow process and fracture network growth. *J. Pet. Sci. Eng.* **2022**, *214*, 110490. [CrossRef]
32. Lei, X.; Kusunose, K.; Rao, M.V.M.S.; Nishizawa, O.; Satoh, T. Quasi-static fault growth and cracking in homogeneous brittle rock under triaxial compression using acoustic emission monitoring. *J. Geophys. Res. Solid Earth* **2000**, *105*, 6127–6139. [CrossRef]
33. Liu, T.; Cui, M.; Li, Q.; Yang, S.; Yu, Z.; Sheng, Y.; Cao, P.; Zhou, K. Fracture and damage evolution of multiple-fractured rock-like material subjected to compression. *Materials* **2022**, *15*, 4326. [CrossRef]
34. Ghamgosar, M.; Erarslan, N. Experimental and numerical studies on development of fracture process zone (FPZ) in rocks under cyclic and static loadings. *Rock Mech. Rock Eng.* **2016**, *49*, 893–908. [CrossRef]
35. Zhang, Z.; Ansari, F. Fracture mechanics of air-entrained concrete subjected to compression. *Eng. Fract. Mech.* **2006**, *73*, 1913–1924. [CrossRef]
36. Durand, R.; Vieira, J.; Farias, M. Numerical analysis of bonded and unbonded prestressed RC beams using cohesive and non-compatible rod elements. *Eng. Struct.* **2023**, *288*, 116157. [CrossRef]
37. Rabczuk, T.; Belytschko, T. Application of particle methods to static fracture of reinforced concrete structures. *Int. J. Fract.* **2006**, *137*, 19–49. [CrossRef]
38. Hussien, O.F.; Elafandy, T.H.K.; Abdelrahman, A.A.; Baky, S.A.; Nasr, E.A. Behavior of bonded and unbonded prestressed normal and high strength concrete beams. *HBRC J.* **2012**, *8*, 239–251. [CrossRef]
39. Tao, X.; Du, G. Ultimate stress of unbonded tendons in partially prestressed concrete beams. *PCI J.* **1985**, *30*, 72–91. [CrossRef]
40. Yu, Q.; Zhang, H.; Yang, R.; Cai, Z.; Liu, K. Experimental and numerical study on the effect of electrohydraulic shock wave on concrete fracturing. *J. Pet. Sci. Eng.* **2022**, *215*, 110685. [CrossRef]
41. Wang, Z.; Zhang, W.; Huang, Y. Experimental and Numerical Study of Concrete Fracture Behavior with Multiple Cracks Based on the Meso-Model. *Materials* **2023**, *16*, 6311. [CrossRef] [PubMed]
42. Ghone, M.O.; Long, G.; Yang, K.; Ma, X.; Islam, N. Toughness improvement of low strength ceramsite lightweight concrete by polypropylene fiber and recycled rubber particle. *Constr. Build. Mater.* **2024**, *422*, 135716. [CrossRef]
43. Park, S.H.; Kim, D.J.; Ryu, G.S.; Koh, K.T. Tensile behavior of ultra high performance hybrid fiber reinforced concrete. *Cem. Concr. Compos.* **2012**, *34*, 172–184. [CrossRef]
44. Rong, H.; Dong, W.; Zhao, X.; Zhou, X. Investigation on multi-cracks initiation and propagation of fiber reinforced concrete in restrained shrinkage ring tests. *Theor. Appl. Fract. Mech.* **2021**, *111*, 102856. [CrossRef]
45. Pan, J.; Leung, C.K.; Luo, M. Effect of multiple secondary cracks on FRP debonding from the substrate of reinforced concrete beams. *Constr. Build. Mater.* **2010**, *24*, 2507–2516. [CrossRef]
46. Cho, C.G.; Kim, Y.Y.; Feo, L.; Hui, D. Cyclic responses of reinforced concrete composite columns strengthened in the plastic hinge region by HPFRC mortar. *Compos. Struct.* **2012**, *94*, 2246–2253. [CrossRef]
47. Kachkouch, F.Z.; Noberto, C.C.; Babadopulos, L.F.D.A.L.; Melo, A.R.S.; Machado, A.M.L.; Sebaibi, N.; Boukhelf, F.; El Mendili, Y. Fatigue behavior of concrete: A literature review on the main relevant parameters. *Constr. Build. Mater.* **2022**, *338*, 127510. [CrossRef]
48. Riyar, R.L.; Mansi; Bhowmik, S. Fatigue behaviour of plain and reinforced concrete: A systematic review. *Theor. Appl. Fract. Mech.* **2023**, *125*, 103867. [CrossRef]
49. Elshazli, M.T.; Saras, N.; Ibrahim, A. Structural response of high strength concrete beams using fiber reinforced polymers under reversed cyclic loading. *Sustain. Struct.* **2022**, *2*, 000018. [CrossRef]

50. Li, S.; Chen, D.; Lu, Y.; Liu, Z. Fatigue fracture characteristics of normal concrete and high ductility geopolymer bonding based on DIC technique. *Thin-Walled Struct.* **2024**, *196*, 111469. [CrossRef]
51. Portal, N.W.; Flansbjer, M.; Zandi, K.; Wlasak, L.; Malaga, K. Bending behaviour of novel Textile Reinforced Concrete-foamed concrete (TRC-FC) sandwich elements. *Compos. Struct.* **2017**, *177*, 104–118. [CrossRef]
52. Hernandez, J.; Sawalha, M.; Rivera-Perez, J.; Ozer, H.; Al-Qadi, I.L. Micromechanical modeling of I-FIT asphalt concrete specimens. *Eng. Fract. Mech.* **2018**, *200*, 234–250. [CrossRef]
53. De Sutter, S.; Verbruggen, S.; Tysmans, T.; Aggelis, D. Fracture monitoring of lightweight composite-concrete beams. *Compos. Struct.* **2017**, *167*, 11–19. [CrossRef]
54. Hong, S.; Qin, S.; Dong, P.; Li, G.; Zhang, Y.; Xing, F.; Dong, B. Quantification of rust penetration profile in reinforced concrete deduced by inverse modeling. *Cem. Concr. Compos.* **2020**, *111*, 103622. [CrossRef]
55. Sun, X.; Wang, S.; Jin, J.; Wang, Z.; Gong, F. Computational methods of mass transport in concrete under stress and crack conditions: A review. *J. Intell. Constr.* **2023**, *1*, 9180015. [CrossRef]
56. Gu, Z.; Feng, H.; Gao, D.; Zhao, J.; Wei, C.; Wu, C. Fatigue behavior and calculation methods of high strength steel fiber reinforced concrete beam. *Sustain. Struct.* **2023**, *3*, 000028. [CrossRef]
57. Li, X.; Hallett, S.R.; Wisnom, M.R.; Zobeiry, N.; Vaziri, R.; Poursartip, A. Experimental study of damage propagation in over-height compact tension tests. *Compos. Part A Appl. Sci. Manuf.* **2009**, *40*, 1891–1899. [CrossRef]
58. Garcea, S.; Mavrogordato, M.; Scott, A.; Sinclair, I.; Spearing, S. Fatigue micromechanism characterisation in carbon fibre reinforced polymers using synchrotron radiation computed tomography. *Compos. Sci. Technol.* **2014**, *99*, 23–30. [CrossRef]
59. Moffat, A.J.; Wright, P.; Helfen, L.; Baumbach, T.; Johnson, G.; Spearing, S.M.; Sinclair, I. In situ synchrotron computed laminography of damage in carbon fibre–epoxy [90/0] s laminates. *Scr. Mater.* **2010**, *62*, 97–100. [CrossRef]
60. Ni, X.; Kopp, R.; Kalfon-Cohen, E.; Furtado, C.; Lee, J.; Arteiro, A.; Borstnar, G.; Mavrogordato, M.N.; Helfen, L.; Sinclair, I.; et al. In situ synchrotron computed tomography study of nanoscale interlaminar reinforcement and thin-ply effects on damage progression in composite laminates. *Compos. Part B Eng.* **2021**, *217*, 108623. [CrossRef]
61. Zobeiry, N.; Vaziri, R.; Poursartip, A. Characterization of strain-softening behavior and failure mechanisms of composites under tension and compression. *Compos. Part A Appl. Sci. Manuf.* **2015**, *68*, 29–41. [CrossRef]
62. Nguyen, M.H.; Waas, A.M. Detailed experimental and numerical investigation of single-edge notched tensile cross-ply laminates. *Compos. Struct.* **2022**, *279*, 114731. [CrossRef]
63. Sadowski, T.; Marsavina, L.; Craciun, E.M.; Kneć, M. Modelling and experimental study of parallel cracks propagation in an orthotropic elastic material. *Comput. Mater. Sci.* **2012**, *52*, 231–235. [CrossRef]
64. Rosen, B.W. Tensile failure of fibrous composites. *AIAA J.* **1964**, *2*, 1985–1991. [CrossRef]
65. Sommer, J.; Hajikazemi, M.; De Baere, I.; Van Paepegem, W. Experimental and numerical fatigue damage characterization in multidirectional thermoplastic glass/polypropylene laminates based on in-situ damage observations. *Compos. Part B Eng.* **2023**, *267*, 111028. [CrossRef]
66. Cintra, G.G.; Vieira, J.D.; Cardoso, D.C.; Keller, T. Novel multi-crack damage approach for pultruded fiber-polymer web-flange junctions. *Compos. Part B Eng.* **2024**, *269*, 111102. [CrossRef]
67. Wagih, A.; Maimí, P.; Blanco, N.; Costa, J. A quasi-static indentation test to elucidate the sequence of damage events in low velocity impacts on composite laminates. *Compos. Part A Appl. Sci. Manuf.* **2016**, *82*, 180–189. [CrossRef]
68. Sun, X.C.; Hallett, S.R. Failure mechanisms and damage evolution of laminated composites under compression after impact (CAI): Experimental and numerical study. *Compos. Part A Appl. Sci. Manuf.* **2018**, *104*, 41–59. [CrossRef]
69. Thouless, M.D.; Olsson, E.; Gupta, A. Cracking of brittle films on elastic substrates. *Acta Metall. Mater.* **1992**, *40*, 1287–1292. [CrossRef]
70. Beuth, J.L. Cracking of thin bonded films in residual tension. *Int. J. Solids Struct.* **1992**, *29*, 1657–1675. [CrossRef]
71. Hutchinson, J.W.; Suo, Z. Mixed mode cracking in layered materials. *Adv. Appl. Mech.* **1991**, *29*, 63–191.
72. Xia, Z.C.; Hutchinson, J.W. Crack patterns in thin films. *J. Mech. Phys. Solids* **2000**, *48*, 1107–1131. [CrossRef]
73. Chen, F.L.; He, X.; Prieto-Munoz, P.A.; Yin, H.M. Opening-mode fractures of a brittle coating bonded to an elasto-plastic substrate. *Int. J. Plast.* **2015**, *67*, 171–191. [CrossRef]
74. Ben Cheikh, I.; Parry, G.; Dalmas, D.; Estevez, R.; Marthelot, J. Analysis of the multi-cracking mechanism of brittle thin films on elastic-plastic substrates. *Int. J. Solids Struct.* **2019**, *180*, 176–188. [CrossRef]
75. Shenoy, V.; Schwartzman, A.; Freund, L. Crack patterns in brittle thin films. *Int. J. Fract.* **2001**, *109*, 29–45. [CrossRef]
76. Andersons, J.; Leterrier, Y.; Fescenko, I. Analysis of the initial fragmentation stage of oxide coatings on polymer substrates under biaxial tension. *Thin Solid Film.* **2003**, *434*, 203–215. [CrossRef]
77. Vellinga, W.P.; Van den Bosch, M.; Geers, M.G.D. Interaction between cracking, delamination and buckling in brittle elastic thin films. *Int. J. Fract.* **2008**, *154*, 195–209. [CrossRef]
78. Ramulu, M.; Kobayashi, A.S. Mechanics of crack curving and branching—A dynamic fracture analysis. *Int. J. Fract.* **1985**, *27*, 187–201. [CrossRef]
79. Fineberg, J.; Marder, M. Instability in dynamic fracture. *Phys. Rep.* **1999**, *313*, 1–108. [CrossRef]
80. Bless, S. Using depth-of-penetration tests to design transparent armor. *Exp. Mech.* **2013**, *53*, 47–51. [CrossRef]
81. Schmidt, J.; Zemanová, A.; Zeman, J.; Šejnoha, M. Phase-field fracture modelling of thin monolithic and laminated glass plates under quasi-static bending. *Materials* **2020**, *13*, 5153. [CrossRef] [PubMed]

82. Qiu, Z.; Wang, Y. Multi-tip indenter tool scratch behavior of glass-ceramics. *J. Mech. Behav. Biomed. Mater.* **2021**, *121*, 104617. [CrossRef] [PubMed]
83. Yang, X.; Gao, S. Analysis of the crack propagation mechanism of multiple scratched glass-ceramics by an interference stress field prediction model and experiment. *Ceram. Int.* **2022**, *48*, 2449–2458. [CrossRef]
84. Yang, X.; Qiu, Z.; Wang, Y. Stress interaction and crack propagation behavior of glass ceramics under multi-scratches. *J. Non-Cryst. Solids* **2019**, *523*, 119600. [CrossRef]
85. Zhang, S.; Feng, Y.; Gao, X.; Song, Y.; Wang, F.; Zhang, S. Modeling of fatigue failure for SiC/SiC ceramic matrix composites at elevated temperatures and multi-scale experimental validation. *J. Eur. Ceram. Soc.* **2022**, *42*, 3395–3403. [CrossRef]
86. Jiang, C.P.; Wu, X.F.; Li, J.; Song, F.; Shao, Y.F.; Xu, X.H.; Yan, P. A study of the mechanism of formation and numerical simulations of crack patterns in ceramics subjected to thermal shock. *Acta Mater.* **2012**, *60*, 4540–4550. [CrossRef]
87. Xu, X.; Tian, C.; Sheng, S.; Lin, Z.; Song, F. Characterization of thermal-shock cracks in ceramic bars. *Sci. China Phys. Mech. Astron.* **2014**, *57*, 2205–2208. [CrossRef]
88. Huang, Q.; Alvarez, N.J.; Shabbir, A.; Hassager, O. Multiple cracks propagate simultaneously in polymer liquids in tension. *Phys. Rev. Lett.* **2016**, *117*, 087801. [CrossRef]
89. Fender, M.L.; Lechenault, F.; Daniels, K.E. Universal shapes formed by two interacting cracks. *Phys. Rev. Lett.* **2010**, *105*, 125505. [CrossRef]
90. Belova, O.N.; Stepanova, L.V.; Kosygina, L.N. Experimental study on the interaction between two cracks by digital photoelasticity method: Construction of the Williams series expansion. *Procedia Struct. Integr.* **2022**, *37*, 888–899. [CrossRef]
91. Goehring, L.; Clegg, W.J.; Routh, A.F. Plasticity and fracture in drying colloidal films. *Phys. Rev. Lett.* **2013**, *110*, 024301. [CrossRef] [PubMed]
92. Willmott, G.R.; Field, J.E. A high-speed photographic study of fast cracks in shocked diamond. *Philos. Mag.* **2006**, *86*, 4305–4318. [CrossRef]
93. Chang, P.Y.; Yen, P.C.; Yang, J.M. Fatigue crack growth in fibre metal laminates with multiple open holes. *Fatigue Fract. Eng. Mater. Struct.* **2012**, *35*, 93–107. [CrossRef]
94. Jin, H.; Cui, B.; Mao, L. Fatigue growth behaviour of two interacting cracks with different crack offset. *Materials* **2019**, *12*, 3526. [CrossRef]
95. Han, Z.; Qian, C.; Li, H. Study of the shielding interactions between double cracks on crack growth behaviors under fatigue loading. *Metals* **2020**, *10*, 202. [CrossRef]
96. Hoang, L.; Nguyen, T.T. Facilitation effect of multiple crack interaction on fatigue life reduction and a quantitative evaluation of interactions factor of two parallel Non-coplanar cracks. *Theor. Appl. Fract. Mech.* **2023**, *125*, 103941. [CrossRef]
97. Schackert, S.M.; Riedel, H.; Schweizer, C. Multiple cracking, crack coalescence and fatigue lifetime–model and experiments on an austenitic steel and on a nickel base alloy. *Int. J. Fatigue* **2024**, *189*, 108562. [CrossRef]
98. Deng, L.; Deng, Y. Study on Multi-Crack Damage Evolution and Fatigue Life of Corroded Steel Wires Inside In-Service Bridge Suspenders. *Appl. Sci.* **2024**, *14*, 9596. [CrossRef]
99. Wang, Y.-L.; Wang, X.-S.; Wu, S.-C.; Yang, H.-H.; Zhang, Z.-H. High-Cycle Microscopic Severe Corrosion Fatigue Behavior and Life Prediction of 25CrMo Steel Used in Railway Axles. *Metals* **2017**, *7*, 134. [CrossRef]
100. Williams, M.L. On the stress distribution at the base of a stationary crack. *J. Appl. Mech.* **1957**, *24*, 109–114. [CrossRef]
101. Sih, G.C.; Paris, P.C.; Irwin, G.R. On cracks in rectilinearly anisotropic bodies. *Int. J. Fract. Mech.* **1965**, *1*, 189–203. [CrossRef]
102. Muskhelishvili, N.I. *Some Basic Problems of the Mathematical Theory of Elasticity*; Noordhoff: Groningen, The Netherlands, 1953.
103. Koiter, W.T. An infinite row of collinear cracks in an infinite elastic sheet. *Ingenieur-Archiv* **1959**, *28*, 168–172. [CrossRef]
104. Sneddon, I. *Crack Problems in the Theory of Elasticity//Developments in Theoretical and Applied Mechanics: Proceedings of the Third Southeastern Conference on Theoretical and Applied Mechanics*; Elsevier: Amsterdam, The Netherlands, 2013; p. 73.
105. Horii, H.; Nemat-Nasser, S. Compression-induced microcrack growth in brittle solids: Axial splitting and shear failure. *J. Geophys. Res. Solid Earth* **1985**, *90*, 3105–3125. [CrossRef]
106. Horii, H.; Nemat-Nasser, S. Elastic fields of interacting inhomogeneities. *Int. J. Solids Struct.* **1985**, *21*, 731–745. [CrossRef]
107. Kachanov, M.L. A microcrack model of rock inelasticity part I: Frictional sliding on microcracks. *Mech. Mater.* **1982**, *1*, 19–27. [CrossRef]
108. Kachanov, M. Elastic solids with many cracks: A simple method of analysis. *Int. J. Solids Struct.* **1987**, *23*, 23–43. [CrossRef]
109. Li, Y.P.; Tham, L.G.; Wang, Y.H.; Tsui, Y. A modified Kachanov method for analysis of solids with multiple cracks. *Eng. Fract. Mech.* **2003**, *70*, 1115–1129. [CrossRef]
110. Qing, H.; Yang, W. Characterization of strongly interacted multiple cracks in an infinite plate. *Theor. Appl. Fract. Mech.* **2006**, *46*, 209–216. [CrossRef]
111. Peng, S.; Jing, L.; Li, S.; Wu, D.; Jing, W. Analytical solution of the stress intensity factors of multiple closed collinear cracks. *J. Vib. Eng. Technol.* **2023**, *11*, 3737–3745. [CrossRef]
112. Gao, H.; Qin, Y.; Jia, T.; Zhao, L.; Gu, J. Reliability analysis of plate parts with multiple interacting hole-edge cracks using complex variable function. *Appl. Math. Model.* **2024**, *125*, 482–498. [CrossRef]
113. Grytsenko, T.; Galybin, A.N. Numerical analysis of multi-crack large-scale plane problems with adaptive cross approximation and hierarchical matrices. *Eng. Anal. Bound. Elem.* **2010**, *34*, 501–510. [CrossRef]
114. Chen, Y.Z. Multiple crack problems of antiplane elasticity in an infinite body. *Eng. Fract. Mech.* **1984**, *20*, 767–775. [CrossRef]

115. Lam, K.Y.; Phua, S.P. Multiple crack interaction and its effect on stress intensity factor. *Eng. Fract. Mech.* **1991**, *40*, 585–592. [CrossRef]
116. Cheung, Y.K.; Woo, C.W.; Wang, Y.H. A general method for multiple crack problems in a finite plate. *Comput. Mech.* **1992**, *10*, 335–343. [CrossRef]
117. Yavuz, A.; Phoenix, S.; TerMaath, S.C. An accurate and fast analysis for strongly interacting multiple crack configurations including kinked (V) and branched (Y) cracks. *Int. J. Solids Struct.* **2006**, *43*, 6727–6750. [CrossRef]
118. Chen, Y.Z. A survey of new integral equations in plane elasticity crack problem. *Eng. Fract. Mech.* **1995**, *51*, 97–134. [CrossRef]
119. Chen, Y.Z. Solution of multiple crack problem in a finite plate using an alternating method based on two kinds of integral equation. *Eng. Anal. Bound. Elem.* **2011**, *35*, 1109–1115. [CrossRef]
120. Denda, M.; Dong, Y.F. Complex variable approach to the BEM for multiple crack problems. *Comput. Methods Appl. Mech. Eng.* **1997**, *141*, 247–264. [CrossRef]
121. Wang, G.S. The interaction of doubly periodic cracks. *Theor. Appl. Fract. Mech.* **2004**, *42*, 249–294. [CrossRef]
122. Li, X. The effect of a homogeneous cylindrical inlay on cracks in the doubly-periodic complete plane strain problem. *Int. J. Fract.* **2001**, *109*, 403–411. [CrossRef]
123. Shi, P.P. On the plastic zone size of solids containing doubly periodic rectangular-shaped arrays of cracks under longitudinal shear. *Mech. Res. Commun.* **2015**, *67*, 39–46. [CrossRef]
124. Dong, C.Y.; Lee, K.Y. Numerical analysis of doubly periodic array of cracks/rigid-line inclusions in an infinite isotropic medium using the boundary integral equation method. *Int. J. Fract.* **2005**, *133*, 389–405. [CrossRef]
125. Shi, P.P. Interaction between the doubly periodic interfacial cracks in a layered periodic composite: Simulation by the method of singular integral equation. *Theor. Appl. Fract. Mech.* **2015**, *78*, 25–39. [CrossRef]
126. Monfared, M.M.; Ayatollahi, M.; Bagheri, R. In-plane stress analysis of dissimilar materials with multiple interface cracks. *Appl. Math. Model.* **2016**, *40*, 8464–8474. [CrossRef]
127. Fartash, A.H.; Ayatollahi, M.; Bagheri, R. Transient response of dissimilar piezoelectric layers with multiple interacting interface cracks. *Appl. Math. Model.* **2019**, *66*, 508–526. [CrossRef]
128. Bagheri, R.; Ayatollahi, M. Multiple moving cracks in a functionally graded strip. *Appl. Math. Model.* **2012**, *36*, 4677–4686. [CrossRef]
129. Tian, W.Y.; Gabbert, U. Multiple crack interaction problem in magnetoelectroelastic solids. *Eur. J. Mech.-A/Solids* **2004**, *23*, 599–614. [CrossRef]
130. Cao, T.; Feng, X.; Qin, T. Analysis for multiple cracks in 2d piezoelectric bimaterial using the singular integral equation method. *Acta Mech. Solida Sin.* **2022**, *35*, 261–272. [CrossRef]
131. Lauterbach, B.; Gross, D. Crack growth in brittle solids under compression. *Mech. Mater.* **1998**, *29*, 81–92. [CrossRef]
132. Matsumto, T.; Tanaka, M.; Obara, R. Computation of stress intensity factors of interface cracks based on interaction energy release rates and BEM sensitivity analysis. *Eng. Fract. Mech.* **2000**, *65*, 683–702. [CrossRef]
133. Mykhas'kiv, V.V.; Khay, O.M. Interaction between rigid-disc inclusion and penny-shaped crack under elastic time-harmonic wave incidence. *Int. J. Solids Struct.* **2009**, *46*, 602–616. [CrossRef]
134. Nishimura, N.; Yoshida, K.-I.; Kobayashi, S. A fast multipole boundary integral equation method for crack problems in 3D. *Eng. Anal. Bound. Elem.* **1999**, *23*, 97–105. [CrossRef]
135. Wang, L.; Yin, Z.-Y.; Chen, W. Characteristics of crack growth in brittle solids with the effects of material heterogeneity and multi-crack interaction. *Int. J. Fract.* **2024**, *246*, 77–99. [CrossRef]
136. Wang, Y.; Cui, Y.; Wang, J.; Ju, Y. An h-version adaptive finite element scheme for eigensolutions of free vibration of three-dimensional cracked elasticity utilising element subdivision-based error estimator. *J. Intell. Constr.* **2024**. [CrossRef]
137. Zhang, D.; Zhou, Z.; Gao, C.; Gai, P.; Chen, X.; Chen, J.; Bu, F. A novel hybrid PD-FEM-FVM approach for simulating hydraulic fracture propagation in saturated porous media. *Comput. Geotech.* **2025**, *177*, 106821. [CrossRef]
138. Daux, C.; Moës, N.; Dolbow, J.; Sukumar, N.; Belytschko, T. Arbitrary branched and intersecting cracks with the extended finite element method. *Int. J. Numer. Methods Eng.* **2000**, *48*, 1741–1760. [CrossRef]
139. Belytschko, T.; Moës, N.; Usui, S.; Parimi, C. Arbitrary discontinuities in finite elements. *Int. J. Numer. Methods Eng.* **2001**, *50*, 993–1013. [CrossRef]
140. Budyn, E.; Zi, G.; Moës, N.; Belytschko, T. A method for multiple crack growth in brittle materials without remeshing. *Int. J. Numer. Methods Eng.* **2004**, *61*, 1741–1770. [CrossRef]
141. Mousavi, S.E.; Grinspun, E.; Sukumar, N. Harmonic enrichment functions: A unified treatment of multiple, intersecting and branched cracks in the extended finite element method. *Int. J. Numer. Methods Eng.* **2011**, *85*, 1306–1322. [CrossRef]
142. Richardson, C.L.; Hegemann, J.; Sifakis, E.; Hellrung, J.; Teran, J.M. An XFEM method for modeling geometrically elaborate crack propagation in brittle materials. *Int. J. Numer. Methods Eng.* **2011**, *88*, 1042–1065. [CrossRef]
143. Xu, D.; Liu, Z.; Liu, X.; Zeng, Q.; Zhuang, Z. Modeling of dynamic crack branching by enhanced extended finite element method. *Comput. Mech.* **2014**, *54*, 489–502. [CrossRef]
144. Sutula, D.; Kerfriden, P.; van Dam, T.; Bordas, S.P. Minimum energy multiple crack propagation. Part I: Theory and state of the art review. *Eng. Fract. Mech.* **2018**, *191*, 205–224. [CrossRef]
145. Sutula, D.; Kerfriden, P.; van Dam, T.; Bordas, S.P. Minimum energy multiple crack propagation. Part-II: Discrete solution with XFEM. *Eng. Fract. Mech.* **2018**, *191*, 225–256. [CrossRef]

146. Sutula, D.; Kerfriden, P.; van Dam, T.; Bordas, S.P. Minimum energy multiple crack propagation. Part III: XFEM computer implementation and applications. *Eng. Fract. Mech.* **2018**, *191*, 257–276. [CrossRef]
147. Agathos, K.; Chatzi, E.; Bordas, S.P.A. Multiple crack detection in 3D using a stable XFEM and global optimization. *Comput. Mech.* **2018**, *62*, 835–852. [CrossRef]
148. Chen, J.W.; Zhou, X.P. The enhanced extended finite element method for the propagation of complex branched cracks. *Eng. Anal. Bound. Elem.* **2019**, *104*, 46–62. [CrossRef]
149. Song, J.H.; Areias, P.M.; Belytschko, T. A method for dynamic crack and shear band propagation with phantom nodes. *Int. J. Numer. Methods Eng.* **2006**, *67*, 868–893. [CrossRef]
150. Ding, J.; Yu, T.; Bui, T.Q. Modeling strong/weak discontinuities by local mesh refinement variable-node XFEM with object-oriented implementation. *Theor. Appl. Fract. Mech.* **2020**, *106*, 102434. [CrossRef]
151. Ding, J.; Yu, T.; Yang, Y.; Bui, T.Q. An efficient variable-node XFEM for modeling multiple crack growth: A Matlab object-oriented implementation. *Adv. Eng. Softw.* **2020**, *140*, 102750. [CrossRef]
152. Wen, L.F.; Tian, R.; Wang, L.X.; Feng, C. Improved XFEM for multiple crack analysis: Accurate and efficient implementations for stress intensity factors. *Comput. Methods Appl. Mech. Eng.* **2023**, *411*, 116045. [CrossRef]
153. Wang, L.X.; Wen, L.F.; Tian, R.; Feng, C. Improved XFEM (IXFEM): Arbitrary multiple crack initiation, propagation and interaction analysis. *Comput. Methods Appl. Mech. Eng.* **2024**, *421*, 116791. [CrossRef]
154. Gajjar, M.; Pathak, H.; Kumar, S. Elasto-plastic fracture modeling for crack interaction with XFEM. *Trans. Indian Inst. Met.* **2020**, *73*, 1679–1687. [CrossRef]
155. Hu, Z.; Suo, X.; Wang, M.; Jiang, F.; Huang, H.; Shen, Y. A phase-field-cohesive-zone framework to simulate multiple failure mechanisms of elastoplastic fiber-reinforced composites. *Int. J. Fract.* **2023**, *244*, 43–59. [CrossRef]
156. Zi, G.; Song, J.-H.; Budyn, E.; Lee, S.-H.; Belytschko, T. A method for growing multiple cracks without remeshing and its application to fatigue crack growth. *Model. Simul. Mater. Sci. Eng.* **2004**, *12*, 901. [CrossRef]
157. Singh, I.V.; Mishra, B.K.; Bhattacharya, S.; Patil, R. The numerical simulation of fatigue crack growth using extended finite element method. *Int. J. Fatigue* **2012**, *36*, 109–119. [CrossRef]
158. Shu, Y.; Li, Y.; Duan, M.; Yang, F. An X-FEM approach for simulation of 3-D multiple fatigue cracks and application to double surface crack problems. *Int. J. Mech. Sci.* **2017**, *130*, 331–349. [CrossRef]
159. Zhu, J.; Jie, Z.; Chen, C.; Zheng, H.; Wang, W. Fatigue Crack Propagation of Corroded High-Strength Steel Wires Using the XFEM and the EIFS. *Materials* **2023**, *16*, 4738. [CrossRef]
160. Chen, Z.; Bao, H.; Dai, Y.; Liu, Y. Numerical prediction based on XFEM for mixed-mode crack growth path and fatigue life under cyclic overload. *Int. J. Fatigue* **2022**, *162*, 106943. [CrossRef]
161. Jafari, A.; Broumand, P.; Vahab, M.; Khalili, N. An eXtended finite element method implementation in COMSOL multiphysics: Solid mechanics. *Finite Elem. Anal. Des.* **2022**, *202*, 103707. [CrossRef]
162. Singh, S.K.; Singh, I.V.; Mishra, B.K.; Bhardwaj, G. Analysis of cracked plate using higher-order shear deformation theory: Asymptotic crack-tip fields and XIGA implementation. *Comput. Methods Appl. Mech. Eng.* **2018**, *336*, 594–639. [CrossRef]
163. Bhardwaj, G.; Singh, I.V.; Mishra, B.K.; Kumar, V. Numerical simulations of cracked plate using XIGA under different loads and boundary conditions. *Mech. Adv. Mater. Struct.* **2016**, *23*, 704–714. [CrossRef]
164. Singh, S.K.; Singh, I.V.; Mishra, B.K.; Bhardwaj, G. Analysis of cracked functionally graded material plates using XIGA based on generalized higher-order shear deformation theory. *Compos. Struct.* **2019**, *225*, 111038. [CrossRef]
165. Gu, J.; Yu, T.; Van Lich, L.; Tanaka, S.; Qiu, L.; Bui, T.Q. Adaptive orthotropic XIGA for fracture analysis of composites. *Compos. Part B Eng.* **2019**, *176*, 107259. [CrossRef]
166. Gu, J.; Yu, T.; Van Lich, L.; Nguyen, T.-T.; Yang, Y.; Bui, T.Q. Fracture modeling with the adaptive XIGA based on locally refined B-splines. *Comput. Methods Appl. Mech. Eng.* **2019**, *354*, 527–567. [CrossRef]
167. Gu, J.; Yu, T.; Van Lich, L.; Tanaka, S.; Yuan, H.; Bui, T.Q. Crack growth adaptive XIGA simulation in isotropic and orthotropic materials. *Comput. Methods Appl. Mech. Eng.* **2020**, *365*, 113016. [CrossRef]
168. Yu, T.; Yuan, H.; Gu, J.; Tanaka, S.; Bui, T.Q. Error-controlled adaptive LR B-splines XIGA for assessment of fracture parameters in through-cracked Mindlin-Reissner plates. *Eng. Fract. Mech.* **2020**, *229*, 106964. [CrossRef]
169. Bui, T.Q. Extended isogeometric dynamic and static fracture analysis for cracks in piezoelectric materials using NURBS. *Comput. Methods Appl. Mech. Eng.* **2015**, *295*, 470–509. [CrossRef]
170. Singh, S.; Singh, I. Analysis of cracked functionally graded piezoelectric material using XIGA. *Eng. Fract. Mech.* **2020**, *230*, 107015. [CrossRef]
171. Jiang, K.; Zhu, X.; Hu, C.; Hou, W.; Hu, P.; Bordas, S.P. An enhanced extended isogeometric analysis with strong imposition of essential boundary conditions for crack problems using B++ splines. *Appl. Math. Model.* **2023**, *116*, 393–414. [CrossRef]
172. Aliabadi, M. A new generation of boundary element methods in fracture mechanics. *Int. J. Fract.* **1997**, *86*, 91–125. [CrossRef]
173. Sutradhar, A.; Paulino, G.H. Symmetric Galerkin boundary element computation of T-stress and stress intensity factors for mixed-mode cracks by the interaction integral method. *Eng. Anal. Bound. Elem.* **2004**, *28*, 1335–1350. [CrossRef]
174. Hsieh, J.; Denda, M.; Redondo, J.; Marante, M.; Flórez-López, J. Electronic handbook of fracture: A Java-based boundary element program for fracture analysis of multiple curvilinear cracks in the general anisotropic solids. *Adv. Eng. Softw.* **2008**, *39*, 395–406. [CrossRef]

175. Lei, J.; Yun, L.; Bui, T.Q. Numerical simulation of crack growth in piezoelectric structures by BEM. *Eng. Anal. Bound. Elem.* **2017**, *85*, 30–42. [CrossRef]
176. Fedelinski, P. Analysis of closed branched and intersecting cracks by the boundary element method. *Acta Mech.* **2022**, *233*, 1213–1230. [CrossRef]
177. Denda, M. A dislocation and point force approach to the boundary element method for mixed mode crack analysis of plane anisotropic solids. *J. Chin. Inst. Eng.* **1999**, *22*, 677–693. [CrossRef]
178. Denda, M. Mixed mode I, II and III analysis of multiple cracks in plane anisotropic solids by the BEM: A dislocation and point force approach. *Eng. Anal. Bound. Elem.* **2001**, *25*, 267–278. [CrossRef]
179. Wang, Y.B.; Chau, K.T. A new boundary element method for mixed boundary value problems involving cracks and holes: Interactions between rigid inclusions and cracks. *Int. J. Fract.* **2001**, *110*, 387–406. [CrossRef]
180. Gray, L.J.; Phan, A.V.; Paulino, G.H.; Kaplan, T. Improved quarter-point crack tip element. *Eng. Fract. Mech.* **2003**, *70*, 269–283. [CrossRef]
181. Sáez, A.; García-Sánchez, F.; Domínguez, J. Hypersingular BEM for dynamic fracture in 2-D piezoelectric solids. *Comput. Methods Appl. Mech. Eng.* **2006**, *196*, 235–246. [CrossRef]
182. Guo, Z.; Liu, Y.; Ma, H.; Huang, S. A fast multipole boundary element method for modeling 2-D multiple crack problems with constant elements. *Eng. Anal. Bound. Elem.* **2014**, *47*, 1–9. [CrossRef]
183. Wu, X.; Li, X. Simulations of micron-scale fracture using atomistic-based boundary element method. *Model. Simul. Mater. Sci. Eng.* **2017**, *25*, 085008. [CrossRef]
184. Liu, Y.J.; Li, Y.X.; Xie, W. Modeling of multiple crack propagation in 2-D elastic solids by the fast multipole boundary element method. *Eng. Fract. Mech.* **2017**, *172*, 1–16. [CrossRef]
185. Hwu, C.; Huang, S.-T.; Li, C.-C. Boundary-based finite element method for two-dimensional anisotropic elastic solids with multiple holes and cracks. *Eng. Anal. Bound. Elem.* **2017**, *79*, 13–22. [CrossRef]
186. Cong, L.; Bin, H.; Zongjun, H.; Zhongrong, N. Analysis of multi-crack propagation by using the extended boundary element method. *Eng. Anal. Bound. Elem.* **2021**, *132*, 65–76. [CrossRef]
187. Park, B.; Min, K.-B. Bonded-particle discrete element modeling of mechanical behavior of transversely isotropic rock. *Int. J. Rock Mech. Min. Sci.* **2015**, *76*, 243–255. [CrossRef]
188. Zhong, J.; Wang, J.; Li, X.; Chu, X. Macro-and meso-failure mechanism analysis for shale-like brittle materials under uniaxial compression. *Eng. Anal. Bound. Elem.* **2022**, *141*, 189–198. [CrossRef]
189. Li, Y.; Cai, W.; Li, X.; Zhu, W.; Zhang, Q.; Wang, S. Experimental and DEM analysis on secondary crack types of rock-like material containing multiple flaws under uniaxial compression. *Appl. Sci.* **2019**, *9*, 1749. [CrossRef]
190. Wang, B.; Gerolymatou, E.; Jin, A. Study on mechanical and fracture characteristics of rock-like specimens with rough non-persistent joints by YADE DEM simulation. *Comput. Geotech.* **2023**, *158*, 105382. [CrossRef]
191. Sun, Y.; Kwok, C.Y.; Duan, K. Size effects on crystalline rock masses: Insights from grain-based DEM modeling. *Comput. Geotech.* **2024**, *171*, 106376. [CrossRef]
192. Bai, Q.S.; Tu, S.H.; Zhang, C. DEM investigation of the fracture mechanism of rock disc containing hole (s) and its influence on tensile strength. *Theor. Appl. Fract. Mech.* **2016**, *86*, 197–216. [CrossRef]
193. Yang, S.Q.; Yin, P.F.; Zhang, Y.C.; Chen, M.; Zhou, X.P.; Jing, H.W.; Zhang, Q.Y. Failure behavior and crack evolution mechanism of a non-persistent jointed rock mass containing a circular hole. *Int. J. Rock Mech. Min. Sci.* **2019**, *114*, 101–121. [CrossRef]
194. Duan, K.; Kwok, C.Y.; Zhang, Q.; Shang, J. On the initiation, propagation and reorientation of simultaneously-induced multiple hydraulic fractures. *Comput. Geotech.* **2020**, *117*, 103226. [CrossRef]
195. Li, M.; Zhang, F.; Wang, S.; Dontsov, E.; Li, P. DEM modeling of simultaneous propagation of multiple hydraulic fractures across different regimes, from toughness-to viscosity-dominated. *Rock Mech. Rock Eng.* **2024**, *57*, 481–503. [CrossRef]
196. Hofmann, H.; Babadagli, T.; Yoon, J.; Zimmermann, G. Multi-branched growth of fractures in shales for effective reservoir contact: A particle based distinct element modeling study. *J. Nat. Gas Sci. Eng.* **2016**, *35*, 509–521. [CrossRef]
197. Hofmann, H.; Babadagli, T.; Yoon, J.S.; Blöcher, G.; Zimmermann, G. A hybrid discrete/finite element modeling study of complex hydraulic fracture development for enhanced geothermal systems (EGS) in granitic basements. *Geothermics* **2016**, *64*, 362–381. [CrossRef]
198. Papachristos, E.; Scholtès, L.; Donzé, F.; Chareyre, B. Intensity and volumetric characterizations of hydraulically driven fractures by hydro-mechanical simulations. *Int. J. Rock Mech. Min. Sci.* **2017**, *93*, 163–178. [CrossRef]
199. Lee, H.P.; Olson, J.E.; Schultz, R.A. Interaction analysis of propagating opening mode fractures with veins using the discrete element method. *Int. J. Rock Mech. Min. Sci.* **2018**, *103*, 275–288. [CrossRef]
200. Liu, G.; Sun, W.; Lowinger, S.M.; Zhang, Z.; Huang, M.; Peng, J. Coupled flow network and discrete element modeling of injection-induced crack propagation and coalescence in brittle rock. *Acta Geotech.* **2019**, *14*, 843–868. [CrossRef]
201. Shao, L.; Mao, J.; Zhao, L.; Li, T. A three-dimensional deformable spheropolyhedral-based discrete element method for simulation of the whole fracture process. *Eng. Fract. Mech.* **2022**, *263*, 108290. [CrossRef]
202. Jiao, K.; Han, D.; Wang, D.; Chen, Y.; Li, J.; Gong, L.; Bai, B.; Yu, B. Investigation of thermal-hydro-mechanical coupled fracture propagation considering rock damage. *Comput. Geosci.* **2022**, *26*, 1167–1187. [CrossRef]
203. Zhong, J.; Wang, J.; Li, X.; Chu, X. Experiments and discrete element simulations of crack initiation angle of mixed-mode I/II in PMMA material. *Theor. Appl. Fract. Mech.* **2023**, *125*, 103862. [CrossRef]

204. Fukumoto, Y.; Shimbo, T. 3-D coupled peridynamics and discrete element method for fracture and post-fracture behavior of soil-like materials. *Comput. Geotech.* **2023**, *158*, 105372. [CrossRef]
205. Belytschko, T.; Lu, Y.Y.; Gu, L. Element-free Galerkin methods. *Int. J. Numer. Methods Eng.* **1994**, *37*, 229–256. [CrossRef]
206. Fleming, M.; Chu, Y.A.; Moran, B.; Belytschko, T. Enriched element-free Galerkin methods for crack tip fields. *Int. J. Numer. Methods Eng.* **1997**, *40*, 1483–1504. [CrossRef]
207. Li, D.M.; Liu, J.H.; Nie, F.H.; Featherston, C.A.; Wu, Z. On tracking arbitrary crack path with complex variable meshless methods. *Comput. Methods Appl. Mech. Eng.* **2022**, *399*, 115402. [CrossRef]
208. Pan, J.H.; Li, D.M.; Luo, X.B.; Zhu, W. An enriched improved complex variable element-free Galerkin method for efficient fracture analysis of orthotropic materials. *Theor. Appl. Fract. Mech.* **2022**, *121*, 103488. [CrossRef]
209. Pan, J.H.; Li, D.M.; Cai, S.; Luo, X.B. A pure complex variable enrichment method for modeling progressive fracture of orthotropic functionally gradient materials. *Eng. Fract. Mech.* **2023**, *277*, 108984. [CrossRef]
210. Zhu, H.; Sun, P.; Cai, Y. Independent cover meshless method for the simulation of multiple crack growth with arbitrary incremental steps and directions. *Eng. Anal. Bound. Elem.* **2017**, *83*, 242–255. [CrossRef]
211. Muravin, B.; Turkel, E. Multiple crack weight for solution of multiple interacting cracks by meshless numerical methods. *Int. J. Numer. Methods Eng.* **2006**, *67*, 1146–1159. [CrossRef]
212. Duflot, M.; Nguyen-Dang, H. A meshless method with enriched weight functions for fatigue crack growth. *Int. J. Numer. Methods Eng.* **2004**, *59*, 1945–1961. [CrossRef]
213. Duflot, M. A meshless method with enriched weight functions for three-dimensional crack propagation. *Int. J. Numer. Methods Eng.* **2006**, *65*, 1970–2006. [CrossRef]
214. Singh, I.V.; Mishra, B.K.; Pant, M. A modified intrinsic enriched element free Galerkin method for multiple cracks simulation. *Mater. Des.* **2010**, *31*, 628–632. [CrossRef]
215. Singh, I.V.; Mishra, B.K.; Pant, M. An enrichment based new criterion for the simulation of multiple interacting cracks using element free Galerkin method. *Int. J. Fract.* **2011**, *167*, 157–171. [CrossRef]
216. Pant, M.; Singh, I.V.; Mishra, B.K. A novel enrichment criterion for modeling kinked cracks using element free Galerkin method. *Int. J. Mech. Sci.* **2013**, *68*, 140–149. [CrossRef]
217. Barbieri, E.; Petrinic, N.; Meo, M.; Tagarielli, V.L. A new weight-function enrichment in meshless methods for multiple cracks in linear elasticity. *Int. J. Numer. Methods Eng.* **2012**, *90*, 177–195. [CrossRef]
218. Barbier, E.; Petrinic, N. Multiple Crack Growth and Coalescence in Meshfree Methods with Adistance Function-Based Enriched Kernel. *Key Eng. Mater.* **2013**, *560*, 37–60. [CrossRef]
219. Ai, W.; Bird, R.E.; Coombs, W.M.; Augarde, C.E. A configurational force driven cracking particle method for modelling crack propagation in 2D. *Eng. Anal. Bound. Elem.* **2019**, *104*, 197–208. [CrossRef]
220. Ai, W.; Augarde, C.E. Thermoelastic fracture modelling in 2D by an adaptive cracking particle method without enrichment functions. *Int. J. Mech. Sci.* **2019**, *160*, 343–357. [CrossRef]
221. Memari, A.; Mohebalizadeh, H. Quasi-static analysis of mixed-mode crack propagation using the meshless local Petrov–Galerkin method. *Eng. Anal. Bound. Elem.* **2019**, *106*, 397–411. [CrossRef]
222. Zhao, C.; Hu, Y.; Zhao, J.; Wang, Q.; He, P.; Liu, A.; Song, P. Numerical investigation of hydraulic fracture extension based on the meshless method. *Geofluids* **2020**, *2020*, 8881901. [CrossRef]
223. Nguyen, N.T.; Nguyen, M.N.; Van Vu, T.; Truong, T.T.; Bui, T.Q. A meshfree model enhanced by NURBS-based Cartesian transformation method for cracks at finite deformation in hyperelastic solids. *Eng. Fract. Mech.* **2022**, *261*, 108176. [CrossRef]
224. Xiang, P.; Liu, Z.; Shao, Z.; Chen, Y.; Peng, X.; Wang, Q. Meshfree method for bending and free vibration analysis of laminated plates using the Reissner's mixed variational theorem. *Mech. Adv. Mater. Struct.* **2024**, 1–15. [CrossRef]
225. Xiang, P.; Shao, Z.; Zhao, H.; Zhang, P.; Xie, X.; Liu, X. A stochastic meshless framework for higher-order free vibration analysis and static bending of porous functionally graded plates. *Mech. Based Des. Struct. Mach.* **2024**, 1–28. [CrossRef]
226. Shao, Z.; Zhao, H.; Zhang, P.; Xie, X.; Ademiloye, A.; Xiang, P. A meshless computational framework for a modified dynamic system of vehicle coupled with plate structure. *Eng. Struct.* **2024**, *312*, 118140. [CrossRef]
227. Zhang, X.; Chen, B.; Shao, Z.; Ademiloye, A.; Yang, D.; Xiang, P.; Xianbiao, W. A size-dependent meshfree model based on nonlocal strain gradient theory for trigonometric functionally graded nanoplates on variable elastic foundations. *Structures* **2024**, *69*, 107480. [CrossRef]
228. Zhao, Y.; Zhou, Z.; Bi, J.; Wang, C.; Wu, Z. Numerical simulation the fracture of rock in the framework of plastic-bond-based SPH and its applications. *Comput. Geotech.* **2023**, *157*, 105359. [CrossRef]
229. Zhou, X.P.; Xiao, N. Analyzing fracture properties of the 3D reconstructed model of porous rocks. *Eng. Fract. Mech.* **2018**, *189*, 175–193. [CrossRef]
230. Xia, C.; Shi, Z.; Li, B. A revisit of disaster process of Vajont rockslide using a coupled discontinuous smooth particle hydrodynamics (CDSPH) method. *Landslides* **2024**, *21*, 197–216. [CrossRef]
231. Islam, M.R.I.; Peng, C.; Patra, P.K. A comparison of numerical stability for ESPH and TLSPH for dynamic brittle fracture. *Theor. Appl. Fract. Mech.* **2023**, *127*, 104052. [CrossRef]
232. Kilic, B.; Madenci, E. Prediction of crack paths in a quenched glass plate by using peridynamic theory. *Int. J. Fract.* **2009**, *156*, 165–177. [CrossRef]

233. Gu, X.; Zhang, Q. A modified conjugated bond-based peridynamic analysis for impact failure of concrete gravity dam. *Meccanica* **2020**, *55*, 547–566. [CrossRef]
234. Zhou, L.; Zhu, S.; Zhu, Z.; Yu, S.; Xie, X. Improved peridynamic model and its application to crack propagation in rocks. *R. Soc. Open Sci.* **2022**, *9*, 221013. [CrossRef] [PubMed]
235. Wang, H.; Dong, H.; Cai, Z.; Li, Y.; Wang, W.; Liu, Y. Peridynamic-based investigation of the cracking behavior of multilayer thermal barrier coatings. *Ceram. Int.* **2022**, *48*, 23543–23553. [CrossRef]
236. Agwai, A.; Guven, I.; Madenci, E. Predicting crack propagation with peridynamics: A comparative study. *Int. J. Fract.* **2011**, *171*, 65–78. [CrossRef]
237. Ha, Y.D.; Bobaru, F. Studies of Dynamic Crack Propagation and Crack Branching with Peridynamics. *Int. J. Fract.* **2010**, *162*, 229–244. [CrossRef]
238. Zhao, J.; Chen, Z.; Mehrmashhadi, J.; Bobaru, F. A stochastic multiscale peridynamic model for corrosion-induced fracture in reinforced concrete. *Eng. Fract. Mech.* **2020**, *229*, 106969. [CrossRef]
239. Peng, X.; Chen, Z.; Bobaru, F. Accurate predictions of dynamic fracture in perforated plates. *Int. J. Fract.* **2023**, *244*, 61–84. [CrossRef]
240. Wang, Y.; Zhou, X.; Xu, X. Numerical simulation of propagation and coalescence of flaws in rock materials under compressive loads using the extended non-ordinary state-based peridynamics. *Eng. Fract. Mech.* **2016**, *163*, 248–273. [CrossRef]
241. Zhou, X.; Wang, Y.; Xu, X. Numerical simulation of initiation, propagation and coalescence of cracks using the non-ordinary state-based peridynamics. *Int. J. Fract.* **2016**, *201*, 213–234. [CrossRef]
242. Dai, Z.; Xie, J.; Lu, Z.; Qin, S.; Wang, L. Numerical modeling on crack propagation based on a multi-grid bond-based dual-horizon peridynamics. *Mathematics* **2021**, *9*, 2848. [CrossRef]
243. Shojaei, A.; Hermann, A.; Cyron, C.J.; Seleson, P.; Silling, S.A. A hybrid meshfree discretization to improve the numerical performance of peridynamic models. *Comput. Methods Appl. Mech. Eng.* **2022**, *391*, 114544. [CrossRef]
244. Wang, W.; Zhu, Q.-Z.; Ni, T.; Vazic, B.; Newell, P.; Bordas, S.P. An extended peridynamic model equipped with a new bond-breakage criterion for mixed-mode fracture in rock-like materials. *Comput. Methods Appl. Mech. Eng.* **2023**, *411*, 116016. [CrossRef]
245. Zhou, L.; Zhu, S.; Zhu, Z. Cosserat ordinary state-based peridynamic model and numerical simulation of rock fracture. *Comput. Geotech.* **2023**, *155*, 105240. [CrossRef]
246. Tong, Q.; Li, S. A concurrent multiscale study of dynamic fracture. *Comput. Methods Appl. Mech. Eng.* **2020**, *366*, 113075. [CrossRef]
247. Zhou, Z.; Yu, M.; Wang, X.; Huang, Z. Peridynamic Study on Fracture Mode and Crack Propagation Path of a Plate with Multiple Cracks Subjected to Uniaxial Tension. *CMES-Comput. Model. Eng. Sci.* **2023**, *137*, 2593–2620. [CrossRef]
248. Bie, Y.; Ren, H.; Rabczuk, T.; Bui, T.Q.; Wei, Y. The fully coupled thermo-mechanical dual-horizon peridynamic correspondence damage model for homogeneous and heterogeneous materials. *Comput. Methods Appl. Mech. Eng.* **2024**, *420*, 116730. [CrossRef]
249. Chu, S.; Bai, J.; Zhao, Z.-L.; Liu, Y.; Huang, D.; Li, B.; Li, Q.; Feng, X.-Q. Peridynamic fracture analysis of film–substrate systems. *J. Mech. Phys. Solids* **2024**, *191*, 105757. [CrossRef]
250. Chen, Z.; Wan, J.; Chu, X.; Liu, H. Two Cosserat peridynamic models and numerical simulation of crack propagation. *Eng. Fract. Mech.* **2019**, *211*, 341–361. [CrossRef]
251. Giannakeas, I.N.; Papathanasiou, T.K.; Fallah, A.S.; Bahai, H. Coupling XFEM and Peridynamics for brittle fracture simulation: Part II—Adaptive relocation strategy. *Comput. Mech.* **2020**, *66*, 683–705. [CrossRef]
252. Loehnert, S.; Krüger, C.; Klempt, V.; Munk, L. An enriched phase-field method for the efficient simulation of fracture processes. *Comput. Mech.* **2023**, *71*, 1015–1039. [CrossRef]
253. Sun, Y.; Liu, Z.; Tang, X. A hybrid FEMM-Phase field method for fluid-driven fracture propagation in three dimension. *Eng. Anal. Bound. Elem.* **2020**, *113*, 40–54. [CrossRef]
254. Schänzel, L.; Hofacker, M.; Miehe, C. Phase field modeling of crack propagation at large strains with application to rubbery polymers. *PAMM* **2011**, *11*, 429–430. [CrossRef]
255. Hou, Y.; Wang, L.; Yue, P.; Sun, W. Fracture failure in crack interaction of asphalt binder by using a phase field approach. *Mater. Struct.* **2015**, *48*, 2997–3008. [CrossRef]
256. Mikelić, A.; Wheeler, M.F.; Wick, T. A phase-field method for propagating fluid-filled fractures coupled to a surrounding porous medium. *Multiscale Model. Simul.* **2015**, *13*, 367–398. [CrossRef]
257. Mikelić, A.; Wheeler, M.F.; Wick, T. Phase-field modeling of a fluid-driven fracture in a poroelastic medium. *Comput. Geosci.* **2015**, *19*, 1171–1195. [CrossRef]
258. Ziaei-Rad, V.; Shen, L.; Jiang, J.; Shen, Y. Identifying the crack path for the phase field approach to fracture with non-maximum suppression. *Comput. Methods Appl. Mech. Eng.* **2016**, *312*, 304–321. [CrossRef]
259. Patil, R.; Mishra, B.; Singh, I.; Bui, T. A new multiscale phase field method to simulate failure in composites. *Adv. Eng. Softw.* **2018**, *126*, 9–33. [CrossRef]
260. Heider, Y.; Sun, W. A phase field framework for capillary-induced fracture in unsaturated porous media: Drying-induced vs. hydraulic cracking. *Comput. Methods Appl. Mech. Eng.* **2020**, *359*, 112647. [CrossRef]
261. You, T.; Waisman, H.; Zhu, Q.-Z. Brittle-ductile failure transition in geomaterials modeled by a modified phase-field method with a varying damage-driving energy coefficient. *Int. J. Plast.* **2021**, *136*, 102836. [CrossRef]

262. Zhang, T.; Yu, T.; Ding, J.; Natarajan, S. Low-cycle fatigue crack growth in brittle materials: Adaptive phase-field modeling with variable-node elements. *Comput. Methods Appl. Mech. Eng.* **2024**, *425*, 116917. [CrossRef]
263. Zhuang, X.; Zhou, S. An experimental and numerical study on the influence of filling materials on double-crack propagation. *Rock Mech. Rock Eng.* **2020**, *53*, 5571–5591. [CrossRef]
264. Fei, F.; Choo, J. Double-phase-field formulation for mixed-mode fracture in rocks. *Comput. Methods Appl. Mech. Eng.* **2021**, *376*, 113655. [CrossRef]
265. Yu, Z.; Sun, Y.; Vu, M.N.; Shao, J.F. Modeling of mixed cracks in rock-like brittle materials under compressive stresses by a double-phase-field method. *Rock Mech. Rock Eng.* **2023**, *56*, 2779–2792. [CrossRef]
266. Huang, D.; Yang, Y.Y.; Song, Y.X.; Wu, Z.J.; Yang, Y.T.; Tang, X.; Cen, D. Fracture behavior of shale containing two parallel veins under semi-circular bend test using a phase-field method. *Eng. Fract. Mech.* **2022**, *267*, 108428. [CrossRef]
267. Li, X.; Hofmann, H.; Yoshioka, K.; Luo, Y.; Liang, Y. Phase-field modelling of interactions between hydraulic fractures and natural fractures. *Rock Mech. Rock Eng.* **2022**, *55*, 6227–6247. [CrossRef]
268. Zhang, J.; Yu, H.; Xu, W.; Lv, C.; Micheal, M.; Shi, F.; Wu, H. A hybrid numerical approach for hydraulic fracturing in a naturally fractured formation combining the XFEM and phase-field model. *Eng. Fract. Mech.* **2022**, *271*, 108621. [CrossRef]
269. Zhou, Z.; Zhao, Y.; Bi, J.; Zhang, Y.; Wang, C.; Li, Y. A thermodynamically consistent SPH-PFM model for modelling crack propagation and coalescence in rocks. *Theor. Appl. Fract. Mech.* **2023**, *127*, 104085. [CrossRef]
270. Xu, B.; Xu, T.; Xue, Y.; Heap, M.J.; Wasantha, P.; Li, Z. Phase field modeling of mixed-mode crack in rocks incorporating heterogeneity and frictional damage. *Eng. Fract. Mech.* **2024**, *298*, 109936. [CrossRef]
271. Wang, S.; Yang, S.; Zhang, Q.; Shen, W.; Zhang, J.; Huang, Q. A modified phase-field model simulating multiple cracks propagation of fissured rocks under compressive or compressive-shear conditions. *Theor. Appl. Fract. Mech.* **2024**, *133*, 104549. [CrossRef]
272. Xu, D.; Wu, A.; Li, C. A linearly-independent higher-order extended numerical manifold method and its application to multiple crack growth simulation. *J. Rock Mech. Geotech. Eng.* **2019**, *11*, 1256–1263. [CrossRef]
273. Zhang, H.H.; Liu, S.M.; Han, S.Y.; Fan, L.F. Computation of T-stresses for multiple-branched and intersecting cracks with the numerical manifold method. *Eng. Anal. Bound. Elem.* **2019**, *107*, 149–158. [CrossRef]
274. Zhang, H.H.; Liu, S.M.; Han, S.Y.; Fan, L.F. T-stress evaluation for multiple cracks in FGMs by the numerical manifold method and the interaction integral. *Theor. Appl. Fract. Mech.* **2020**, *105*, 102436. [CrossRef]
275. He, J.; Liu, Q.; Wu, Z. Creep crack analysis of viscoelastic material by numerical manifold method. *Eng. Anal. Bound. Elem.* **2017**, *80*, 72–86. [CrossRef]
276. Yang, Y.; Tang, X.; Zheng, H.; Liu, Q.S.; He, L. Three-dimensional fracture propagation with numerical manifold method. *Eng. Anal. Bound. Elem.* **2016**, *72*, 65–77. [CrossRef]
277. Wang, Y.; Yang, Y.; Zheng, H. On the implementation of a hydro-mechanical coupling model in the numerical manifold method. *Eng. Anal. Bound. Elem.* **2019**, *109*, 161–175. [CrossRef]
278. Li, G.; Wang, K.; Tang, C.; Qian, X. An NMM-based fluid-solid coupling model for simulating rock hydraulic fracturing process. *Eng. Fract. Mech.* **2020**, *235*, 107193. [CrossRef]
279. Sun, H.; Xiong, F.; Wei, W. A 2D hybrid NMM-UPM method for waterflooding processes modelling considering reservoir fracturing. *Eng. Geol.* **2022**, *308*, 106810. [CrossRef]
280. Zeng, Q.; Bo, L.; Liu, L.; Li, X.; Sun, J.; Huang, Z.; Yao, J. Analysis of fracture propagation and shale gas production by intensive volume fracturing. *Appl. Math. Mech.* **2023**, *44*, 1385–1408. [CrossRef]
281. Yang, C.X.; Yi, L.P.; Yang, Z.Z.; Li, X.G. Numerical investigation of the fracture network morphology in multi-cluster hydraulic fracturing of horizontal wells: A DDM-FVM study. *J. Pet. Sci. Eng.* **2022**, *215*, 110723. [CrossRef]
282. Cheng, W.; Wang, R.; Jiang, G.; Xie, J. Modelling hydraulic fracturing in a complex-fracture-network reservoir with the DDM and graph theory. *J. Nat. Gas Sci. Eng.* **2017**, *47*, 73–82. [CrossRef]
283. Miao, C.; Wei, Y.; Yan, X. Two collinear square-hole cracks in an infinite plate in tension. *Theor. Appl. Fract. Mech.* **2015**, *75*, 32–38. [CrossRef]
284. Yan, X.; Miao, C. Interaction of multiple cracks in a rectangular plate. *Appl. Math. Model.* **2012**, *36*, 5727–5740. [CrossRef]

mathematics

Article

A New Fault Diagnosis Method for Rolling Bearings with the Basis of Swin Transformer and Generalized S Transform

Jin Yan [1,2], Xu Zhu [1], Xin Wang [1] and Dapeng Zhang [1,*]

1 Guangdong Provincial Key Laboratory of Intelligent Equipment for South China Sea Marine Ranching, Guangdong Ocean University, Zhanjiang 524088, China
2 Shenzhen Research Institute, Guangdong Ocean University, Shenzhen 518120, China
* Correspondence: zhangdapeng@gdou.edu.cn

Abstract: In view of the rolling bearing fault signal non-stationarity, strong noise can lead to low fault diagnosis accuracy. A Swin Transformer and generalized S Transform fault diagnosis method is proposed to solve the problems of difficult signal feature extraction and low diagnostic accuracy. Generalized S transform is used to improve the resolution of bearing fault signals, the Swin Transformer model is used to master the shallow weight required for identifying rolling bearing faults for highly fault characteristic expression signals, and the deep weight is obtained by backpropagation training. Finally, the extracted features are input into the improved Softmax classifier for fault classification. The various signal processing methods for the bearing signal processing ability are compared, and this model's diagnosis ability and the ability to resist noise are verified. The experimental results show that the method has a remarkable ability and an accuracy of above 90% in the anti-noise test and also has a good robustness.

Keywords: rolling bearing; vibration signal; fault diagnosis; Swin Transform; generalized S transform

MSC: 37M10

Academic Editors: Joaquim Infante Barbosa, José Alberto Rodrigues, Yiu Yin Raymond Lee and Carlos Conceicao Antonio

Received: 6 October 2024
Revised: 6 December 2024
Accepted: 23 December 2024
Published: 26 December 2024

Citation: Yan, J.; Zhu, X.; Wang, X.; Zhang, D. A New Fault Diagnosis Method for Rolling Bearings with the Basis of Swin Transformer and Generalized S Transform. *Mathematics* **2025**, *13*, 45. https://doi.org/10.3390/math13010045

1. Introduction

In recent years, in the context of the era of the continuous development and integration of techniques like deep learning, "Internet Plus (+)", Internet of Things (IOT), intelligent detection, etc., the industrial field is experiencing a huge leap from Industry "3.0" to Industry "4.0" [1]. The operational status of bearings, as the core components of modern machinery, which has a growing tendency to be high-speed and high-precision, directly affect the safety and efficiency of the entire production process. It is important to note that at the moment, 30% of all problems in rotating machinery equipment, including centrifugal fans, impellers, conveyors, etc., are caused by bearing failures in the great majority of industrial machinery [2]. Therefore, real-time, rapid, and precise diagnostics of rotating machinery's bearings have significant scientific relevance as well as practical utility. Traditional techniques include vibration signal analysis [3], sound signal analysis [4], lubricating oil analysis [5], acoustic emission detection [6], and so forth. The most popular of them is the vibration signal analysis approach.

Nowadays, with the rise of artificial intelligence technology, data-driven intelligent fault diagnosis methods based on machine learning algorithms have been widely studied [7–11]. Conventional machine learning algorithms for diagnostics mainly consist of characteristic extraction and pattern classification processes [10,11], and the feature extraction usually uses fast Fourier transform [12], variation mode decomposition [13], statistical features [14], spectral analysis [15], wavelet transform [16], and Hilbert–Huang transform [17], as well as other advanced signal processing methods to extract time domain, frequency domain, and time–frequency domain features from raw fault data. Zhang [18] used a one-dimensional CNN for the fault diagnosis of rolling bearings, eliminating the need for noise reduction preprocessing in traditional fault diagnosis, directly inputting the original one-dimensional vibration signal into the CNN for feature extraction and classification, and introducing a certain degree of interference to enhance the anti-noise ability of the model. Fuan [19] proposed an adaptive one-dimensional CNN rolling bearing fault diagnosis method based on particle swarm optimization for the uncertainty of hyperparameter selection in a one-dimensional CNN, making the algorithm have a higher diagnostic accuracy and robustness. Eren [20] proposed a compact one-dimensional CNN fault diagnosis method, which takes the original vibration signal as the input and performs one-dimensional convolution, which greatly reduces the computing cost. XiaM et al. proposed a CNN-based fault diagnosis method for rotating machinery, which uses the structural characteristics of the CNN network to achieve the fusion of multi-sensing information, which has a higher diagnostic accuracy than traditional methods [21].

For environments with high noise levels and fluctuating workloads, Wei Zhang [22] suggested a rolling bearing problem diagnostic approach based on convolutional neural networks to eliminate the need for human feature extraction. Based on the bearing defect diagnosis framework, Xiaoli Zhao et al. [23] presented a normalized conditional variation auto-encoder with adaptive focal loss (NCVAE-AFL) to improve the dataset's feature learning capacity and achieve a better diagnostic accuracy. By combining supervised learning with episodic metric meta-learning, Duo Wang et al. suggested a meta-learning model based on feature space metrics and demonstrated the viability of the method via tests [24]. Using two phases of data reconstruction and meta-learning, the novel hierarchical recursive technique for data reconstruction suggested by Hao Su et al. is appropriate for small-sample bearing failure detection under various operating situations [25]. Li [26] put out a bearing failure diagnostic technique that can combine data from several sensors. This technique employs a binary tree support vector machine (BT-SVM) for pattern identification and defect diagnostics. The energy values of many sensors are employed as feature vectors. It successfully cuts down on the feature extraction time while increasing diagnostic precision. Ding Xu [27] et al. proposed a time–frequency manifold image synthesis method to realize bearing fault diagnosis. The above study builds images based on time–frequency methods to transform fault diagnosis problems into image classification problems.

Ville et al. [28] proposed the Wigner–Ville distribution (WVD) for secondary time–frequency analysis, which effectively improved the focus of time–frequency analysis. Aboud et al. [29] suggested an enhanced square envelope spectroscopy approach based on the time domain filtering theory. This method had an excellent anti-interference effect and was effective in diagnosing the vibration signal's fault type. Time–frequency analysis provides additional benefits over time domain and frequency domain analysis when processing non-stationary signals. It can also define more fault features that are not accessible in the time domain or frequency domain. However, for non-stationary signals, time domain analysis and frequency domain analysis have several restrictions that might result in the loss of identifying information. In this paper, we combine time–frequency analysis and new deep learning models to use end-to-end methods for rolling bearing fault diagnosis. In order to deal with a large amount of data, there are shortcomings of a slow processing speed, which greatly limits the development of rolling bearing fault diagnosis technology. The one-dimensional bearing signal is first transformed into a two-dimensional image signal using the generalized S transform, and then this image signal is fed into the Swin Transformer model to identify faults. The Xichu big and small bearing dataset was used to test the model's efficacy, and a rolling bearing fault detection bench was constructed to test the model's generalization capabilities.

Recently, there are still two shortcomings that are difficult to be solved. Firstly, machine learning-based approaches inevitably need to resort to generating discriminative features with the help of signal processing methods, but the manual extraction of features still requires a high level of professional knowledge. Secondly, the features obtained after careful manual extraction and selection according to the requirements of specific tasks are not always effective in the face of unknown working conditions or application scenarios. As the vibration signals in real industry are becoming more and more complicated, and the time–frequency imagery obtained from the existing time–frequency analysis methods is still poorly focused and has serious cross-terms, and its resolution is not enough to fully reflect the frequency and energy distribution information, it is essential to further research the novel time–frequency analysis methods.

In this article, the GST is applied to convert 1D bearing signals into 2D image signals, which are then introduced into a Swin Transformer model for fault identification. Using Case Western Reserve University's large and small bearing datasets to demonstrate the validity of the model, a rolling bearing fault diagnostic bench was built to demonstrate the generalizability of the model.

2. Materials and Methods

2.1. Swin Transformer

Swin Transformer is an upgraded image processing network based on the concept of Vision Transformer with excellent image classification capability. It has four base models, which are Swin_T, Swin_S, Swin_B, and Swin_L. Considering the complexity of the input signals and the calculative cost, Swin_T is chosen as the basic structural model. The architecture of the Swin Transformer (Swin_T) appears in Figure 1.

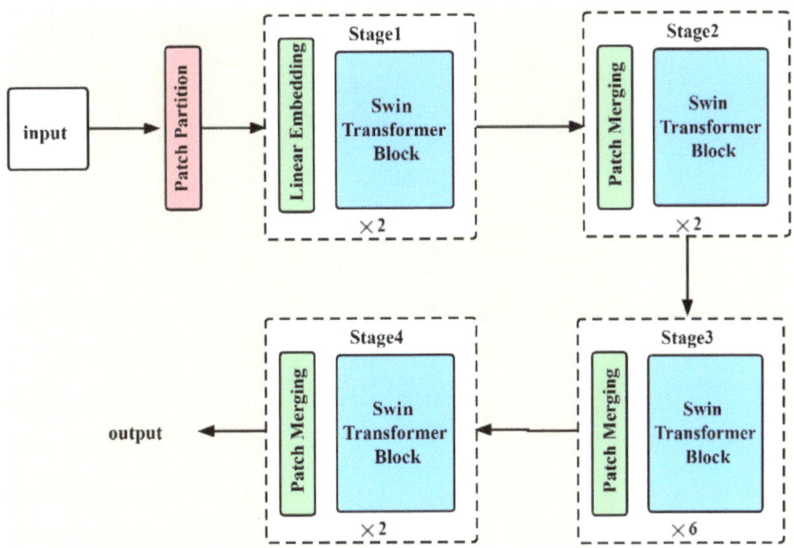

Figure 1. Swin Transformer network structure (Swin-T).

The algorithmic process of the Swin Transformer has the following general steps: take the three-channel RGB image signals as the input, cut the original image by module partition (patch partition) operation, and obtain the non-overlapping image block (patch). After expanding the block, the obtained feature is then input into the linear inlay layer to reduce the dimensionality of the feature. Next, generate a feature block, and input this feature block into the Swin Transformer block to perform feature extraction. After the block splicing (patch merging) operation, the image feature size is cut to half of its original size, and the number of channels is increased to twice their original size. The output after each stage is the input features to the classifier for performing the image classification task.

1. Patch Merging

Patch merging is a down-sampling operation similar to pooling in convolutional neural networks. In each stage block, it is necessary to carry out patch merging, as depicted in the figure; input a $(H \times W \times C)$ feature, the feature points at one position apart are labeled with the same number. After completing the labeling, the labeled feature points are extracted and combined together in the direction of the channel. After splicing, a new feature $((H/2) \times (W/2) \times 4C)$ is formed in the direction of the channel, after the LayerNorm layer to normalize the pixel points, and finally, the feature is linearly processed along the direction of the channel by the all-connected layer, and the feature is transformed into $((H/2) \times (W/2) \times 2C)$ output. The whole patch merging process is to cut the input feature size to half of its original size and increase the number of channels to twice their original size. This operation can save computation and improve network computing efficiency. Moreover, the patch merge does not lose signal and the entire patch merging process is demonstrated in Figure 2.

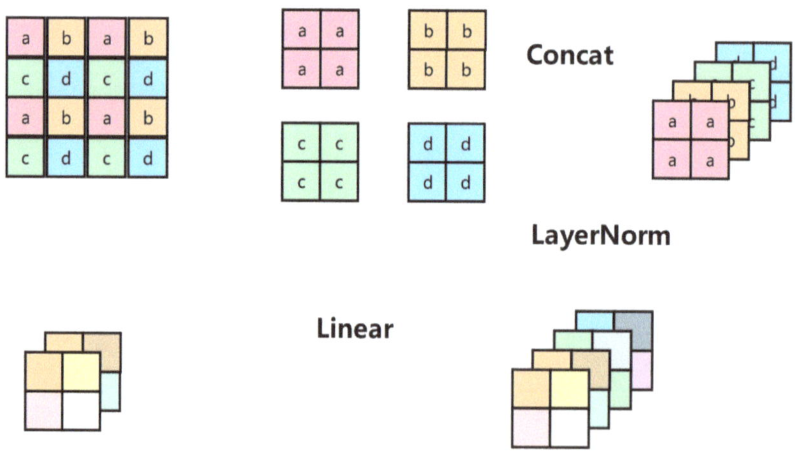

Figure 2. Patch merging process.

2. Swin Transformer Block

As shown in Figure 3, Swin Transformer Block consists of a Windows Multi-head Self-Attention (W-MSA) module and a Shifted Windows Multi-Head Self-Attention (SW-MSA) module. Windows Multi-Head Self-Attention (SW-MSA) module. And two multilayer perceptrons (MLPs) are connected after it, and the nonlinear ability of the whole network is enhanced by (GELU) activation function between them, which in turn improves the fitting ability of the whole network. And there is a normalization layer (LN) before W-MSA, SW-MSA and MLP, and a residual connection is connected after each module.

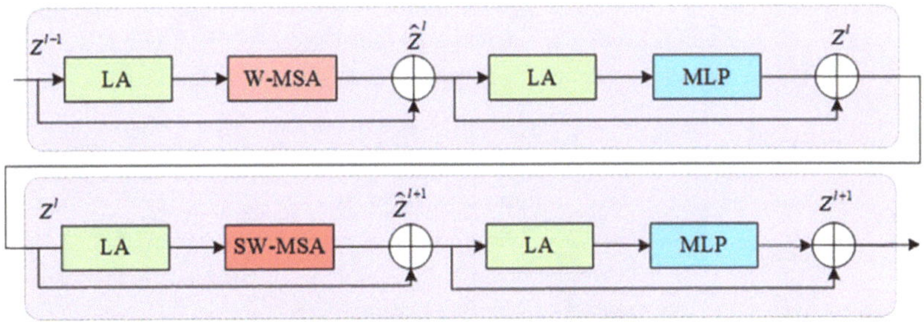

Figure 3. Swin Transformer block module structure.

- Multi-head self-attention mechanism

With the development in neural networks, Ashish Vaswani et al. [30] proposed a network structure based entirely on the attention mechanism in 2017, which significantly reduces the time required for network training. The self-attention layer can compute the weights of local features by localizing them into global features, and then the global features can be obtained from the sum of the local features. Nevertheless, due to the high computational complexity of MSA, it is necessary to introduce a window module in the Swin Transformer to reduce the computational effort of MSA. Figure 4 illustrates the differences between MSA and window-based self-attention approaches (windowed multiple self-attention, W-MSA).

(**a**) Multi-headed self-attention (**b**) Windows multi-head self-attention

Figure 4. Differences between the two attention mechanisms.

As Figure 4a shows, the weights for each pixel point in the feature are computed for the ordinary multi-attention mechanism as follows in Equation (1):

$$Q(MSA) = 4hwC^2 + 2(hw)^2C \quad (1)$$

Figure 4b represents the multi-attention mechanism after the addition of windows, where the features are first divided into window spaces by windows, and then the weights of each window space are calculated in a single degree, as follows in Equation (2):

$$Q(W - MSA) = 4hwC^2 + 2MhwC \quad (2)$$

where Q denotes the computational complexity of the multi-attention mechanism, h denotes the height of the feature, w denotes the width of the feature, C denotes the number of channels of the feature, and M denotes the size of the window. Since the size of the window is much smaller than the size of the feature, the computational complexity of using the window is much lower than that of the non-windowed computation, which can effectively improve the computational speed of the model.

- Offset window self-attention mechanism (SW-MSA)

Adding windows may greatly speed up the computation of weights in the feature map, but doing so breaks the connections between windows and reduces the correlation between local and global data. To address this problem, the Swin Transformer performs weight adjustment with the SW-MSA module (also known as Shifted W-MSA). Figure 5 depicts the shifted feature block.

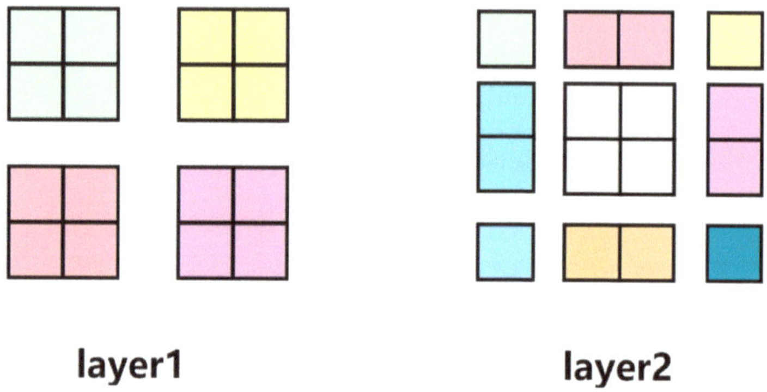

Figure 5. Output module after two attention calculations in Swin Transformer block.

As shown in the figure above, the features output from layer 1 circularly shift the window to the upper left $(\frac{M}{2}, \frac{M}{2})$ pixels to obtain the output from layer 2. When calculating the weights, nine windows of different sizes are spliced into four feature blocks, with the grey feature block in the middle remaining unchanged as a separate window; the feature blocks on the four corners are spliced into a new computational window: the feature blocks on the left, right, top, and bottom are spliced into a single window. At this time, each window contains elements of other windows with interrelated weights, and MSA calculations are performed fast for each feature separately, thus reducing the amount of computation and correlating the local features with the global ones. Figure 6 shows the schematic diagram of pixel shifting in the computation.

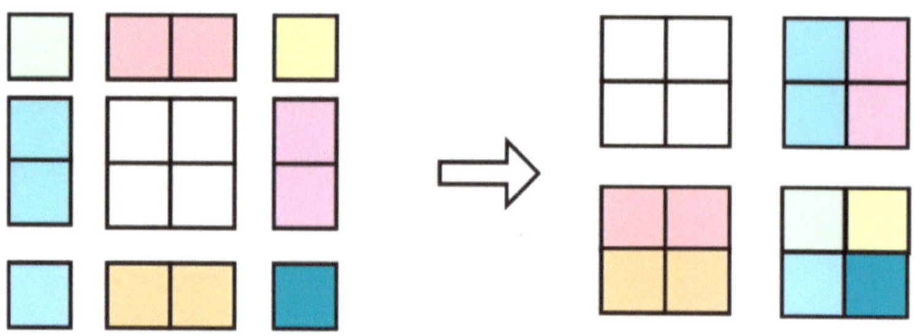

Figure 6. Schematic diagram of SW-MSA window calculation.

2.2. Multi-Classification Algorithm

Softmax classifiers are commonly used to deal with multiple classification problems. In this article, we improve the multi-classification algorithm based on the Softmax function.

The mathematical expression of the Softmax function [31–36] can be expressed as illustrated in Equation (3) below

$$h_\omega(x^{(i)}) = \begin{bmatrix} \varphi(y^{(i)} = 1 \middle| x^{(i)} : \omega \\ \varphi(y^{(i)} = 2 \middle| x^{(i)} : \omega \\ \varphi(y^{(i)} = k \middle| x^{(i)} : \omega \end{bmatrix} = \frac{1}{\sum_{j=1}^{p} e^{\omega_m{}^T x(i)}} \begin{bmatrix} e^{\omega_1^T x^{(i)}} \\ e^{\omega_1^T x^{(i)}} \\ \vdots \\ e^{\omega_p^T x^{(i)}} \end{bmatrix} \tag{3}$$

Among them, $h_\omega(x^{(i)})$ is the output value after being processed and normalized by the Softmax classifier, $\{\omega_1, \omega_2, \cdots\cdots, \omega_p\}$ is the model parameter of the Softmax classifier, and $\frac{1}{\sum_{j=1}^{p} e^{\omega_m{}^T x(i)}}$ is to normalize the output value and reduce the output value of the model to between 0 and 1. The ith sample in the input signal is denoted by $x^{(i)}$, and the probability that this sample's classification prediction belongs to k is $\varphi\left(y^{(i)} = 1 \middle| x^{(i)} : \omega\right)$.

The Softmax classifier optimizes the model by using the cross-entropy loss function [25], which is computed as follows:

$$Loss = \frac{1}{\text{n}} \sum_{i=1}^{m} \left(-y^{(i)} \log\left(h_\omega\left(x^{(i)}\right)\right) - \left(1 - y^{(i)}\right) \log\left(1 - h_\omega\left(x^{(i)}\right)\right)\right) \tag{4}$$

where n is the number of input samples; m is the number of categories; $y^{(i)}$ is the label corresponding to the sample; when using the Softmax classifier, the parameter is usually expressed in a matrix, and the expression of the matrix is as follows:

$$\omega = \begin{bmatrix} \omega_1^T \\ \omega_2^T \\ \vdots \\ \omega_{\text{P}}^T \end{bmatrix} \tag{5}$$

Substituting the parameters into the loss function, the loss function expression is as follows:

$$Loss = -\frac{1}{m} \left(\sum_{i=1}^{n} \sum_{i=1}^{k} \psi[y^{(i)} = j] \log \frac{e^{\omega_j^T x^{(i)}}}{\sum_{j=1}^{k} e^{\omega j^T x(i)}}\right. \tag{6}$$

where $\psi(\cdot)$ is 1 when the predicted result is the same as the real value, and 0 when it is different.

Due to the existence of countless vectors in the vector space, when any two of them with an appropriately large span are given a category meaning, the sample points will be clustered towards the corresponding category vectors, and the difference in the distance values will be greater when the distance calculation is performed on the samples using the standard base coordinates; thus, the category differences will be more obvious. Therefore, the aggregation of similar features in the mapping space can be enhanced by increasing the distance between different feature clusters, which can successfully improve the accuracy of classification. The similarity between samples and parameters is represented by the cosine distance, which is used together with the feature amplitude to determine the weight of the feature vector that belongs to the final class. The modified weight formula is as follows:

$$W_c x = ||W_c|| \cdot ||x|| \cos(\omega_c) \tag{7}$$

where c is the classification category, and W_C is the weight index that divides features into categories in the classifier. For a feature, the cosine distance between the value of the feature vector and the angle between the weight vectors will determine the final classification result.

The Softmax classification impact is the best after updating the Softmax settings to obtain the ideal loss amount. The following formula is obtained by substituting the modified weight parameters into the loss function.

$$Loss_i = -\log\left(\frac{e^{\|W_{y_i}\|\cdot\|x_i\|\cos(\omega_{y_i})}}{\sum\limits_{j=1}^{k} e^{\|W_j\|\cdot\|x_i\|\cos(\omega_j)}}\right) \tag{8}$$

Among them, W_{y_i} represents the column of the W weight matrix, x_i, y_i are the feature and label of the instance, ω_{y_i} represents the angle between W_{y_i} and x_i, and W_j refers to all weights of class j.

2.3. Troubleshooting Process

In this research, a fault classification model based on time–frequency pictures is developed as a way to effectively raise the accuracy of fault detection. The time–frequency characteristics of the vibration signal will be converted to a time–frequency picture, and then the time–frequency image signals will be input into the Swin Transformer model to carry out the automatic extraction of the features and select the Swin-T model with a smaller specification according to the characteristics of the vibration signals. Then, the extracted features are processed by linear full connectivity, and finally, the software classifier of the reformer is used for the multi-classification prediction of faults. The construction of the classification model built using the time–frequency diagram and Swin Transformer is depicted in Figure 7. Figure 8 depicts the process for diagnosing a rolling bearing failure using a time–frequency graph and a Swin Transformer.

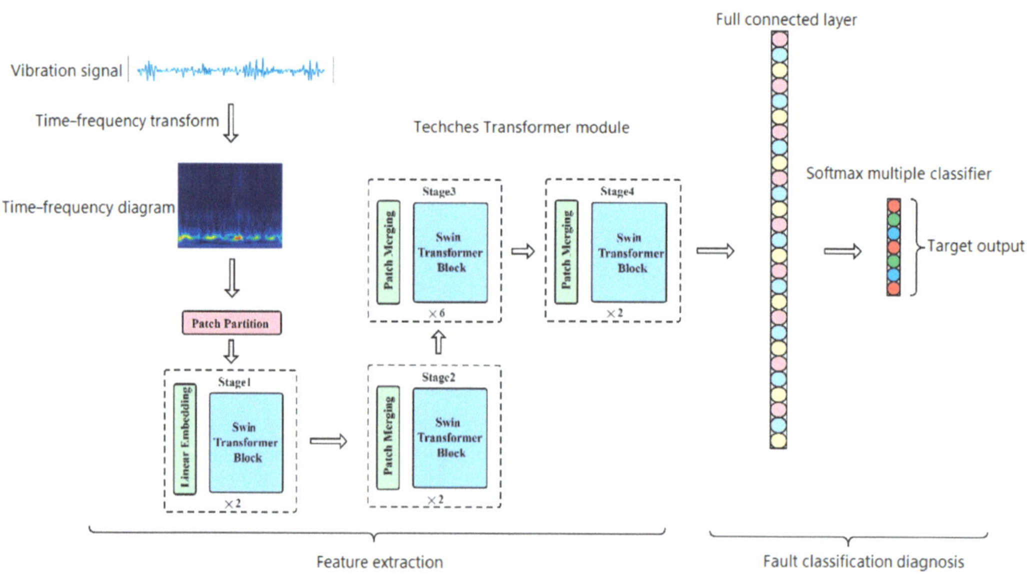

Figure 7. Classification model structure based on time–frequency diagram and Swin Transformer.

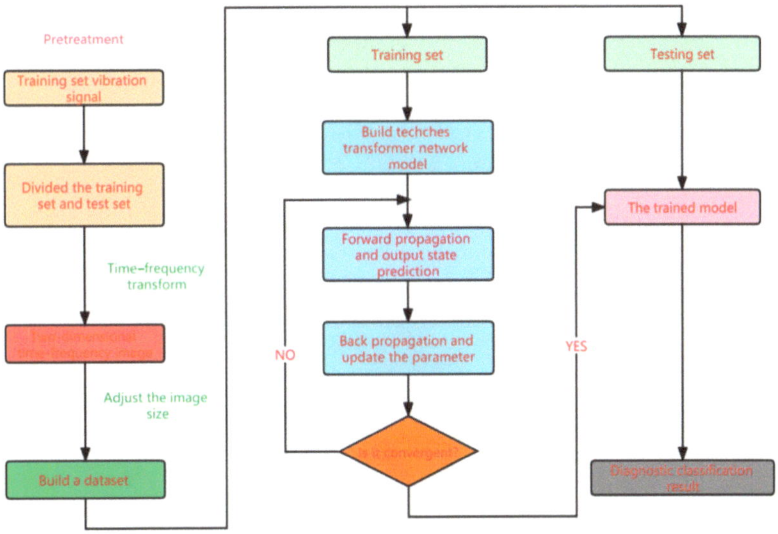

Figure 8. Experimental flow chart.

This experiment uses the bearing dataset from the experimental dataset of Case Western Reserve University, and the bearing failure data under different working conditions at 48 kHz are selected. The experiment includes three steps: data pretreatment, model training, and its prediction. The following are the details regarding the experiment:

(1) The acquired vibration signal data are divided into the training set and test set in the ratio of 8:2, the 1D vibration signal is transformed into a 2D time–frequency picture, the size of the image output is modified, and the image is labeled with fault categories for subsequent training and testing

(2) The model of the Swin Transformer network is constructed, its hyperparameters (such as the number of iterations, learning rate, decay rate, batch size, etc.) are configured, its weights and biases are initialized at random, and the training data are fed into it. Using block splicing (patch merging), the window self-attention mechanism (W-MSA), the offset window self-attention (W-MSA), the Shift Window Self-Attention (SW-MSA), and multilayer perceptron (MLP) are used to extract image features, the predicted value of the output state by forward propagation is calculated, and the parameters of the network are updated by back propagation to make the error between the labeled value and the predicted value smaller until the loss function reaches convergence, and then the parameters are saved to complete the training.

(3) The test set is imported into the trained model, the classification diagnostics are run, and the effectiveness of its classification recognition is checked.

3. Results

3.1. Experimental Data

As Figure 9 shows, this experimental bench is mainly composed of the following parts: on the left side is a motor with a power of 1.5 KW, in the middle is a torque transducer, and on the right side is a power tester. In the data collection experiment, a single-point fault bearing is used, and EDM is used to manufacture faulty bearings with fault diameters of 0.007 inches, 0.014 inches, 0.021 inches, 0.028 inches, and 0.040 inches. On the other hand, the datasets used for model training in this article are from Case Western Reserve University's bearing dataset, which is commonly used to measure the performance of rolling bearing defect detection models. The bearings on the bearing test rig were replaced with bearings of different failure sizes, and the vibration signal data were captured by using accelerometers mounted on the test rig and stored at both 12 kHz and 48 kHz sampling frequencies throughout the data acquisition experiment. Datasets under four distinct operating situations, namely 0 hp, 1 hp, 2 hp, and 3 hp loads, of which 0.007 inch, 0.014 inch, and 0.021 inch are the same bearing type, are collected for this experiment. This experiment selects the above three kinds of fault size of the bearing, which includes the inner ring failure, outer ring failure, and rolling body failure; together with the normal operation data of the bearing, the whole dataset can be divided into 10 kinds of operating states, and according to the different loads are divided into three datasets, A, B, and C. Each dataset is taken as 100 samples for each kind of operating state and randomly disrupted according to 9:1. The training set and test set are divided, and dataset D is a multi-operating condition dataset containing three kinds of loads, and the specific dataset division is depicted in Table 1 below:

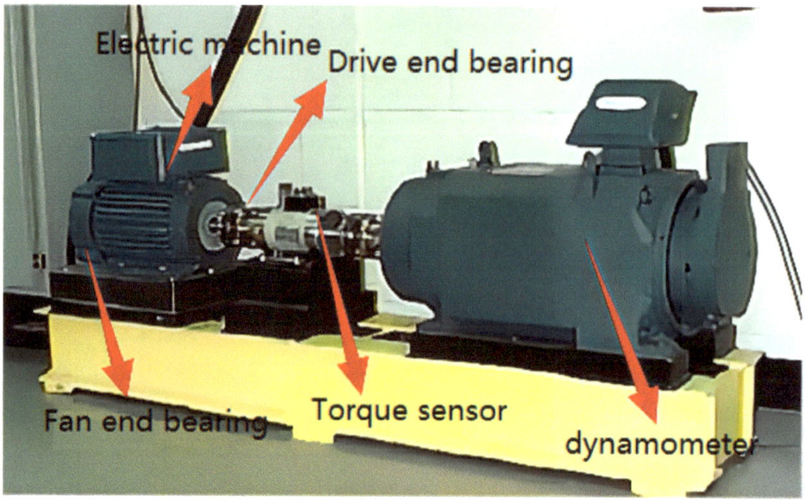

Figure 9. Case Western Reserve University bearing test bench.

Table 1. Dataset division.

Damage Position		**Normal**	**Inner Ring**			**Outer Ring**			**Rolling Element**			**Load**
Label		0	1	2	3	4	5	6	7	8	9	
Damage diameter		0	0.007	0.014	0.021	0.007	0.014	0.021	0.007	0.014	0.021	
A	Training	900	900	900	900	900	900	900	900	900	900	0
	Testing	100	100	100	100	100	100	100	100	100	100	
B	Training	900	900	900	900	900	900	900	900	900	900	1
	Testing	100	100	100	100	100	100	100	100	100	100	
C	Training	900	900	900	900	900	900	900	900	900	900	2
	Testing	100	100	100	100	100	100	100	100	100	100	
D	Training	2700	2700	2700	2700	2700	2700	2700	2700	400	2700	0~2
	Testing	300	300	300	300	300	300	300	300	300	300	

3.2. Comparison and Analysis of Time–Frequency Analysis Approaches

In an effort to acquire models with higher diagnostic accuracy, we employed a comparative validation approach utilizing the Case Western Reserve University bearing dataset to achieve the best-performing time–frequency analysis approach. In the following, the vibration signals will be analyzed and corresponding time–frequency images will be generated using the linear STFT, WT, and GST, and the nonlinear WVD, respectively.

(i) Short-time Fourier analysis

In short-time Fourier analysis, the choice of window length will directly affect the resolution of the time–frequency diagram; when the window exceeds the appropriate size, the time resolution will deteriorate, or even become a Fourier transform, which will result in a loss of time scale information; when the window is smaller than the appropriate size, the frequency resolution will also deteriorate, which will cause the loss of part of the frequency information. Here, we choose 64, 128, 256, and 512 window size lengths for the STFT, and the obtained time–frequency diagram is depicted in Figure 10 below.

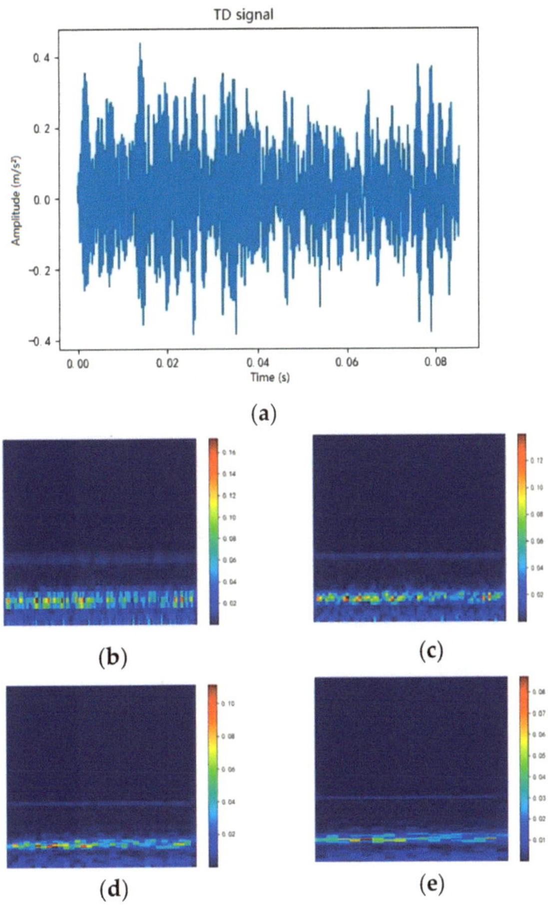

Figure 10. Short-time Fourier transform time–frequency diagram. (**a**) Time domain waveform of bearing rolling element failure. (**b**) Window size 64. (**c**) Window size 128. (**d**) Window size 256. (**e**)Window size 512.

From the above four time–frequency diagrams, it has been found that the frequency resolution of the time–frequency diagrams increases gradually when the window size increases, and when the window size reaches 512, the frequency resolution is the best, and the time resolution is also more obvious.

(ii) Continuous wavelet transform

In wavelet analysis, due to the choice of wavelet basis having a greater impact on the effect of the time–frequency diagram, different wavelet bases are chosen to deal with different signals, and so the effect is different; in order to obtain the best wavelet analysis effect, we intercepted the Case Western Reserve University bearing failure of the subsequent analysis of the dataset, the Grid wavelet basis, Hill's wavelet basis, and the complex Mossy's wavelet basis for the signal to carry out a continuous wavelet transform, and the time–frequency diagrams are shown in Figure 11 below.

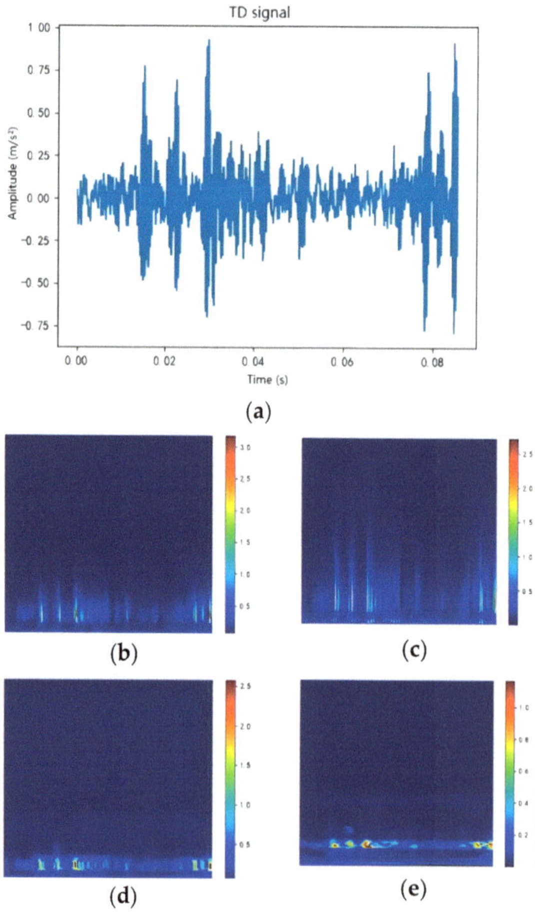

Figure 11. Continuous wavelet transform time–frequency diagram. (**a**) Time domain waveform of bearing rolling element failure. (**b**) Haar wavelet basis. (**c**) Mesh wavelet basis. (**d**) Shan wavelet basis. (**e**) Complex Morlet wavelet basis.

(iii) Generalized S transform

The generalized S transform is developed from the S transform, which is very similar to the fundamental wavelet transform of the Morlet wavelet. However, only the Gaussian function part of the S transform changes the size of the window function with the frequency and performs translational changes in the time dimension, and the chi-square harmonic waveform part only performs telescopic changes, which makes the S transform defective for the feature representation of non-smooth signals. So, the parameters a and b are added to adjust the shape of the Gaussian window to optimize its resolution in the time and frequency domains, as shown in the following equation:

$$GST(\tau, f) = \int_{-\infty}^{\infty} x(t) \frac{a|f|^b}{\sqrt{2\pi}} e^{[-\frac{1}{2}a^2 f^{2b}(t-\tau)^2]} e^{(-i2\pi f t)} dt \tag{9}$$

The generalized S transform combines the strengths of the STFT and the WT, effectively avoiding the limitation of the short-time Fourier window size and the problem of selecting the wavelet basis function, which is very advantageous in the domain of time–frequency analysis. The time–frequency diagram obtained from the GST is illustrated in Figure 12.

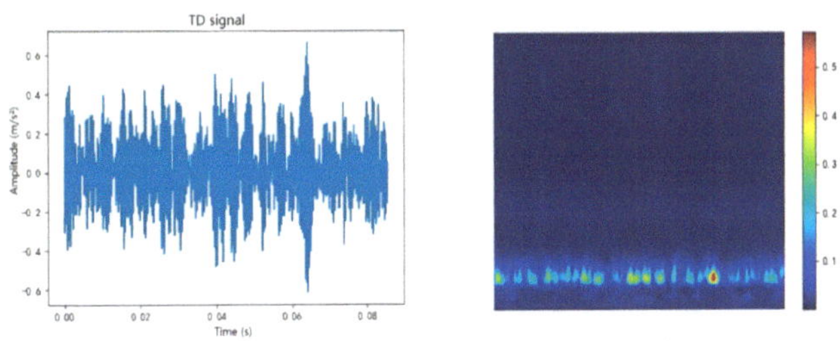

(a) (b)

Figure 12. Generalized S transform. (**a**) Time domain waveform of bearing rolling element failure. (**b**) Generalized S-transform time-frequency diagram.

The time–frequency analysis of the Case Western Reserve University data by the GST gives time–frequency maps with clear time–frequency resolution, and the GST can be better characterized by the characteristic information of vibration and its energy characteristics are clearer.

(iv) Wigner–Ville distribution

From the time–frequency plot of the WVD in Figure 13 above, it can be noticed that the WVD is less efficient in analyzing the bearing vibration signals, with a lower time–frequency resolution and pseudo-distribution of superimposed interference.

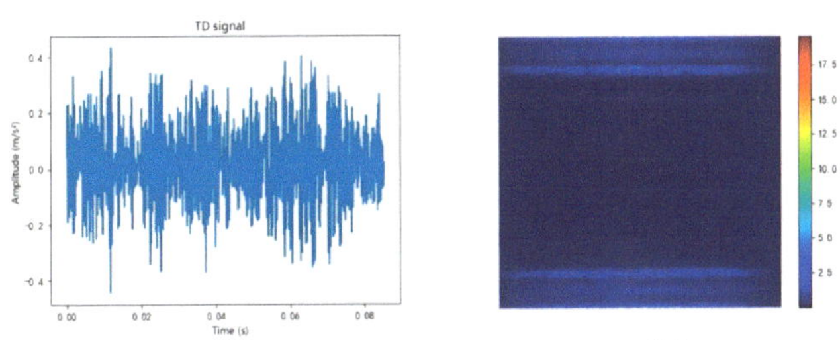

(a) (b)

Figure 13. Wigner–Ville Distribution.(**a**) Time domain waveform of bearing rolling element failure. (**b**)Wigner-Ville Distribution.

3.3. Data Preprocessing

In this experiment, firstly, the STFT, the CWT, the GST, and the WVD are compared. Figure 14 demonstrates the acquisition capability of the time–frequency resolution.

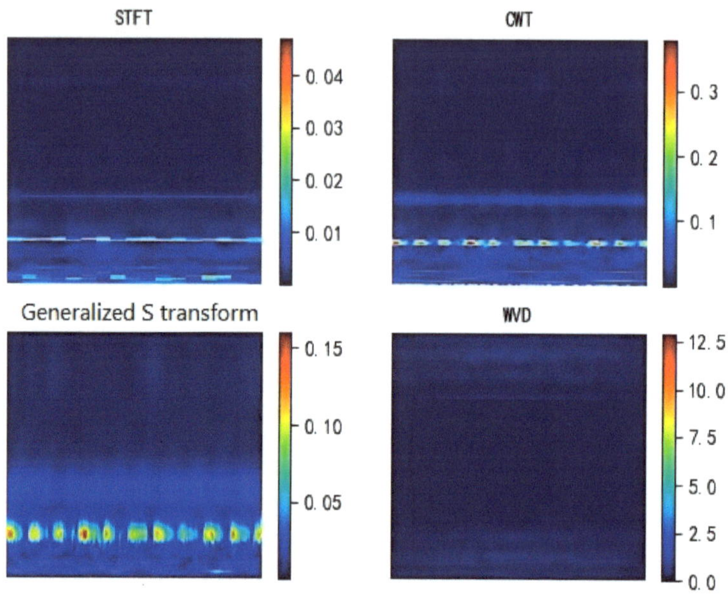

Figure 14. Comparison of four kinds of time–frequency diagrams.

Figure 14 compares the four time–frequency analysis approaches, from which a conclusion can be drawn that the time–frequency resolution of the STFT is low, while the wavelet analysis approach can more obviously be a time–frequency resolution, which can be seen in the ability of the generalized S transform characteristics. Compared with the STFT and WT, the GST has more obvious energy characteristics and more prominent signal characteristics, while the WVD has a lower time–frequency resolution and still has pseudo-distributed signal interference.

In the final analysis, 4096 consecutive sample points were randomly intercepted from the original vibration data to obtain a new sample. Under the same conditions, 100 samples were selected for each running state and the remaining 1000 samples were randomly partitioned into a training set and test set in the ratio of 9:1. The time domain signals of the training and test sets were converted into 2D image signals utilizing the continuous wavelet transform approach, and the output size of the selected images was 64×64, as shown in Figure 15.

3.4. Experimental Verification

The experiment is based on a Python-based PyTorch deep learning platform. The computer operating system is Windows 10, the graphics card is NVIDIA Quadro RTX5000, the edition of PyTorch is 1.11.0, and the running memory is 128 G. The following hyperparameter values are input to the network (Table 2).

The model has been trained and validated utilizing the above four datasets (A, B, C, and D), and its loss functions and accuracies are depicted in Figures 16 and 17, respectively.

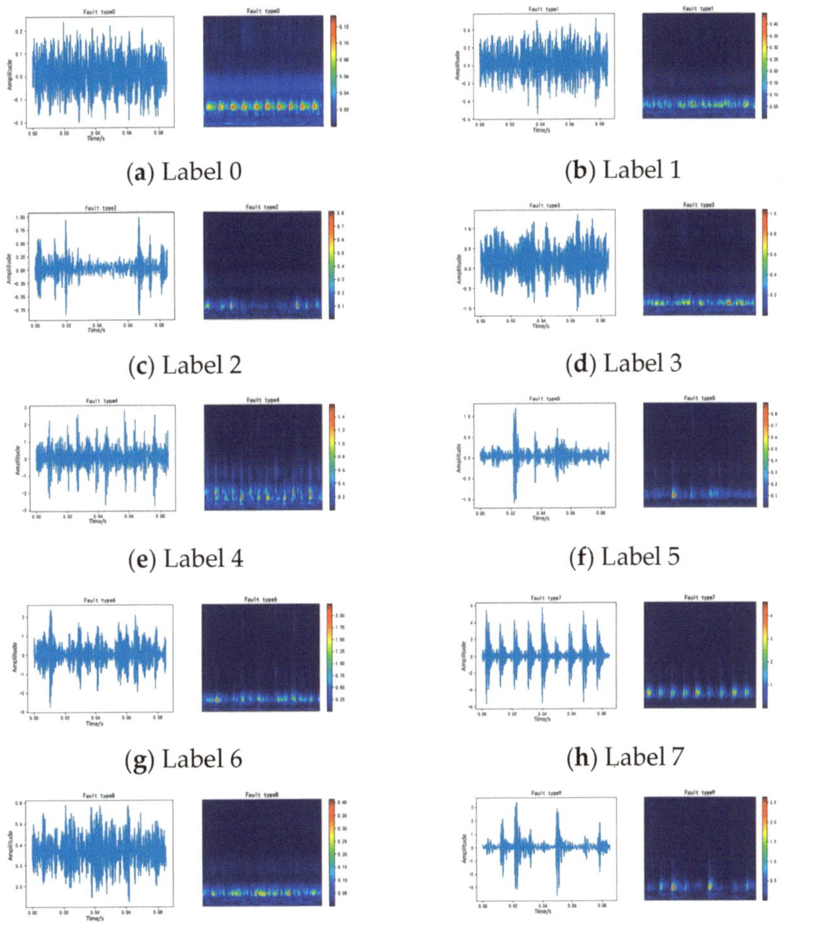

(a) Label 0 (b) Label 1 (c) Label 2 (d) Label 3 (e) Label 4 (f) Label 5 (g) Label 6 (h) Label 7 (i) Label 8 (j) Label 9

Figure 15. Graph of generalized S transform results.

Table 2. Hyperparameter settings.

Image Size	64 × 64 × 3
Batch_size	8
Learning_rate	10^{-3}
Weight_decay	10^{-5}
Epoch	50
Optimizer	SGD

The loss function curve shows that after 50 iterations in the single condition, the loss value of the training set and the loss value of the test set are basically equal to 0, and the loss value of the training set and the test set in the multi-condition is close to 0. From the accuracy curve, it can be seen that the final accuracy of the dataset in the single condition is stable at 1, and that the accuracy of the dataset in the multi-condition is close to 1. The model achieves the accurate prediction of the fault type and performs slightly better than the single-condition dataset.

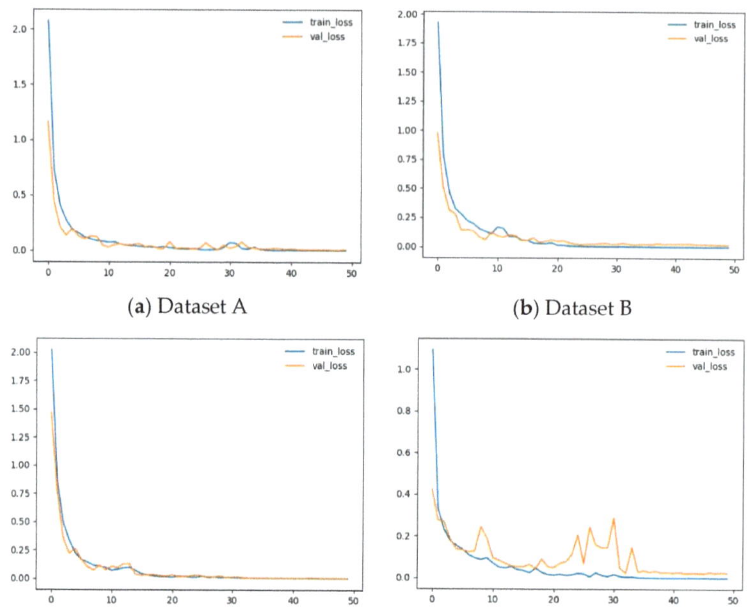

(**a**) Dataset A (**b**) Dataset B

(**c**) Dataset C (**d**) Dataset D

Figure 16. Transformation curve of loss value with the number of iterations.

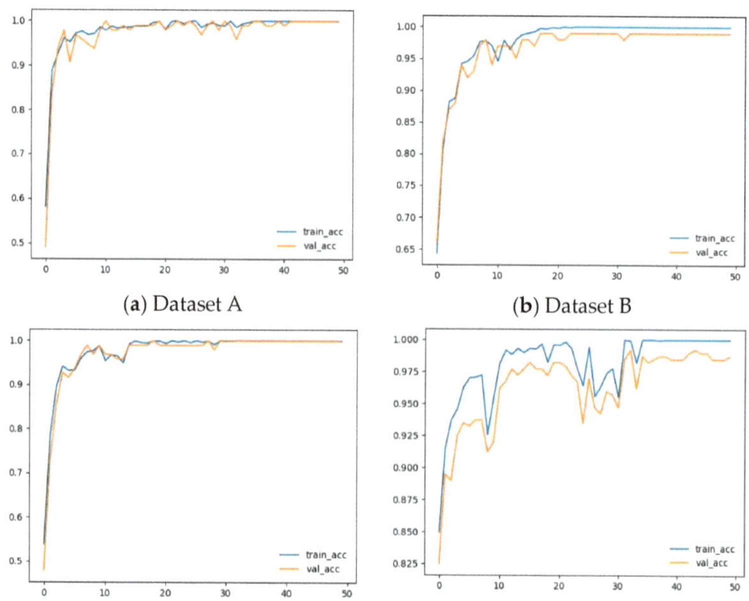

(**a**) Dataset A (**b**) Dataset B

(**c**) Dataset C (**d**) Dataset D

Figure 17. Accuracy variation curve with the number of iterations.

In order to specify the accuracy of the method proposed in this article, the performance of the model is illustrated using Accuracy, Precision, Recall, and F1 Score, and then

10 repetitions of the experiment are performed for each dataset and the average is taken and the results are shown in Table 3 below.

Table 3. Model performance evaluation table.

	Accuracy	Precision	Recall Rate	F1 Score
Data A	100	100	100	100
Data B	99.25	99.48	99.32	99.82
Data C	100	100	100	100
Data D	99.37	99.45	99.26	99.28

Table 3 shows that the model can successfully recognize both single-condition data and multiple-condition data with a ten-time average accuracy of more than 99%. The prediction process of the Swin Transformer model can be visualized and analyzed by the T-SNE downscaling technique, which is a common downscaling method for mapping high-dimensional data into 2D or 3D data, and then visualized and analyzed, as shown in Figure 18, which displays the visualization result graph of dataset A.

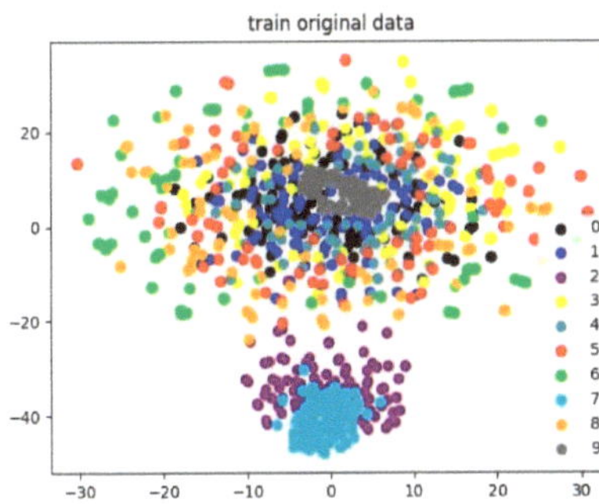

(**a**) Original features of the training set

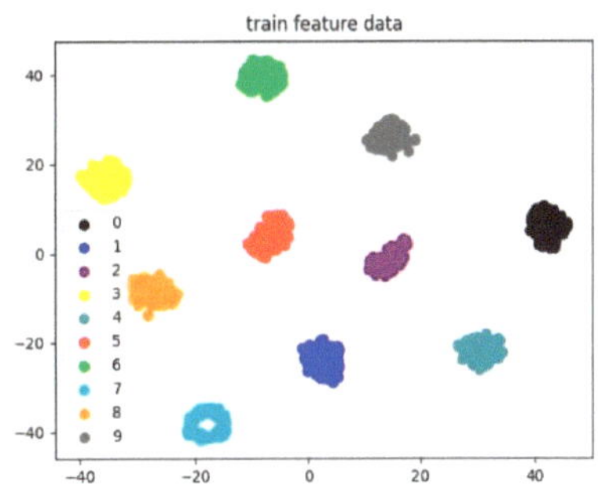

(**b**) Output features of the training set

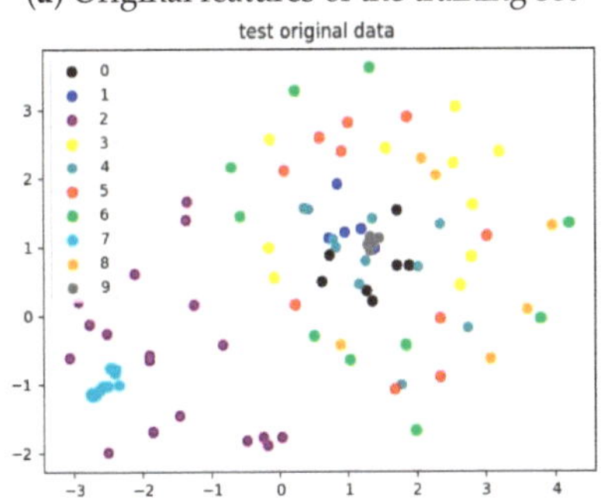

(**c**) Original features of the testing set

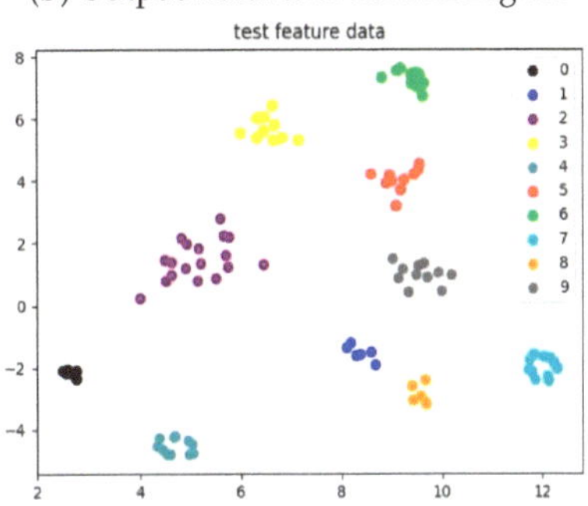

(**d**) Output features of the testing set

Figure 18. Feature visualization.

The initial features of the training set are shown in Figure 18a. The distribution of the original traits is chaotic, as can be seen in the image, making it difficult to categorize them precisely. Figure 18b displays the characteristics after 50 training iterations. It is evident that the characteristics of different types of bearing failures are effectively differentiated. The model can also successfully delineate distinct borders between various characteristics in the test set. These all demonstrate that the time–frequency graph and Swin Transformer-based rolling bearing fault detection model has outstanding feature learning capacity and can recognize various bearing failure kinds.

In this article, we choose to utilize the more popular machine learning techniques and deep learning models for comparative validation and analysis to further validate the effectiveness of the rolling bearing defect detection model based on time–frequency diagrams and the Swin Transformer suggested in this article. The dataset used in the follow-up approach is consistent with the dataset provided in this study. Table 4 below presents the classification accuracy rate of the various diagnostic techniques for different datasets. The method of this paper is denoted as S+ST, which can show the capability of each model more intuitively. The consequences of the research are depicted in Figure 19. As can be viewed from the figure, the approach suggested in this article outperforms several common diagnostic approaches on all four datasets. This comparative experiment further demonstrates that the Swin Transformer model has a powerful feature learning capability and is able to accurately perform the task of fault classification and identification in the domain of fault diagnosis.

Table 4. Accuracy rates of different experimental methods.

Diagnostic Methods	Accuracy			
	Data A	Data B	Data C	Data D
SVM	82.56	84.58	86.93	80.29
CNN	88.27	84.35	86.95	81.26
LSTM	87.53	88.40	84.58	86.53
WT + CNN	93.65	92.14	95.58	85.27
STFT + SVM	94.47	92.33	93.08	89.23
CNN + LSTM	96.59	98.24	97.28	92.05
S + ST	100	99.25	100	99.37

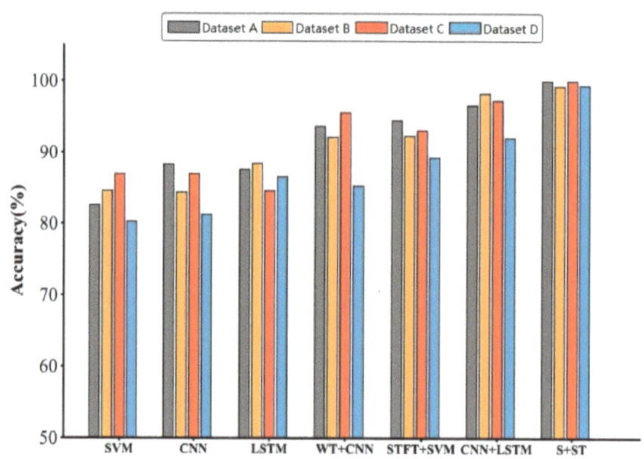

Figure 19. Diagnostic accuracy of different models.

4. Analysis of the Impact of Noise on Model Performance

In practical industrial applications, the presence of noise often influences the diagnostic accuracy rate of the model. In this research, experimental validation will be carried out by introducing white noise into the vibration signal to test the model's ability to resist noise. As the capability of white noise to hide signal features varies with its intensity, therefore, this paper will test the model's immunity to noise by using white noise with diverse signal-to-noise rates to approximate the true noise intensity in various cases. Choosing the added noise signal-to-noise ratios of 2 db, 4 db, and 8 db, respectively, and taking the 0-loaded dataset A as the original vibration signal dataset, the time domain signals have been analyzed by time–frequency analysis after the addition of the noise, as illustrated in Figure 20 below.

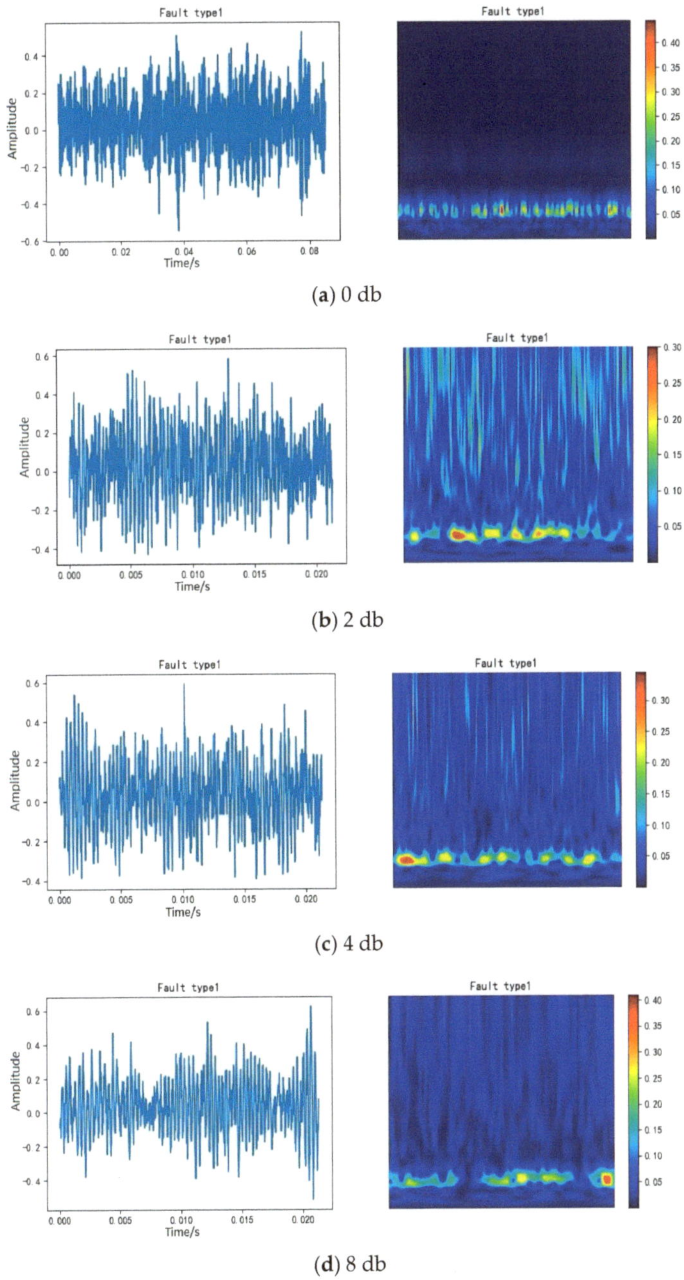

Figure 20. Time–frequency diagram after adding white noise.

Figure 20 shows the time–frequency pattern obtained by the continuous wavelet transform of the original vibration signal labeled 1 in dataset A, where the signal-to-noise ratios of the white noise interference signals are 2 dB, 4 dB, and 8 dB, respectively. Signals from the three noise environments are input into the network model for training and validating the trained model by using the test set, and the confusion matrix is used to evaluate the performance of the model in the different environments, and the diagnostic performance is evaluated using the confusion matrices of the multiple noise environments. The test set confusion matrices are shown in Figure 21 with noise additions of 0 dB, 2 dB, 4 dB, and 8 dB. The test set with no noise addition and a noise addition of 8 dB has the highest accuracy of 100%. The accuracy rate for the test set with 4 dB of noise added is 98.95%, and the test set with 2 dB of added noise has an accuracy of 96%. It is clear that the ability to adapt to noise disturbances has been improved.

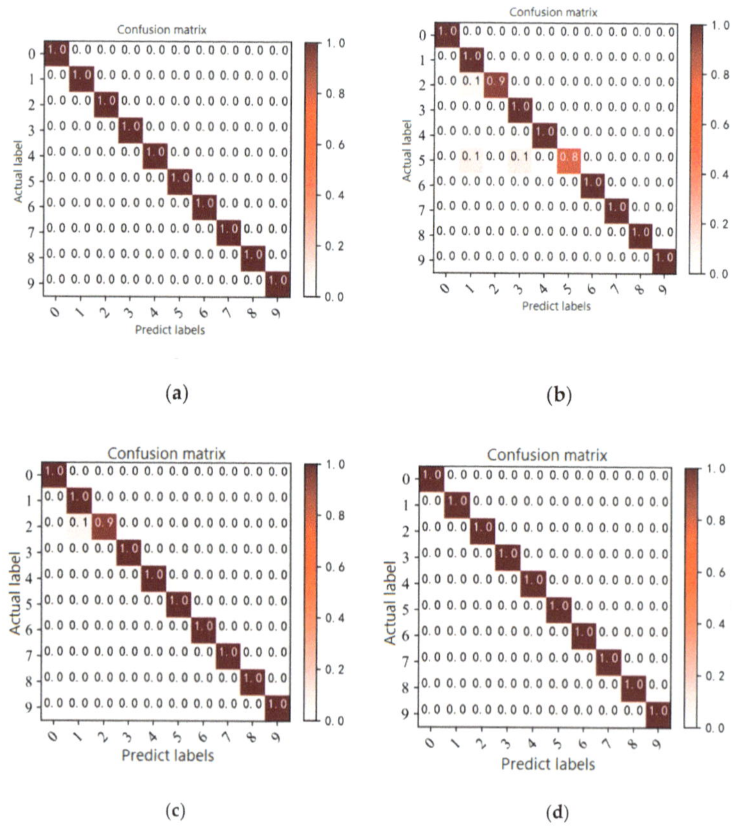

Figure 21. Confusion matrix under different white noises: (**a**) 0 db, (**b**) 2 db, (**c**) 4 db, and (**d**) 8 db.

The experimental results show that the rolling bearing problem detection technique based on the time–frequency diagram and Swin Transformer suggested in this article has good noise robustness. The accuracy is most stable under the influence of various disturbances compared to other methods, as shown in Table 5 below. The single recognition accuracy under various noise disturbances is higher than the other three widely used techniques, which indicates the strong noise robustness of the method. As shown in Figure 22, we depict the comparative results of several methods in a histogram to visualize the noise immunity of this method.

Table 5. Diagnostic accuracy of different models under noise interference.

	CNN	MLP	LSTM	S + ST
0 db	88.43	65.59	87.82	100
2 db	92.01	74.06	89.28	96.00
4 db	93.07	79.25	93.06	98.95
8 db	95.02	85.06	95.35	100
Average	92.1325	75.99	91.3775	98.7375

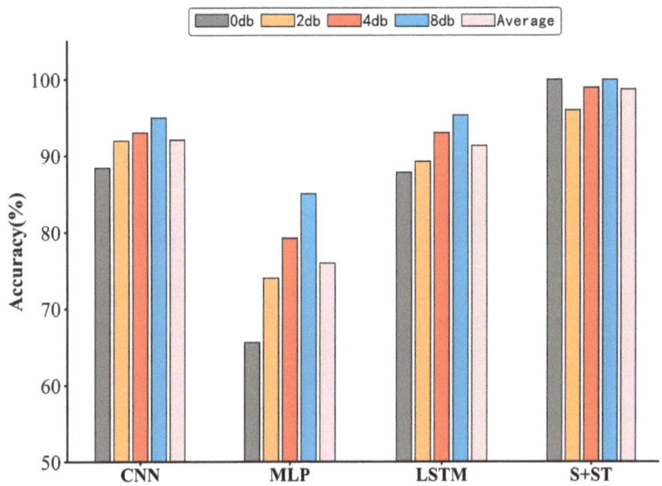

Figure 22. Diagnostic accuracy of different models under noise interference.

5. Conclusions

Aiming at the non-smooth characteristics of bearing signals, this paper compares and discusses the advantages and disadvantages of several commonly used time–frequency analysis methods, including linear STFT, WT, GST, and nonlinear WVD. The time–frequency images obtained by these four different methods are compared, analyzed, and validated using publicly available datasets. The experimental results show that the generalized S transform converts the 1D vibration signals into 2D image signals and retains the time–frequency feature information in the signals more effectively. On this basis, the GST is combined with the Swin Transformer algorithm in the image field, and the experimental results show that, compared with the traditional methods, the method proposed in this paper obtains more accurate and complete time–frequency information in feature extraction, has a higher accuracy in fault classification and identification, and still has a more accurate diagnosis and better noise robustness under noisy conditions.

Author Contributions: Conceptualization, J.Y. and D.Z.; methodology, J.Y. and D.Z.; software, D.Z.; validation, D.Z. and X.Z.; formal analysis, X.Z. and D.Z.; investigation, X.W. and X.Z.; resources, J.Y.; data curation, X.Z.; writing—original draft preparation, X.Z.; writing—review and editing, D.Z.; visualization, J.Y.; supervision, J.Y.; funding acquisition, J.Y. All authors have read and agreed to the published version of the manuscript.

Funding: The authors gratefully acknowledge the support provided for this research by the Natural Science Foundation of Guangdong Province (2022A1515011562) and National Natural Science Foundation of China (52201355), by Guangdong Provincial Special Fund for promoting high quality economic development (Yuerong Office Letter [2020]161, GDNRC [2021]56), and Development of intelligent early warning system for regional equipment failure (CY-ZJ-19-ZC-005).

Data Availability Statement: The Case Western Reserve University dataset used in this paper is available at this URL: https://gitcode.com/open-source-toolkit/78d4f/overview?utm_source=tools_gitcode&index=top&type=card&&isLogin=1 (accessed on 6 October 2024).

Conflicts of Interest: The authors declare no conflict of interest.

References

1. Coutinho, R.W.; Boukerche, A. Modeling and Analysis of a Shared Edge Caching System for Connected Cars and Industrial IoT-Based Applications. *IEEE Trans. Ind. Inform.* **2019**, *16*, 2003–2012. [CrossRef]
2. Li, C.; De Oliveira, J.V.; Cerrada, M.; Cabrera, D.; Sánchez, R.V.; Zurita, G. A Systematic Review of Fuzzy Formalisms for Bearing Fault Diagnosis. *IEEE Trans. Fuzzy Syst.* **2018**, *27*, 1362–1382. [CrossRef]
3. Pacheco-Chérrez, J.; Fortoul-Díaz, J.A.; Cortés-Santacruz, F.; Aloso-Valerdi, L.M.; Ibarra-Zarate, D.I. Bearing Fault Detection with Vibration and Acoustic Signals: Comparison among Different Machine Leaning Classification Methods. *Eng. Fail. Anal.* **2022**, *139*, 106515. [CrossRef]
4. Mian, T.; Choudhary, A.; Fatima, S. An Efficient Diagnosis Approach for Bearing Faults Using Sound Quality Metrics. *Appl. Acoust.* **2022**, *195*, 108839. [CrossRef]
5. Sadegh, H.; Mehdi, A.N.; Mehdi, A. Classification of Acoustic Emission Signals Generated from Journal Bearing at Different Lubrication Conditions Based on Wavelet Analysis in Combination with Artificial Neural Network and Genetic Algorithm. *Tribol. Int.* **2016**, *95*, 426–434. [CrossRef]
6. Motahari-Nezhad, M.; Jafari, S.M. Experimental and Data Driven Measurement of Engine Dynamometer Bearing Lifespan Using Acoustic Emission. *Appl. Acoust.* **2023**, *210*, 109460. [CrossRef]
7. Wen, L.; Li, X.; Gao, L.; Zhang, Y. A New Convolutional Neural Network-Based Data-Driven Fault Diagnosis Method. *IEEE Trans. Ind. Electron.* **2017**, *65*, 5990–5998. [CrossRef]
8. Gong, W.; Wang, Y.; Zhang, M.; Mihankhah, E.; Chen, H.; Wang, D. A Fast Anomaly Diagnosis Approach Based on Modified CNN and Multisensor Data Fusion. *IEEE Trans. Ind. Electron.* **2021**, *69*, 13636–13646. [CrossRef]
9. Liu, R.; Yang, B.; Zio, E.; Chen, X. Artificial Intelligence for Fault Diagnosis of Rotating Machinery: A Review. *Mech. Syst. Signal Process.* **2018**, *108*, 33–47. [CrossRef]
10. Shao, S.; McAleer, S.; Yan, R.; Baldi, P. Highly Accurate Machine Fault Diagnosis Using Deep Transfer Learning. *IEEE Trans. Ind. Inform.* **2018**, *15*, 2446–2455. [CrossRef]
11. Li-Hua, W.; Xiao-Ping, Z.; Jia-Xin, W.; Yang-Yang, X.; Yong-Hong, Z. Motor Fault Diagnosis Based on Short-Time Fourier Transform and Convolutional Neural Network. *Chin. J. Mech. Eng. Ji Xie Gong Cheng Xue Bao* **2017**, *30*, 1357–1368.
12. Jalayer, M.; Orsenigo, C.; Vercellis, C. Fault Detection and Diagnosis for Rotating Machinery: A Model Based on Convolutional LSTM, Fast Fourier and Continuous Wavelet Transforms. *Comput. Ind.* **2021**, *125*, 103378. [CrossRef]
13. Xu, C.; Yang, J.; Zhang, T.; Li, K.; Zhang, K. Adaptive Parameter Selection Variational Mode Decomposition Based on a Novel Hybrid Entropy and Its Applications in Locomotive Bearing Diagnosis. *Measurement* **2023**, *217*, 113110. [CrossRef]
14. Jegadeeshwaran, R.; Sugumaran, V. Fault Diagnosis of Automobile Hydraulic Brake System Using Statistical Features and Support Vector Machines. *Mech. Syst. Signal Process.* **2015**, *52*, 436–446. [CrossRef]
15. Muruganatham, B.; Sanjith, M.A.; Krishnakumar, B.; Murty, S.S. Roller Element Bearing Fault Diagnosis Using Singular Spectrum Analysis. *Mech. Syst. Signal Process.* **2013**, *35*, 150–166. [CrossRef]
16. Zhou, K.; Tang, J. A Wavelet Neural Network Informed by Time-Domain Signal Preprocessing for Bearing Remaining Useful Life Prediction. *Appl. Math. Model.* **2023**, *122*, 220–241. [CrossRef]
17. Wei, B.; Xie, B.; Li, H.; Zhong, Z.; You, Y. An Improved Hilbert–Huang Transform Method for Modal Parameter Identification of a High Arch Dam. *Appl. Math. Model.* **2021**, *91*, 297–310. [CrossRef]
18. Zhang, W.; Li, C.; Peng, G.; Chen, Y.; Zhang, Z. A Deep Convolutional Neural Network with New Training Methods for Bearing Fault Diagnosis under Noisy Environment and Different Working Load. *Mech. Syst. Signal Process.* **2018**, *100*, 439–453. [CrossRef]
19. Fuan, W.; Hongkai, J.; Haidong, S.; Wenjing, D.; Shuaipeng, W. An Adaptive Deep Convolutional Neural Network for Rolling Bearing Fault Diagnosis. *Meas. Sci. Technol.* **2017**, *28*, 095005. [CrossRef]
20. Eren, L.; Ince, T.; Kiranyaz, S. A Generic Intelligent Bearing Fault Diagnosis System Using Compact Adaptive 1D CNN Classifier. *J. Signal Process. Syst.* **2019**, *91*, 179–189. [CrossRef]
21. Xia, M.; Li, T.; Xu, L.; Liu, L.; De Silva, C.W. Fault Diagnosis for Rotating Machinery Using Multiple Sensors and Convolutional Neural Networks. *IEEE/ASME Trans. Mechatron.* **2017**, *23*, 101–110. [CrossRef]
22. Zhao, X.; Yao, J.; Deng, W.; Jia, M.; Liu, Z. Normalized Conditional Variational Auto-Encoder with Adaptive Focal Loss for Imbalanced Fault Diagnosis of Bearing-Rotor System. *Mech. Syst. Signal Process.* **2022**, *170*, 108826. [CrossRef]

23. Wang, D.; Zhang, M.; Xu, Y.; Lu, W.; Yang, J.; Zhang, T. Metric-Based Meta-Learning Model for Few-Shot Fault Diagnosis under Multiple Limited Data Conditions. *Mech. Syst. Signal Process.* **2021**, *155*, 107510. [CrossRef]
24. Su, H.; Xiang, L.; Hu, A.; Xu, Y.; Yang, X. A Novel Method Based on Meta-Learning for Bearing Fault Diagnosis with Small Sample Learning under Different Working Conditions. *Mech. Syst. Signal Process.* **2022**, *169*, 108765. [CrossRef]
25. Li, X.J.; Yang, D.L.; Jiang, L.L. Bearing Fault Diagnosis Based on Multi-Sensor Information Fusion with SVM. *Appl. Mech. Mater.* **2010**, *34*, 995–999. [CrossRef]
26. Ding, X.; He, Q.; Shao, Y.; Huang, W. Transient Feature Extraction Based on Time–Frequency Manifold Image Synthesis for Machinery Fault Diagnosis. *IEEE Trans. Instrum. Meas.* **2019**, *68*, 4242–4252. [CrossRef]
27. Ville, J. Theorie et Application Dela Notion de Signal Analysis. *Câbles Transm.* **1948**, *2*, 61–74.
28. Abboud, D.; Antoni, J.; Sieg-Zieba, S.; Eltabach, M. Envelope Analysis of Rotating Machine Vibrations in Variable Speed Conditions: A Comprehensive Treatment. *Mech. Syst. Signal Process.* **2017**, *84*, 200–226. [CrossRef]
29. Vin Koay, H.; Huang Chuah, J.; Chow, C.-O. Shifted-Window Hierarchical Vision Transformer for Distracted Driver Detection. In Proceedings of the 2021 IEEE Region 10 Symposium (TENSYMP), Jeju, Republic of Korea, 23–25 August 2021; pp. 1–7.
30. Vaswani, A.; Shazeer, N.; Parmar, N.; Uszkoreit, J. Attention Is All You Need. In Proceedings of the Advances in Neural Information Processing Systems 30 (NIPS 2017), Long Beach, CA, USA, 4–9 December 2017; pp. 5998–6008.
31. Yao, Y.; Zou, J.; Wang, H. Model Constraints Independent Optimal Subsampling Probabilities for Softmax Regression. *J. Stat. Plan. Inference* **2023**, *225*, 188–201. [CrossRef]
32. Kumar, H.S.; Gururaj, U. Fault Diagnosis of Rolling Element Bearing Using Continuous Wavelet Transform and K- Nearest Neighbour. *Mater. Today Proc.* **2023**, *92*, 56–60. [CrossRef]
33. Bai, R.; Meng, Z.; Xu, Q.; Fan, F. Fractional Fourier and Time Domain Recurrence Plot Fusion Combining Convolutional Neural Network for Bearing Fault Diagnosis under Variable Working Conditions. *Reliab. Eng. Syst. Saf.* **2023**, *232*, 109076. [CrossRef]
34. Yuan, P.-P.; Zhang, J.; Feng, J.-Q.; Wang, H.-H.; Ren, W.-X.; Wang, C. An Improved Time-Frequency Analysis Method for Structural Instantaneous Frequency Identification Based on Generalized S-Transform and Synchroextracting Transform. *Eng. Struct.* **2022**, *252*, 113657. [CrossRef]
35. Mirzaeian, R.; Ghaderyan, P. Gray-Level Co-Occurrence Matrix of Smooth Pseudo Wigner-Ville Distribution for Cognitive Workload Estimation. *Biocybern. Biomed. Eng.* **2023**, *43*, 261–278. [CrossRef]
36. Talebitooti, R.; Zarastvand, M.R.; Gheibi, M.R. Acoustic transmission through laminated composite cylindrical shell employing Third order Shear Deformation Theory in the presence of subsonic flow. *Compos. Struct.* **2016**, *157*, 95–110. [CrossRef]

mathematics

MDPI

Article

Extending the Meshless Natural-Neighbour Radial-Point Interpolation Method to the Structural Optimization of an Automotive Part Using a Bi-Evolutionary Bone-Remodelling-Inspired Algorithm

Carlos Oliveira [1], Ana Pais [2] and Jorge Belinha [2,3,*]

[1] ISEP, Polytechnic of Porto, Rua Dr. António Bernardino de Almeida, n.431, 4200-072 Porto, Portugal
[2] INEGI—Institute of Science and Innovation in Mechanical and Industrial Engineering, Rua Dr. Roberto Frias, 400, 4200-465 Porto, Portugal; anapais@fe.up.pt
[3] Department of Mechanical Engineering, ISEP, Polytechnic of Porto, Rua Dr. António Bernardino de Almeida, n.431, 4200-072 Porto, Portugal
* Correspondence: job@isep.ipp.pt

Abstract: Topological structural optimization is a powerful computational tool that enhances the structural efficiency of mechanical components. It achieves this by reducing mass without significantly altering stiffness. This study combines the Natural-Neighbour Radial-Point Interpolation Method (NNRPIM) with a bio-inspired bi-evolutionary bone-remodelling algorithm. This combination enables non-linear topological optimization analyses and achieves solutions with optimal stiffness-to-mass ratios. The NNRPIM discretizes the problem using an unstructured nodal distribution. Background integration points are constructed using the Delaunay triangulation concept. Nodal connectivity is then imposed through the natural neighbour concept. To construct shape functions, radial point interpolators are employed, allowing the shape functions to possess the delta Kronecker property. To evaluate the numerical performance of NNRPIM, its solutions are compared with those obtained using the standard Finite Element Method (FEM). The structural optimization process was applied to a practical example: a vehicle's suspension control arm. This research is divided into two phases. In the first phase, the optimization algorithm is applied to a standard suspension control arm, and the results are closely evaluated. The findings show that NNRPIM produces topologies with suitable truss connections and a higher number of intermediate densities. Both aspects can enhance the mechanical performance of a hypothetical additively manufactured part. In the second phase, four models based on a solution from the optimized topology algorithm are analyzed. These models incorporate established design principles for material removal commonly used in vehicle suspension control arms. Additionally, the same models, along with a solid reference model, undergo linear static analysis under identical loading conditions used in the optimization process. The structural performance of the generated models is analyzed, and the main differences between the solutions obtained with both numerical techniques are identified.

Keywords: meshless methods; natural-neighbour radial-point interpolation method; structural optimization; bone remodelling algorithm; evolutionary optimization; automotive industry

MSC: 74B10; 74P15

Academic Editors: Joaquim Infante Barbosa and José Alberto Rodrigues

Received: 25 October 2024
Revised: 13 December 2024
Accepted: 19 December 2024
Published: 7 January 2025

Citation: Oliveira, C.; Pais, A.; Belinha, J. Extending the Meshless Natural-Neighbour Radial-Point Interpolation Method to the Structural Optimization of an Automotive Part Using a Bi-Evolutionary Bone-Remodelling-Inspired Algorithm. *Mathematics* **2025**, *13*, 178. https://doi.org/10.3390/math13020178

1. Introduction

The past two decades have witnessed a technological revolution, with numerical methods becoming a cornerstone for advancements across various engineering disciplines, and mechanical engineering is no exception. This progress has been further accelerated by the remarkable evolution of computational power observed since the late 20th century. The availability of increasingly fast, efficient, versatile, and practical computational tools has driven the widespread adoption of advanced numerical methods in engineering simulations [1]. In particular, its uses have revolutionized the entire mechanical construction industry, allowing for the design of optimized components based on the manufacturer's imposed constraints, allowing for a close approximated prediction of the component's behaviour when subjected to real-life working conditions. In the automotive industry, the structural optimization of various parts is a preponderant factor in the vehicle's components' performance and behaviour when subjected to stress throughout the driving procedure, demonstrating promising results in weight reduction while maintaining the necessary resistance to ensure that the component fulfils all its mechanical requirements [2].

In the field of vehicle manufacturing, weight reduction across various components presents an avenue for manufacturers to enhance profitability. Weight reduction often allows for the use of less material per vehicle, further decreasing production costs [3]. By implementing weight reduction strategies and regular optimization processes on the part-design phase, manufacturers can achieve substantial financial gains through these combined effects. In addition to the financial incentive, growing demand and legislative requirements in the automotive industry have created the need to evolve and develop all types of components involved in the various functional sets of a vehicle so that they are lighter, safer, more efficient in relation to production costs, and, specifically for certain components, more comfortable [4]. With the need to meet these requirements, the application of structural optimization methods in the automotive field has grown exponentially over the years, keeping with the improvement and evolution of the computational techniques.

The structural evaluation of automotive components is crucial for the development of efficient and safe parts. One way to perform this is through experimental techniques. For example, Liu et al. [5] developed load spectrum editing for fatigue bench testing, which avoids the need to use the full load spectrum, which could sometimes have minimal impact and significantly increase the testing time. Additionally, computational structural assessment techniques provide engineers with powerful tools to analyse the behaviour of components and systems under various load and stress conditions and complement the overall process of optimization of the studied structure. Through computer simulation, stresses, strains, and displacements can be predicted, allowing the identification of critical failure points to be identified and a efficient optimization of design. For instance, Komurcu et al. [6] took advantage of numerical techniques to tailor the design of a composite suspension control arm to the required manufacturing considerations.

Weight reduction without compromising the structural integrity of the part can be carried out through structural optimization approaches. The suspension control arm has been the object of study combined with structural optimization techniques; for example, Viqaruddin and Ramana Reddy [7] designed a suspension control arm with a 30% weight reduction. Also regarding the same component, Llopis-Albert et al. [8] tested several optimization algorithms to achieve a multiobjective solution for the part. Song et al. [9] had surrogate models, namely the response surface model and the Kriging model, supporting the stuctural optimization of a suspension control arm and achieved weight reduction between 4.13% and 5.22%. Stiffness optimization is also important in addition to the scope of automotive components. For example, Wang et al. [10] used a homogenous stiffness domain index to create an optimization model to improve the stiffness of a machining robot. Finally, optimization approaches are not limited to the optimization of stiffness or weight minimization, along with other aspects such as the friction in bearings [11]. The optimization approach, in this case particle swarm optimization, could also be employed in other applications.

The field of computational mechanics has always been dominated by the use of FEM as the most popular discretization technique in research, development, and education [12]. However, new techniques have been developed to overcome some of the limitations of the FEM related with its rigid mesh dependency. In areas such as fracture and impact mechanics, areas that approach problems that require meshing due to transient domain boundaries, meshless methods have been shown to be a more accurate alternative to FEM due to not being affected by mesh distortion and not requiring meshing. Unlike FEM, in meshless methods, the nodes are distributed in an arbitrary way, and the field functions are approximated based on a domain of influence, rather than an element. In addition, the rule established in FEM that elements cannot overlap does not apply to the domains of influence of meshless methods: they can and should overlap [13].

The first meshless method applied in the context of computational mechanics was the DEM (Diffuse Element Method), developed by Nayroles et al. [14], which used the approximating functions of the Moving Least Squares to construct the approximation functions, a technique previously suggested by Lancaster and S. [15], Dinis et al. [16], Poiate et al. [17]. Later, Belytschko et al. [18] improved the DEM method and developed one of the most popular and widely used meshless methods: the Element Free Galerkin Method (EFGM). Over time, other methods have also been developed, such as the Petrov–Galerkin Local Meshless Method (MLPG) [19], the Finite Point Method (FPM) [20], and the Finite Sphere Method (FSM) [21].

Although these methods have been successfully employed for a variety of issues in the computational mechanics domain, they all present problems and limitations, one of the main ones being the effect of using approximation functions instead of interpolation functions. The PIM (Point Interpolation Method), developed by Liu and Gu [22], proved to be a highly attractive approach, as it effectively solves the challenge of imposing essential boundary conditions by constructing shape functions with the Kronecker's delta property. Furthermore, PIM simplifies the process of obtaining the derivatives of shape functions. Meanwhile, PIM has evolved with the incorporation of radial basis functions for solving partial differential equations [13,23]. One of the first truly meshless methods to emerge was the NEM (Natural Element Method) [24]. Later, new meshless interpolation methods were proposed, such as PIM (Point Interpolation Method) [22], MFEM (Meshless Finite Element Method) [25], NREM (Natural Radial Element Method) [26], and RPIM (Radial-Point Interpolation Method) [23].

Later, Dinis et al. [16] introduced the Natural-Neighbour Radial-Point Interpolation Method (NNRPIM), a truly meshless method that leverages the connectivity advantages of the Natural Element Method (NEM) and the interpolation capabilities of the Radial-Point Interpolation Method (RPIM). NNRPIM solely relies the on nodal discretization of the problem domain. It then utilizes this spatial information to autonomously distribute integration points and establish nodal connectivity, eliminating the need for a separate background integration mesh as required by EFGM or RPIM [16]. This method differs from RPIM as the connectivity between nodes is not described using domains of influence. Instead, it uses influence cells determined by the Voronoï diagram space decomposer [27] and complemented by the use of Delaunay triangulation [28]. The Voronoï diagram takes on the task of creating the influence cells from a set of unstructured nodes in the domain. The Delaunay triangulation is applied in order to create a background grid with nodal dependence, which is then used in the integration of the interpolation functions of this method. Thus, when compared with a conventional meshless method, NNRPIM can be considered a truly meshless method, since the set of integration points is totally dependent on the nodal distribution [13].

The aim of this study is to utilize a bio-inspired bi-evolutionary optimization algorithm, combined with a natural-neighbour meshless method, for a suspension control arm that has undergone prior accurate modelling and replication. The design of the control arm is based on the geometry of an established industry-standard suspension arm. In automotive mechanical engineering, product development often relies on design philosophies informed by empirical knowledge from engineers. By employing automated techniques to selectively remove material from specific stressed components, it becomes possible to achieve designs that meet manufacturer requirements while significantly reducing mass. Recent literature also highlights a preference for meshless methods, which not only serve as an alternative to FEM but also offer potential advantages [29,30]. Being a truly meshless method possesses some advantages. NNRPIM is capable of discretizing the problem domain using only a nodal distribution. All the other mathematical constructions (nodal connectivity, background integration mesh, shape functions, etc.), required to build the system of equations governing the studied phenomenon, are obtained using only the spatial information of the nodes. In the automotive industry, this feature is an advantage since it allows us to obtain the discretization directly from sketches of CAD software (SOLIDWORKS Student Edition 2023 SP2.1) or the output of 3D scanning. Moreover, as the literature shows, NNRPIM shows a high convergence rate and accuracy, which is convenient in structural optimization algorithms depending on the stress field mapping (as the one used in this work). Accurate predictions of the higher and lower stress levels will lead to better remodelling designs.

2. Natural-Neighbour Radial-Point Interpolation Method

Like any other node-dependent numerical discretization method, NNRPIM discretizes the problem domain with a set of nodes, following a regular or irregular distribution. Then, the Voronoï diagram of the nodal set is constructed, using the mathematical concept of the natural neighbours [31]. For the sake of simplicity, the natural-neighbour procedure will be demonstrated for a 2D Euclidean space, but it can be applied to any n-D space [13]. Considering the set of nodes $\mathbf{N} = \{n_1, n_2, ..., n_N\}$, discretizing the $\Omega \subset \mathbb{R}^d$ domain, with $\mathbf{X} = \{\mathbf{x}_1, \mathbf{x}_2, ..., \mathbf{x}_N\} \in \Omega$. The Voronoï diagram of $\mathbf{N}$ is the partitioning of the spatial domain discretized by $\mathbf{X}$ into V_i. Each sub-region V_i is associated with a node n_i so that any point within V_i is closer to n_i than to any other node $n_j \in N \wedge j \neq i$. The set of Voronoï cells $\mathbf{V}$ defines the Voronoï diagram, which is $\mathbf{V} = \{V_1, V_2, ..., V_N\}$. The Voronoï cell can be defined by

$$\mathbf{N} = \left\{ \mathbf{x}_I \in \Omega \subset \mathbb{R}^d : \|\mathbf{x}_I - \mathbf{x}_i\| < \|\mathbf{x}_I - \mathbf{x}_j\|, \forall \neq j \right\} \tag{1}$$

Figure 1 depicts the Voronoï diagram for a general nodal discretization. The natural neighbours of node $\mathbf{x}_i$ are all the nodes whose Voronoï cells share a common edge with the Voronoï cell of node x_i (represented by the light gray cells surrounding the Voronoï cell of node $\mathbf{x}_i$ in Figure 1A). The concept of natural neighbours in NNRPIM replaces the need for a pre-defined connectivity information. The Voronoï diagram automatically generates influence domains (called influence cells in the NNRPIM formulation). With this process, it is possible to define a lower-connectivity influence cell and a higher-connectivity influence cell:

- First-degree influence cells (Figure 1A): These comprise node $\mathbf{x}_i$ itself and its immediate natural neighbours. The Voronoï diagram identifies these neighbours as nodes sharing a common edge with the Voronoï cell of $\mathbf{x}_i$.

- Second-degree influence cells (Figure 1B): These encompass node $\mathbf{x}_i$, its first-degree neighbours (including natural neighbours of $\mathbf{x}_i$), and the natural neighbours of those first-degree neighbours.

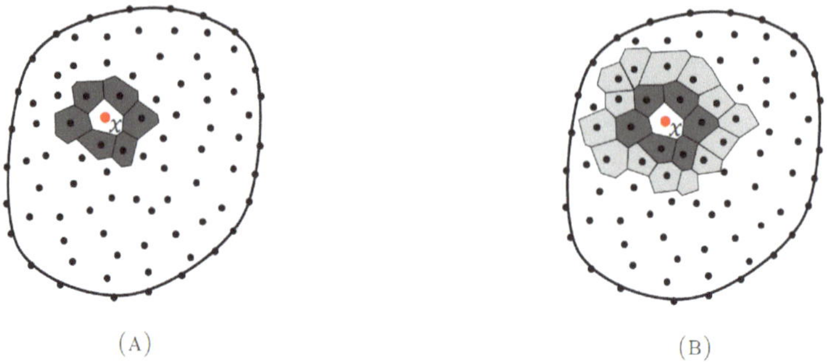

Figure 1. Nodal connectivity. (**A**) First-degree influence cell. (**B**) Second-degree influence cell.

After the nodal connectivity is established, it is time to build the grid of background integration points. Thus, in order to integrate the integro-differential equation ruling the physical phenomenon, it is necessary to establish the background integration cells. In NNRPIM, the background integration cells are constructed using only the spatial information of the nodal distribution. This is achieved by applying the Delaunay triangulation numerical technique [13,28], which is product of the Voronoï diagram of the initial nodal distribution [13]. Thus, consider a Voronoï cell V_i of a node $\mathbf{x}_i$, as in Figure 2. It is possible to discretize V_i into smaller quadrilaterals and then apply the Gauss–Legendre quadrature integration scheme to determine the position and weight of integration points within the quadrilaterals. As Figure 2 shows, NNRPIM employs a two-step process to define such integration points. First, each quadrilateral element in a Voronoï cell is transformed into a unit isoparametric square, which allows for the distribution of the integration points within the isoparametric square in compliance with the Gauss–Legendre integration scheme. Then, the isoparametric coordinates are converted back to the actual Cartesian coordinates of the integration. This process is repeated for each Voronoï cell V_i discretizing the problem domain. As suggested in the literature, only one integration point is inserted inside each quadrilateral [13]. Thus, the position of each quadrilateral's integration point is the quadrilateral's geometric centre, and its integration weight corresponds to the quadrilateral's area. A detailed description of the numerical integration procedure of NNRPIM can be found in the literature [13].

Regarding the connectivity of each integration point, integration points located within the Voronoï cell V_i inherit the nodal connectivity of node $\mathbf{x}_i$ (i.e., inherit its influence cell). In the NNRPIM, nodal connectivity arises naturally from the overlap of influence cells associated with each integration point. These influence cells define the set of nodes contributing to the shape function construction and stiffness matrix assembly [13].

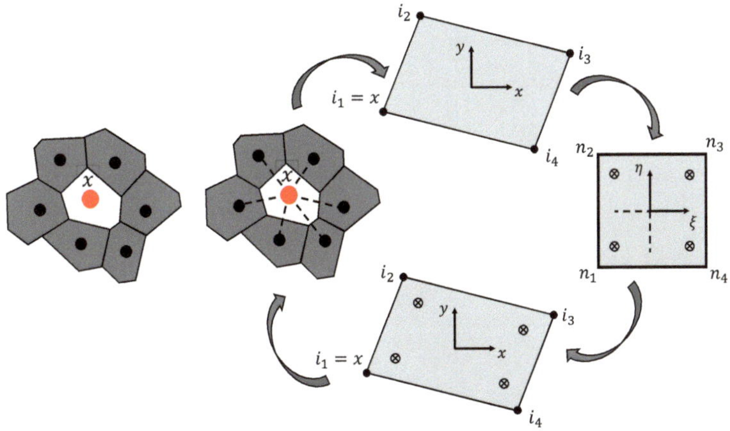

Figure 2. Adopted NNRPIM procedure for constructing the set of background integration points based on the Voronoï diagram.

The next step is the construction of the shape functions. The NNRPIM uses the radial point interpolators (RPI) technique, which allows the interpolation of the variable field at an integration point $\mathbf{x}_I$. Thus, consider a function $u(\mathbf{x})$, defined in the domain Ω, discretized by a set of nodes $\mathbf{N}$, and assuming that only the nodes included in the influence domain of the point of interest $\mathbf{x}_I$ have an effect on $u(\mathbf{x}_I)$. The value of the function at the point $\mathbf{x}_I$ can be obtained from the following expression:

$$u(\mathbf{x}_I) = \sum_{i=1}^{n} R_i(\mathbf{x}_I)a_i(\mathbf{x}_I) + \sum_{j=1}^{m} p_j(\mathbf{x}_I)b_j(\mathbf{x}_I) = \left\{\mathbf{R}^{\mathrm{T}}(\mathbf{x}_I), \mathbf{p}^{\mathrm{T}}(\mathbf{x}_I)\right\}\begin{Bmatrix}\mathbf{a}\\ \mathbf{b}\end{Bmatrix} \quad (2)$$

in where R_i represents a radial basis function, n is the number of nodes inside the influence cell of $\mathbf{x}_I$, and $a_i(\mathbf{x}_I)$ and $b_j(\mathbf{x}_I)$ are non-constant coefficients of $R_i(\mathbf{x}_I)$ and $p_j(\mathbf{x}_I)$, respectively.

Several radial basis functions can be used, and several have been studied and developed over the years. In this work, as recommended in the literature [13], the multiquadratic radial basis function (MQ-RBF) function will be used [32]. The MQ-RBF can be described as follows:

$$R(r_{Ii}) = (r_{Ii}^2 + (\omega_I \cdot c)^2)^p \quad (3)$$

for which r_{Ii} is defined as

$$r_{Ii} = \sqrt{(x_I - x_i)^2 + (y_I - y_i)^2} \quad (4)$$

The variable ω_I is the integration weight of integration point $\mathbf{x}_I$, and c and p are MQ-RBF shape parameters. In the literature, it is possible to find works studying the influence of the MQ-RBF shape parameters on the constructed shape functions [13]. It was found that assuming $c = 0.0001$ and $p = 0.9999$ leads to shape functions with the delta Kronecker [13]. Thus, these are the values used in this work. In order to guarantee a unique solution [23], the following system of equations is added:

$$\sum_{i=1}^{n} p_j(\mathbf{x}_I)a_i(\mathbf{x}_I) = 0, \;\; j = 1, 2, ..., m \quad (5)$$

Assuming a linear polynomial basis $p(\mathbf{x}_I) = \{1, x_I, y_I\}^T$, with $m = 3$, it is possible to present Equation (2) as

$$\begin{Bmatrix} \begin{bmatrix} u_1 \\ u_2 \\ \vdots \\ u_n \end{bmatrix} \\ \begin{bmatrix} 0 \\ 0 \\ 0 \end{bmatrix} \end{Bmatrix} = \begin{bmatrix} \begin{bmatrix} R(r_{11}) & R(r_{12}) & \cdots & R(r_{1n}) \\ R(r_{21}) & R(r_{22}) & \cdots & R(r_{2n}) \\ \vdots & \vdots & & \vdots \\ R(r_{n1}) & R(r_{n2}) & \cdots & R(r_{nn}) \end{bmatrix} & \begin{bmatrix} 1 & x_1 & y_1 \\ 1 & x_2 & y_2 \\ \vdots & \vdots & \vdots \\ 1 & x_n & y_n \end{bmatrix} \\ \begin{bmatrix} 1 & 1 & \cdots & 1 \\ x_1 & x_2 & \cdots & x_n \\ y_1 & y_2 & \cdots & y_n \end{bmatrix} & \begin{bmatrix} 0 & 0 & 0 \\ 0 & 0 & 0 \\ 0 & 0 & 0 \end{bmatrix} \end{bmatrix} \begin{Bmatrix} \begin{bmatrix} a_1 \\ a_2 \\ \vdots \\ a_n \end{bmatrix} \\ \begin{bmatrix} b_1 \\ b_2 \\ b_3 \end{bmatrix} \end{Bmatrix} \tag{6}$$

solving this system of equations allows us to define the non-constant coefficients $a_i(\mathbf{x}_I)$ and $b_j(\mathbf{x}_I)$,

$$\begin{Bmatrix} \mathbf{u}_s \\ 0 \end{Bmatrix} = \mathbf{G} \begin{Bmatrix} \mathbf{a} \\ \mathbf{b} \end{Bmatrix} \Longrightarrow \begin{Bmatrix} \mathbf{a} \\ \mathbf{b} \end{Bmatrix} = \mathbf{G}^{-1} \begin{Bmatrix} \mathbf{u}_s \\ 0 \end{Bmatrix} \tag{7}$$

Inserting $a_i(\mathbf{x}_I)$ and $b_j(\mathbf{x}_I)$ into Equation (2), the following interpolation is obtained:

$$\mathbf{u}(\mathbf{x}_I) = \left\{ \mathbf{R}^{\mathbf{T}}(\mathbf{x}_I), \mathbf{p}^{\mathbf{T}}(\mathbf{x}_I) \right\} \mathbf{G}^{-1} \begin{Bmatrix} \mathbf{u_s} \\ 0 \end{Bmatrix} = \boldsymbol{\varphi}(\mathbf{x}_I) \mathbf{u_s} \tag{8}$$

And, finally, the RPI shape function is defined,

$$\boldsymbol{\varphi}(\mathbf{x}_I) = \left\{ \mathbf{R}^{\mathbf{T}}(\mathbf{x}_I), \mathbf{p}^{\mathbf{T}}(\mathbf{x}_I) \right\} \mathbf{G}^{-1} = \{\varphi_1(\mathbf{x}_I), \varphi_2(\mathbf{x}_I), \cdots, \varphi_n(\mathbf{x}_I)\} \tag{9}$$

In elasto-static problems, the equilibrium equations governing the partial differential equilibrium can be summarized as: $\nabla\sigma + \mathbf{b} = 0, \ \in \Omega$, in which ∇ represents the gradient vector, σ the Cauchy stress tensor, and $\mathbf{b}$ the body force vector. Regarding the boundary surface, it can be divided into two types: natural boundaries (Γ_u), where $\sigma\mathbf{n} = \bar{\mathbf{t}}$, and essential boundaries (Γ_t), where $\mathbf{u} = \bar{\mathbf{u}}$. The imposed displacement at the essential boundary Γ_u is represented as $\bar{\mathbf{u}}$, and the traction force on the natural boundary Γ_t is defined by $\bar{\mathbf{t}}$ (where $\mathbf{n}$ is a unit vector normal to the natural boundary Γ_t).

The Cauchy stress tensor can be represented in Voigt notation, $\sigma = \left\{ \sigma_{xx} \ \ \sigma_{yy} \ \ \sigma_{zz} \ \ \tau_{xy} \ \ \tau_{yz} \ \ \tau_{zx} \right\}^T$, as well as the strain tensor, $\varepsilon = \left\{ \varepsilon_{xx} \ \ \varepsilon_{yy} \ \ \varepsilon_{zz} \ \ \gamma_{xy} \ \ \gamma_{yz} \ \ \gamma_{zx} \right\}^T$. Applying Hooke's law, it is possible to relate the stress state with the strain state, $\sigma = \mathbf{c} \cdot \varepsilon$, being the strain obtained from the displacement field: $\varepsilon = \mathbf{L} \cdot \mathbf{u}$. For a generic 3D problem, the differential operator matrix L and the material constitutive matrix c can be represented as

$$\mathbf{L} = \begin{bmatrix} \frac{\partial}{\partial x} & 0 & 0 & \frac{\partial}{\partial y} & 0 & \frac{\partial}{\partial z} \\ 0 & \frac{\partial}{\partial y} & 0 & \frac{\partial}{\partial x} & \frac{\partial}{\partial z} & 0 \\ 0 & 0 & \frac{\partial}{\partial z} & 0 & \frac{\partial}{\partial y} & \frac{\partial}{\partial x} \end{bmatrix}^T \tag{10}$$

$$\mathbf{c} = \mu_1 \begin{bmatrix} 1 & v & v & 0 & 0 & 0 \\ v & 1 & v & 0 & 0 & 0 \\ v & v & 1 & 0 & 0 & 0 \\ 0 & 0 & 0 & \mu_2 & 0 & 0 \\ 0 & 0 & 0 & 0 & \mu_2 & 0 \\ 0 & 0 & 0 & 0 & 0 & \mu_2 \end{bmatrix} \tag{11}$$

where $\mu_1 = \frac{E}{1-v^2}$ and $\mu_2 = \frac{1-v}{2}$. To establish the system of equations, the virtual work principle is assumed, and energy conservation is imposed:

$$\Psi = \int_{\Omega} \delta\varepsilon^T \sigma \, d\Omega - \int_{\Omega} \delta \mathbf{u}^T \sigma \, b\Omega - \int_{\Gamma_t} \delta \mathbf{u}^T \mathbf{t} \, d\Gamma = 0 \tag{12}$$

With the simplification of the above expression, the following can be obtained:

$$\mathbf{\Psi} = \delta \mathbf{u}^T (\mathbf{K} \cdot \mathbf{u} - \mathbf{f_b} - \mathbf{f_t}) = 0 \tag{13}$$

which results in the simplified expression $\mathbf{K} \cdot \mathbf{u} = \mathbf{f_b} + \mathbf{f_t}$, where $\mathbf{K}$ represents the global stiffness matrix, which can be numerically calculated with:

$$\mathbf{K} = \int_{\Omega} \mathbf{B^T} \cdot \mathbf{c} \cdot \mathbf{B} \, d\Omega = \sum_{i=1}^{n_Q} \mathbf{B}(\mathbf{x}_I)^{\mathbf{T}} \cdot \mathbf{c} \cdot \mathbf{B}(\mathbf{x}_I) \widehat{w_I} \tag{14}$$

The $\mathbf{B}$ matrix, known as the deformability matrix, can be defined as

$$\mathbf{B} = \begin{bmatrix} \frac{\partial \varphi_1(\mathbf{x_I})}{\partial x} & 0 & 0 & \cdots & \frac{\partial \varphi_n(\mathbf{x_I})}{\partial x} & 0 & 0 \\ 0 & \frac{\partial \varphi_1(\mathbf{x_I})}{\partial y} & 0 & \cdots & 0 & \frac{\partial \varphi_n(\mathbf{x_I})}{\partial y} & 0 \\ 0 & 0 & \frac{\partial \varphi_1(\mathbf{x_I})}{\partial z} & \cdots & 0 & 0 & \frac{\partial \varphi_n(\mathbf{x_I})}{\partial z} \\ \frac{\partial \varphi_1(\mathbf{x_I})}{\partial y} & \frac{\partial \varphi_1(\mathbf{x_I})}{\partial x} & 0 & \cdots & \frac{\partial \varphi_n(\mathbf{x_I})}{\partial y} & \frac{\partial \varphi_n(\mathbf{x_I})}{\partial x} & 0 \\ 0 & \frac{\partial \varphi_1(\mathbf{x_I})}{\partial z} & \frac{\partial \varphi_1(\mathbf{x_I})}{\partial y} & \cdots & 0 & \frac{\partial \varphi_n(\mathbf{x_I})}{\partial z} & \frac{\partial \varphi_n(\mathbf{x_I})}{\partial y} \\ \frac{\partial \varphi_1(\mathbf{x_I})}{\partial z} & 0 & \frac{\partial \varphi_1(\mathbf{x_I})}{\partial x} & \cdots & \frac{\partial \varphi_n(\mathbf{x_I})}{\partial z} & 0 & \frac{\partial \varphi_n(\mathbf{x_I})}{\partial x} \end{bmatrix} \tag{15}$$

With Equation (12), the body force ($\mathbf{f_b}$) and external force vectors ($\mathbf{f_t}$) can also be defined:

$$\mathbf{f_b} = \int_{\Omega} \mathbf{H^T} \cdot \mathbf{b} \, d\Omega = \sum_{i=1}^{n_Q} \mathbf{H}(\mathbf{x}_I)^{\mathbf{T}} \cdot \mathbf{b} \widehat{w_I} \tag{16}$$

$$\mathbf{f_t} = \int_{\Gamma} \mathbf{H^T} \cdot \bar{\mathbf{t}} \, d\Gamma = \sum_{i=1}^{n_Q^*} \mathbf{H}(\mathbf{x}_I)^{\mathbf{T}} \cdot \mathbf{f} \cdot \widehat{w_I^*} \tag{17}$$

where w_I^* represents the weight of the integration point on the surface where the external force $\mathbf{f_t}$ is being applied, n_Q^* is the number of integration points defining the boundary where the force is applied, and $\mathbf{H}$ is the interpolation matrix.

$$\mathbf{H} = \begin{bmatrix} \varphi_1(\mathbf{x}_I) & 0 & 0 & \cdots & \varphi_n(\mathbf{x}_I) & 0 & 0 \\ 0 & \varphi_1(\mathbf{x}_I) & 0 & \cdots & 0 & \varphi_n(\mathbf{x}_I) & 0 \\ 0 & 0 & \varphi_1(\mathbf{x}_I) & \cdots & 0 & 0 & \varphi_n(\mathbf{x}_I) \end{bmatrix} \tag{18}$$

The essential boundary conditions are imposed directly on the stiffness matrix $\mathbf{K}$, since RPI shape functions possess the Kronecker delta property. If the problem can be analysed assuming a plane stress simplification, the problem reduces to a 2D analysis, and all components associated with the Oz direction are removed, thus, reducing the size of all algebraic structures previously presented. For instance, the constitutive matrix and the stress and strain vectors become

$$\mathbf{c} = \mu_1 \begin{bmatrix} 1 & v & 0 \\ v & 1 & 0 \\ 0 & 0 & \mu_2 \end{bmatrix} \quad ; \quad \sigma = \begin{Bmatrix} \sigma_{xx} \\ \sigma_{yy} \\ \tau_{xy} \end{Bmatrix} \quad ; \quad \boldsymbol{\varepsilon} = \begin{Bmatrix} \varepsilon_{xx} \\ \varepsilon_{yy} \\ \gamma_{xy} \end{Bmatrix} \tag{19}$$

and the deformability and interpolation matrices are reduced to

$$\mathbf{B} = \begin{bmatrix} \frac{\partial \varphi_1(\mathbf{x}_I)}{\partial x} & 0 & \cdots & \frac{\partial \varphi_n(\mathbf{x}_I)}{\partial x} & 0 \\ 0 & \frac{\partial \varphi_1(\mathbf{x}_I)}{\partial y} & \cdots & 0 & \frac{\partial \varphi_n(\mathbf{x}_I)}{\partial x} \\ \frac{\partial \varphi_1(\mathbf{x}_I)}{\partial y} & \frac{\partial \varphi_1(\mathbf{x}_I)}{\partial x} & \cdots & \frac{\partial \varphi_n(\mathbf{x}_I)}{\partial y} & \frac{\partial \varphi_n(\mathbf{x}_I)}{\partial y} \end{bmatrix} \tag{20}$$

$$\mathbf{H} = \begin{bmatrix} \varphi_1(\mathbf{x}_I) & 0 & \cdots & \varphi_n(\mathbf{x}_I) & 0 \\ 0 & \varphi_1(\mathbf{x}_I) & \cdots & 0 & \varphi_n(\mathbf{x}_I) \end{bmatrix} \tag{21}$$

3. Structural Topology Optimization

In computational mechanics, topological optimization is one of the most studied types of optimization due to its ability to generate more efficient and innovative designs. A topological optimization involves the strategic redistribution of material in a structure, resulting in shapes and geometries that are optimized to meet specific criteria, such as strength, stiffness, or other mechanical performance criteria. Assuming a standard topological optimization problem for a given structure, where the aim is to achieve a layout that is as rigid as possible while constraining the structure's mass, the problem can be formulated by minimizing the average compliance, with the material's weight constrained. The problem may be described as follows:

$$\begin{aligned} &Minimize\ C = \frac{1}{2} \cdot \mathbf{f}^T \cdot \mathbf{u} \\ &s.t.: W^* - \sum_{i=1}^{n} W_i x_i = 0 \\ &x_i = 0\ or\ 1 \end{aligned} \tag{22}$$

where C represents the average compliance of the structure, W^* the mass of the selected structure, and W_i the mass of node i. The design variable x_i indicates the presence ($x_i = 1$) or absence ($x_i = 0$) of a node in the layout of the defined domain.

Evolutionary computation is a search technique inspired by biological evolution, which uses selection, reproduction and variation to find optimized solutions to complex problems [33]. In relation to the more conventional optimization techniques, evolutionary techniques are more robust, exploratory and flexible, making them ideal for complex problems with challenging cost functions. Methods such as ESO (Evolutionary Structural Optimization), developed by Xie and Steven [34], have been widely applied to structural optimization problems in recent years [34]. The technique is based on the removal of material from a specific domain through an iterative process, material that is considered inefficient and redundant, in order to obtain a design that is considered optimal [35]. Despite the widespread use of the ESO method, this method presents problems and limitations that have led to the necessity of investigating new techniques. In order to improve the viability of the solutions obtained in the optimization, the need to create a bidirectional algorithm appears, which would allow not only the removal of material in order to eliminate areas that demonstrated low stress but also the addition of material to compensate for areas of high stress. This led to the creation of the bidirectional evolutionary structural optimization method, or BESO (Bi-Directional Evolutionary Structural Optimization), a method inspired not only by the material removal capabilities of ESO but also by the additive material capabilities of AESO [36], an additive evolutionary structural optimization method (Addition Evolutionary Structural Optimization), which allows for a more careful search of the design domain while also offering a superior ability to find the global minimum [37].

An elasto-static analysis step initiates each optimization iteration, returning the displacement, strain, and stress fields. As such, it is possible to calculate the equivalent von Mises stress for each integration point, as well as the cubic average of the von Mises stress field, which serves as a reference to help detecti sudden stress changes. With a high value of stress, the cubic average is highly affected. Meanwhile, with low values of stress, the average is practically unaltered.

$$\overline{\sigma}(\mathbf{x}_I) = \sqrt{\frac{(\sigma_{xx} - \sigma_{yy})^2 + (\sigma_{yy} - \sigma_{zz})^2 + (\sigma_{zz} - \sigma_{xx})^2 + 6(\tau_{xy}^2 + \tau_{yz}^2 + \tau_{zx}^2)}{2}} \quad (23)$$

$$\overline{\sigma}_{cube} = \sqrt[3]{\frac{1}{n_Q} \sum_{i=1}^{n_Q} \overline{\sigma}(\mathbf{x}_I)^3} \quad (24)$$

Next, a penalty system is applied in order to describe and attribute a specific parameter, in this specific case the density, to each integration point. In this work, the interval values for the penalty are assumed to be $\xi \in [10^{-3}, 1]$, where 1 represents the rewarded domains, or solid material, and 10^{-3} the penalized domain, or removed material. The BESO procedure performance depends on the reward ratio, α_R, and the penalization ratio, α_P. The $n_Q^{\alpha_R} = \alpha_R \cdot n_Q$ integration points with the highest $\sigma(\mathbf{x}_I)$ and the $n_Q^{\alpha_P} = \alpha_P \cdot n_Q$ integration points with the lowest $\sigma(\mathbf{x}_I)$ are identified. The $n_Q^{\alpha_R}$ points are rewarded with $\xi(\mathbf{x}_I) = 1$, while the $n_Q^{\alpha_P}$ points are penalized with $\xi(\mathbf{x}_I) = 10^{-3}$. Each node $\mathbf{x}_I$ is then assigned a penalty parameter $\eta(\mathbf{x}_i)$. For each integration point $\mathbf{x}_I$, the closest nodes update their penalty values with $\eta(\mathbf{x}_i)^{new} = 0.5(\eta(\mathbf{x}_i)^{old} + \xi(\mathbf{x}_I))$. After updating all nodes, the penalty parameters for each integration point are recalculated in order to filter and smooth the selected penalty parameters using the interpolation function $\xi(\mathbf{x}_I) = \sum_{i=1}^{n} \varphi_i(\mathbf{x}_I) \cdot \eta(\mathbf{x}_i)$, where n is the number of nodes inside the analyzed influence domain of $\mathbf{x}_I$, and $\varphi(\mathbf{x}_I)$ is the shape function vector of the integration point $\mathbf{x}_I$. At the end of the first iteration, some ξ values differ from one, indicating the absence of material. The process can then proceed to the next iteration. In iteration j, the penalty parameters ξ will be used to modify the material constitutive matrix. Consequently, the penalized constitutive material matrix $c_p(\mathbf{x}_I) = \xi(\mathbf{x}_I) \cdot c(\mathbf{x}_I)$ is calculated. In the following iteration j, the stiffness matrix is calculated, using $c_p(\mathbf{x}_I)$ instead of $c(\mathbf{x}_I)$. The same steps follow, and a new equivalent von Mises stress field is obtained. Through it, the new cubic average stress is calculated, and the comparison $\sigma_{cubic}^{j} \geq \delta \cdot \sigma_{cubic}^{j-1}$ is made. If the condition is true, the integration points with $\xi(\mathbf{x}_I) > \lambda$ are rewarded with $\xi(\mathbf{x}_I) = 1$. The penalty parameters are recalculated, updating the material domain for the next iteration $j + 1$.

The structural optimization algorithm used in the present work is a BESO - inspired algorithm, developed for applications in the biomechanics field, namely bone-remodelling applications. In a relation known as Wolff's law, bone tissue directionality increases its stiffness in response to external applied loads [38]. In order to predict this behaviour, several researchers have developed laws based on observations and experimental tests able to predict bone behaviour based on the different load cases considered. The created models are the basis for computational bone analysis, and the model used affects the results of the simulations carried out. Various models have been established, ranging from the Pauwels' model [39] to other models with extra considerations or different approaches to the problem, such as the Corwin's [40] and Carter's [41].

Carter's model is identical to Pauwels' model in that it requires a mechanical stimulus for remodelling to occur. This stimulus is calculated based on the effective stress, which takes into account both the local stress and the bone density, as well as the number of load cycles to which the bone is subjected (represented by the exponent k). The higher the magnitude of stress, the stronger the stimulus for remodelling.

$$S_n \propto \sum_{i=1}^{l} m_i \, \overline{\sigma_i}^k \tag{25}$$

The model assumes that the applied stress acts as a built-in optimization tool. The goal is to achieve a balance between maximizing the structural integrity of the bone (strength) and minimizing its mass. This can be achieved by minimizing an objective function that mathematically represents this goal.

The model also offers the option of using stress or strain energy as the basis for optimization. Strain energy focuses on maximizing the bone's stiffness (resistance to bending), while stress focuses on optimizing the material's strength. By using strain energy, the model relates the apparent density of the bone to the local strain energy it experiences. This makes it possible to estimate the bone's density at the remodelling equilibrium, a state in which bone resorption and formation are balanced.

$$\rho_{app} \propto \left(\sum_{i=1}^{l} m_i \, U_i^k\right) \tag{26}$$

If the bone is under stress from several directions, the model combines the effects of each stress pattern in a single direction. This direction is referred to as the normal vector ($\mathbf{n}$) and represents the ideal alignment for the bone's internal support structures (trabeculae) for optimum strength. To calculate this ideal direction, the model considers the normal stress acting on the entire bone, which is specified in Equation (27).

$$\overline{\sigma_n}(n) = \left(\sum_{i=1}^{l} \frac{m_i}{\sum_{j=1}^{l}} \, \overline{\sigma}_{n_i}^k(\mathbf{n})\right)^{\frac{1}{k}} \tag{27}$$

The algorithm, originally developed for this work, was incorporated in the previous codes already programmed by the research team, which included a bone-remodelling model adapted for meshless methods developed by Belinha et al. [42]. This new approach assumes that a mechanical stimulus, adequately represented by stress and potentially strain metrics, serves as the key factor influencing the bone-tissue-remodelling process. A detailed description of the entire model can be found in the literature [13]. Through the described bone-remodelling procedure, the remodelling itself functions as a topological optimization algorithm. Thus, in each iteration, only the points with high/low values of energy deformation density optimize the density based on its mechanical stimulus. A detailed description of the procedure can be found in the literature [13]. Figure 3 presents a scheme of how the optimization topology algorithm inspired by the bone-remodelling flowchart would present the NNRPIM method. As the flowchart shows, the structural optimization algorithm applied in this work is iterative. Thus, in each iteration, for a given material distribution, the stiffness matrix is calculated and the variable fields are obtained (displacements, strains, and stresses). Then, the $N_Q \cdot \alpha_P$ integration points with lower stress levels have their material density reduced, which will reduce their mechanical properties (notice that N_Q is the total number of integration points and α_P is the penalization ratio, established in the beginning of the analysis). A similar procedure occurs for the $N_Q \cdot \alpha_R$ integration points a with a higher stress level; their material density will increase, which will increase their mechanical properties (where α_R is the reward ratio, established at the beginning of the analysis). Then, in the next iteration, the material distribution changes, leading to new variable fields and a consequent new remodelling scenario. The remodelling process ends when the average density of the model is lower than a threshold valued initially defined by the user. Since the FEM and NNRPIM formulations are different (from a mathematical point of view), for the same material model, they lead to different variable fields (very close, but different). Because the adopted optimization algorithm is iterative, and since the solution of the next iteration is dependent on the solution of the previous iteration, it is not straightforward that the FEM and NNRPIM analyses tend to the same solution.

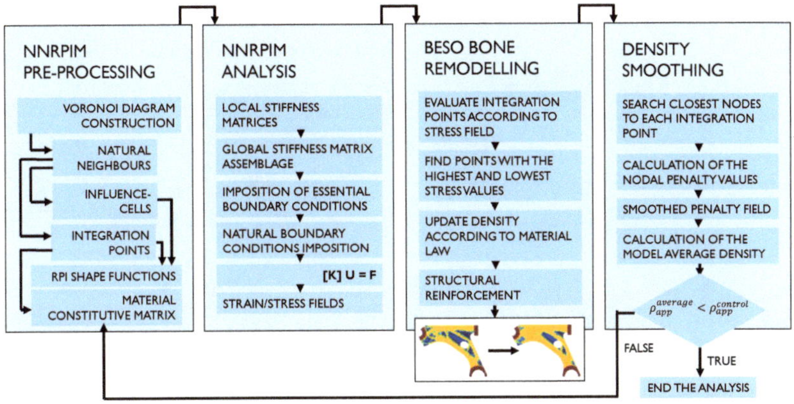

Figure 3. Flowchart of the topology optimization algorithm combined with the NNRPIM.

4. Numerical Results

This section presents the numerical results obtained in the optimization study of a vehicle's control arm; a comparison of the results obtained with NNRPIM, which involves the implementation of the numerical methodology presented previously; and FEM. For all numerical simulations, the dimensional approach to the numerical analysis was for plane stress, so the stress vector normal to the xy plane is equal to zero. In this work, the following formulations were used to perform the optimization analyses:

- FEM: three-node 2D linear triangular elements with constant strain;
- NNRPIM: second-degree influence cells, MQ-RBF shape parameters $c = 0.0001$ and $p = 0.9999$, constant polynomial basis, and 1×1 integration points per quadrilateral integration sub-cell.

4.1. Control Arm Optimization

In this subsection, the proposed optimization numerical technique is used to optimize the stiffness of a standard suspension control arm using the FEM and the NNRPIM as solvers. The BESO algorithm is inspired in a bone-remodelling model, allowing as output nonbinary density distributions. This approach avoids chess pattern solutions.

The parameters associated with the optimization algorithm were selected based on the literature [43,44]. The literature shows that that as the nodal mesh becomes denser, the solution becomes more complex, with more trusses and more micro-trusses [43,44]. Additionally, the solution complexity is also related to the penalization and reward ratios. For instance, a very dense nodal mesh assuming a large penalization ratio will lead to simpler solutions (lower number of trusses and almost no micro-trusses); at the same time, this solution will be very well defined (with the contours of the trusses being well defined). It was found that, for the nodal mesh density considered in this paper, the best penalization ratio is about 2% and 5% [43,44]. However, for denser meshes, a penalization ratio of 10%

is also admissible. Thus, taking into consideration the nodal mesh density of the models analyzed in this work, penalization ratios α_P of 5% and 10% will be considered, and the reward ratio will be kept at $\alpha_R = 1\%$.

The effective von Mises stress criterion will be used exclusively. The working procedure consisted of searching for a three-dimensional CAD model of a relatively functional component, where its geometry would be simplified to a two-dimensional format in Solidworks® Student Edition 2023 SP2.1 (Figure 4). Subsequently, the 2D sketch created was exported to FEMAP 2021.2 MP1 (student version), where its mesh was created and then imported into the code written by the authors.

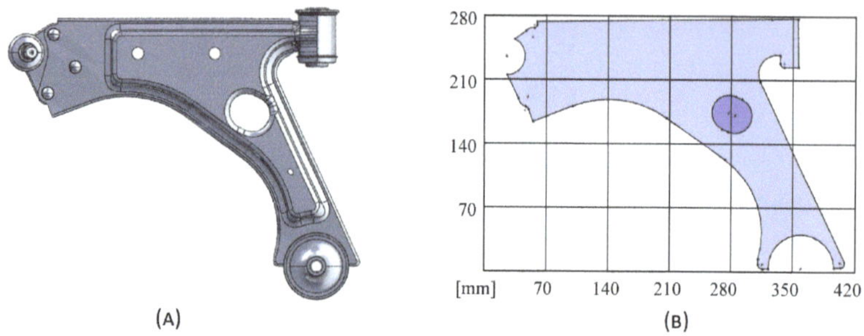

Figure 4. Standard suspension control arm models: (**A**) 3D CAD and (**B**) 2D CAD.

Four meshes were built, corresponding to four different case studies that will be analysed: a mesh without the arm's characteristic perforation, a mesh with the perforation, and the respective versions created by dividing sections of the arm to avoid reducing the density of the material in the areas with applied boundary conditions (Figure 5).

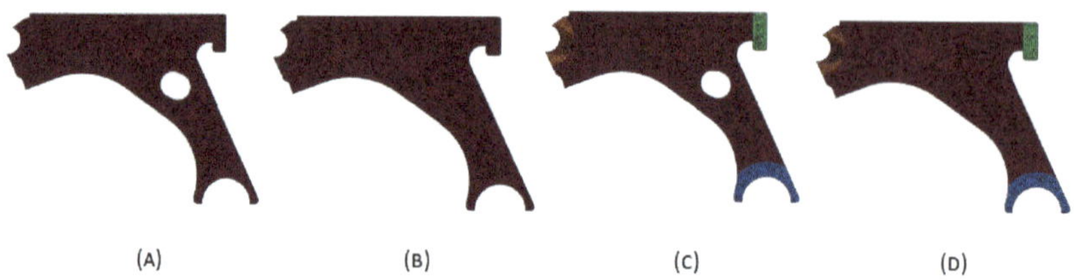

Figure 5. Adopted nodal discretizations of the solid domain. (**A**) Model D1—discretization with central perforation. (**B**) Model D2—discretization of the solid model without perforation. (**C**) Model D3—discretization of the model with central perforation, assuming remodelling domain constraints. (**D**) Model D4—discretization of the solid model (without perforation) with remodelling domain constraints.

The purely academic material properties considered were as follows: Young's modulus $E = 1$ MPa and Poisson's ratio $\nu = 0.3$. Since the variable fields (displacement, strain, and stress fields) are obtained assuming a material linear-elastic behaviour, and only small strains are considered, the stress field does not depend on the Young's modulus. Thus, the solution obtained using these purely academic material properties is equal to the solution obtained with any other positive Young's modulus value. The essential and natural boundary conditions presented in Figure 6 were assumed, allowing us to simulate the displacement constrains and external loads of the control arm. At the circular surface, a distributed load of $q = 1$ N/mm was applied. The described boundary conditions simulate bending (flexion) of the analysed component, a common mechanical behaviour experienced during its operation.

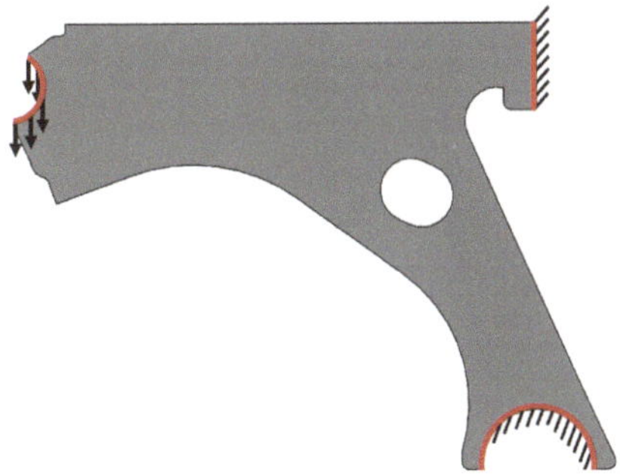

Figure 6. Schematic representation of the natural and essential boundary conditions considered.

The obtained topologies for the different meshes and control arm arrangements considered are presented in Tables 1–4. In each one of these tables, is possible to find the FEM and NNRPIM results, obtained at distinct iterations. Thus, in the first two lines of the tables, the FEM and NNRPIM results obtained for a penalization ratio of $\alpha_R = 5\%$ are presented. Notice that the mass obtained for each iteration (m_i) decreases as the remodelling procedure evolves and the iteration increases. In the last two lines of the tables, the results obtained for both FEM and NNRPIM (considering $\alpha_P = 10\%$) are shown. The colormap of the figures included in the tables corresponds to the volume fraction distribution and follows the corresponding colorbar shown in each table.

Recalling the flowchart in Figure 3, in each iteration using FEM or NNRPIM, the displacement field is obtained; then, the strain and stress fields are calculated, and the von Mises stress field is defined. With the von Mises stress field, it is possible to decide which material points (integration points) will be remodelled. Thus, $\alpha_P\%$ integration points (with lower stress levels) will reduce their volume fraction (and consequently their mechanical properties), and $\alpha_R\%$ integration points (with higher stress levels) will increase their volume fraction and mechanical properties. Atthe end of each iteration, based in this information, the volume fraction of each material point is actualized, leading to a transient material map. In Tables 1–4, it is possible to visualize the modification of the material map, where the results of only four iterations (three intermediary interesting iterations and the last iteration of the analysis) are presented.

The analysis of the design solutions revealed that the perforation in the control arm corresponds to a null stress zone. Situated in the primary zone of material removal, this perforation serves solely to reduce the component's overall mass. Therefore, the perforation has no impact on the mechanism's functionality. The solutions obtained reflect that there is the possibility of more drastic material removal in relation to the original removal. The obtained topologies reveal highly binary structures (topologies) across the entire density field. It is possible to observe that $\alpha_P = 5\%$ yielded the most successful solutions. These solutions showcased a clear improvement and connection between generated sections, particularly evident in the initial and final iterations of the NNRPIM method. A difference between the FEM and NNRPIM solutions was observed in the final iteration volume fraction.

Table 1. Material remodelling solutions obtained with the discretized model D1. For each analysis, four iterations are represented, and the iteration number and corresponding mass m_r (with respect to the initial mass m_i) are presented.

α_P	Method	Solution			
		Volume fraction  0 … 1			
5%	FEM	8 it. $m_r = 0.8606 m_i$ 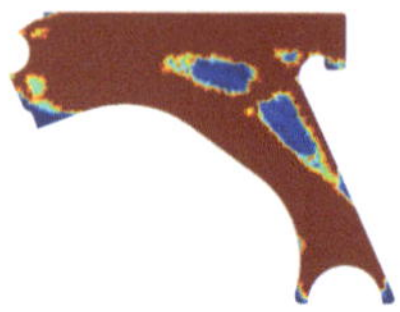	15 it. $m_r = 0.7700 m_i$ 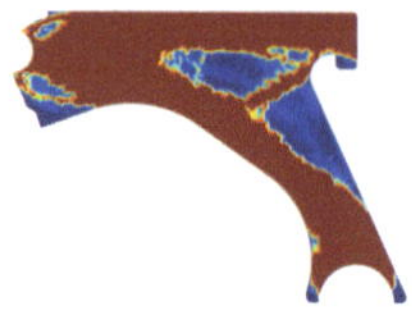	24 it. $m_r = 0.6373 m_i$ 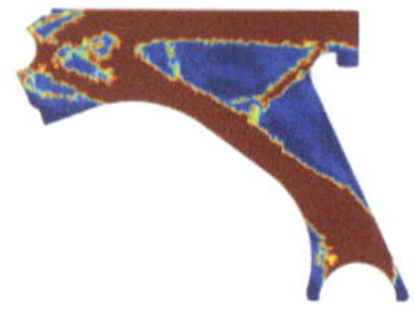	33 it. $m_r = 0.5189 m_i$ 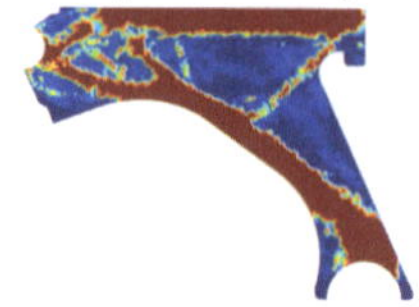
5%	NNRPIM	8 it. $m_r = 0.8824 m_i$ 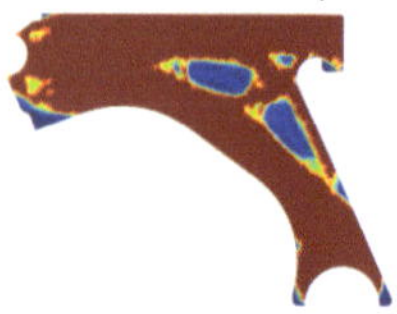	15 it. $m_r = 0.7718 m_i$ 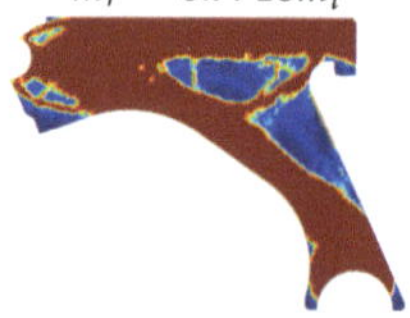	24 it. $m_r = 0.6441 m_i$ 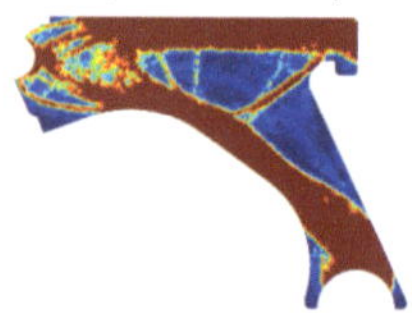	33 it. $m_r = 0.5420 m_i$ 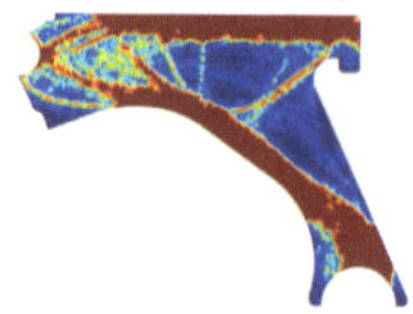
10%	FEM	4 it. $m_r = 0.9012 m_i$ 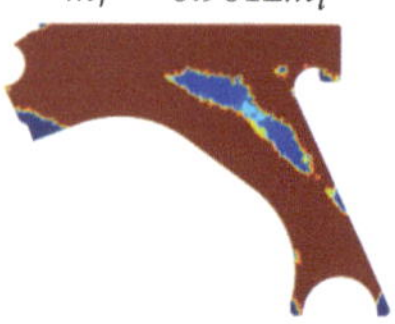	9 it. $m_r = 0.7203 m_i$ 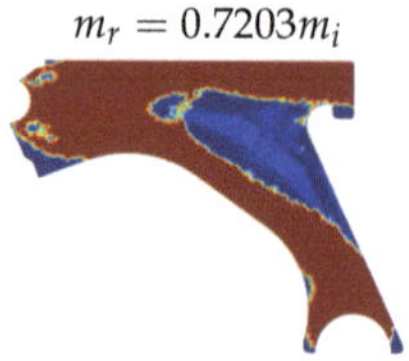	13 it. $m_r = 0.6158 m_i$ 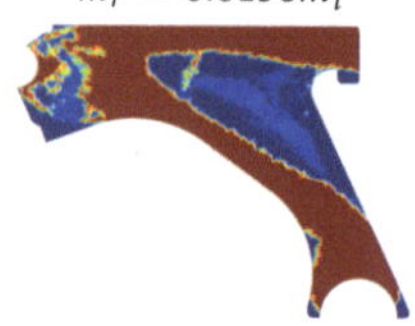	18 it. $m_r = 0.4984 m_i$ 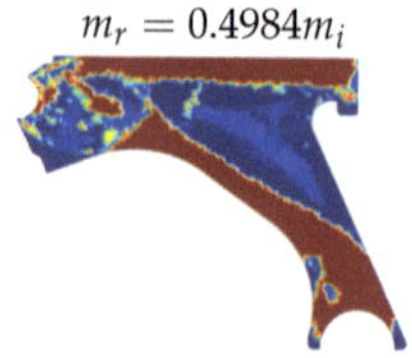
10%	NNRPIM	4 it. $m_r = 0.9047 m_i$ 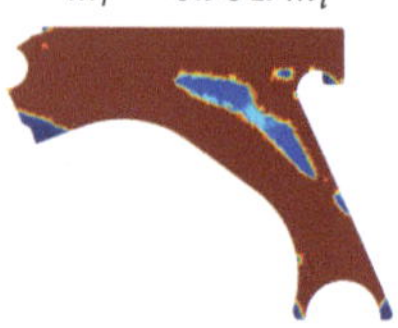	9 it. $m_r = 0.7240 m_i$ 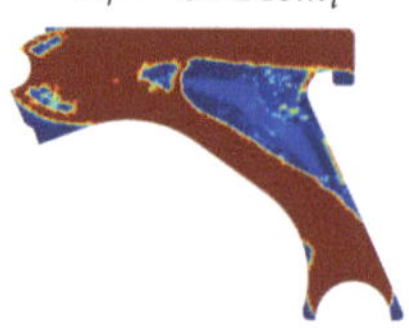	13 it. $m_r = 0.6219 m_i$ 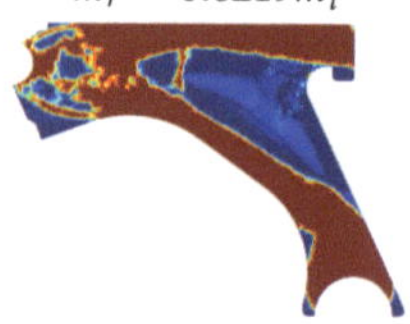	18 it. $m_r = 0.5086 m_i$ 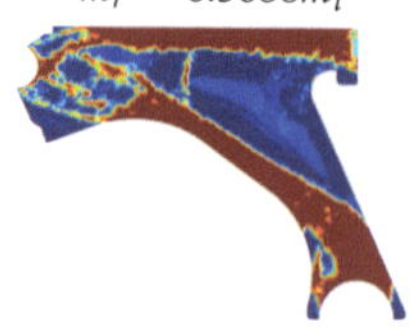

Table 2. Material remodelling solutions obtained with the discretized model D2. For each analysis, four iterations are represented, and the iteration number and corresponding mass m_r (with respect to the initial mass m_i) are presented.

<table>
<tr><th>α_P</th><th>Method</th><th colspan="4">Solution</th></tr>
<tr><td></td><td></td><td colspan="4">Volume fraction

0 … 1</td></tr>
<tr><td rowspan="2">5%</td><td>FEM</td><td>8 it.
$m_r = 0.8776m_i$
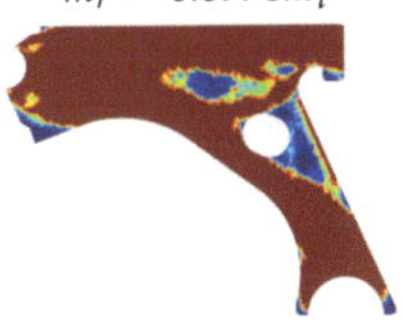</td><td>15 it.
$m_r = 0.7712m_i$
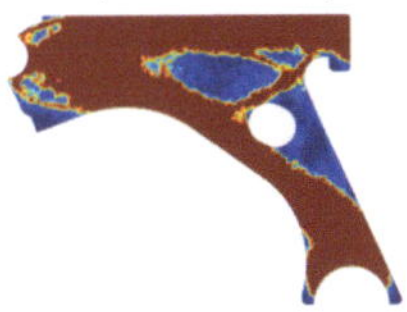</td><td>24 it.
$m_r = 0.6550m_i$
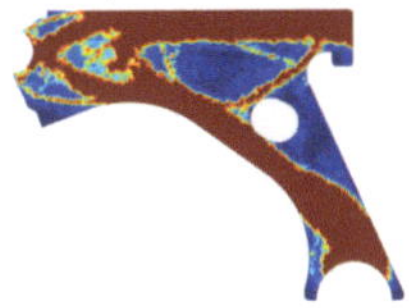</td><td>33 it.
$m_r = 0.5593m_i$
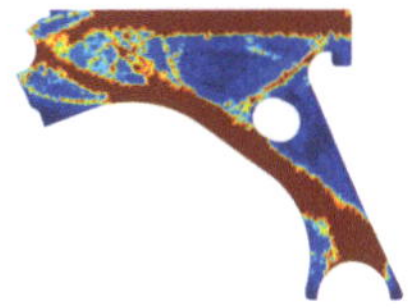</td></tr>
<tr><td>NNRPIM</td><td>8 it.
$m_r = 0.8753m_i$
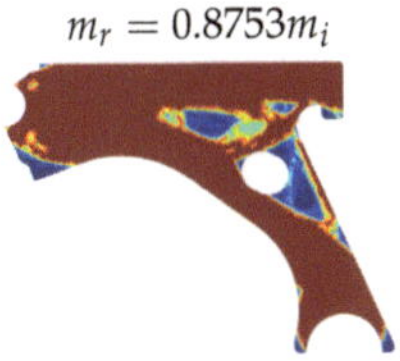</td><td>15 it.
$m_r = 0.7666m_i$
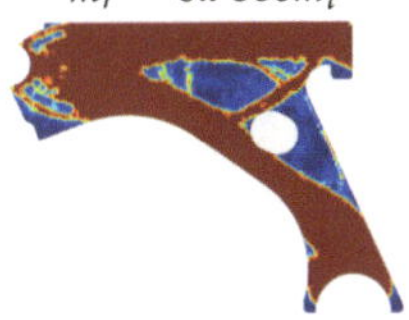</td><td>24 it.
$m_r = 0.6378m_i$
</td><td>33 it.
$m_r = 0.5337m_i$
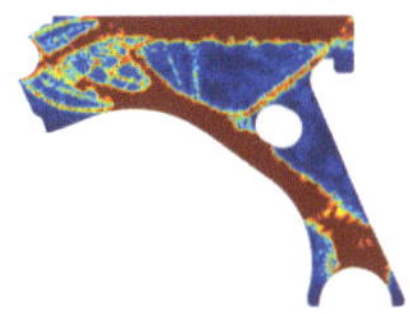</td></tr>
<tr><td rowspan="2">10%</td><td>FEM</td><td>4 it.
$m_r = 0.9024m_i$
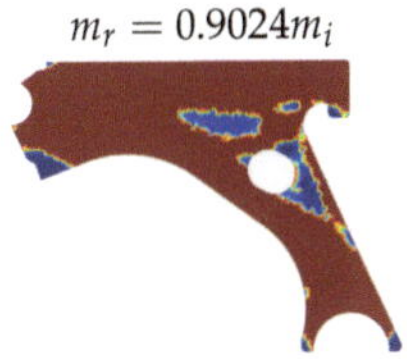</td><td>9 it.
$m_r = 0.7208m_i$
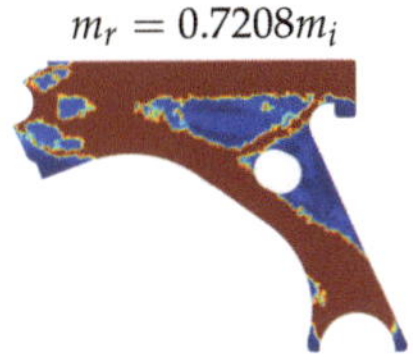</td><td>13 it.
$m_r = 0.6216m_i$
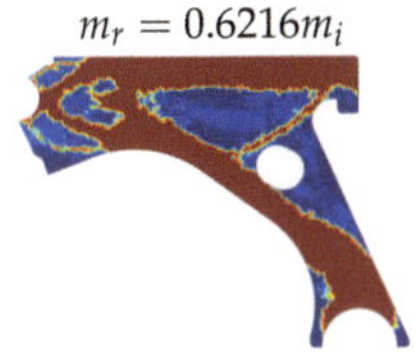</td><td>18 it.
$m_r = 0.5081m_i$
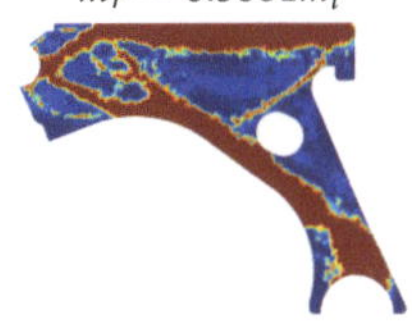</td></tr>
<tr><td>NNRPIM</td><td>4 it.
$m_r = 0.9022m_i$
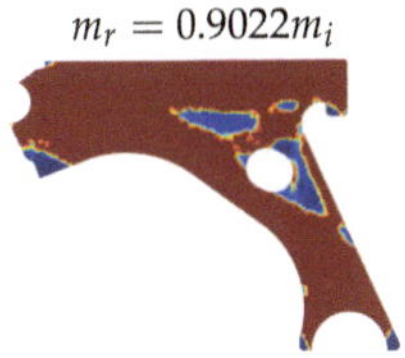</td><td>9 it.
$m_r = 0.7223m_i$
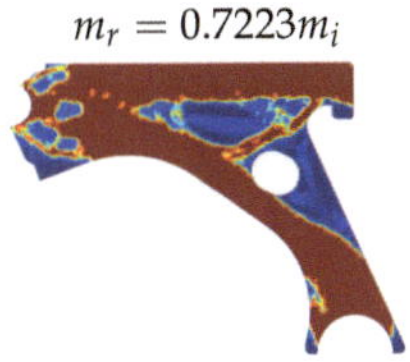</td><td>13 it.
$m_r = 0.6226m_i$
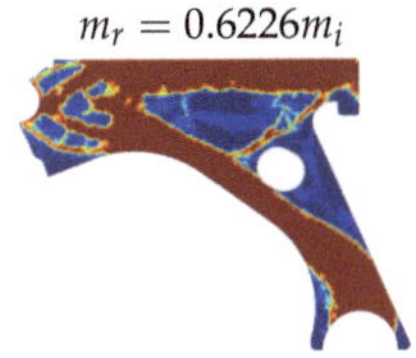</td><td>18 it.
$m_r = 0.5068m_i$
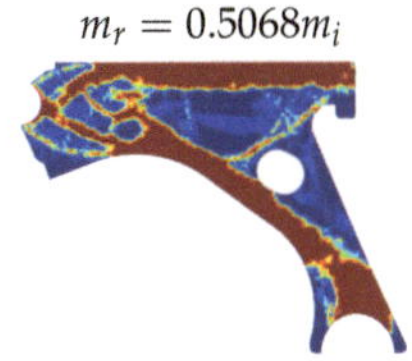</td></tr>
</table>

Table 3. Material remodelling solutions obtained with the discretized model D3. For each analysis, four iterations are represented, and the iteration number and corresponding mass m_r (with respect to the initial mass m_i) are presented.

α_P	Method	Solution			
		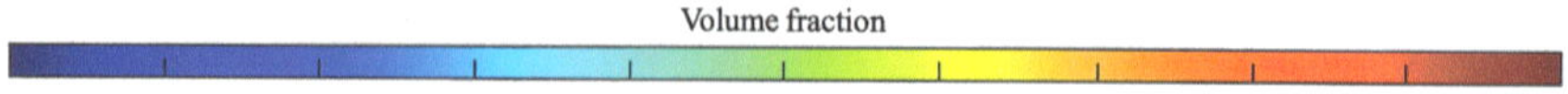			
5%	FEM	8 it. $m_r = 0.8811m_i$ 	15 it. $m_r = 0.7853m_i$ 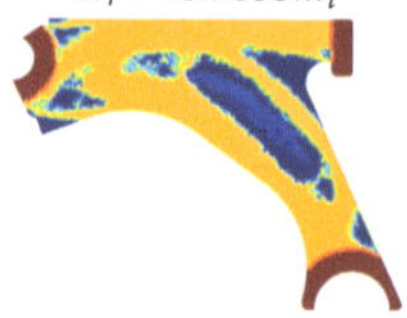	24 it. $m_r = 0.6557m_i$ 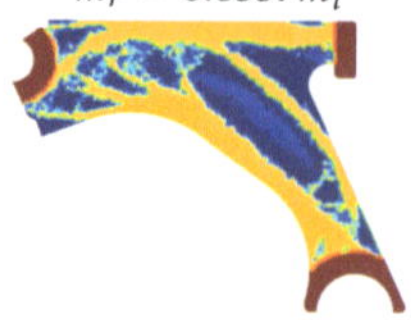	30 it. $m_r = 0.6049m_i$ 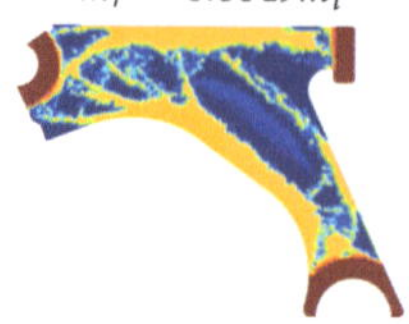
	NNRPIM	8 it. $m_r = 0.8801m_i$ 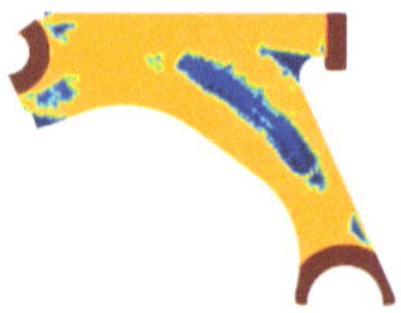	15 it. $m_r = 0.7872m_i$ 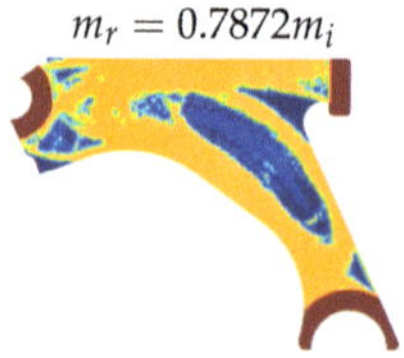	24 it. $m_r = 0.6696m_i$ 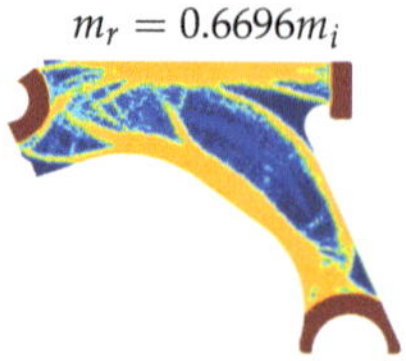	30 it. $m_r = 0.6206m_i$ 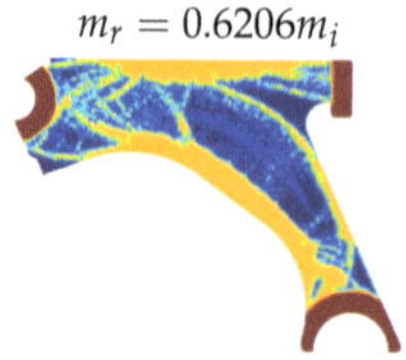
10%	FEM	4 it. $m_r = 0.9154m_i$ 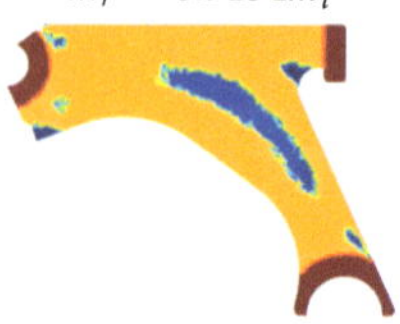	9 it. $m_r = 0.7482m_i$ 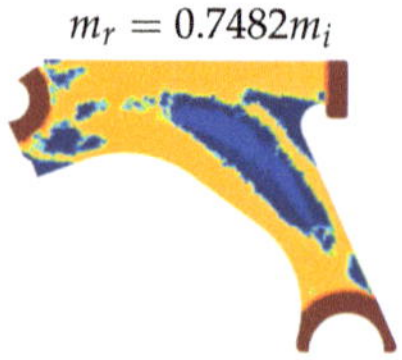	13 it. $m_r = 0.6520m_i$ 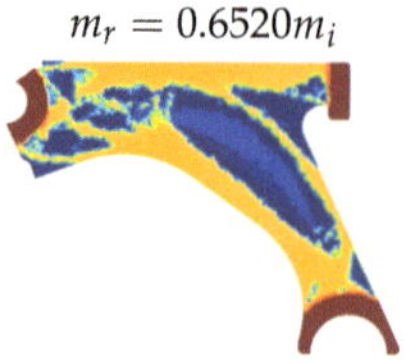	17 it. $m_r = 0.5939m_i$ 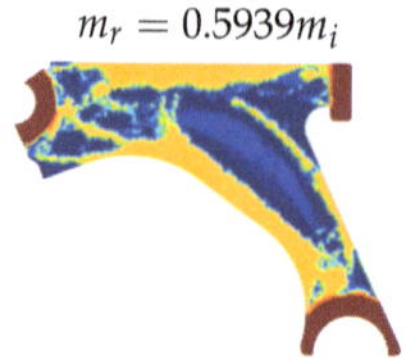
	NNRPIM	4 it. $m_r = 0.9124m_i$ 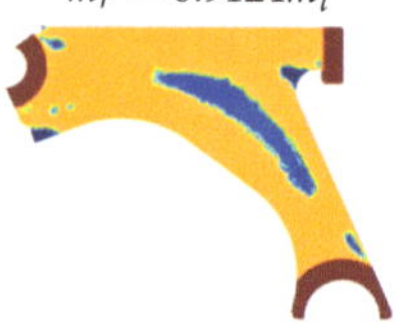	9 it. $m_r = 0.7446m_i$ 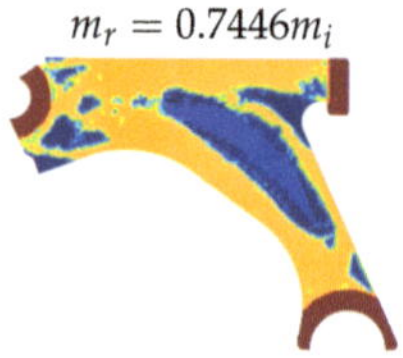	13 it. $m_r = 0.6453m_i$ 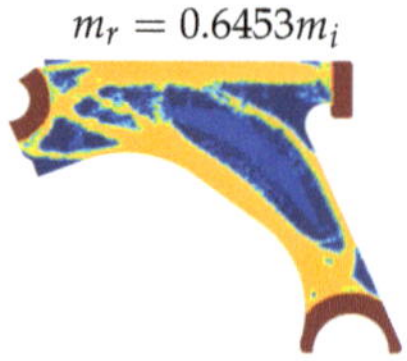	17 it. $m_r = 0.5888m_i$ 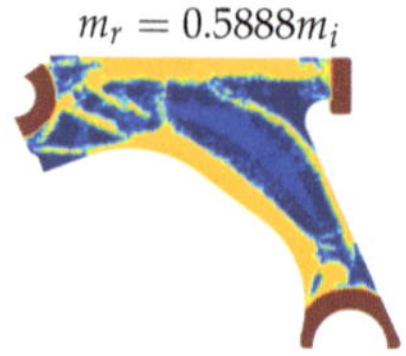

Table 4. Material remodelling solutions obtained with the discretized model D4. For each analysis, four iterations are represented, and the iteration number and corresponding mass m_r (with respect to the initial mass m_i) are presented.

α_P	Method	Solution			
		Volume fraction  0 1			
5%	FEM	8 it. $m_r = 0.8776m_i$ 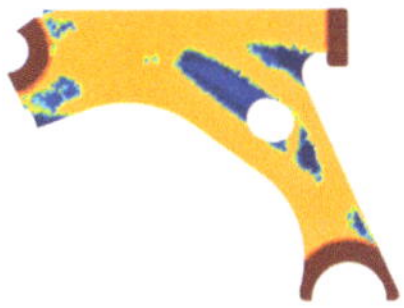	15 it. $m_r = 0.7712m_i$ 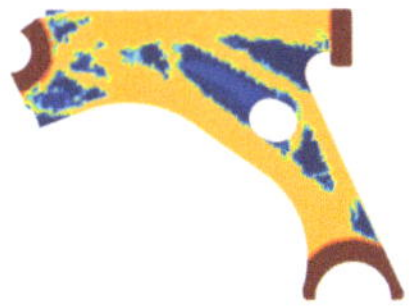	24 it. $m_r = 0.6550m_i$ 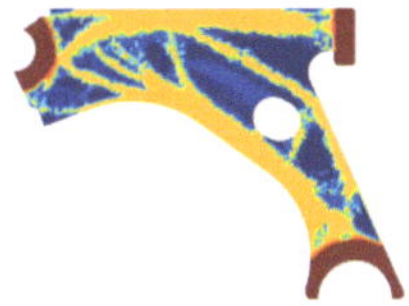	30 it. $m_r = 0.5593m_i$ 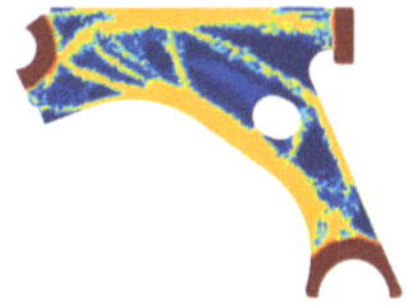
	NNRPIM	8 it. $m_r = 0.8753m_i$ 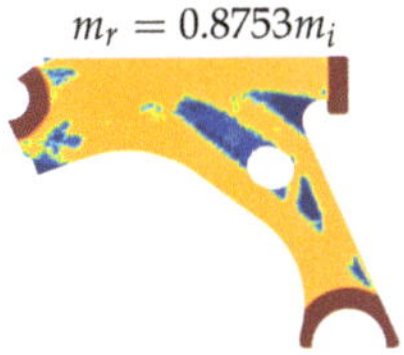	15 it. $m_r = 0.7666m_i$ 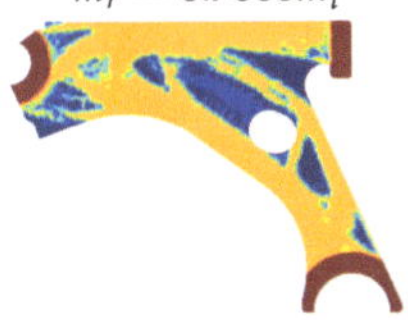	24 it. $m_r = 0.6378m_i$ 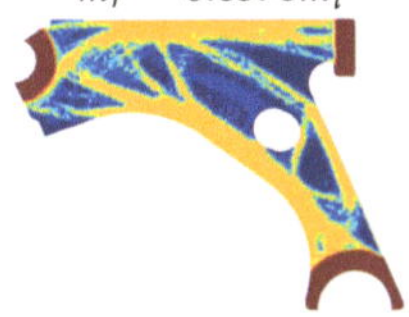	30 it. $m_r = 0.5337m_i$ 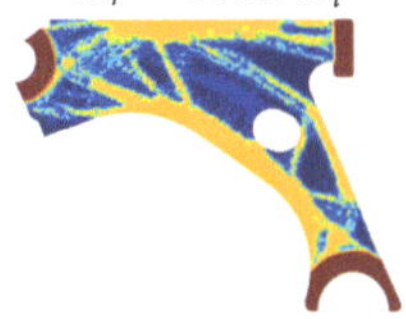
10%	FEM	4 it. $m_r = 0.9024m_i$ 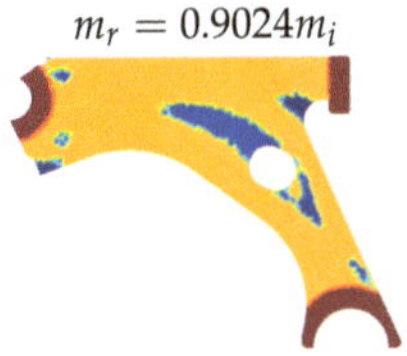	9 it. $m_r = 0.7208m_i$ 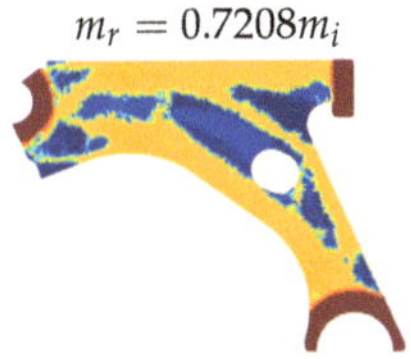	13 it. $m_r = 0.6216m_i$ 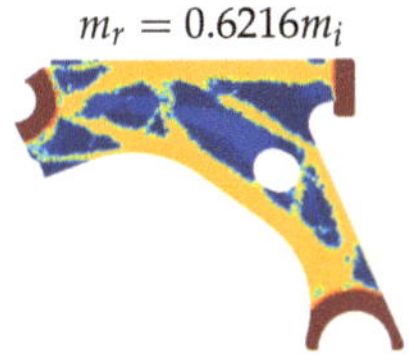	17 it. $m_r = 0.5081m_i$ 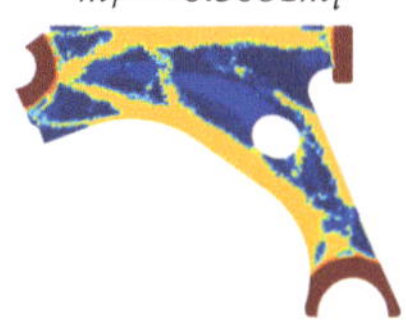
	NNRPIM	4 it. $m_r = 0.9022m_i$ 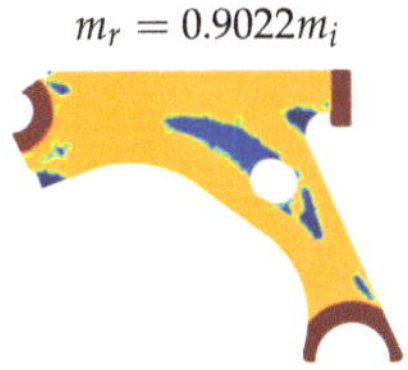	9 it. $m_r = 0.7223m_i$ 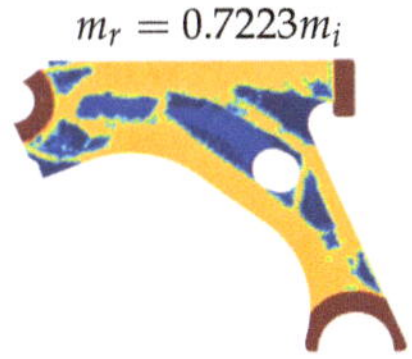	13 it. $m_r = 0.6225m_i$ 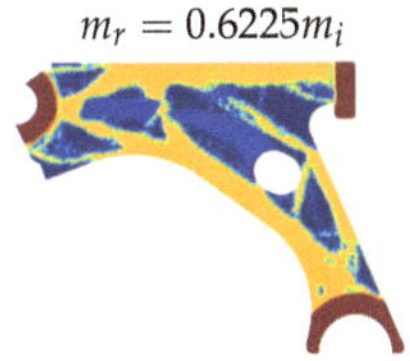	17 it. $m_r = 0.5068m_i$ 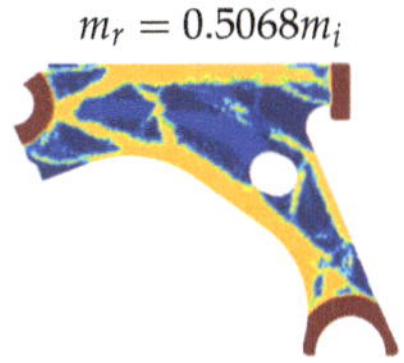

For a more practical and direct comparison, two solutions from each method (FEM and NNRPIM) were separated from Table 4. Figure 7 shows two solutions of the previously presented optimization of the control arm (corresponding to the model with no inside perforation) with density reduction restriction in the boundary condition zone, for $\alpha_P = 5\%$. The iteration chosen to analyse the final result of the algorithm used was the very last one.

Visually, the superior truss connection and the creation of a greater number of intermediate densities in the NNRPIM are noticeable. Both these aspects would be potentially important factors in additive manufacturing production, since they are both prevalent to the component's structural performance.

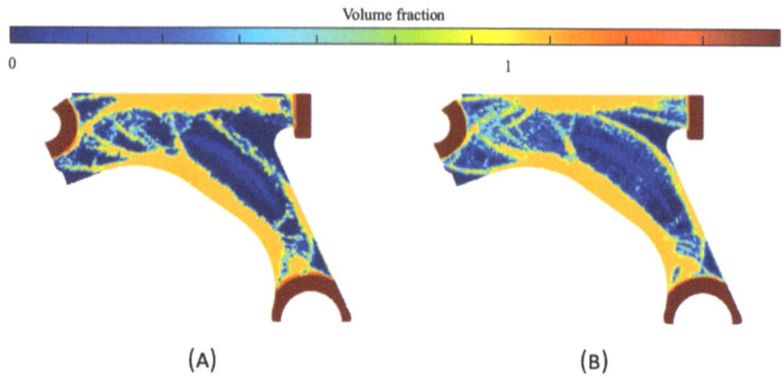

Figure 7. Remodelling material solutions obtained at iteration 30, with discretization D4 (assuming a density reduction restriction in the boundary conditions sections), for $\alpha_P = 5\%$ with (**A**) the FEM method and (**B**) the NNRPIM method.

4.2. Topology Design and Structural Analysis

Three models based on the previously obtained optimized solutions were built Figure 8A,C,D. These three models do not resemble the designs used in the automotive industry, which prefers designs with less sharp angles in the inner voids to reduce local stress concentrations. Generally, the industrial automotive solutions include circular holes, which are able to reduce the stress concentration phenomenon [45]. Therefore, a commonly used design for the control arm was considered as well, as Figure 8B shows. Model 1 is inspired ny the solutions assuming a central perforation (Table 4). Model 3 is a reinforced version of the solutions suggested in Table 3. Model 4 is based on model 3 with a modified boundary contour. The thickness of the boundary contour is increased by 50% (1.5 times the nominal thickness) relatively to the baseline model, using a 6 mm offset in relation to the outer delineation of the model.

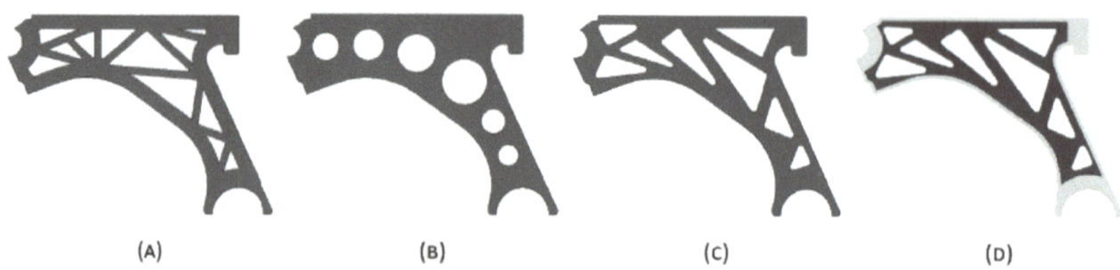

Figure 8. Constructed models for the linear elasticity analysis. (**A**) Model 1, (**B**) Model 2, (**C**) Model 3 and (**D**) Model 4.

Then, to each model of Figure 8, the essential and natural boundary conditions described in Figure 6 were imposed and static linear analyses were performed.

Table 5 provides the displacement and von Mises stress distributions calculated using FEM and NNRPIM for the fully solid model. A comparison of the two methods shows reduced differences in the displacement and von Mises effective stress fields.

It is possible to observe that model 2 demonstrated the best mechanical performance, justified by the lower von Mises stress and higher stiffness than the other models designed and an even higher specific stiffness than the solid arm. These results support initial expectations, as the removal of material in a circular shape allows for a more uniform distribution of stresses in the structure. As a result, the stress is not concentrated at specific points, which leads to a reduction in the risk of structural failure and an increase in the overall stiffness of the part.

Table 5. Variable fields of interest (displacement and von Mises stress) obtained for the solid control arm.

	FEM	NNRPIM
σ_{VM}	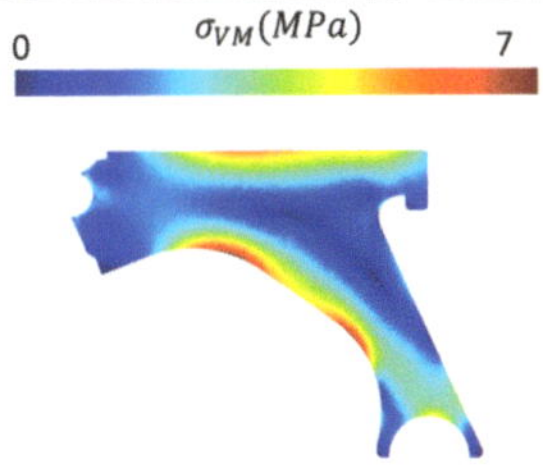	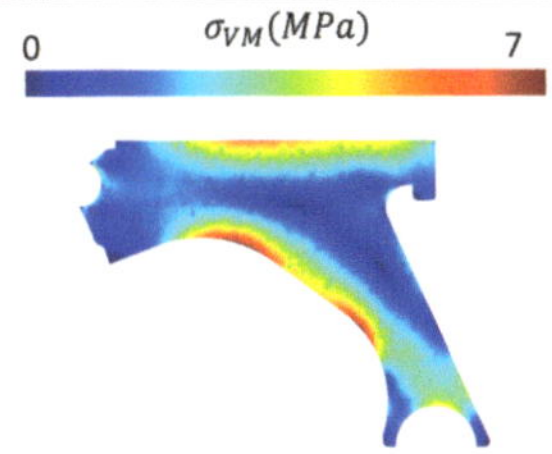
$\|\|u\|\|$	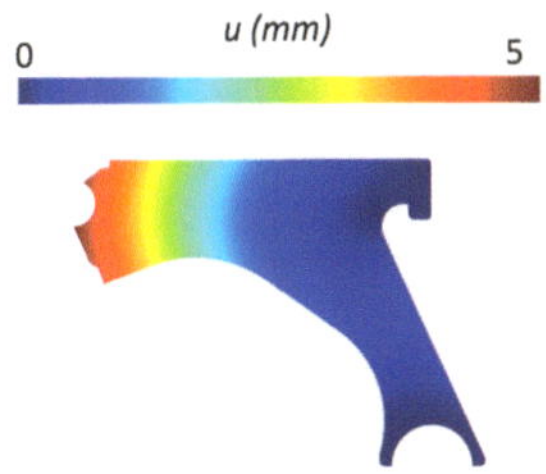	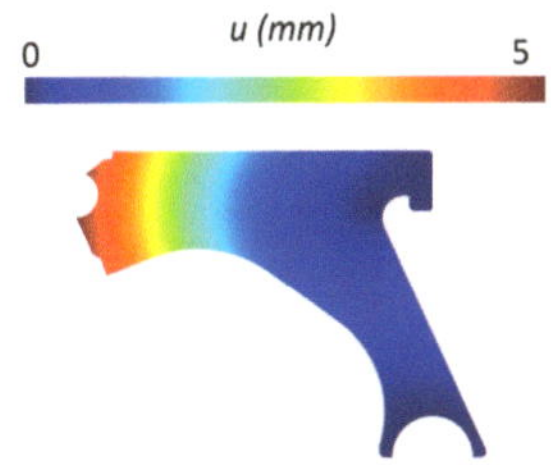

Triangular material removal leaves behind a pattern resembling interconnected triangles. This process effectively creates a truss-like structure that is more efficient in transferring loads, as well as easier to manufacture. Regarding the behaviour of models 1, 3 and 4, based on triangular material removal, model 4 presented the higher stiffness. However, this stiffness is due to the increased thickness of the outside struts, which has an effect on specific thickness as it increases less than models 1 and 3. Between model 1 and 3, the specific stiffnesses are equal. However, a distinction between both can be made regarding the smoothness of the obtained stress fields. It can be seen in Tables 6 and 7 that the stresses are only slightly better distributed in Model 3, which presents a lower peak von Mises stress.

The displacement and von Mises stress fields are shown in Tables 6 and 7 for the FEM and NNRPIM, respectively. Comparing both tables, the two methods present very similar solutions. Recall that the objective function of the adopted optimization procedure, Equation (3), aims to reduce the mass and at the same time maximize the stiffness of the mechanical component (by the minimization of the structural compliance). Therefore, in Table 8, the mass and directional stiffness of each model are calculated with the results obtained with both methods. The directional stiffness K is calculated with

$$K = \frac{1}{n} \cdot \sum_{i=1}^{n} \frac{f_i}{d_i}, \tag{28}$$

where n is the number of nodes along the natural neighbour, f_i is the force applied at node n_i of the natural boundary in direction Oy, and d_I is the displacement obtained at the same node n_i in the same direction Oy.

Compared to FEM analysis, the NNRPIM solutions obtained for models 2, 3, and 4 exhibited higher maximum von Mises stress values. Similarly, FEM displayed slightly lower displacements compared to NNRPIM, suggesting a stiffer solution. The FEM formulation used is the constant-strain triangular element, and the literature shows that this formulation produces stiffer results for bending problems (such as the one analysed in this work) [46]. Nonetheless, both these discrepancies are very small, allowing us to conclude that both techniques produce similar results.

Finally, both methods are quantitatively compared in Table 9, which shows the relative difference between the interest metrics calculated through the FEM and NNRPIM. The relative difference between methodologies is calculated by

$$\mathcal{D} = \frac{\zeta_{NNRPIM} - \zeta_{FEM}}{\zeta_{FEM}}, \tag{29}$$

where ζ_{NNRPIM} is the variable value obtained with NNRPIM and ζ_{FEM} is the same variable value obtained by FEM. Table 9 shows that the relative differences between both methods are very reduced. Regarding the displacement, the relative difference is generally about 1.5%, being even lower in model 1 (0.33%). Concerning the maximum von Mises stress, the relative difference shows more variation, being low for the solid model and higher for models 2, 3 and 4. For the relative difference of the directional stiffness, it is interesting to observe that FEM and NNRPIM produce similar results, and that the relative difference between all the other models is very low (between 1.48% and 3.57%).

Table 6. Obtained variable fields of interest (displacements and von Mises stresses) with FEM, for each of the four analysed models.

	Model 1	Model 2	Model 3	Model 4
σ_{VM}	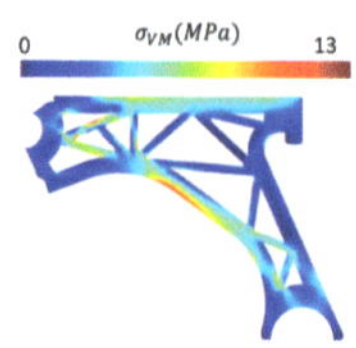	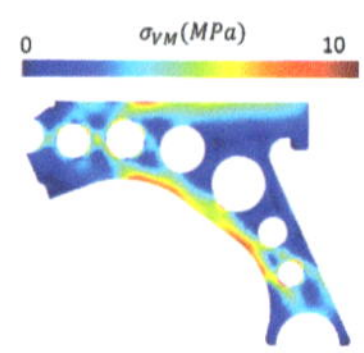	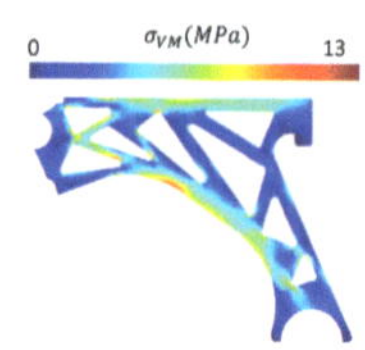	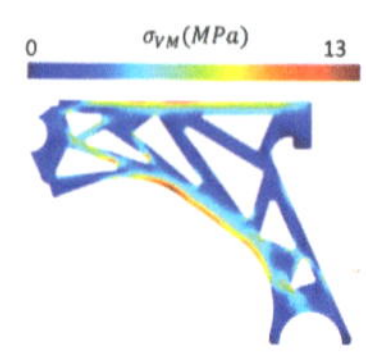
$\|\|u\|\|$	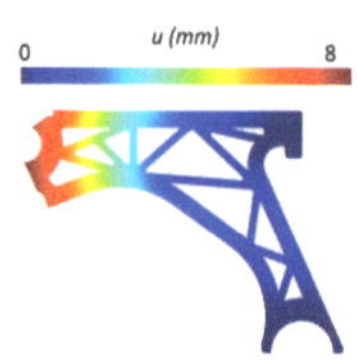	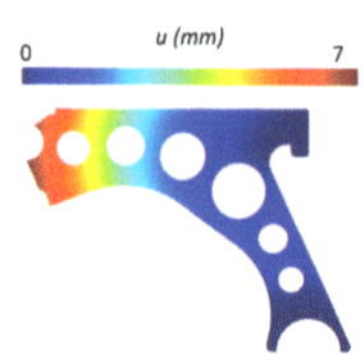	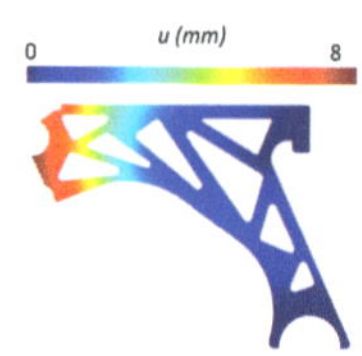	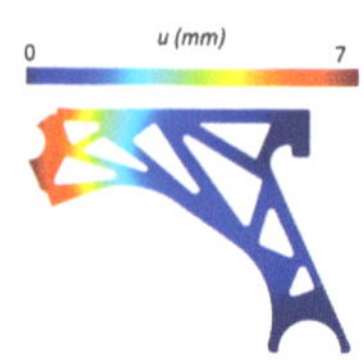

Table 7. Obtained interest variable fields (displacements and von Mises stresses) with NNRPIM, for each of the four analysed models.

	Model 1	Model 2	Model 3	Model 4
σ_{VM}	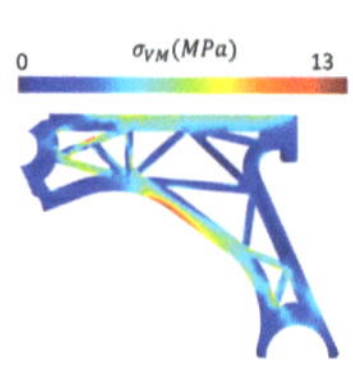	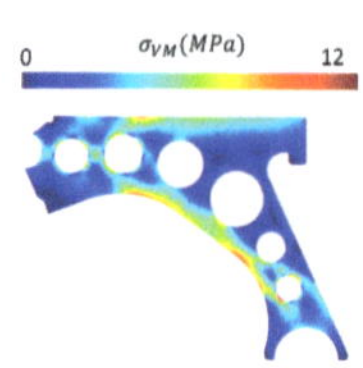	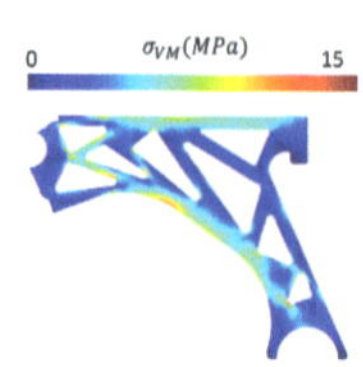	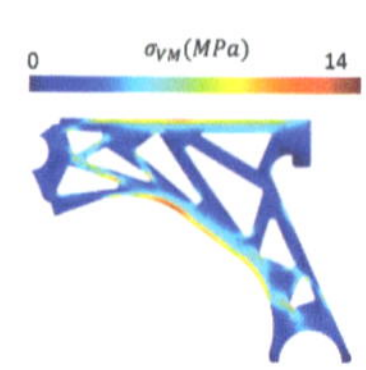
$\|\|u\|\|$	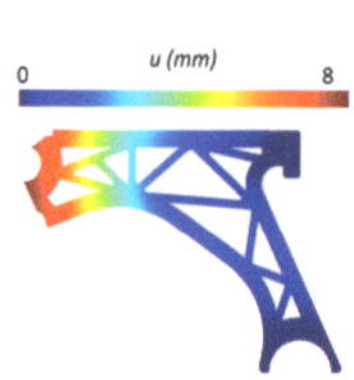	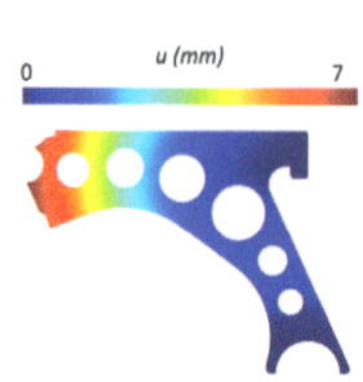	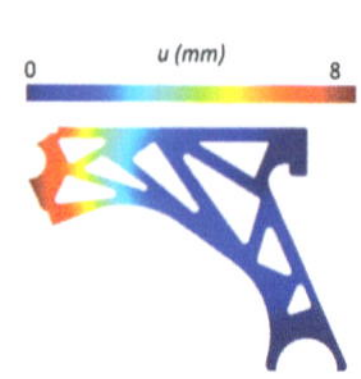	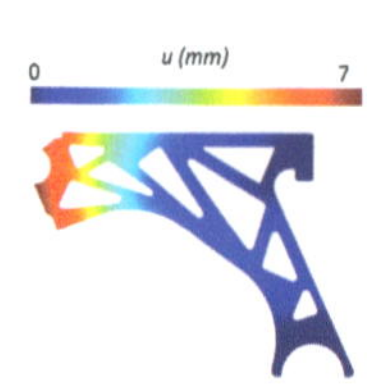

Table 8. Results obtained with the model of the solid structure and with the proposed designed models M1 to M4.

		Solid Control Arm	Model 1	Model 2	Model 3	Model 4
$V_f^{\%}$ (%)		100	70.06 (−29.94 %)	76.78 (−23.22 %)	68.50 (−31.50 %)	81.70 (−18.30 %)
$\|\|u\|\|$ [mm]	FEM	5.408	8.505 (+57.27%)	7.422 (+37.24%)	8.689 (+60.67%)	7.165 (+32.49%)
	NNRPIM	5.495	8.477 (+54.27%)	7.537 (+37.16%)	8.821 (+60.53%)	7.389 (+34.47%)
σ_{max}^{VM} [MPa]	FEM	7.567	13.922 (+83.98%)	10.789 (+42.58%)	13.896 (+83.64%)	13.311 (+75.91%)
	NNRPIM	7.629	13.746 (+80.18%)	12.458 (+63.30%)	15.203 (+99.28%)	14.743 (+89.71%)
K [N/mm]	FEM	0.185	0.118 (−36.22%)	0.135 (−27.03%)	0.115 (−37.84%)	0.140 (−24.32%)
	NNRPIM	0.182	0.118 (−35.17%)	0.133 (−26.92%)	0.113 (−37.91%)	0.135 (−25.82%)
$K/V_f^{\%}$ [N/mm]	FEM	0.185	0.168 (−9.19%)	0.175 (−5.41%)	0.168 (−9.19%)	0.171 (−7.57%)
	NNRPIM	0.182	0.168 (−7.69%)	0.173 (−4.95%)	0.165 (−9.34%)	0.165 (−9.34%)

Table 9. Relative difference $\mathcal{D}$ between the critical variables calculated through FEM or NNRPIM.

	Solid	Model 1	Model 2	Model 3	Model 4
|u| [mm]	0.0161	−0.0033	0.0155	0.0152	0.0171
stress [MPa]	0.0082	−0.0126	0.1547	0.0941	0.1076
K [N/mm]	−0.0162	0.0000	−0.0148	−0.0174	−0.0357
Kf [N/mm]	−0.0162	0.0000	−0.0114	−0.0179	−0.0351

5. Conclusions

The focus of this work was the application of the NNRPIM, combined with a bi-evolutionary topological optimization algorithm, for the analysis of a standard automotive mechanical component. In parallel, a well-known FEM formulation was also used for comparison purposes. The analysed mechanical component was a standard suspension control arm, in which the 3D CAD was converted to a simplified two-dimensional layout in order to streamline and minimize the computational cost of the numerical simulations conducted.

When assessing the obtained solutions, it was noticeable that NNRPIM generated topologies with better truss connection and a higher number of intermediate densities (intricate bone-like trabecular distributions), features that would greatly benefit the mechanical performance of an hypothetical part manufactured by means of additive manufacturing. Subsequently, four designs were built based on a solution obtained from the previously mentioned algorithm, following material-removal approaches commonly applied in the automotive industry for the studied component: a model with a trussed design, a model with circular material removal, a model with triangular material removal, and a model equivalent to the previously mentioned, albeit with an increase in the boundary contour thickness to 1.5 times the nominal thickness of the remaining model. By means of an linear static analysis in the same conditions applied to the optimization algorithm, it was observable that the design based on circular material removal demonstrated the best stiffness and specific stiffness, proving the original hypothesis, since the circular shape allows for a more uniform distribution of stresses in the structure. This kind of solution is recurrent in the automotive industry, and the results presented show that this simple solution is efficient and practical. The trussed and triangular models exhibited similar behaviour, as the principle for their material removal is similar. Model 4 (reinforced at the contour), as expected, displayed a lower displacement, and consequently a higher stiffness, compared to model 3. However, as a result, its increase in mass and total volume led to a negligible difference in specific stiffness between models 3 and 4. There were minor discrepancies observed in the von Mises stress fields and maximum stress values obtained with FEM and NNRPIM. Similarly, small differences were observed in the displacement values, which can be attributed to the higher rigidity of triangular elements.

Regarding the relative difference between both formulations, the obtained results show that concerning the displacement, NNRPIM is able to produce results very close to FEM. For instance, for model 1, the relative difference is 0.33%, and for all the other models, the relative difference ranges between 1.52% and 1.71%. Regarding the maximum von Mises stress, the results show that the relative differences obtained for the solid model and model 1 are 0.82% and 1.26%, respectively, which are very close. However, for models 2, 3 and 4, the relative difference increases, ranging from 9.41% and 15.47%, indicating that some stress-concentration zones produce distinct von Mises stress values. The directional stiffness of both formulations is very close, ranging between 0% and 3.57%. These results reinforce the idea that NNRPIM is a valid numerical alternative to the FEM.

In other applications associated with remodelling and BESO algorithms, NNRPIM already proved to be efficient, delivering optimal solutions for automotive parts, such as wheels and brake pedals [44], or the development of new optimized functional materials [47] and their cellular foam structure [48]. In this work, it was shown again that NNRPIM is able to produce results with satisfactory similarity to FEM, indicating that it could represent a viable alternative to FEM topological optimization analyses. Future research directions on this topic will include the extension of the application to 3D analyses in order to include out-of-plane forces and torsion effects; the inclusion of functionally foam material (to fill the voids and reduce stress concentration phenomena) and its prototype production and experimental validation using 3D printing techniques; and the inclusion of artificial neural networks to surrogate the FEM/NNRPIM processing block, allowing for much faster computational analysis [49].

Author Contributions: Conceptualization, J.B. and A.P.; methodology, J.B. and A.P.; software, J.B. and A.P.; validation, J.B., C.O. and A.P.; formal analysis, J.B., C.O. and A.P.; investigation, J.B., C.O. and A.P.; resources, J.B. and A.P.; data curation, J.B., A.P. and C.O.; writing—original draft preparation, C.O.; writing—review and editing, J.B. and A.P.; visualization, J.B. and A.P.; supervision, J.B.; project administration, J.B.; funding acquisition, J.B. All authors have read and agreed to the published version of the manuscript.

Funding: This research received no external funding.

Institutional Review Board Statement: Not applicable.

Informed Consent Statement: Not applicable.

Data Availability Statement: The original contributions presented in the study are included in the article, further inquiries can be directed to the corresponding author.

Conflicts of Interest: The authors declare no conflicts of interest.

References

1. Oanta, E.; Raicu, A.; Menabil, B. Applications of the numerical methods in mechanical engineering experimental studies. *IOP Conf. Ser. Mater. Sci. Eng.* **2020**, *916*, 012074. [CrossRef]
2. Jones, D. Optimization in the Automotive Industry. In *Optimization and Industry: New Frontiers*; Springer: Boston, MA, USA, 2003. [CrossRef]

3. Witik, R.; Payet, J.; Michaud, V.; Ludwig, C.; Månson, J. Assessing the life cycle costs and environmental performance of lightweight materials in automobile applications. *Compos. Part A Appl. Sci. Manuf.* **2011**, *42*, 1694–1709. [CrossRef]
4. Matsimbi, M.; Nziu, P.K.; Masu, L.M.; Maringa, M. Topology Optimization of Automotive Body Structures: A review. *Int. J. Eng. Res. Technol.* **2021**, *13*, 4282–4296.
5. Liu, X.; Tan, J.; Long, S. Multi-axis fatigue load spectrum editing for automotive components using generalized S-transform. *Int. J. Fatigue* **2024**, *188*, 108503. [CrossRef]
6. Komurcu, E.; Kefal, A.; Abdollahzadeh, M.; Basoglu, M.; Kisa, E.; Yildiz, M. Towards composite suspension control arm: Conceptual design, structural analysis, laminate optimization, manufacturing, and experimental testing. *Compos. Struct.* **2024**, *327*, 117704. [CrossRef]
7. Viqaruddin, M.; Ramana Reddy, D. Structural optimization of control arm for weight reduction and improved performance. *Mater. Today Proc.* **2017**, *4*, 9230–9236. [CrossRef]
8. Llopis-Albert, C.; Rubio, F.; Zeng, S. Multiobjective optimization framework for designing a vehicle suspension system. A comparison of optimization algorithms. *Adv. Eng. Softw.* **2023**, *176*, 103375. [CrossRef]
9. Song, X.G.; Jung, J.H.; Son, H.J.; Park, J.H.; Lee, K.H.; Park, Y.C. Metamodel-based optimization of a control arm considering strength and durability performance. *Comput. Math. Appl.* **2010**, *60*, 976– 980. [CrossRef]
10. Wang, Z.; Gao, D.; Deng, K.; Lu, Y.; Ma, S.; Zhao, J. Robot base position and spacecraft cabin angle optimization via homogeneous stiffness domain index with nonlinear stiffness characteristics. *Robot. Comput.-Integr. Manuf.* **2024**, *90*, 102793. [CrossRef]
11. Shi, J.; Zhao, B.; He, J.; Lu, X. The optimization design for the journal-thrust couple bearing surface texture based on particle swarm algorithm. *Tribol. Int.* **2024**, *198*, 109874. [CrossRef]
12. Rao, S. *The Finite Element Method in Engineering*, 6th ed.; Butterworth-Heinemann: Oxford, UK, 2018. [CrossRef]
13. Belinha, J. *Meshless Methods in Biomechanics—Bone Tissue Remodelling Analysis*; Springer International: Berlin/Heidelberg, Germany, 2014; Volume 16. [CrossRef]
14. Nayroles, B.; Touzot, G.; Villon, P. Generalizing the finite element method: Diffuse approximation and diffuse elements. *Comput. Mech.* **1992**, *10*, 307–318. [CrossRef]
15. Lancaster, P.; Salkauskas, K. Surfaces generated by moving least squares methods. *Math. Comput.* **1981**, *37*, 141–158. [CrossRef]
16. Dinis, L.; Natal Jorge, R.; Belinha, J. Analysis of 3D solids using the natural neighbour radial point interpolation method. *Comput. Methods Appl. Mech. Eng.* **2007**, *196*, 2009–2028. [CrossRef]
17. Poiate, I.; Vasconcellos, A.; Mori, M.; Poiate, E. 2D and 3D finite element analysis of central incisor generated by computerized tomography. *Comput. Methods Programs Biomed.* **2011**, *104*, 292– 299. [CrossRef]
18. Belytschko, T.; Lu, Y.; Gu, L. Element-free Galerkin methods. *Int. J. Numer. Methods Eng.* **1994**, *37*, 229–256. [CrossRef]
19. Atluri, S.; Zhu, T. A new meshless local Petrov–Galerkin (MLPG) approach. *Comput. Mech.* **1998**, *22*, 117–127. [CrossRef]
20. Oñate, E.; Idelsohn, S.; Zienkiewicz, O.; Taylor, R. A finite point method in computational mechanics. Applications to convective transport and fluid flow. *Int. J. Numer. Methods Eng.* **1996**, *39*, 3839–3866. [CrossRef]
21. De, S.; Bathe, K. Towards an efficient meshless computational technique: The method of finite spheres. *Int. J. Numer. Methods Eng.* **2001**, *170*, 3839–3866. [CrossRef]
22. Liu, G.; Gu, Y. A point interpolation method for two-dimensional solid. *Int. J. Numer. Methods Eng.* **2001**, *50*, 937–951. [CrossRef]
23. Wang, J.; Liu, G. A point interpolation meshless method based on radial basis functions. *Int. J. Numer. Methods Eng.* **2002**, *54*, 1623–1648. [CrossRef]
24. Sukumar, N.; Moran, B.; Belytschko, T. The Natural Element Method in Solid Mechanics. *Int. J. Numer. Methods Eng.* **1998**, *43*, 839–887. [CrossRef]
25. Idelsohn, S.; Oñate, E.; Calvo, N.; Del Pin, F. Meshless finite element method. *Int. J. Numer. Methods Eng.* **2003**, *58*, 893–912. [CrossRef]
26. Belinha, J.; Dinis, L.; Natal Jorge, R. The natural radial element method. *Int. J. Numer. Methods Eng.* **2013**, *93*, 1286–1313. [CrossRef]
27. Voronoï, G. Nouvelles applications des paramètres continus à la théorie des formes quadratiques. Deuxième mémoire. Recherches sur les parallélloèdres primitifs. *J. Für Die Reine Und Angew. Math.* **1908**, *134*, 198–287. [CrossRef]
28. Ito, Y. Delaunay Triangulation. In *Encyclopedia of Applied and Computational Mathematics*; Engquist, B., Ed.; Springer: Berlin/Heidelberg, Germany, 2015; pp. 332–334. [CrossRef]
29. Juan, Z.; Shuyao, L.; Yuanbo, X.; Guangyao, L. A Topology Optimization Design for the Continuum Structure Based on the Meshless Numerical Technique. *Comput. Model. Eng. Sci.* **2008**, *34*, 137–154. [CrossRef]
30. Zou, W.; Zhou, J.; Zhang, Z.; Li, Q. A Truly Meshless Method based on Partition of Unity Quadrature for Shape Optimization of Continua. *Comput. Mech.* **2007**, *39*, 357–365. [CrossRef]
31. Sibson, R. A brief description of natural neighbour interpolation. In *Interpreting Multivariate Data*; John Wiley & Sons: Hoboken, NJ, USA, 1981; pp. 21–36.

32. Hardy, R. Theory and applications of the multiquadric-biharmonic method 20 years of discovery 1968–1988. *Comput. Math. Appl.* **1990**, *19*, 163–208. [CrossRef]
33. Bendsøe, M.; Sigmund, O. *Topology Optimization. Theory, Methods, and Applications*, 2nd ed.; Corrected Printing; Springer International: Berlin/Heidelberg, Germany, 2004. [CrossRef]
34. Xie, Y.; Steven, G.P. Optimal design of multiple load case structures using an evolutionary procedure. *Eng. Comput.* **1994**, *11*, 295–302. [CrossRef]
35. Abolbashari, M.; Keshavarzmanesh, S. On various aspects of application of the evolutionary structural optimization method for 2D and 3D continuum structures. *Finite Elem. Anal. Des.* **2006**, *42*, 478–491. [CrossRef]
36. Querin, O.; Steven, G.; Xie, Y. Evolutionary structural optimisation using an additive algorithm. *Finite Elem. Anal. Des.* **2000**, *34*, 291–308. [CrossRef]
37. Querin, O.; Young, V.; Steven, G.; Xie, Y. Computational efficiency and validation of bi-directional evolutionary structural optimisation. *Comput. Methods Appl. Mech. Eng.* **2000**, *189*, 559–573. [CrossRef]
38. Fuchs, R.; Warden, S.; Turner, C. 2—Bone anatomy, physiology and adaptation to mechanical loading. In *Bone Repair Biomaterials*; Planell, J.A., Best, S.M., Lacroix, D., Merolli, A., Eds.; Woodhead Publishing Series in Biomaterials; Woodhead Publishing: Sawston, UK, 2009; pp. 25–68. [CrossRef]
39. Pauwels, F. *Gesammelte Abhandlungen zur Funktionellen Anatomie des Bewegungsapparates*; Springer: Berlin/Heidelberg, Germany, 1965. [CrossRef]
40. Cowin, S. The relationship between the elasticity tensor and the fabric tensor. *Mech. Mater.* **1985**, *4*, 137–147. [CrossRef]
41. Carter, D.; Fyhrie, D.; Whalen, R. Trabecular bone density and loading history: Regulation of connective tissue biology by mechanical energy. *J. Biomech.* **1987**, *20*, 785–794. [CrossRef] [PubMed]
42. Belinha, J.; Natal Jorge, R.; Dinis, L. A meshless microscale bone tissue trabecular remodelling analysis considering a new anisotropic bone tissue material law. *Comput. Methods Biomech. Biomed. Eng.* **2013**, *16*, 1170–1184. [CrossRef]
43. Gonçalves, D.; Lopes, J.; Campilho, R.; Belinha, J. Topology optimization using a natural neighbour meshless method combined with a bi-directional evolutionary algorithm. *Math. Comput. Simul.* **2022**, *194*, 308–328. [CrossRef]
44. Gonçalves, D.; Lopes, J.; Campilho, R.; Belinha, J. Topology optimization of light structures using the natural neighbour Radial-Point Interpolation Method. *Meccanica* **2022**, *57*, 659–676. [CrossRef]
45. Crawford, R. CHAPTER 2—Mechanical Behaviour of Plastics. In *Plastics Engineering*, 3rd ed.; Crawford, R., Ed.; Butterworth-Heinemann: Oxford, UK, 1998; pp. 41–167. [CrossRef]
46. Muftu, S. Chapter 8—Rectangular and triangular elements for two-dimensional elastic solids. In *Finite Element Method*; Muftu, S., Ed.; Academic Press: Cambridge, MA, USA, 2022; pp. 257–291. [CrossRef]
47. Pais, A.; Alves, J.; Belinha, J. A bio-inspired remodelling algorithm combined with a natural neighbour meshless method to obtain optimized functionally graded materials. *Eng. Anal. Bound. Elem.* **2022**, *135*, 145–155. [CrossRef]
48. Pais, A.; Alves, J.; Belinha, J. Functional Gradients of the Gyroid Infill for Structural Optimization. *Mater. Proc.* **2022**, *8*, 72. [CrossRef]
49. Pais, A.; Alves, J.; Belinha, J. Predicting trabecular arrangement in the proximal femur: An artificial neural network approach for varied geometries and load cases. *J. Biomech.* **2023**, *161*, 111860. [CrossRef]

MDPI AG
Grosspeteranlage 5
4052 Basel
Switzerland
Tel.: +41 61 683 77 34

Mathematics Editorial Office
E-mail: mathematics@mdpi.com
www.mdpi.com/journal/mathematics

MDPI

www.ingramcontent.com/pod-product-compliance
Lightning Source LLC
Chambersburg PA
CBHW041406210926
51850CB00013B/3195